MASTERING MODERN ENGLISH
A Certificate Course

Mastering Modern English

A Certificate Course

A. R. B. ETHERTON
M.A. (Lond.), PH.D.

Illustrations by Michael ffolkes

LONGMAN

LONGMAN GROUP LIMITED
London

*Associated companies, branches and representatives
throughout the world*

First published* 1966
Twentieth impression 1979

ISBN 0 582 52573 X

Printed in Singapore by
Four Strong Printing Company

Contents

Contents

Foreword

This book is intended to be used by students preparing for G.C.E. 'O' level or Overseas School Certificate examinations in English. It may also be used in training colleges and other institutions of an appropriate standard. The book is divided into two parts: the first dealing with the topics most commonly tested in examinations, and the second providing revision of such basic language difficulties as agreement between subject and verb, and the use of tenses, prepositions, articles and pronouns. Formal descriptive grammar (including clause analysis) has been deliberately omitted since it is of very doubtful value in the teaching of English.

The book is primarily designed for use in the classroom but it can also be used with advantage by students who prepare by means of a correspondence course or have to rely on their own resources. Use has been made of extracts from examiners' reports so that candidates may be fully aware of the standards expected from them, of the techniques available and the mistakes most commonly made. Students who are preparing by means of private study are urged to obtain copies of recent examiners' reports and to study them carefully. They contain much helpful advice.

In preparing this book account has been taken of the possible effects of the recommendations contained in two important reports:

(a) *The Examining of English Language* – Eighth Report of the Secondary School Examinations Council, Department of Education and Science, U.K., H.M.S.O.

(b) D. W. Grieve: *Report of an Inquiry into English Language Examining* for The West African Examinations Council.

These reports are bound to have considerable beneficial effect on the examining of English in future years and, as far as is practicable at this stage, this book is indebted to them.

vii

Foreword

The author wishes to emphasize that students are not expected to work through every exercise in the book. The aim has been to provide a sufficient variety of work to meet the requirements of students at different levels of attainment, and it is presumed that teachers will be selective in their use of material.

Chapter 1

The Mechanics of Composition

Fire

Contents

A composition topic may be vague or it may be very clear and specific:

i. *a vague topic:* Write a composition on 'The cinema'.

ii. *a specific topic:* Write an account of a film which you have seen and enjoyed. You can use any or all of the following points as the basis of your account:

    a. Give the title of the film and say what type it was, e.g. a comedy, a detective story, a love story etc.

    b. Briefly outline the plot in one paragraph of about eight to twelve lines.

    c. Comment on any or all of these aspects: the originality and handling of the plot; the use of suspense; the acting and characterization; the music; the skill of the cameramen; the background scenery; any special effects.

    d. Criticize anything which you thought was weak or bad.

    e. Point out the features of the film which specially appealed to you. Explain why you enjoyed the film.

You must be prepared to write about topics which are vague

1

and those which are quite specific. In this book the writing of composition is considered as a craft which can be studied, practised and learnt.

1. Finding a theme, making it clear and sustaining it

Bernard Shaw said, 'He who has nothing to say cannot write.' This is **the most important point** in writing a composition. You must have a message to pass to your reader: ONE IDEA which dominates all your work and which gives it unity and shape. We call this idea *the theme*. It is a summary of your whole composition.

In some composition subjects the theme is obvious. For example, these two subjects tell you exactly what to write about:

   i. 'Describe your journey to the building in which you are now taking this examination.'
   ii. 'Write a composition about a very old person whom you know.'

In the first case, your theme will be 'I will describe the journey.' In the second case it may be 'I will describe my grandfather.' However, some subjects are vague and do not appear to have any definite theme, e.g.

iii. Food	v. Parents	vii. Fire
iv. Water	vi. Patience	viii. Friendship

If possible, it is better to avoid subjects like these in an examination unless you enjoy writing a composition and are good at it. In most cases it is easier to choose a subject in which the theme is given. If you do have to write about a subject like (iii) to (viii) above, you can use the method described below.

Use ONE of these ways of finding a theme. Try each method in turn until you find the most suitable one.

a. P = Describe the **part** which your subject plays in the life of man.
b. C = Describe the **chronological** or historical development of your subject.
c. F = Give a **factual** account of your subject.
d. A = Describe the **advantages** and disadvantages of your subject.
e. T = Give an account of different **types** of your subject OR of different attitudes to it.

If we take the first letter of the words in bold type, we can make the letters PC FAT. We can pretend that 'PC' stands for 'police constable' so you must remember 'a fat police constable'. This will give you five ways of finding a theme.

Learn PC FAT and the five ways by heart.

In addition to these five methods of finding a theme, there is a sixth one for use with proverbs and controversial topics:

f. B = Describe **both sides** of an argument. Don't agree blindly with a quotation or proverb about which you are asked to write. Consider both sides, *give your own opinion* and then sum up if necessary.

If we add this sixth method to PC FAT, we shall have the mnemonic PC FATB to remember. Let us now apply this method to some topics:

Examples

i. *Topic:* 'Patience'
Theme: 'I will write about the times when patience is a virtue and the times when it can be a disadvantage.' (Type A)

ii. *Topic:* 'Fire'
Theme: 'I will write about the part which fire plays in the life of man, showing how it can be a good thing and a bad thing.' (Types P and A together)

iii. *Topic:* 'Food'
Theme: 'I will give a historical account of the food eaten by the human race, starting in very primitive times and finishing by speculating about the time when we may live on tablets produced by chemists.' (Type C)

OR

'I will describe the different attitudes which people have to food, ranging from the starving man to the gourmet who suffers from gout.' (Type T)

iv. *Topic:* 'Radar'
Theme: 'I will give a factual account of radar, as well as I can, explaining what it is and how it works.' (Type F)

v. *Topic:* 'All men are born equal.'
Theme: 'I will try to show in what respects this statement is true and in what ways it is wrong or misleading. Then I will briefly sum up my arguments.' (Type B)

3

The Mechanics of Composition

Exercise 1

a. Say which of the following composition subjects have definite themes. In each case, say what the theme is.

b. Say which of the subjects have NOT got a definite theme. Use PC FATB to find a theme suitable to each of these subjects.

1. Describe your own school building.
2. What changes do you expect the next ten years to bring in your life?
3. The wind   4. Toys
5. The wonders of modern science
6. Traditional games and amusements of your country
7. 'Parents always know best.'
8. Sources of power in my country today. (ambiguous)
9. Growing up
10. Transport in my country
11. Maps   12. Friendship
13. Babies   14. A journey by river
15. Rain   16. My favourite game or sport
17. Describe an airport *or* a seaport *or* a railway station.
18. Tradition   19. Trees
20. Food   21. My family
22. My country's greatest problem
23. The kind of entertainment I most enjoy
24. 'Man to lead, woman to follow.'
25. Clocks and other timepieces used by man to mark the passing of the hours
26. Write a description of your country or part of the country so that it can be used in a brochure designed to attract tourists.

Exercise 2

Write a single sentence which shows the theme you would use in writing a composition on each of these subjects:

1. Animals   2. Finding a job
3. An eye-witness description of *either* a disastrous fire *or* a disastrous flood
4. Films   5. What I enjoy in my work
6. Give an account of *either* the animal life *or* the national pastimes of your country
7. The work of any craftsman   8. Newspapers
9. What foreign country would you most like to visit? Give your reasons fully, and say what you would hope to see there.

10. Discuss fully any *one* important problem facing your community, your country, or the world, today.
11. Describe the arrival *or* departure of a steamship *or* an airliner *or* a railway train.
12. Traffic accidents   13. The sea
14. Describe the historical character you would most like to have met, showing your reasons.
15. The pleasantest season of the year
16. Cooking   17. Dreams
18. How I have changed in character in the last ten years
19. The type of book I like to read
20. 'Look before you leap.'

Exercise 3

You know that by using the mnemonic PC FATB you can find the theme for a composition in one of six ways. In each case say how many of the six ways could be used to write a composition about the subjects below. Assume that you are considering different ways of writing about each subject.

Example: Subject: Honour
Answer: 'P' is possible but difficult.
        'C' is not really suitable.
        'F' is not really suitable.
        'A' is possible but difficult.
        'T' (different attitudes to it) is possible.
        'B' does not apply in this case.

Thus 'T' might be the easiest way of finding a suitable theme although 'P' or 'A' could be used instead.

1. Fame   6. Advertising
2. Patriotism   7. Solitude
3. Success   8. Darkness
4. Writing letters   9. Music
5. Public opinion   10. Insurance

Exercise 4

Write the opening sentence of a composition on each of the subjects given below. In your sentence make your theme quite clear.

1. The most interesting person in my town or village

5

2. Your country's main crop *or* industry
3. Charity   4. Tolerance
5. Describe the parts of a newspaper which interest you most.
6. The problems of a shopkeeper *or* a farmer.
7. 'The road to Hell is paved with good intentions.'
8. 'He who hesitates is lost.' Discuss.
9. Equal pay for equal work
10. 'A woman's place is in the kitchen.' What are your views?

Summary

a. In each composition there must be a theme or single idea which dominates the work and gives it unity.

b. In some composition subjects the theme is quite clear.

c. When a theme is not given it can be found by using the method known here as PC FATB.

We ought to add two further points which are often overlooked by examination candidates:

d. **Make your theme clear to your reader.** The best way of doing this is by stating your theme in your opening sentence. Do *not* waste time with an introduction. Get straight to the point and tell your reader exactly what you are going to write about. *Many candidates seem to know what they are trying to write about but never make the point clear to the examiner.*

e. **Sustain your theme right through your composition** and do not wander off into little stories, irrelevant details or matters which do not concern your theme. As you write, glance back at your theme from time to time. In this way you will prevent yourself from wandering from the point. Every sentence and paragraph should contribute to the working out of your theme.

2. Planning AFTER the theme has been found

If you have made sure that you have chosen a clear theme, it will be easy to make a plan. Without a theme, it is impossible to make an effective plan.

Imagine that you want a builder or an architect to draw up the plan of a new house for you. If you say to him, 'I want a plan for a new house' he will not know how to start. First you must give him a general idea of the house. You can say, 'I want a bungalow with three bedrooms, costing not more than five thousand pounds.' That will give him a general idea. That is your theme and his theme. He can ask a few questions and then start to make a plan.

Once you have found your theme, make some rough notes (preferably in pencil) as you think about your theme. Sometimes it is useful to ask yourself 'Why?' each time. In this way you can gradually build up a plan which fits your theme. Your main aim is to **give all the facts in the right order**. Remember these points when you make a plan:

a. *You can spend up to a quarter of your time making a plan.* If you have an hour in which to write one composition, you can spend 10 to 15 minutes on your plan. If you have to write two compositions in an hour, you can spend just over 5 minutes on each plan.

b. *Arrange the ideas in your plan so that they fit into 4 to 6 paragraphs* if you have an hour for the whole composition. If you have only 30 minutes, two or three paragraphs will be sufficient.

c. *There is no need for your plan to be elaborate.* The more intelligent you are, the less elaborate your plan needs to be. However, if you always find it difficult to think of something to write about, it might be safer to make a fairly detailed plan.

d. You should be able to write your composition straight from your theme and plan. *It is a waste of time to make a rough copy of the whole composition* and then to make a final copy for the examiner.

e. *Do not include an introduction in your plan.* This is boring to the reader, dangerous to the writer (because it leads to irrelevance) and quite unnecessary. Aim to get to the point in your opening sentence.

Exercise 5

Choose ONE of the following subjects. Write down your theme in a single sentence. Then make a plan to fit the theme. Your plan can be in the form of notes and should not take you longer than 15 minutes.

1. The main street in your town or village
2. The advantages and disadvantages of speed in present-day life

3. The way in which the climate in your country or district affects the agriculture of the region
4. Rivers   5. An interesting hobby   6. Television

Exercise 6

Choose ONE of the following subjects. Write down your theme in a single sentence. Then make a plan, spending not more than 15 minutes on the task.

1. Tell the story of a quarrel you saw, and its results.
2. Opportunities for women in the professions
3. Changes in methods of transport in your country in the last fifty years
4. Fishing   5. Nursing   6. Exploring

Exercise 7

Choose TWO of the following subjects. In each case, write down your theme and make a plan. The two plans must be completed within 20 minutes.

1. Describe a ceremony *or* important function you have witnessed recently.
2. How to spend a rainy day
3. Describe some piece of handiwork that you have recently completed *or* a job you have undertaken successfully.
4. Which method of travelling do you prefer for longer journeys —road, sea, river, railway or air? Give your choice and then explain why you prefer it to the alternative methods.
5. A visit to a relative   6. Films*

Note: *Notice that the subject in 6 is NOT 'Describe a film you have seen.'

Exercise 8

Choose TWO of the following subjects. In each case, write down your theme and then make a plan. The two plans must be completed with 15 minutes.

1. Describe any interesting journey which you have made. Explain why the journey was interesting.
2. A windy day
3. A visit to your house by a relative or some relatives

8

4. Compose a dialogue between yourself and a native of your town or village who has returned after living abroad for many years.

5. The choice of a career*　　　6. A visit to a hospital

Note: *Notice that the subject in 5 is NOT 'Describe the career in which you are interested.'

Exercise 9

Choose TWO of the following subjects. In each case, write down your theme and then make a plan. The two plans must be completed within 20 minutes.

1. Explain how ONE of the following works: a refrigerator, a pump of any kind, a car battery, a tape recorder, radar.
2. Describe the best way of looking after any pet, giving details of its food, liability to disease, special problems etc.
3. Explain clearly how to do ONE of these things: repair a broken fuse wire, grow any vegetable, cook any dish.
4. Write a report for your school magazine of any game which you have seen recently. Do not explain the rules of the game. Describe the game itself.
5. Explain some of the problems of collecting ONE of the following: stamps, shells, coins, badges, labels, autographs.

3. Methods of starting

Think of 'Fed up' and learn FADAP. The five letters in FADAP show you different ways of starting a composition:

a. F = Start with a simple **factual statement** which will usually be your theme. (easy)

b. A = Start with **action** which is relevant to your theme. (fairly easy)

c. D = Start with **dialogue** which is relevant to your theme. (fairly easy)

d. A = Start with an **anecdote** or little story which is relevant to your theme. (difficult and NOT recommended)

e. P = Start with a **proverb** or a **quotation** which is relevant to your theme. (fairly difficult)

Learn by heart the mnemonic FADAP and what it represents.

Notice that method *d* above is not recommended unless you are very good at composition. Too often a writer allows his opening anecdote to grow too long so that the reader begins to feel that the whole composition is irrelevant.

Here are examples of methods *a*, *b*, *c* and *e* at work:

Example

Topic: Floods

Method (*a*) In my part of the country floods are not so dangerous or widespread today as they were many years ago.

(I shall then write about floods in the past, the measures taken to control them and the present position in my own country.)

Method (*b*) Desperately my brother and I filled sandbags and passed them to my father. We were trying to protect our shop from the rising flood.

Method (*c*) 'I don't like the look of the river,' my uncle said. 'What's the matter?' I asked him. 'It's rising rapidly,' he replied. 'It may burst its banks during the night.'

Method (*e*) The saying 'It never rains but it pours' certainly applies to my country, where tropical storms are frequent.

When you use action, dialogue, a proverb or a quotation to start your composition make sure that it is relevant to the theme. Do not get carried away by your action or diaolgue. Bring in your theme as soon as possible. **Your first task in starting your composition is to make your theme absolutely clear to your reader.**

Exercise 10

Make up the opening sentence or two for each of the following subjects, using one of the methods explained above.

1. Give an account of a sports meeting you have recently attended.
2. My favourite season and why I like it
3. Describe, with as much detail as you can, an important person in your community.
4. A public holiday   5. Sounds which annoy me

Exercise 11

Start each of these compositions in THREE different ways, giving the opening 1–3 sentences in each case.

1. Useful animals   2. Weddings*
3. Describe an interesting scene at a river, a market or a port.
4. My neighbours
5. The handicaps to progress in my country

Note: *In (2) the subject is NOT 'Describe a wedding.'

Exercise 12

Write the first three sentences of each of the following subjects, making sure that you show your theme within the opening sentences:

1. The house I should one day like to live in
2. How my life may change in the next ten years
3. Write about an occasion when somebody cheated you or tried to do so.
4. Describe what happens in your home on the public holiday which you most enjoy.
5. Make up a story in which you save somebody from danger. (The story can be based on fact if you like.)

Exercise 13

Find an interesting report or article in any newspaper or magazine. Read it and then write down:
a. The title or headline
b. The theme
c. The method used to start it

Exercise 14

Listen to any talk at school, at work, on the radio or on television. Then write down:
a. When and where you heard the talk
b. The theme or what it was about
c. The method used to start it

Exercise 15

Write the opening paragraph of 8 to 12 lines for ONE of these subjects:

1. The time when I was ill
2. Shopping
3. My favourite radio or television programme

Exercise 16

Write the opening paragraph of 8 to 12 lines for ONE of these subjects:

1. A book which I have read and enjoyed
2. Write a composition on the ways in which rivers help us and can hinder us. You can consider the following points if you wish: They help us by providing a means of transport, water for irrigation and washing, water for hydro-electric power, an opportunity for recreation and swimming, and a supply of food. They can hinder us by being an obstacle to communication and by flooding.
3. You have been asked to take a friend of the family to visit some interesting places in your district. Describe the places you would visit and explain how they are interesting.

4. Continuity and paragraphing

a. Paragraphing: As a rough guide, try to produce about four to six paragraphs in an hour, or two to three in 30 minutes. Each paragraph should be about 8 to 12 lines in length, and successive paragraphs should be linked to each other in one of the ways explained below in *b*. Of course, the number of paragraphs will vary with the type of composition you write. If you use a lot of dialogue, you will naturally use more paragraphs. The guide given above will apply in most cases to factual, narrative and descriptive compositions. On the whole, it is better to have short paragraphs rather than long ones which can cause the reader to lose interest.

Without looking back at the previous paragraph, say about how many lines you will try to have in each of your paragraphs.

b. Continuity:

Exercise 17

In each of the examples below we have the end of one paragraph and the start of the next one. Try to explain in each case:

i. Why the writer decided to start a new paragraph.
ii. What idea links the two paragraphs.

1. (*A badly injured man is trying to escape from the secret police. He manages to climb up a tree.*)

. . . I couldn't fall, wedged in as I was between the little branches of that prolific tree. When I climbed into the narrowing of the cone and the boughs were thicker and smaller and greener, I got jammed. That suited me well enough, so I fainted again. It was luxury, almost sin.

When I became conscious, the tree was swaying in the light wind and smelling of peace. I felt deliciously secure . . .

(*Rogue Male* by Geoffrey Household)

2. (*The police have brought dogs to track down the injured man.*)

. . . The dogs might have found me, but their master, whoever he was, never gave them a chance. He wasn't wasting time by putting them on a trail that he could follow himself; he was casting up and down the stream.

When night fell I came down from my tree. I could stand, and, with the aid of two sticks, I could shuffle slowly forwards. . .

(*Rogue Male* by Geoffrey Household)

3. (*During the Japanese occupation, a party of British women are being marched from place to place in Malaya. The first paragraph tells us something about a woman called Jean.*)

. . . but Jean carried the bundle of blankets and small articles, and the baby, and led Jane by the hand. She went barefoot as before; after some experiments she found that the easiest way to carry the baby was to perch him on her hip, as the Malay women did.

The baby, curiously, gave them the least anxiety of any of the children. They fed it on rice and gravy from the fish soup or stew, and it did well. Once in the six weeks it had seemed to be developing dysentery. . . .

(*A Town Like Alice* by Nevil Shute)

4. (*At one of their halts, the women try to get some mosquito repellent but to do so they have to evade their guards.*)

As an experiment she attracted the attention of the sentry and pointed to her mosquito bites; then she pointed to the village and got down from the veranda on to the ground. Immediately he brought his bayonet to the ready and advanced towards her; she got back on to the veranda in a hurry. That evidently wouldn't do. He scowled at her suspiciously, and went back to his position.

There was another way. The latrine was behind the building up against a wall; there was no sentry there because the wall prevented any exit. . . .   (*A Town Like Alice* by Nevil Shute)

5. (*The author is describing the time when his family moved to a house in the country. He was three years old then. The first of these paragraphs describes the author and his sisters.*)
. . . We were washed up in a new land, and began to spread out searching its springs and treasures. The sisters spent the light of that first day stripping the fruit bushes in the garden. The currants were at their prime, clusters of red, black, and yellow berries all tangled up with wild roses. Here was bounty the girls had never known before, and they darted squawking from bush to bush, clawing the fruit like sparrows.

Our Mother too was distracted from duty, seduced by the rich wilderness of the garden so long abandoned. All day she trotted to and fro, flushed and garrulous, pouring flowers into every pot and jug she could find . . .

(*Cider With Rosie* by Laurie Lee)

We often start a new paragraph when one of the following conditions exists:

a. **There is a change in time.** This is usually a step forward in time but you may sometimes wish to refer to past events. It was a change in time which led Geoffrey Household to start new paragraphs in examples 1 and 2 above.

When there is a change in time, the next paragraph often starts with an expression similar to these:

Not long after this . . .   Later that day/morning . . .
Four days later . . .   The next day . . .

These expressions warn the reader of a change in the time of the action.

b. **There is a change in place.** In a narrative composition we may wish to explain what was happening in another place. In a factual composition we may wish to explain, for example, how a certain problem is tackled in different countries. In a descriptive composition we may wish to move the scene slightly. Whatever the reason, expressions similar to the following are often used:

| Not far away . . . | In colder countries . . . |
| In my own country, however . . . | A few miles away . . . |

c. There is a change in the topic or in emphasis. In example 3 on page 13, Nevil Shute starts a new paragraph when he moves from Jean to the baby. In example 4 he starts a new paragraph when he describes a different method of trying to get some mosquito repellent. In example 5 Laurie Lee starts a new paragraph when he moves from the children to their mother. Notice that in each case the different topics are linked to each other in some way.

d. There is a similarity between people, actions or topics. This similarity is then used to introduce a new topic. When this happens, we meet expressions like these:

| In a similar way . . . | Similar conditions exist . . . |
| We find exactly the same thing . . . | A similar reason . . . |

e. There is a modification of an idea already expressed. Sometimes this takes the form of contrast; sometimes it is merely a less striking change in the line of thought. The new paragraph may start in this way:

Not everybody behaves like this . . .
However, there are some important exceptions to the rule and we ought to consider them . . .

The five reasons given above cover the majority of occasions when new paragraphs are started.

Exercise 18

Look at the comprehension passages in Chapter 4 and in each case:

a. Find out why a new paragraph has been started. See which of the five reasons above applies to each new paragraph.

b. Point out the ideas which connect the end of one paragraph with the beginning of the next paragraph.

5. Methods of ending

Try to show as much skill in ending your composition as you do in starting it. First and last impressions are important. You can use one of these methods:

a. **Sum up your arguments or ideas**. This method is essential if you have been discussing two sides of an opinion or problem. Do not introduce new ideas in your summing up. Give a final or personal verdict if one is required.

In a similar way you can sum up what you have said if you have been describing a person or a place. This time your summing up will give a final impression and may be very similar to the sentences with which you started the composition.

Notice that the final paragraph should usually be of a reasonable length, i.e. from 8 to 12 lines. It should NOT be two or three lines hurriedly scribbled with an eye on the clock. This type of ending is common in the work of candidates who have not learnt the craft of composition.

Exercise 19

Imagine that you have been writing a composition on each of the following subjects. Write a concluding paragraph which sums up your arguments or ideas.

1. Do you agree that life in a big town is better than life in a country village?
2. Describe anybody whom you particularly admire. (The person can be alive or dead.)
3. Describe the view from the place where you live OR from any part of your school.

b. **Finish by looking into the future.** This method of ending a composition is particularly useful when you are writing about such factual subjects as Tradition, Transport, Rivers, Education in My Country, Handicrafts, etc. Having finished with the past and present, you can briefly attempt to explain what might happen in the future. In this case your final paragraph will probably start by referring to present or past events but the last two or three sentences will refer to the future. If necessary, the whole paragraph can deal with future developments.

Exercise 20

Imagine that you have been writing a composition on each of the following subjects. Write a concluding paragraph which looks forward to the future.

1. The use of rivers in my country
2. Recent developments in building houses
3. Education in my country

c. Finish a story by bringing it to its climax or point of greatest interest and by ending as soon as possible after that point.

d. Use a sentence which has an air of finality about it. This is useful when you are explaining how to do or make something. When you have reached the last step, make sure that your reader can see that your account has finished. Don't leave him mentally hanging in the air. If you have been explaining how to repair a puncture in a bicycle tyre, you can finish '. . . Once I have got the tyre on again, there is only one thing left for me to do: I pump up the inner tube and make sure that my repair is a good one.' If you have been describing how to cook something, you can finish in this way: 'Then, when the food is all ready, I call my brothers and sisters and we put the final touch to the meal: we eat it.'

Exercise 21

Imagine that you have been writing a composition on each of the following subjects. Write *the last two sentences* for each subject.

1. Explain how you can do ONE of these things: repair a broken fuse wire, clean and overhaul a bicycle, make a blouse or dress.
2. Explain how you would do ONE of these things:

a. Treat a person who has just burnt her arm on a hot iron.
b. Revive a semi-conscious person who has just been rescued from the sea or a river and was nearly drowned.
c. Treat a wound in your hand or foot. Imagine that the wound was made by a rusty piece of metal found in the ground.

6. Summary of the chapter

So far we have learnt the points mentioned below. Read them again and then use them when you write compositions during the year.

1. *PC FATB shows you how to find a theme when the subject does not contain one. Once you have found your theme, make it clear and sustain it right to the end.*

2. *The plan is based on the theme. The main problem is to get all the facts in the right order. The examiners are looking for 'the orderly presentation of material'.*
3. *FADAP gives you five ways of starting a composition. Of these, the first three—F, A and D—are the most suitable.*
4. *A new paragraph may start because of a change in time, place or topic. It may show a similarity of ideas or a modification. Successive paragraphs should be linked by the ideas they contain.*
5. *We can finish by summing up, by looking into the future or by using a sentence with an air of finality about it.*

Now that we have dealt with the mechanics of composition, our next task is to consider the ideas to be put into an essay and the words in which they can be expressed.

Chapter 2

Subject Matter
Language and Style

Toads

1. Originality and interest

Try to be original and interesting in the way you tackle your subject, in the way you start and in the way you end. Later in this section we shall consider ways of achieving these aims. Right from the start, probe deeply into your subject. Try to present the reader with something he will enjoy reading. Nearly every report by the examiners complains of dull essays. You may avoid this mistake if you start with the determination to give your reader a composition which is more interesting than most of the others.

Remember that the examiner wants your own work and **not** a memorized composition. Do not try to hand in a memorized

19

essay. If you do, your attempt will probably be detected because the standard of accuracy will be different from that seen in your other answers. In that case you may get no marks for your composition.

2. Length

The examiners have stated in their reports that they expect between 450 and 500 words in an hour—or *a total* of this length if you have to write two essays in the same time. As a rough guide, you can say that this is *a line a minute of actual writing time.* It follows that if, for example, you had to write 3 essays in a total time of 90 minutes you would make each of them about 20–25 lines in length, having spent about 20–25 minutes planning your work.

Do NOT waste time counting the number of words you use. Before you go into the examination room, count the average number of words you write per line of examination paper. Then you will know whether you have to write about 50 lines (10 words to a line) in an hour or only 40 lines (12 words to a line). If you know how many lines there are on a sheet of examination paper, you will soon be able to judge whether or not you have written enough.

You have already been warned NOT to waste time by making a rough copy which has to be turned into a 'fair' copy. A recent examiners' report contained this comment: 'Many candidates write out a complete essay in rough, and then make a fair copy. Often there is not time to complete this, so that the examiner finds an incomplete—and therefore often short—essay to mark.' If you have chosen a sensible subject and theme, and made a good plan, you ought to be able to do without the help of a rough copy.

3. Relevance

Study the exact meaning of each word in your topic and don't start to find a theme or make a plan until you are CERTAIN that you know exactly what the subject is. Look at these past questions and see from the examiners' reports where candidates went wrong. Learn from their mistakes.

i. *Topic:* The pleasure of craftwork (for example, carving, pottery, and weaving) *or* cooking

Examiners' Comment: *This was attempted chiefly by girls, who wrote on cooking, but usually without any attempt to suggest the pleasure derived from it. Candidates who chose to write on craftwork tended to give a dull account of the making of some object, again without any suggestion of pleasure, and some interpreted the suggestion in the question as an instruction to write on all the topics mentioned as examples.*

ii. *Topic:* Transport in my country

Examiners' Comment: *Some candidates read the question carelessly, overlooking 'in my country', and thus spoke of sea transport to far-off countries, or long-distance flights by aeroplane.*

iii. *Topic:* The machine in modern life

Comment: *Many candidates neglected to read the question carefully, and as a result spent time on the history and development of machines, often revealing an ignorance here of the chronology of development.*

iv. *Topic:* A public holiday

Comment: *This was frequently taken as an opportunity to present a prepared essay, as, for example, an account of a visit to an exhibition, or to the seaside. Many candidates used it as a basis for narrative, telling a story with little reference to a holiday. Very rarely was there any emphasis on 'public', and most essays were accounts of a visit to the beach, or a picnic, with no suggestion whatsoever of there being a 'public' holiday. Some candidates wrote on holidays in general, having missed the point of the indefinite article at the beginning of the title.*

Every year the examiners' reports contain similar comments. Sometimes the subject is misunderstood and general topics are confused with specific ones. Notice the difference between the following subjects:

General	*Specific*
Neighbours	Your neighbours
Films	Describe a film you have seen.
Fire	A fire
Good books	A good book
The excitement of travelling	An exciting journey
Food	Food you like and dislike

Be very careful, too, with anecdotes, incidents which support your theme, and details which illustrate a point. It is easy to get so interested in one of these that you forget your theme and wander off on to your story or incident. Remember the advice

21

given earlier: keep on glancing back at your subject and theme as you write so that you can be sure you are keeping to the subject.

Finally, don't panic if you want to change your mind half-way through your composition. If you are dealing with a controversial quotation, proverb or subject, and find that you want to change your attitude do NOT start again. This wastes time. Continue with your composition and explain why you have changed your mind. This is quite a natural thing to do. Be as honest with your reader as possible.

Exercise 1

To show that you understand these topics and can write about them relevantly, write down a suitable theme for each one.
1. The problems of a boy OR girl of school age
2. Write about any important natural event.
3. 'Films do more harm than good.' Discuss this statement. (Warning: 'Discuss' here means 'consider both sides'. It does *not* mean that you must agree.)
4. Ambition
5. Describe some of the problems connected with a hobby in which you are particularly interested.
6. The house you would like to live in
7. Drums
8. Describe some of the new industries in your country or region.
9. The future of the town or village in which you now live
10. The handicaps to progress in my country

Exercise 2

Write down your theme for each of the following subjects and then make a plan which is based on your theme. Do NOT write the composition.
1. Those who .have taught me. (*Note: Does this mean only teachers in schools?*)
2. The music of my people. (*Notes: When? Now—or in the past and future as well? Who are 'my people'?*)
3. Turning over a new leaf. (*Note: Usually it is better to avoid a subject like this one—but here you can't avoid it. See page 21*

and ask yourself whether this topic is general or applies specifically to you alone.)

4. Money. (*Note: You* **must** *use PC FAT to find a theme. Without it you may be lost.*)

5. Write a short story *or* an account concerning an accident, a fire, a rescue, a surprise *or* a great disappointment in which you are concerned yourself. (*Note: Which one are you going to write about?*)

4. The use of detail

a. A lorry

The lorry that arrived to take me up to the mountains was worse than anything I had seen before: it tottered on the borders of senile decay. It stood there on buckled wheels, wheezing and gasping with exhaustion from having to climb up the gentle slope to the camp, and I consigned myself and my loads to it with some trepidation. The driver, who was a cheerful fellow, pointed out that he would require my assistance in two very necessary operations: first, I had to keep the hand brake pressed down when travelling downhill, for unless it was held thus almost level with the floor it sullenly refused to function. Secondly, I had to keep a stern eye on the clutch, a wilful piece of mechanism, that seized every chance to leap out of its socket with a noise like a strangling leopard.

(The Bafut Beagles by Gerald Durrell)

b. Rifles

These fearsome weapons were incredibly ancient, and their barrels were pitted and eroded with rust holes, as though each gun had suffered an acute attack of smallpox.

(The Bafut Beagles by Gerald Durrell)

c. Toads

Above its large eyes the skin is hitched up into two little points, so that the creature has its eyebrows raised at the world in a markedly sardonic manner. The immensely wide mouth adds to this impression of aristocratic conceit by drooping gently at the corners, thus giving the toad a faintly sneering expression that can only be achieved by one other animal that I know of, the camel. Add to this the slow swaggering walk, and the fact that the creature squats down every two or three steps and gazes at you with a sort of pitying disdain, and you begin to feel that superciliousness could not go much farther. (*The Bafut Beagles* by Gerald Durrell)

 i. What details in *a* make the lorry a distinctive and unusual one? Do you agree that these details make the description more interesting?

 ii. What words in passage *b* help to make the description of the old rifles more interesting?

 iii. What details are given about the toads in passage *c* and what effect is obtained by giving them?

Exercise 3

Write a short description of any common object in a way similar to that seen in *a* and *b*. Make your description interesting by the use of significant details. You can describe ONE of the following things or anything else: a bicycle, a desk, a building, a person's hand, a pair of shoes, a bus or coach, some furniture in a room, a ship or a boat, a taxi.

Exercise 4

Write a short description of an animal OR a person. Use significant details to make your work really striking and interesting. If your description is not interesting to the reader, it is no good.

In the passages and exercises above, we have seen the importance of using significant details in describing people and things. We use the expression *significant details* because we mean details which are significant or important in the way that they reveal the character or personality of the thing being described. For example, wrinkles on a person's face show not merely age but something of the person's character and past experiences. The act of smiling gradually creates wrinkles which turn upwards at the corners of the mouth. A person who is usually dissatisfied, very critical or rather sad gradually develops wrinkles which turn down at the mouth. In a similar way each wrinkle on a person's face sends a message to a thoughtful observer. The deeper the wrinkles, the stronger the message is. Look at your own face when you go home; peer into a mirror and see what messages you can find. Then study the faces and hands of old people. Watch how the old people walk, sit down, stand up and eat; watch for their personal mannerisms; listen to them cough, breathe and speak.

You must try to develop the art of finding significant details in people and things which you meet. You will not always have the time to do this, and in some cases there are no details worth noticing. But if you open your eyes and ears more widely, you will begin to notice details which will eventually make your writing more interesting to read. You may happen to notice some of these things:

A person: the face (wrinkles, scars, fatness or emaciated look), clothes (many things to notice), hands (size, roughness, where put when the person is talking or sitting down), feet, way of walking etc.

A building: colour, material, age, squeaking doors, peeling paint, badly fitting windows etc.

A river: its smell and colour, the currents, any changes in it from time to time, things in and around it.

A car: scratches and dents, a crooked registration plate, a loose silencer, the condition inside, things in and on the car.

Look for these things in life. Then use them, sparingly but effectively, when you write.

5. The use of local colour

In the expression 'local colour' the word 'colour' refers to much more than colours such as green, red, blue etc. It means the whole of the background of a place, particularly the more interesting parts. It refers to the people, buildings, scenery, rivers and everything else. These are the things which bring your writing to life—if they are chosen carefully and described sensitively.

Read these two extracts from the examiners' reports. They are typical:

i. 'Local detail and colour which might have lifted their essays [= made them more interesting than the average essays] were ignored.'

ii. 'Overseas candidates start with one advantage: if they have kept their eyes open, their everyday experience, accurately and sincerely recorded, can provide novel material, of great interest to their distant readers. But few realized this.'

The point is worth emphasizing. If you want to write well, think of your reader when you write. Give him what he wants. If you know that your reader is an examiner who lives in England, try to bring in the things which YOU know well and which will interest him because he does not know much about them. Don't give him a lecture on London or England. Tell him about the hopes and fears of your own people, about their customs, faces, clothes, food, means of transport; tell him about your trees, flowers, rivers, hills and animals. Enjoy yourself as you write— and he will enjoy reading what you have written.

Exercise 5

Write a composition on ONE of the following subjects, bringing in 'local colour'. Imagine that your composition will be read by somebody outside your own country.

1. Describe the life in your town or village.
2. Give an account of your daily life.
3. A street scene
4. The attraction of shops OR markets. (*Warning:* Notice the importance in this subject of the word 'attraction'.)
5. The town by night, OR the country by night

6. Powers of observation

You have five senses: those of sight, hearing, smell, touch and taste. Use them fully in life and try to use them in your essays. Your reader can more easily imagine a place if you describe not merely what it looks like but some of the sounds and smells of the place also. If possible read the poem, 'The Great Lover' by Rupert Brooke. In it he describes some of the sights, sounds and smells he liked as well as things he liked to taste or touch.

Exercise 6

1. Listen carefully for a few moments. Then make a list of the different noises you can hear.
2. Say what noises you can hear outside your house (a) early in the morning at about 6 a.m., and (b) in the evening.
3. What different smells can you notice in the shops of your town? Which of them are pleasant?
4. What things do you dislike touching? What do these things

26

feel like: worms, snakes, buttons, sandpaper, velvet, raw liver, feathers, silk, wool?

7. Personal views and experiences

If possible, choose an essay subject which will allow you to give your personal views or to write from your own experiences. Compare these two subjects:

a. The advantages and disadvantages of speed in present-day life.
b. How my life may change in the next ten years.

Obviously *b* will enable you to give your own views whereas in writing about *a* you will have to be more impersonal and thus less interesting. Compare these two subjects:

c. Your country's main crop *or* industry.
d. The pleasantest season of the year.

It will not be easy to write an interesting essay about *c*. In *d*, however, you can deal with the subject from a purely personal angle, if you wish.

In a recent report the examiners complained that 'in all these essays one saw far too little of the candidates' own feelings and experiences; most essays were far too general in treatment . . .'

So don't be shy. Wherever possible, give your own feelings and experiences but:

i. Remember that an essay often reveals the personality of the writer. Don't reveal a boastful, arrogant or unpleasant personality in your work. This may make your reader hostile. Always try to be courteous to the reader and fair in your arguments.
ii. Avoid dogmatic statements, wild claims and exaggeration.
iii. Don't ask the reader questions. Give him information.

Exercise 7

Write a composition of about 40 to 50 lines on ONE of the following subjects. Assume that the reader will be your teacher in your school. Write frankly but courteously. Be careful! When you feel very strongly about a subject, there is a danger that you may be discourteous unintentionally.

1. Homework

2. The system of discipline in our school
3. How I would like to improve my town or village
4. The future of my country

8. Legibility

Illegible handwriting is a discourtesy to your reader and may annoy him—with disastrous results in an examination or in a job. These are extracts from examiners' reports:

i. 'Write letters like *c* and *s* carefully, so that the examiner can see immediately whether you intend a capital or a small letter. The candidates who pass are those who take care over all these details.'

ii. 'Write as clearly and legibly as possible, avoiding excessively sloping writing or huddling letters and words closely together.'

iii. 'There is still much slipshod presentation of material. It is often difficult to distinguish between capital letters and small letters, corrections are not made clearly, the revised form often being written over the original word, resulting in complete illegibility, and rough work is not clearly cancelled.'

Writing illegibly is rather like trying to carry on a conversation with your hand in your mouth—and it has about the same effect on the person with whom you are trying to communicate. Your ideas may be brilliant, your language may be faultless, but it will all be wasted if your handwriting is illegible.

Make your capital letters about twice as high as your small letters. Form *each letter* carefully. Be certain that the letters given here in brackets do not look alike: (*b*, *h* and *k*), (*d* and *cl*), (*e* and *i*), (*l* and *t*), (*m*, *n*, *r* and *w*), (*s* and *r*), (*u* and *v*).

When you cross the small letter 't', put the horizontal stroke through the letter and not above it. Don't put unnecessary 'tails' and flourishes on your letters.

Exercise 8

1. Copy out the last three paragraphs above and then get the legibility of your handwriting checked. If you are in a school, your teacher will do it for you. If you have left school, get a friend to read through your work and comment on its legibility.

2. Practise individual letters and groups of letters as advised by the person who checks the work done in 1.

3. If necessary, improve your handwriting steadily during the year. The only person who can't write neatly is somebody who has a temporary muscular or other physical defect in the hand or arm.

9. Vocabulary

In matters of vocabulary and language generally, textbooks can give you only limited assistance—and certainly not enough to bring you up to the required standard. Again, the examiners' reports show you the way:

i. 'The best way to prepare . . . is to read interesting books on many different subjects.'

ii. 'Success can be achieved only through the elimination of mechanical errors of spelling, grammar and punctuation, the acquirement of a command of the patterns and idiom of the language and a more complete understanding of what they read. Candidates would be well advised to spend more time in the careful reading of good authors.'

iii. 'Behind most of the scripts, even the weaker ones, lay much hard, steady work—much memorizing of model essays, and lists of quotations, proverbs and "useful" words, which had to be dragged in at all costs. Unfortunately, candidates still have too narrow an idea of what this examination demands. More of them would pass if, abandoning their futile search for short cuts, they could only bring themselves to enjoy their study of English, and, above all, to surround themselves with attractive books of all kinds, and read for the sheer fun of it.'

Follow the advice given by these very experienced examiners. On page 407 you will find an appendix which lists books you may find interesting and useful. Get a good dictionary, buy or borrow cheap editions of the books, and try to read at least one book a week throughout the year.

Meanwhile there are several points of style which we can consider in a moment, and the second part of this book deals with language problems which must be revised and practised.

a. A good general standard is expected in the use of such things as articles, prepositions, pronouns, verbs, sequence of tenses etc. Part II of the book will help you but sustained reading will be of even greater value.

b. **Do NOT clutter up your work with memorized proverbs, idioms and quotations.** The examiners have rightly complained of 'the extensive use of glib quotations learned by heart and dragged into essays with little or no relevance'. Such proverbs as 'Too many cooks spoil the broth' and 'All that glitters is not gold' are occasionally used in speech but are very rarely used in writing. A good composition will normally contain **none** of these proverbs at all. If they are forced into an essay, they merely make it seem ridiculous.

You may perhaps have a separate examination question which asks you to explain the meaning of certain proverbs or idiomatic expressions. Because of this you may study them at school. When you do so, remember that they should NOT be pushed into your composition.

c. **Never use a long or unusual word if a shorter or more common one is available.** You won't impress your reader; you will only make your work seem odd or ridiculous. Aim at simplicity and sincerity of expression.

d. Unless you are using dialogue, **avoid the use of colloquial expressions and slang**. Thus *children* must be used instead of 'kids', and *I have* instead of 'I've'.

e. By using synonyms, try to bring some variety into your vocabulary. This is particularly necessary when your subject consists of a single word such as 'Transport'. The reader does not want to find 'transport' on every line.

f. Notice that we **never** use the following words in the plural form and that they are all followed by a *singular* verb: scenery, furniture, laughter, equipment, apparatus, luggage, news.

Vocabulary exercises will be found in the chapter on 'Comprehension' and in Part II of this book.

10. Sentence structure

We cannot here review the many sentence patterns which can occur in English. You will find some of them in Part II. However, we can consider a few guides to sentence structure in composition:

a. Your aim is to convey information to your reader. When in doubt, therefore, keep your sentences short. Do not go to the extreme of making every sentence a simple one. But do avoid lengthy qualifying and modifying statements. They can make it difficult for the reader to find the meaning of your sentences. Remember that if your sentence exceeds two lines you may be in danger of confusing your reader. Keep him in mind when you write.

b. Sentences can vary in these ways:

i. In their structure. (Here 'structure' refers to the order of subject, verb, indirect object and object, and to the order of clauses and phrases.)

ii. In their length.

iii. In their pace or emotional intensity. (For example, an order, prohibition or question arouses a little more emotion than most statements.)

As far as possible, try to prevent monotony by varying the types of sentences you use.

11. Use of tenses

The correct use of individual tenses, and problems involving sequence of tenses are left to Part II.

Before you start your composition, look and see which tenses you are likely to use. For example:

i. *My hobby* This will probably involve the Simple Present tense mainly.

ii. *Describe an accident* This will make you use the Simple Past tense quite a lot.

iii. *Which country would you most like to visit? Why?* This will involve the use of the Present Conditional tense and the Simple Present tense.

iv. *Fishing* The main tense will depend on the theme you choose. When you are wondering which composition subject to choose, think about the tenses involved. Don't choose a subject like (iii) if you cannot use conditional tenses properly.

When you have chosen your subject and the theme, decide what your main tense will be. Don't change from the present to the past unless you have a good reason.

12. Summary of the chapter

1. *Your work should be original and as interesting as possible.*

2. *You are expected to write about 40 to 50 lines in an hour. If you have to write more than one essay, try to produce a total of about a line per minute of writing time.*

3. *It is vital that the composition should be relevant to the subject set. The exact words of the topic must be studied carefully.*
4. *Your work will be more interesting if you make use of significant details, local colour, your five senses and your personal views and experiences.*
5. *Your handwriting MUST be easily legible.*
6. *Vocabulary and linguistic accuracy can best be improved through wide and sustained reading.*
7. *While variety is desirable in both vocabulary and sentence structure, simplicity is also very necessary. Unnecessarily long words, the use of proverbs and complicated sentences should be avoided.*
8. *Care must be taken to use the corrrect main tense in a composition.*

Chapter 3

Some Types of Composition

A plot

1. Story-telling or narrative

In this section we will consider the writing of stories not merely in an examination but for magazines, newspapers etc. as well. If you become interested in this type of work, buy a book on the art of the short story and perhaps one which deals with the problems of novelists. A book called *The Writer's and Artist's Year Book* will tell you how and where to sell your stories in England, America and many other countries. It is not easy to write and sell good stories but many people succeed.

In a story we must have these things:

a. A plot
b. Some characters.

c. Suitable language
d. An interesting background.

We will consider them separately.

a. The plot

Most plots are based on a conflict of some kind. We can have these types:

33

i. A person *in conflict with himself* because he is acting abnormally, e.g. an intensely jealous or ambitious person.

ii. A person is *in conflict with other people* or with another person, a jealous husband or employee, a disappointed suitor.

iii. A person is *in conflict with some outside circumstance* over which he has little or no control, e.g. a sailor caught in a fierce tropical storm, a housewife caught by a hurricane, a motorist stranded by puncture or breakdown.

Exercise 1

1. Think of the plot of some films or plays which you know, or some books or stories you have read. Say whether the plot is based on type (i), (ii) or (iii) above.

2. By using conflict we create a problem. The story then becomes interesting when attempts are made to solve the problem or work it out. Write down an example of a problem created by using, in turn, each of the three types of conflict mentioned at the top of this page.

Once the problem has been created, the story usually follows a definite pattern:

i. It must have **an interesting start** which quickly presents the reader with the problem on which the plot is based.

ii. Obstacles appear. These are peaks of interest, each more exciting than the last.

iii. The story comes to a climax, probably when the problem is finally worked out. After this, the story ends abruptly.

Exercise 2

Choose any story which you have read or seen as a film. Write down the title. Then analyse the plot. Explain:

i. How the start was made interesting and what problem was presented.

ii. What incidents held your interest after that.

iii. How and when the climax came.

Exercise 3

To make sure that you understand the structure of a plot, repeat Exercise 2, but with a different story.

34

Exercise 4

1. Write the opening paragraph of a detective story or thriller. Make it interesting and don't copy it from an existing book because (a) that would be an infringement of copyright and (b) we learn by doing and not by copying.
2. Write the opening paragraph of a love story OR of a sea story.

Exercise 5

Write the outline of the plot for ONE of the following stories. Do not write the complete story. You should be able to explain the outline in less than 10 lines.

1. A young man (or woman) is travelling in a car on his way to an interview which, he hopes, will bring him his first job after leaving school. Some miles from his destination, the car breaks down.
2. A simple fisherman finds a pearl of very great value. (This is the basis of the plot in John Steinbeck's fine story, *The Pearl*.)
3. A girl is jealous of another one who is more attractive than she is.

b. The characters

The characters in your story should be:

i. credible, i.e. reasonably true to life.
ii. clearly differentiated from each other so that we do not mix them up.
iii. vividly presented so that we can easily visualize them.

To make your characters credible (and not incredible) you must study people and take a real interest in them and their motives. You can make them different from each other if you try hard enough. It is merely a matter of effort. You can present them sharply and clearly by using significant details which readily give a clue to the nature of each person. Read the following descriptions:

1. The manager of the factory was a short, restless man. His voice never fell below a deafening roar as he led us on a tour of inspection. He strode through the building like an emperor surveying his troops before battle. Nothing daunted him; nothing even checked him. If a foreman approached him with a problem, he jerked his scrawny neck round and barked out a series of orders which practically swept the poor man

35

off his feet. With his head held high and his large nose scenting out the way before us, he breathed an air of supreme confidence—and we followed him in awe, mildly astonished to find such a dynamic personality in such a scanty frame.

(*Knock and Wait* by K. S. Lee)

2. Mary was much more than merely pretty. Her dark curly hair, her smiling brown eyes and her face were all that one could wish for. But there was something else—something of greater importance. In some subtle way she radiated a degree of goodness which all admire but few attain. It shone in her eyes and fashioned her smile. It dominated her personality and drew me towards her. (*The Tasek Road* by Brian Deroy)

3. Elias Strorm at the age of 45 was a husky man, a dominating man, and a man fierce for rectitude. He had eyes that could flash with evangelical fire beneath bushy brows. Respect for God was frequently on his lips, and fear of the devil constantly in his heart. (*The Chrysalids* by John Wyndham)

4. . . . his confidential servant, Ivan, the old man with a scar and a face almost as grey as his moustache . . .

(*The Secret Garden* by G. K. Chesterton)

It is not necessary to use a paragraph to build up an effective picture of a person. A few well-chosen words will serve to introduce a character. After that, a person's actions and words should reveal his nature.

Exercise 6

What qualities do you associate with each of the following?

1. tight or thin lips
2. restless eyes
3. untidy hair (of an adult)
4. a heavily lined or wrinkled forehead

Exercise 7

Using not more than 3 lines in each case, write a brief description of each of the following, making your account as striking as possible but credible.

a. a nervous prisoner on trial for theft
b. the magistrate or judge trying the case in *a*

c. the efficient lawyer prosecuting the prisoner in *a*

d. an old man or woman

e. a wealthy trader who is rather unscrupulous

Exercise 8

In this exercise you may answer 2 before 1 if you wish. Do not write more than 10 lines about each couple.

1. Describe two girls or women who are present in the same place but very different in character.
2. Do a similar thing with two boys or men.

c. Suitable language

Your story should be written in language suitable for a particular class or type of reader. To give an extreme case, we must write much more simply for children under the age of 8. *Your* task at the moment is to make your work suitable for an examiner but you may have to use different styles if you ever try to write for the public. You must study the people who read the magazine or newspaper to which you hope to sell your story. Then you may have to adjust your language to suit their known tastes.

Exercise 9

Write the opening paragraph of ONE of these:

1. A story or legend intended for children under the age of 5. Suggest an illustration to accompany your first paragraph. Make sure you use language which very young children can understand and try to read.
2. A story for any comic, magazine or publication popular with young people aged 12–18. Say whether you are writing for boys or for girls. Do not try to write for both.
3. A short story for any newspaper popular with adults. (*Note:* This does **not** give you a licence to use long words.)
4. A short story for your school magazine. Assume that it will be read by some pupils and parents.

Note: If you become very interested in your story, you can complete it but this is not necessary. It applies to 1, 2, 3 and 4.

d. An interesting background

If possible, a short story should be set against a background

37

which interests the reader because it teaches him something he does not know. For example, a story set in a tin mine may lead us to a better understanding of the working of such a mine. A story set in a hospital is likely to improve our knowledge of medicine or hospital routine. This factor is not as important as the plot, characterization or language but it can make a worthwhile contribution. It is of more importance in a novel—as the works of Dickens, Thomas Hardy, Gerald Durrell and Ian Fleming demonstrate.

Exercise 10

EITHER 1. Write an original short story on any subject you like, paying special attention to the plot, characterization, language and background.

OR 2. Write a complete short story of up to 70 lines on ONE of the subjects in Exercise 5.

2. Descriptive compositions

A descriptive composition can deal with a person, a place, a lifeless object or, in some cases, with an action such as an accident. In each case, the best effect is obtained **not** by giving quantity but by carefully selecting the most apt words. A general impression can be given in a few words as we see in these descriptions of two cafés:

The Café des Amateurs was a sad, evilly run café where the drunkards of the quarter crowded together and I kept away from it because of the smell of dirty bodies and the sour smell of drunkenness.

I came to *a good café* that I knew on the Place St-Michel. It was a pleasant café, warm and clean and friendly.

(*A Moveable Feast* by Ernest Hemingway)

For longer descriptive passages see the works of any of the novelists mentioned in 1*d* above, or read the first chapter of Daphne du Maurier's *Rebecca*.

We need not linger in our consideration of descriptive compositions because we have already seen (in Chapter 2) what is required: significant detail, the full use of the five senses, local colour etc. Your aim is to get the maximum effect (on your reader) with the minimum number of words. Flowery and ostentatious expressions, as well as the so-called 'purple patches' should be avoided since they merely make a composition appear ridiculous. Your first task is to decide on the general impression you want to convey. This becomes your theme, e.g.

My best friend Bunmi never takes anything seriously. For her, life is one long joke . . .

A shopkeeper Success had made Mr. Brown indifferent to his customers and was now slowly ruining his business. He left most of the business of running the shop to his assistants, and only served behind the counter when the spirit moved him. Then he was studiously formal and impersonal so that his customers suspected that he had been rude to them but could not decide what to complain about.

The main street The main street in my village consists of three houses, a coffee shop, a standpipe with a dripping tap, and the remains of a bus stop sign. It is asleep by day but sometimes rouses itself into activity at night.

Once you have decided on the general impression of the person, place or thing, you use the techniques already described when you deal with the details. They should develop the general impression and drive it home as graphically as possible.

Exercise 11

Write the opening two or three sentences of a description of each of the following, disclosing to the reader the general impression which will be worked out in the full description.

a. A room in a hotel OR in somebody else's house.
b. An inspector of any kind OR a dentist.
c. A scene in a large town OR in the country.
d. A pet OR a wild animal.

Exercise 12

Write about 30 lines on ONE of the following:

a. The most unpleasant season OR month of the year.
b. Choose any scene or building you please, and describe it as it might have appeared hundreds of years ago.
c. Describe an airport OR a seaport OR a railway station.
d. Describe the character and achievements of a person whom you admire.

39

3. Explanatory or argumentative composition

a. Explanatory composition

Examples of this type of composition include:

    i. Explain how to mend a puncture OR make a blouse.

    ii. Explain why any important festival is celebrated in your country or by your community.

    iii. Give detailed instructions for one of the following: raising poultry, growing vegetables, making any article which you have made at school or at home as a hobby.

The principles to be followed when writing this type of composition are few but important. Don't try to make your composition vivid and interesting as you would when writing a narrative or descriptive composition. Make your work intelligible and accurate. Assemble *all* the facts. Put them in the right order. A detailed plan is very necessary to make sure that you include each important step in the account.

b. Argumentative composition

Examples of this type of composition include:

    i. 'Parents always know best.' Discuss.

    ii. Comment on the opinion that tradition is an obstacle to progress.

    iii. Do you agree that it is better not to have co-educational schools?

    iv. 'Man to lead; woman to follow.' What do you think?

Some detailed comments on these topics may help you to understand the attitude you should show in a composition of this type. The guiding principle is that you should **consider both sides.**

    i. *Parents always know best*

This is wrong but it contains a germ of truth or sound advice. No parent *always* knows best. Some very able parents *often* know best. Some very stupid parents rarely know best. Because of their age and greater experience, parents can usually offer sound advice and this should be heeded. There are times, however, when parents are faced with an entirely new situation or way of life and the child may be better equipped to make a decision. The most desirable state is a compromise in which the advice of the parent is usually sought but not necessarily followed.

    ii. *Tradition as an obstacle to progress*

This is not always the case. Tradition is sometimes a safe guide for young or inexperienced people and shows them a safe path to follow. However, when it prevents people from exploring new paths and methods, it can become an obstacle.

iii. *Do you agree that it is better not to have co-educational schools?*

On the whole, I think it is better to have both co-educational and 'single sex' schools. Each system has its good points and disadvantages but I should prefer to have both systems to allow parents to choose. Certainly I should not agree with the abolition of co-educational schools, because many countries cannot afford to replace one co-educational school with two separate schools.

iv. *Man to lead; woman to follow*

As a guiding principle this is illogical and unfair. In general, women have every right to equal treatment and should not be regarded as inferior. In some (but not all) tasks which require physical strength, men lead and will probably continue to do so since women have no wish to oust them. In others such as nursing and the teaching of very young children, women often do the leading.

In these summaries, we can see the type of approach to controversial topics. A word of warning should be added. Some of these topics can be very dangerous unless you are quite a tolerant, fair-minded and thoughtful person. Many candidates would be tempted to agree with (iv) above and may be penalized for holding an uncivilized view. If you are doubtful about a controversial topic, therefore, avoid it lest you expose a weakness in thinking or experience.

If you do tackle one of these topics, BE FAIR. Think deeply when you are making your plan and searching for arguments. Remember that you can have only one theme: present the arguments of both sides. If necessary, sum up and give your personal view—but remember the reader for whom you will be writing.

Exercise 13

Using not more than 5 to 10 lines in each case, give summaries of the attitude you would show when writing about each of the topics below. Your summaries should consider both sides as in the examples (i) to (iv) above.

1. 'You can judge a man by his clothes.' Do you agree?

2. 'Education should be free and compulsory to the age of 16.' What do you think?

3. Do you agree that a woman's place is in the home?

4. Personal reflective essays

This is the type of essay in which a person reflects on such wide subjects as 'Food', 'Leisure', 'Money', 'Clothes'. This type of essay used to be fashionable in examinations but, perhaps fortunately, it is becoming less common.

If you are faced with this type of subject, use PC FAT to find a definite theme, after which you will find that the topic is not so difficult to deal with. There are so many aspects to such topics as 'Food' and 'Money' that it is almost impossible to write about them satisfactorily unless you limit the scope of your subject by using PC FAT. Once you have done this, you merely follow the procedure outlined in Chapter 1.

5. Factual or imaginative approach

The aim of this section is to remind you that in many cases you can choose between a factual or an imaginative approach to your composition subject. A factual approach is usually easier (and thus safer for less able candidates) but an imaginative approach sometimes produces a more interesting essay. These examples show you the different approaches:

i. *'The main street in my town'*

Factual: Write a descriptive composition of the main street as it is now, bringing in plenty of detail, movement and sensitive observation. Describe the appearance of the street, some of its noises and users and even perhaps its smells.

Imaginative: Describe the main street as it was many years ago, as it is now, and as it may be in a hundred years' time.

ii. *'Animals in captivity'*

Factual: Deal with the problems of animals in captivity, e.g. whether they should be kept in captivity at all and, if so, under what conditions; the breeding in captivity of animals which might otherwise become extinct; national animal reserves as a form of captivity etc.

Imaginative: Deal only with the most important animal in captivity—Man. There are then alternative ways of developing this theme. You can write only about prisons and the 'animals' in captivity in them. You can write about Man as held captive by his own superstitions and prejudices etc. There are other methods but you can use only one of them in a single essay.

These two examples show you the difference in the approaches but you can see that the imaginative approach requires considerable skill and experience. There is always a danger that an inexperienced writer might become completely irrelevant. For this reason, the imaginative approach must be handled with great care.

Exercise 14

As has been done above, outline (i) a factual approach and then (ii) an imaginative approach to ONE of these subjects:

1. The jungle
2. Space travel
3. A public holiday
4. Music

6. Summary of the chapter

1. *In writing a story special attention must be paid to the choice and construction of the plot, to the characterization and language, and to the type of background used.*
2. *In a descriptive composition it is wise to give a general impression of the object first and then to build up a detailed description by the use of significant detail, the five senses etc.*
3. *In an explanatory composition it is important to make sure that the account is easy to understand and contains all the facts in the right order.*
4. *In an essay on a controversial topic both sides of the question must be discussed thoroughly. The issue can then be summed up and a personal opinion given. Automatic agreement with a quotation can be highly dangerous.*
5. *With such topics as 'Food' and 'Leisure', PC FAT must be used to find a definite theme.*
6. *Some topics can be dealt with from a factual point of view OR from an imaginative point of view but the latter requires considerable skill on the part of the writer.*

Note: Appendix B on page 410 contains further composition topics.

Chapter 4

Some Problems of Factual Composition

meteors and things from space

1. The theme is given but the facts are not provided

You may sometimes have to write about a subject for which the theme is given but for which the facts are not provided. Two examples are:

a. Write about the problems of improving communications in your country.

b. Write about the damage caused by the wild forces of nature.
   In such cases you must:

i. Make a note of all the relevant facts. Sometimes it is helpful to ask yourself 'Why?' 'What else?' 'When?' or 'Where?' until you have built up a sufficient store of facts.

ii. Organize your facts into a logical order so that they develop a definite theme or central idea. This is very necessary. Do NOT present your ideas in a random or unconnected manner.

We can illustrate this procedure by considering subject *b* above. When I first thought about this topic, these ideas came into my mind and I jotted them down as *notes:*

Fire	Volcanoes	Storms
Floods	? disease	Icebergs (but are they 'wild'?)
Earthquakes	? meteors and things from space	
Hurricanes, cyclones etc.	Slower forces such as wind erosion (?)	
Man (he is sometimes a very 'wild force' of nature)?		

I have put these ideas down exactly as they came into my mind but you can see that (a) they do not follow any special order and (b) I am uncertain whether or not to include some of them.

Finding a theme
Looking at them I see that I can put them into groups. I shall not use the headings in my composition but they are useful as guides to me.

Land	*Air*	*Water*	*? Man*
Earthquakes	Hurricanes etc.	Storms	Diseases
Volcanoes	? Wind erosion	Floods	War etc.
Fire	? Meteors	Icebergs	

I am now ready to start my composition. My theme will be: 'I will give a factual account of the damage caused by the wild forces of nature, dividing my work into matters arising from the land, the movement of the air, water and ice and, perhaps, from man himself.' When I come to deal with man I shall explain that it is possible to consider man a 'wild force' of nature because his actions are sometimes very rash and uncontrolled. The bulk of my answer will be on the more conventional 'wild forces' affecting the land, the air and water. I shall deal with each group at a time and not have to leap from topic to topic with no logical development.

Exercise 1

a. Make notes on each of the following subjects. Write down the facts or points which you may need when you write your composition.

b. Group your facts under two or more headings.

c. Work out and write down the theme which unites all your headings in a logical order. (This is difficult at first but becomes easier with practice.)

   i. Write about the problems of improving communications in your country.

   ii. What steps are being taken to develop industries in your country?

iii. In what ways could your local radio (or television) programmes be improved?
iv. Discuss the attractions which your country can offer to tourists.

2. Some or all of the facts are provided

You may sometimes be given some or all of the facts which concern your topic. For example:

Discuss the effects which the increase in population is now having in your country and consider what steps can be taken to deal with any problems which arise. You can take the following points into consideration when writing your answer and can also provide material of your own:

a. The possible effects on the educational system; the need for new schools and better facilities; possible changes and their cost.
b. Problems concerning housing, health and social services.
c. The need to create more opportunities for employment; the development of industries; the increase in domestic markets.
d. Changes in traditional family attitudes and customs.
e. The need to provide food for the increasing population; matters affecting agriculture and imports; possible lack of land.
f. Transport, communications and other problems arising from the sudden development of urban areas.

When you have to deal with this type of topic, consider two points:

i. Is sufficient information given? Are there any other factors which ought to be brought in? Does the wording of the question permit me to bring in additional material?
ii. Is the material already arranged in a logical order? How can I rearrange the material so that I use it to develop a unifying theme in a logical way?

In this example, we are given six points, *a* to *f*. They deal fairly well with the subject but do not consider the question of checking the increase in the population. We might therefore wish to add this point. With a little thought, we can rearrange the order of the points in this way:

Social Services	*Keeping Alive*	*Personal and Family Matters*
a and *b*	*c* and *e*	*d* and the question of con-
f		trolling the birth rate

In which order would you deal with these three groups? Which would you write about first? One method would be to take 'Keeping Alive' first, and to deal with the question of finding food and employment. We could then consider the 'Social Services' group. Next we could consider the changes in family customs and traditions. Finally we could consider what steps, if any, could be taken to deal with the rise in population and to try to check it.

Exercise 2

Consider the following composition subject.

a. Say what extra material, if any, should be inserted.

b. Explain how you would rearrange the facts so that you can develop a unifying theme in a logical manner.

What qualities do you consider make an ideal husband (or wife) for you?

You can consider the following points and any others which are necessary:

i. Personal appearance, face, clothes etc.
ii. Wealth, social position etc.
iii. Education, training, ability to earn a living and contribute to the family income.
iv. Race, cultural background etc.
v. Religion or other beliefs, perhaps including political views.
vi. Age and maturity.
vii. Personal interests, hobbies, sports etc.

3. Using statistics

Be careful when you use statistics or see them used. If they are used properly, they are very helpful. Unfortunately, these tricks are quite common:

a. The speaker chooses only the statistics that support his point of view; he deliberately suppresses those against his opinion, e.g.

'In our school there are 25 male teachers but only 6 lady teachers. This proves that women are no good as teachers.'

47

b. The statistics may be based on unreliable evidence—or on no real evidence at all. The public are then led to believe that the statistics are reliable, e.g.

'More people smoke Coffing Cigarettes than any other cigarette.'

'Leading doctors recommend Onk's Oily Ointment For Perforated Pimples. It has proved successful in 98 per cent of the most difficult cases.'

In other cases the statistics may be prepared honestly but they are unreliable because they do not take into account all the relevant factors.

The following figures show the total amount of money spent on food in two areas in two different years:

	Rural Area	*Urban Area*
1965	£6,410,000	£7,075,000
1966	£4,650,000	£8,165,000

It would be wrong to assume that the standard of living in the rural area declined in 1966. The reduction in the amount spent may have been caused by (a) the movement of large numbers of people from the rural area to the urban area, or by (b) improvements in farming in the rural area, making the purchase of food less necessary, or by (c) another unstated factor.

Conversely, we cannot conclude that the standard of living rose in the urban area. If the population rose by 25 per cent in 1966, the standard of living might have fallen since less money would have been spent by each person.

Exercise 3

Consider the following statistics and then answer the questions about them.

Crime in the period 1964–1966

	1964	*1965*	*1966*
Murder	27	31	39
Manslaughter	14	12	8
Serious assaults	264	340	243
Kidnapping	48	30	12
Rape and indecent assault	1	4	2
Other offences against the person	112	124	118
Against public order	12	78	68
Robbery	212	224	198

Burglary	684	857	864
Larceny	463	586	283
Fraud and embezzlement	113	275	285
Loitering and trespass	362	583	785

1. Say whether each of the following statements is true or false. If you think a statement is false, give your reasons for your opinion.

   a. There has been a steady increase in the number of murders since 1964.

   b. The increase in murders proves that more crime was committed in 1966 than in (i) the two previous years, (ii) any previous year.

   c. An examination of the figures for murder shows that morals fell sharply in 1966.

   d. An examination of the figures for rape and indecent assault shows that morals rose sharply in 1966 and, indeed, are twice as high as in 1965.

   e. The figures for rape and indecent assault show that in 1966 the men were at least twice as immoral as in 1964. This is a grave reflection on our society and, in particular, on our educational system. Steps should be taken immediately to deal with this grave menace.

   f. The figures for serious assaults and kidnapping prove how efficient our police force has been in suppressing crime recently. We may conclude that the day of the criminal is past in our country, thanks largely to the enlightened nature of our educational system and to the high civic spirit of our people.

   g. The figures for crimes against public order prove that:
      i. The Government was more popular in 1966 than in 1965.
      ii. There was a serious riot in 1965.
      iii. The law was enforced more severely in 1965 than in 1964.

   h. The figures for crimes against public order do not enable us to draw any conclusions at all unless we know what is meant by 'against public order'.

   i. From the figures for robbery we may deduce that:
      i. More robbers were convicted in 1965 than in 1966.
      ii. More robberies were committed in 1965 than in 1966.
      iii. It is impossible to say whether the number of robberies committed in 1965 did or did not exceed the number in 1966.

2. In commenting on the figures for crime, what would you want to know about the increase in population at this period?
3. Would you want to consider (i) the size of the police force and (ii) its efficiency when commenting on the figures?
4. In what way are the following factors relevant to the statistics for crime?

   a. In January, 1965, a new law was passed making it an offence for a person to enter the compound of another person without permission. This offence is listed as 'trespass'.

   b. In 1965 seventy-two people took part in a peaceful demonstration outside a foreign embassy. They were all arrested and fined for an offence against public order.

   c. In 1966 an offence which had previously been considered to be larceny was reclassified as burglary.

   d. The number of tourists in 1965 was nearly five times the number in 1964.

   e. The population increased by about 5 per cent in 1965 and by a further 8 per cent in 1966.

Exercise 4

The following figures show the number of lessons per week in the timetables of pupils in Sixth Form (Arts) of two different schools. In each school English is the medium of instruction but is not the mother tongue of the pupils. Assume that the pupils are preparing for entrance to a university.

	High School	*Modern School*
Mother tongue	—	2
English	10	
Geography	9	
History	10	9 each for any three subjects
Economics	9	
Physical Education	—	2 (organized games)
Religion or Ethics	—	1
Private Study	2	8 (including 2 optional periods of Art)
Total	40	40

Pupils from the High School offer 4 subjects at H.S.C. Principal level (or G.C.E. 'A' level) but those from the Modern School offer only 3 subjects. The university concerned will accept candidates who get good results in 2 or 3 subjects at this level.

Use the material given above to make a written comparison of the usefulness of the two timetables.

4. Appraising a photograph or a picture

You may sometimes want to discuss the merits of a photograph or a picture. Unfortunately there is no space in this book for an adequate discussion of the very interesting factors involved in photography and in art. These topics are mentioned here only as a reminder to you to pursue them if the opportunity occurs. If possible:

a. Persuade an expert photographer (who may be a pupil, a teacher or somebody outside the school) to give you an illustrated talk on his craft.

b. Persuade your Art teacher to give you a talk on the appreciation of pictures of various types.

5. Summary of the chapter

1. *Sometimes you are required to write about a factual subject but the facts are not provided. When this happens, you must find the facts and arrange them in a logical order. This may involve finding a unifying theme.*

2. *When the facts are provided, check that they are sufficient. Provide extra ones if necessary and permissible. Arrange the facts in a logical order.*

3. *Statistics are often misused, and their correct interpretation requires great care and honesty.*

4. *The appraisal of photographs and pictures is an interesting type of composition and should be studied if possible.*

6. Further exercises

Exercise 5 (45 minutes)

Write a story based on the following points:

a. A motorist left a hotel one evening. He was in a hurry to catch the last car-ferry some miles away.

b. He was delayed by dense traffic in the town but managed to get out of the town at last.

c. He hurried on and drove quickly through a storm.

  d. He nearly had an accident when he found the road obstructed by a very large branch torn from a tree.
  e. With the aid of another motorist, he managed to move the branch after some delay.
  f. Eventually he reached the ferry station but found that the last ferry had already gone. He was very angry.
  g. He returned to his hotel and there heard on the radio that the ferry had sunk during the storm, with great loss of life.

Exercise 6 (45 minutes)

  Write an account of a shop, using the material given below:
  a. Give a brief account of its location and the general area or neighbourhood.
  b. Describe the outside of the shop—its size and appearance; the goods on display; the entrance.
  c. Give an outline of the inside of the shop—a first impression of the size, the location of the counters etc., and the number of customers and assistants.
  d. Describe in greater detail some of the goods, the staff and a few customers.
  e. Perhaps give a snatch of conversation or some action in the shop.
  f. Finish with a summary of the atmosphere of the shop or the impression this particular shop makes on you.

Exercise 7 (45 minutes)

  Study the statistics below. They refer to road accidents in a country in one year. Use the information contained in them as the basis for an account entitled 'Accidents on the Road'. Do not introduce material not found in the statistics.

  Percentages refer to the number of all road accidents in the year.

Place	%	*Weather*	%
Slight bend	5	Fine	62
Sharp bend	10	Misty	2
Crest of hill	3	Slight rain	9
Road junction	7	Heavy rain	14
Straight, open road	54	Overcast or	
Busy city street	21	growing dark	13

Apparent cause	%	Time	%
Poor lighting	3	6–8 a.m.	21
Animals	2	8–10 a.m.	9
Excessive speed	43	10 a.m.–noon	4
Mechanical defect	6	noon–2 p.m.	15
Lack of care or error		2–4 p.m.	5
of judgment	31	4–6 p.m.	26
Faulty road surface	2	6–8 p.m.	12
Drink or drugs	9	at night	8
Over-loading	4		

Exercise 8 (30 minutes)

Use the following notes to write an account of the way in which you repair a puncture in a bicycle tyre. You need not follow the notes at all steps if your own method is different in some way.

a. Using a lever to take the tyre off the wheel. Unscrewing the valve cap and pulling out the inner tube.

b. Finding the puncture by inspection or by using a bowl of water.

c. Cleaning the tube, sticking on the patch, dusting the area with chalk to stop it from sticking to the tyre.

d. Putting the tube and tyre on again. Replacing the valve cap. Pumping up the tyre.

Exercise 9 (45 minutes)

Write 8 to 15 lines about each of the two following photographs:

(See page 54)

a. Explain what you would do if you were driving along a road through some hills, heard the rumbling noise of a landslide ahead of you, and came round the corner to find the scene in the photograph. Start your answer in this way: 'If I came on a scene like this, I would . . .'

b. Explain what events possibly led to this picture. The snake is a python which has recently eaten something but not yet digested it.

Exercise 10 (45 minutes)

Write about *one* of the following subjects:

1. Here is an item taken from a daily newspaper:
   John Smith, aged 34, was arrested at London Airport today, and charged with attempting to evade Customs duty on uncut diamonds estimated to be worth nearly £250,000.
   Make up a story about John Smith and the diamonds, explaining where he got them, where he was going and how he came to be arrested.

2. A publisher approaches you and explains that he is about to start a new magazine intended to appeal to young people. He asks you to act as adviser on the contents of the magazine. Give an account of the things you would advise him to put in the magazine to make it attractive to people of your own age. You can assume that the magazine is intended for females only, males only or for males and females. The choice is up to you.

Exercise 11 (45 minutes)

Write an article for a newspaper discussing the good and bad points of setting homework in secondary schools. You may use the information given below and you may add to it. Make sure that you discuss each side fairly and fully.

Suggested advantages

a. It keeps the pupils busy at home and does not give them time to get into trouble in the streets.

b. It enables the school to cover more work and a wider syllabus.

c. It helps to maintain a standard of education which is high by comparison with that of other countries.

d. It helps to stop pupils from forgetting work done at school. This is particularly the case with homework set for the holidays.

e. It keeps children out of the way of their tired or busy parents at home.

Suggested disadvantages

a. It seriously limits the free time which pupils have for sports, their hobbies, social service etc. and thus has a narrowing effect on their education.

b. The same amount of work could be covered at school by using smaller classes and more efficient methods.

c. It is a strain for conscientious pupils, some of whom worry or lose sleep through excessive amounts of homework. It can thus have an adverse effect on mental or physical development.

d. In some homes, conditions are unsuitable for homework, i.e. there is insufficient room or lack of peace, so that some children are penalized through no fault of their own.

e. It makes too much marking for teachers who are thus unable to give their best in the classroom.

Note: See Appendix B on page 410 for further composition topics.

Chapter 5

Comprehension

fish that the rest respect

1. Examination techniques

In this chapter we are concerned with comprehension in examinations and in the normal activities of life. We will start by considering two past questions, together with comments made by the examiners.

i. Read carefully through the following passage, and then answer the questions below, *using your own words* as far as possible:

I became more and more convinced that sharks are not as formidable as most people think and that a prudent and experienced diver does not have to be a heroic superman, or endanger his life by challenging them to mortal combat, so long as he has a precise understanding of their nature and habits. 5

In reality, just like a great many other people who have preceded me, I was much attracted by the new sport of diving for amusement. Undersea exploration, even when confined to the coastal waters extending from the shore itself to shallow depths, can be carried out by any modern diver. Yet 10

it reveals to him a vast and multifarious world hitherto
believed closed to mankind, and one in which human beings
can now move with ease, no longer the slaves of gravity and
released from all the common restrictions imposed on physical
activity above water.   15
    Moreover, the feelings he experiences below the surface
cannot be compared with any others. For he discovers a new
world of a different kind altogether. He enters it in reliance
upon his lungs alone, the precarious independence afforded
by the human respiratory system. For a few precious moments 20
he becomes part of those submarine realms.
    When I set out to discover the secrets of the sea and to
move in a liquid atmosphere eight hundred times denser than
that of earth, playing the part of an unauthorized tourist among
its biological and architectural treasures, I came to know its 25
carnivorous and vegetarian inhabitants and its sovereign lords.
I contemplated its peaceful meadows, its sumptuous gardens,
its virgin forests. I was spellbound by the splendours of its
dizzy, wildly overgrown abysses, its perpendicular cliffs and
grandiose cathedrals.   30

a. Give a word or phrase of equivalent meaning for each of *four*
    of the following words as used in the passage:
    convinced (l. 1), formidable (l. 2), prudent (l. 2), precise (l. 5),
    preceded (l. 8), confined (l. 9), spellbound (l. 29).
b. i. What two kinds of treasures are suggested to you by
         'biological and architectural' (l. 26)?
     ii. What two types of inhabitants are suggested by 'carnivorous
         and vegetarian' (l. 27)?
c. In what sense is the writer an 'unauthorized tourist' (l. 25)?
d. Express the following simply in words of your own, so as to
    bring out their full meaning:
      i. 'a vast and multifarious world' (l. 12).
     ii. 'released from all the common restrictions imposed on
         physical activity' (ll. 15–16).
    iii. 'the precarious independence afforded by the human
         respiratory system' (ll. 20–21).
e. What ideas does the author convey to the reader by the follow-
    ing metaphorical expressions? Study the sample answer first.

Example: 'its sovereign lords' (l. 27).
Answer: Just as in any country in the world there will be
           found one or more rulers governing and controlling

57

> the people, so in the depths of the sea are found fish that the rest respect as their mighty rulers.
>   i. 'the slaves of gravity' (l. 14).
> ii. 'its sumptuous gardens, and its virgin forests' (ll. 28–29).
>
> (University of London)

Before you read any further, write down your answers to the questions given above.

This is what the examiners said about the candidates' answers:

'In [this question] many candidates had low marks simply because they did not understand the passage, and this can be remedied only by constant practice in answering this type of question. There is evidence of long and meticulous 'drilling' of candidates in the grammar question. The time would be better spent in testing comprehension of the candidates' reading.

'There were, however, faults which did not arise from lack of comprehension of the passage, the commonest being carelessness in reading the questions. Answers were often too long especially in *b*, *c* and *d*, and many candidates wasted time by writing out the question as well as the answer.

'In *a* the rubric was often ignored: candidates should realize that if four words are asked for, only the first four will be marked, and the rest ignored. They should also make sure that the equivalent they give will fit the word as it is used in the passage. Often a correct dictionary definition of a word will be the wrong one for the passage in question. Candidates should be careful not to change the part of speech. The question asked for the word to be defined in a single word or short phrase; often the answers were far too long, in some cases a complete sentence being used. If a phrase is used it should not contain more than four or five words. Many candidates offer several attempts in the hope that one may be correct. When a candidate offers four or five alternatives, with one correct and the rest hopelessly wrong, it is clear that the candidate does not know the word, and is merely guessing. When a string of unconnected alternatives are offered, all will be ignored after the first. In *b* there was far too much copying, and evidence of lack of care in reading the question. Specific *examples* of plants, fishes and animals were given, although the question asked for types, and in the first part the idea underlying "treasures" was nearly always ignored.

The same mistake was to be seen in *c*, where, for example, "unauthorized" was carefully paraphrased, but "tourist" was ignored. The same lack of attention to detail was seen in *d*, where, for example, the two elements of "multifarious" were not explained. This section was not well done, and in *e*, in spite of the example provided, candidates showed little ability to explain the metaphorical usage. Few candidates made intelligent use of the example offered: they did not follow the suggested pattern, which showed clearly that what was required was (i) the literal meaning of the word used metaphorically, (ii) the meaning of the word as it was used in the passage, and (iii) the connection between the two. Few candidates gave more than the meaning as it appeared in the passage. In the last example there was again clearly a lack of attention to the demands of the question as a whole, the only word to receive attention being "virgin". Finally, in most answers it was clear that the candidates did not pay the same attention to spelling, punctuation, grammar and syntax that they had done in the essay and summary questions. They must remember that errors of this kind are penalized in every part of the paper.'

Exercise 1

The questions on the comprehension passage were lettered *a* to *e*. Go through the comments of the examiners and make notes of the points which seem to you to be important to candidates. Arrange your notes under these headings: *a*, *b*, *c*, *d*, *e* and *General*.

Exercise 2

Compare your own answers to the comprehension questions with the following specimen answers (which are NOT supplied by the examiners):

a. (*To enable you to check your answers, all seven words are explained. For the same reason, alternatives are given.*)

convinced: made certain OR strongly persuaded
formidable: fearsome OR (much) to be dreaded
prudent: careful OR cautious OR sensible
precise: (an) exact OR thorough
preceded: come before OR gone before
confined: restricted
spellbound: completely fascinated OR most impressed.

b. i. 'Biological treasures' suggests to me comparatively rare plants, fishes and other forms of marine life which the author had not seen before. 'Architectural treasures' suggests the uneven form of the sea-bed, rock pillars and arches, and undersea hills and valleys; these, too, were 'treasures' to the author because of their novelty.

ii. 'Carnivorous inhabitants' suggests creatures which eat flesh or meat and refers to various types of fish, crustaceans etc. 'Vegetarian inhabitants' suggests plant-eating fish.

c. The writer is an 'unauthorized tourist' in the sense that he is making a comparatively rare visit to a place which is new to him and he is doing so without first having obtained permission from the local inhabitants, i.e. the marine life.

d. (*The meanings given here are those which the expressions have in the passage.*)

i. a very extensive region (possibly self-contained) in which are found many different objects and forms of life.

ii. freed from all the normal limitations which are put on movements of the body.

iii. the rather uncertain and vulnerable ability given to human beings by their system of breathing so that they can move about freely (wherever oxygen is available).

e. i. Just as men once forced others to serve them as unpaid servants so men are forced to order their movements in accordance with the law of gravity, being unable to rise far above the surface of the land.

ii. On land one can find beautiful gardens, on which much money appears to have been spent, and forests (apparently) unvisited by men. In a similar way, beneath the sea one can find rich displays of marine plants which can be likened to the sumptuous gardens seen on land; one can also find darker areas and taller plants which are similar to the virgin forests found on land.

Let us now consider another past question. Read the passage and answer the questions *before* you read the examiners' comments or look at the specimen answers. Your aim is to study mistakes which are personal to yourself, to understand where and how you went wrong, and to avoid the mistakes in future work. This aim can be achieved only by doing the exercise **before** you look at the comments and answers below it.

ii. Read the passage below carefully, and then answer the questions that follow, *using your own words as far as possible:*

One summer a school of seventeen bottle-nosed dolphins spent a whole week in the Camusfeàrna bay, and they would seem almost to hang about waiting for the boat to come out and play with them. They never leapt and sported unless the human audience was close at hand, but when we were out 5 among them with the outboard motor they would play their own rollicking and hilarious games of hide-and-seek with us, and a sort of aquatic blind-man's-buff, in which we in the boat were all too literally blind to them, and a target for whatever surprises they could devise. The beginning followed an invari- 10 able routine; they would lead, close-packed, their fins thrust-ing from the water with a long powerful forward surge every five or ten seconds, and we would follow to see how close we could get to them. When we were within fifty feet or so there would be a sudden silence while, unseen, they swooped back 15 under the boat to reappear dead astern of us. Sometimes they would remain submerged for many minutes, and we would cut the engine and wait. This was the dolphins' moment. As long as I live, and whatever splendid sights I have yet to see, I shall remember the pure glory of the dolphins' leap as they 20 shot up a clear ten feet out of the sea, one after the other in high parabolas of flashing silver at the very boat's side. At the time it gave me a *déjà-vu** sensation that I could not place; afterwards I realized that it recalled irresistibly the firing in quick succession of pyrotechnic rockets, the tearing sound of 25 the rockets' discharge duplicated by the harsh exhalation of air as each dolphin fired itself almost vertically from the waves.

In this school of dolphins there were some half a dozen calves, not more than four or five feet long as against their parents' twelve. The calves would keep alongside their 30 mothers' flanks—the right-hand side always—and I noticed that when the mothers leapt they kept their acrobatics strictly within the capabilities of their offspring, rising no more than half the height of those unencumbered by children.

*déjà-vu—suggesting something already seen; familiar.

a. Give, each in a single word or a *short* phrase, the exact meaning of *four* of the following words as they are used in the above passage: rollicking (l. 7); aquatic (l. 8); devise (l. 10); sub-merged (l. 17); parabolas (l. 22); flanks (l. 32).

Comprehension

b. i. Why do you think the people in the boat 'cut the engine' (l. 18)?

    ii. What does the author mean by 'This was the dolphins' moment' (l. 18)?

c. What is 'an invariable routine'? Give an example of an invariable routine from the first paragraph, and another from the second.

d. Give *four* distinct and separate reasons why the dolphins' leap (l. 20) recalled the firing of rockets.

e. 'The mothers . . . kept their acrobatics strictly within the capabilities of their offspring' (ll. 33–34). Express this idea in simple words of your own. What evidence does the writer give in support of his statement?   (University of London)

Before you read any further, write down your answers to the questions given above.

This is what the examiners said about the candidates' answers: 'The questions on the passage set for comprehension are carefully designed to find out whether you have understood the passage *as a whole*. If you fully understand the simpler words and phrases of the original, you should be able to make a sensible guess at the meaning of some of the more difficult parts, and, although you will probably make some mistakes, you should be able to earn the nine or ten marks needed on this question if you are to pass. The best way to prepare for this question is to read interesting books on many different subjects. Make it a regular habit to choose a few pages, and examine them thoroughly with the help of a good dictionary, until you are certain that you have understood the full meaning. Most overseas candidates read very little, and what they read is mostly newspapers and political pamphlets. For this reason, their answers to the comprehension question are far below the required standard.

'The passage in the main paper gives a clear, and even vivid, description of the habits of dolphins; yet many candidates did not realize that dolphins are fish-like creatures. They must have misunderstood almost every word in the passage, and they should not have entered for the examination. Read the questions carefully. If, as in *a*, you are asked to explain *four* words, only your first four answers can be given any marks; so the many candidates who gave guesses for all six words were only wasting valuable time. Good candidates answer each of these comprehension questions in one or two short, clear sentences. It is only the weak candidates who write long, muddled answers, containing many different guesses; and these lose marks for unnecessary length. Most candidates understood that the phrase "cut the engine" means that the boat was stopped, but not many realized that the people in the boat wanted to see the exciting performance of the dolphins, and therefore wished to attract them as close as possible. In section *c*, you are asked to explain what is meant by "an invariable routine"; most candidates explained only the word "invariable", and therefore lost half their marks for the question. In giving examples from the passage, it is best to express them in your own words, unless you are definitely told to answer by quotation; for instance, do not say, "The dolphins always *went close-packed*", but rather, "The dolphins always *kept close together*". In section *d*, most candidates did not understand the word "recalled", and they ignored the apostrophe in "dolphins'." Instead of answering the question set, they tried to explain why the dolphins leapt. They should have realized that the leap of the dolphins was like the discharge of a rocket because (i) both go at great speed, (ii) both reach a great height, (iii) both are similar in colour and brightness, and (iv) both make the same sort of noise. (There are several other possible reasons.) Many candidates misunderstood the phrase "dead astern". They had never seen the word "dead" used with the meaning "exactly". Yet this is a very common idiom. The mistakes caused by this gap in their knowledge were often comical.'

Exercise 3

Answer these questions, which refer to the examiners' comments above.

1. What is recommended as the best way of preparing for comprehension questions?
2. What are you going to do about this advice? What materials will you need and where will you get them?
3. What advice or information in the second paragraph of the comments was new to you?

Exercise 4

Compare your own answers to the comprehension questions with the following specimen answers (which are NOT supplied by the examiners). Alternatives are given, and all parts of every question are answered only to help you check your work.

a. rollicking: boisterously playful OR high-spirited
   aquatic: in the water OR marine version of
   devise: think of OR think up
   submerged: below the surface OR under the water
   parabolas: arcs OR curves
   flanks: sides

b.   i. They wanted to stop the boat so that they could watch the dolphins leap into the air.
      ii. This could mean that this was the point for which the dolphins had been waiting.

c. 'An invariable routine' is a method of procedure which does not change. An example in the first paragraph is to be found in the action of the dolphins in allowing the boat to approach within about fifty feet after which they swam back under the boat and appeared behind it. In the second paragraph the calves always kept to the right of their mothers who, in turn, always moderated the extent of their leaps to allow the young dolphins to accompany them safely.

d. (In an examination *any four* of these reasons would be given.)
      i. They both rise unexpectedly and abruptly.
     ii. They both move upwards at a great speed.
    iii. They make a similar sound as they shoot upwards.
     iv. They both present a splendid sight to watch.
      v. Both are first seen as an upward-moving streak of silvery light.
     vi. Considering their sizes, both go surprisingly high.
    vii. Both fall back to the element from which they came, after moving through an arc.

e. The mother dolphins leapt only as high as they knew their calves could leap, that they would not exceed the physical ability of the young ones. The writer noticed that dolphins which were accompanied by their young rose only about half the height attained by those without calves.

From these and other passages, and the comments on them, we may learn these points of examination technique:

   1. The best preparation is sustained reading with the aid of a good dictionary.
   2. Read the rubric (= instructions to the candidate at the start

of a question) and the question most carefully and be sure that you understand what is wanted.

3. Answer the correct number of questions and parts of questions. It is a waste of time to do more.

4. When necessary and when giving an explanation of a word, make sure that your equivalent fits the word *as it is used in the particular passage*. Use the correct tense and part of speech.

5. When asked to explain the meaning of an expression, explain all the major words in the expression and do not repeat them in your explanation.

6. A short phrase is expected to contain not more than four or five words.

7. Use your own words as far as possible and do not copy from the passage unless asked to do so.

8. Answers to comprehension questions should be given in 'one or two short, clear sentences.'

9. Remember that you will lose marks for errors of spelling, punctuation, grammar and syntax. Even if your facts are correct, you won't pass if you make errors of expression.

10. Be on the watch for multiple questions and make sure that you answer each part.

With these points in your mind, you can now do your best at some exercises before we consider some problems concerned with the use (and misuse) of words.

Exercise 5

Read the following passage carefully and then answer the questions *a*, *b*, *c*, **and** *d* which follow.

In the evening we decided to pitch camp as the weather was not encouraging. The wind was high and gathering storm clouds predicted a wild wet night. Moreover we had arrived at a spot which looked promising for a camp. A level expanse in the lee of a high hill afforded some shelter from the wind;   5 fresh water was near at hand in a stream which flowed across the plain; a copse of trees provided adequate supplies of fuel; and the dry grasses which abounded on the hillside would enhance the comfort of our beds.

Each member of the party was allotted a task. Some erected   10 the tents; others prepared a scanty meal; yet others attended to the needs of the ponies, now exhausted after a very strenuous day. As the angry sun sank, the bustle of activity was hushed into silence and each man settled down to sleep.

a. For each of the following words, which are taken from the above passage, give a word or short phrase which **could be used to replace it in the passage without change of meaning:**
i. high (l. 2); ii. predicted (l. 3); iii. afforded (l. 5); iv. adequate (l. 7); v. abounded (l. 8); vi. enhance (l. 9); vii. allotted (l. 10); viii. erected (l. 10).

b. Explain what is meant by 'bustle of activity' in line 13.

c. Why do you think the men were silent as they went to bed?

d. Name *five* features of the site chosen by the travellers for a camping ground, and state how each feature helped to make the site suitable. (University of Cambridge Overseas School Certificate and G.C.E.)

Exercise 6

Read the following passage carefully, and then answer *a*, *b* and *c*.

Primitive man was probably more concerned with fire as a source of warmth and as a means of cooking food than as a source of light. Before he discovered less laborious ways of making fire, he had to preserve it, and whenever he went on a journey he carried a firebrand with him. His discovery that 5 the firebrand, from which the torch may well have developed, could be used for illumination was probably incidental to the primary purpose of preserving a flame.

Lamps, too, probably developed by accident. Early man may have had his first conception of a lamp while watching 10 a twig or fibre burning in the molten fat dropped from a roasting carcass. All he had to do was to fashion a vessel to contain fat and float a lighted reed in it. Such lamps, which were made of hollowed stones or sea-shells, have persisted in identical form up to quite recent times. 15

a. For each of the following words, which are taken from the above passage, give a word or a short phrase **which could be used to replace it in the passage without change of meaning:**
i. laborious (l. 3); ii. developed (l. 6); iii. accident (l. 9); iv. conception (l. 10); v. fashion (l. 12).

b. Explain concisely the meaning of each of the following phrases, which are taken from the passage, without using the words underlined:

   i. was <u>incidental</u> to the <u>primary</u> purpose (ll. 7–8);

   ii. have <u>persisted</u> in <u>identical</u> form (ll. 14–15).

c. Describe briefly the part which the author suggests may have been played by each of the following in the discovery and use of 'artificial' lighting by primitive man:

   i. the firebrand;

   ii. cooking;

   iii. hollowed stones.   (University of Cambridge Overseas School Certificate and G.C.E.)

Exercise 7

Read the passage below carefully, and then answer the questions that follow:

To be mocked as a foreigner, a gringo*, an inferior being, was what Jack could not stand, and the result was that he had to fight, and it then came as a disagreeable revelation that when he fought, he fought to kill. This was considered bad form; for though men were often killed when fighting, the 5 gaucho's idea is that you do not fight with that intention, but rather to set your mark upon and conquer your adversary, and so give yourself fame and glory. Naturally, they were angry with Jack and became anxious to get rid of him, and by-and-by he gave them an excuse. He fought with and killed a man, 10 a famous young fighter, who had many relations and friends, and some of these determined to avenge his death. And one night a band of nine men came to the rancho where Jack was sleeping, and, leaving two of their number at the door to kill him if he attempted to escape that way, the others burst into 15 his room, their long knives in their hands. As the door was thrown open Jack woke, and, instantly divining the cause of the intrusion, he snatched up the knife near his pillow and sprang like a cat out of his bed; and then began a strange and bloody fight, one man, stark naked, with a short-bladed knife 20 in his hand, against seven men with their long *facons*, in a small, pitch-dark room. The advantage Jack had was that his bare feet made no sound on the clay floor, and that he knew the exact position of a few pieces of furniture in the room. He

had, too, a marvellous agility, and the intense darkness was 25
all in his favour, as the attackers could hardly avoid wounding
one another. At all events, the result was that three of them
were killed and the other four wounded, all more or less
seriously. And from that time Jack was allowed to live among
them as a harmless, peaceful member of the community, so 30
long as no person twitted him with being a gringo.

   gringo—among Spanish Americans, a contemptuous name
for an Englishman.

(In answering the questions below, you must use your own
words as far as possible.)

a. Give, in a single word or a *short* phrase, the exact meaning
of each of *four* of the following words as they are used in the
above passage: stand (l. 2); adversary (l. 7); determined (l. 12);
agility (l. 25); community (l. 30); twitted (l. 31).
b. Using the evidence given in the first *two* sentences, contrast
Jack's idea of fighting with that of the gauchos.
c. Using *two* separate pieces of evidence given in the passage,
prove in your own words that Jack had been expecting an
attack.
d. Show how each of the following facts helped Jack to win his
fight:
   i. that he was one against seven;
   ii. that he was naked;
   iii. that his knife was short-bladed;
   iv. that his room contained furniture.
e. Two words in the last sentence come as a surprise. Quote them,
and explain why they are unexpected.

(University of London G.C.E. 'O' level.
Paper for Overseas Candidates.)

Exercise 8

Read the passage below carefully, and then answer the
questions that follow:

It was the first lion that we met that I particularly remember. He was a huge, black-maned beast, and he was stretched
out comfortably on the grass on his four paws like a monumental statue. Evidently he had just eaten, for when we
approached to within twenty yards he did nothing more than 5
favour us with a slow and casual stare. Then the yellow eyes
closed, the jaws opened in a wide yawn, and in a deep daze of

weariness the animal rolled over on his back. All around him in the sunshine herds of zebras and gazelles were quietly grazing. The hyenas sat and waited. 10

It was a little later in the morning that we saw the other side of this picture. We were driving along a watercourse on the opposite side of the crater when another lion got up suddenly in front of us, a younger beast with very little mane as yet, but he looked very fine as he lifted his head and made 15 the air vibrate with a deep short throaty roar. Ker stopped the car at once. 'Now watch,' he said; 'he's hunting.' Over to the left, some two hundred yards away from the lion, a mingled herd of zebra and wildebeest were grazing, and they were now standing very still with their heads turned towards 20 the point of danger. But for the moment the lion did nothing more. He sank down on his haunches and gently sniffed the breeze. Then again he got up in full view of his quarry, moved forward with a few slow paces, and again emitted his awful threatening growl. This time the zebras and the wildebeest 25 bolted. They ran full tilt for fifty yards or so and then turned uncertainly and faced the lion again. Ker explained what was happening.

'You feel the breeze? It's blowing directly over the herd towards that gully over there; and in that gully somewhere a 30 lioness is waiting. She is the one that will make the kill. She will wait until her mate has driven the zebras on to her hiding-place and then she'll spring out on the nearest animal.'

'But don't the zebras know what is happening? Don't they ever learn from experience?' 35

'No, they never learn.'

(*In answering the questions below, you must use your own words as far as possible. You will lose marks if your answers are needlessly long, or if they contain material you have not been asked for.*)

a. Give, in a single word or a *short* phrase, the exact meaning of each of the following words as they are used in the above passage: vibrate (l. 16); quarry (l. 23); emitted (l. 24); bolted (l. 26); gully (l. 30).

b. The lion in the first paragraph is compared to a 'monumental statue' (ll. 3–4). What does this comparison suggest about the appearance of the lion?

c. Write *three* short sentences, each giving a different piece of evidence to prove that the first lion had just eaten.

Comprehension

   d. From the second paragraph, quote, each on a separate line, *four* separate words or *short* expressions which suggest that the zebras and wildebeest were frightened of the second lion.

   e. Very briefly, outline the contrasting parts played in the hunt (i) by the lioness and (ii) by the lion. Show in detail how the lion's actions were well fitted to his purpose, and explain why he was interested in the direction of the wind.

(University of London G.C.E. 'O' level.
Paper for Overseas Candidates.)

For further comprehension exercises please turn to section 3 of this chapter on page 75.

2. The use of words

The aim of this section is to make you more alert to the power and importance of individual words. If possible, buy and read an excellent book by Dr. R. H. Thouless called *Straight and Crooked Thinking*. It will help you to defend yourself against advertisers and other skilful manipulators of words and ideas.

The emotive value of words

Read these seven sentences and say which of the people you would like to know and which you would want to avoid.

a. 'Yes, I did it,' said Mr. Cole.

b. 'Yes, I did it myself,' Mr. Olude agreed cheerfully.

c. 'Yes, I did it myself,' snapped Mr. Williams.

d. 'Yes, I did it,' Bayo said firmly.

e. 'Yes, I did it myself,' Mary retorted sharply.

f. 'Yes, I did it,' Mr. Smith whined at last.

g. 'Yes,' Margaret admitted begrudgingly, 'I did it.'

Exercise 9

  1. From the sentences above, what impression can you gain of the personality of these people?

a. Mr. Smith	*c.* Mr. Olude
b. Mary	*d.* Mr. Williams

  2. Say whether these words create in your mind a good impression, a bad one or no special effect (= neutral):

a. cheerfully	*d.* begrudgingly	*g.* retorted
b. whined	*e.* admitted	*h.* sharply
c. snapped	*f.* agreed	*i.* said

As you can see from the above examples and exercise, it is possible to choose a word for the emotional or emotive effect which it has. In general terms, we can say that words produce a good, unfavourable or neutral effect on a listener or reader. Sometimes the same word may have a different effect on different people. For example, the word 'beer' may make a very favourable impression on some men; it may annoy others, and it may have no effect at all on some people.

Exercise 10

The words below are arranged in lists according to the effect which they have on my mind. Study each word and think about the effect it has on *you*. Say whether you would put it in a different column. Remember that it is unlikely that we will agree about every word.

A good effect	A bad impression	Neutral = no effect
food	hospital	typewriter
money	homework	cardboard
work	storm	cotton
water	severely	road
television	ill	shop
gardening	cancer	walking
football	punishment	replied
ice	cakes	impression
beautiful	handsome	answer
forest	plain	stamps

Exercise 11

1. Arrange these words in three columns as in Exercise 10. Arrange them to show the effect which they have on you.

slaves	stupid	perfume	chickens
red	cooking	white	crimson
green	black	ink	woman
biology	lady	scent	keys
history	smell	spiders	odour
electricity	luxury	proud	chocolate
helpless	elegant	humble	ambitious

2. Now compare your lists with those of another person. You may have a surprise to see how somebody else has arranged the

words. It will prove that individual words have a different effect on different people.

Now let us go a step farther and attempt to measure the emotive effect of words. Let us give a mark of up to +10 for words which create a favourable impression; words which have a bad effect can be marked from − 1 down to − 10. 'Neutral' words can be given 0. We may then have these marks:

1.	food + 6	6.	pencil 0	11.	bucket − 2
2.	money + 8	7.	butterfly + 2	12.	gentleman − 7
3.	dirt − 5	8.	dictionary 0	13.	pigs − 7
4.	smoke − 1	9.	teeth − 3	14.	agony − 6
5.	water + 7	10.	mirror 0	15.	camera 0

Do you agree with the scores given above?

Exercise 12

1. Your teacher will call out these words, one at a time. Write down a plus or minus number (to a maximum of 10) to show the effect which the word has on *you*.

1. centre	8. shoes	15. swindle
2. trumpet	9. stomach	16. lottery
3. dogs	10. nectar	17. pillow
4. tap	11. cigarettes	18. security
5. curry	12. chalk	19. soap
6. filthy	13. comics	20. thunder
7. hygiene	14. belly	

2. Do the same with these words:

1. marriage	8. jewellery	15. onions
2. prison	9. undulating	16. boys
3. discreet	10. mosquito	17. fame
4. funeral	11. relief	18. thirteen
5. science	12. boil	19. pleasant
6. company	13. hockey	20. healthy
7. mine	14. grey	

Exercise 13

1. Read the following advertisement:

'Ram Shackle brings you fabulous furniture at practical prices—exquisite designs for contemporary living, the finest traditional craftsmanship, gorgeous fabrics and rugged strength.

'The discerning housewife doesn't compromise on quality—
she expects Ram Shackle.'

a. Is this advertisement aimed at men or at women? Give
evidence in support of your opinion.

b. In what type of paper or magazine would you expect to find
this advertisement? Give reasons for your opinion.

c. Say which words or expressions seem to have been chosen for
their emotive effect on the reader. Explain the intended appeal.

2. Cut an advertisement from a paper or magazine and make
an analysis of its effectiveness and the reasons for this effectiveness (or lack of it).

Exercise 14

At a meeting of the City Council of an imaginary city, the
councillors were discussing a proposal to build a new sports
stadium. Here is the speech made by Councillor Williams of the
Blank Party. His party wishes to oppose the proposal.

Mr. Williams: 'I agree with the project entirely but not with
the proposed site. It's not that I'm against the idea of helping the
youth of our city but I think a better site could be found—one
which would do greater honour to the fine youth of our great
city. Remember that the youth of today are the leaders of
tomorrow. Sport is important but health and education are vital
and more pressing. The time may not be opportune for the
expenditure of £100,000 on a stadium so I suggest we defer the
scheme for the time being.'

　1. What arguments has Mr. Williams used to support his view
　　that the scheme should be deferred?
　2. What expressions has he used to create the impression that
　　he is keen to help young people in his city?

Now read these two reports of Mr. Williams's speech:

Report No. 1 (From a newspaper hostile to Mr. Williams's party).

Representing the reactionary Blank Party, Williams admitted
that he was against the idea of helping the young people of our
city. He did not agree with the site and claimed that other matters
were more important than sport, especially when it came to
spending a little money. He voted against the proposal.

　1. How does the report create an unfavourable impression of
　　Mr. Williams?

2. What dishonesty can you find in the report?

Report No. 2 (From a newspaper supporting Mr. Williams's party).

Speaking on behalf of the democratic and freedom-loving Blank Party, Councillor Williams expresses his entire agreement with the fine principles behind the proposal. He looked forward to a time when the city would provide the magnificent facilities to which the young people were entitled. He pointed out the importance of health and education in the life of the young worker and urged the Council to find the best possible site. His aim, he declared passionately, was to force the Council to pay greater honour to the city's youth than they had done before. He warned the opposition that the young men and women of today would be the leaders of tomorrow, despite barriers put in their way, and mentioned the expenditure of £100,000 on a stadium in the near future.

1. How does this report create a favourable impression of Mr. Williams?
2. What dishonesty does it contain?

Exercise 15

Study advertisements and reports in newspapers and magazines, and see if you can find examples of the following:

a. Opinions given as facts
b. Opinions and facts cleverly mixed together to create the impression that all the statements are facts
c. Dishonesty by exaggeration
d. Dishonesty by distortion of facts
e. Dishonesty by suppression of facts vital to the case
f. Dishonesty of attitude or tone
g. Misleading claims made by the use of words with a strong emotive appeal

3. Further exercises: literary and non-literary passages

1. Read the following passage carefully, and then answer *a*, *b*, *c* and *d*.

My look-out is built for comfort as well as for efficiency. The platform is solidly constructed to avoid creaking and one

section is protected from the rain by a roof of banana-leaves.
In this section I have a comfortable seat, with a back (to
avoid cramp) and a cushion, and under the seat I keep a flask 5
of coffee, provisions, first-aid equipment, some dry clothes
and a book. The platform is covered with sacks which effectively deaden my footsteps. There is a primitive rack for guns
in case of emergency. My powerful spotlight, which my
assistant operates as soon as it is dark, is fixed to a branch. 10
The whole contraption is concealed by leafy branches through
which I can easily watch the arrival of the tiger and, when my
luck is in, photograph his subsequent movements.

a. For each of the following words, which are taken from the
   above passage, give another word or a short phrase **which
   could be used to replace it in the passage without change
   of meaning:** i. solidly (l. 2); ii. effectively (ll. 7–8); iii. deaden
   (l. 8); iv. primitive (l. 8); v. operates (l. 10); vi. concealed
   (l. 11); vii. subsequent (l. 13).
b. Give **four** examples of the arrangements made for the writer's
   comfort.
c. Give **three** reasons why it was unlikely that animals would
   detect the presence of a man in the look-out.
d. How do we know that it was not the writer's intention to
   shoot tigers? Give **two** reasons.

(University of Cambridge,
Overseas School Certificate and G.C.E.)

   2. Read the passage below carefully, and then answer the questions that follow, *using your own words as far as possible:*

Here the beach was interrupted abruptly by the square
motif of the landscape; a great platform of pink granite thrust
up uncompromisingly through forest and terrace and sand
and lagoon to make a raised jetty four feet high. The top of
this was covered with a thin layer of soil and coarse grass and 5
shaded with young palm trees. There was not enough soil
for them to grow to any height and when they reached perhaps twenty feet they fell and dried, forming a criss-cross
pattern of trunks, very convenient to sit on. The palms that
still stood made a green roof, covered on the underside with a 10
quivering tangle of reflections from the lagoon. Ralph hauled
himself on to this platform, noted the coolness and shade,
shut one eye, and decided that the shadows on his body were
really green. He picked his way to the seaward edge of the

platform and stood looking down into the water. It was clear 15
to the bottom and bright with the efflorescence of tropical
weed and coral. A school of tiny, glittering fish flicked hither
and thither. Ralph spoke to himself, sounding the bass strings
of delight.

'Whizzoh!' 20

Beyond the platform there was more enchantment. Some
act of God—a typhoon, perhaps, or the storm which had
accompanied his own arrival—had banked sand inside the
lagoon so that there was a long, deep pool in the beach with
a high ledge of pink granite at the further end. Ralph had 25
been deceived before now by the specious appearance of
depth in a beach pool and he approached this one preparing
to be disappointed. But the island ran true to form and the
incredible pool, which was only invaded by the sea at high
tide, was so deep at one end as to be dark green. Ralph 30
inspected the whole thirty yards carefully and then plunged
in. The water was warmer than his blood and he might have
been swimming in a huge bath.

a. Give, each in a single word or a *short* phrase, the exact meaning
of *four* of the following words as they are used in the above
passage: abruptly (l. 1); uncompromisingly (l. 3); jetty (l. 4);
lagoon (l. 11); hauled (l. 11); school (l. 17); specious (l. 26).
b. i. What do you think caused the 'quivering' of the 'tangle
of reflections' (l. 11)?
ii. Why did Ralph have to 'pick his way' (l. 14)?
c. Describe briefly, in your own words, the tone of voice and the
mood in which Ralph 'spoke to himself' (l. 18).
d. What is the meaning of the expression 'act of God' (l. 22)?
e. i. What disappointment was Ralph prepared for when he
approached the 'incredible pool'?
ii. Mention a detail from the first paragraph which Ralph at
first found incredible. What made him change his mind?
f. i. From the final paragraph, quote *one* word which sums up
the atmosphere of the island.
ii. 'The island ran true to form' (l. 28). What do you think
the author means by this statement?

(University of London,
G.C.E. 'O' level for overseas candidates)

3. Read the following passage carefully and then answer the
questions below, **using your own words as far as possible:**

Suddenly a strange distant noise made us aware that something peculiar was going on. We slid out of our shelter, ready for any eventuality, only to become transfixed with astonishment. About a hundred yards from L'Hérétique, to port, a strange white mass, intangible yet vast, appeared out of the 5 sea like some prehistoric monster. The apparition slowly came nearer while I feverishly loaded my underwater harpoon gun as a last desperate defence measure. Stupefied, I recognized that the beast, some eighty or a hundred feet long, was an extremely rare albino whale, of a type unknown 10 in the Mediterranean.

Not only did we need to prove to ourselves that we had not become light-headed, but we should require some evidence if people were to believe our description. Throwing down my totally inadequate weapon, I seized my ciné- 15 camera and recorded the monster's menacing approach. We held our breath, expecting anything to happen. I was fascinated by the beast's red eyes, but Jack watched with increasing terror each flick of its enormous flukes, which could easily have shattered the dinghy at a single blow. I 20 tried to calm our fears by recalling the peaceable school of whales we had recently seen, but this failed to dispel the menace implicit in the slow approach of this solitary and unexpected creature. It dived underneath the dinghy, and then swam round us as if to show off its astonishing snow- 25 white skin. Then it slowly turned away and disappeared into the mist.

Hardly recovered from the shock and still discussing this extraordinary apparition, we cocked our ears to a new danger. It was almost as if the whale had been the precursor of a series 30 of trials designed to break our spirit. Barely an hour after the monster had disappeared we heard the ululation of a siren. We both sat bolt upright. In fact, I had heard a faint sound of the same sort several times before, but so indistinctly that I had thought my hearing was probably playing me tricks and 35 had made no mention of it. It had occurred to me for a moment that perhaps we were not so far from land, but I saw no point in awakening vain hopes in my companion. Now there was no further doubt. The noise, which almost drowned the sound of our voices, could come only from 40 some man-made device and the effort to determine its direction made us slightly hysterical.

a. Give, each in a single word or **short** phrase, the exact meaning
of **four** of the following words as they are used in the passage:
eventuality (l. 3); transfixed (l. 3); intangible (l. 5); feverishly
(l. 7); stupefied (l. 8); device (l. 41); determine (l. 41).

b. i. Quote **three** separate and different expressions from the
first paragraph showing why the men in the story felt that
they would need some evidence if people were to believe
their description.

ii. What steps did they take to provide that evidence?

c. What ideas about the whale does the writer suggest by describing it as:

i. like some prehistoric monster (l. 6).

ii. The apparition (l. 6)?

d. Explain the word 'flick' (l. 19), and show how its use here
emphasizes the strength of the monster.

e. Express the following extracts in simple words of your own
so as to bring out the full meaning:

i. this failed to dispel the menace implicit in the slow
approach of this solitary and unexpected creature (ll.
22–24).

ii. the precursor of a series of trials designed to break our
spirit (ll. 30–31).

(University of London, G.C.E. for overseas candidates)

4. Read the following passage carefully, and then answer the
questions below:

His eyes widened as they fell upon something strange.
Something was moving slowly and cautiously along the gutter
—a snake. The pale yellow and brown of the snake's body
glistened like a stream of flowing metal. By what mistake had
the creature strayed into this unlikely place? Impossible to   5
say. Yet there it was; and its slow movements betrayed un-
easiness and confusion.

As he watched it his instinctive antipathy melted away. He
could understand so well what the snake was feeling. He
entered into its cold, narrow intelligence, and shared its angry   10
perplexity. Its movements were cramped, its advance difficult,
and it was in constant danger of slipping over the edge. Now
and then it lay still in dull reflection, nursing a cold anger
that could find no vent.

Meanwhile the little plant, bent downwards by every puff   15
of wind, was beating its thin twigs against the gutter like a

birch. The snake seemed not to see the plant. It moved forward until a light touch from the twigs fell upon its head. At this it stopped and lifted its neck. The little plant was now doing no more than lightly sway and dip. The snake, its head 20 still reared, waited with flickering tongue. One could feel the angry heaving and straining in the sluggish brain—the dull, red anger waiting to explode. Then came a strong gust sweeping along the wall, and at once the twigs thrashed down upon the furious head—thrashed down and beat it with a move- 25 ment that seemed to Jali both comic and dreadful. In a flash the head reared itself higher, the neck drew back, and there was a lunge at the twigs and the empty air. O fatal act! To strike, the snake had been obliged to coil, and its coiled body could not support itself upon the narrow ledge. No recovery 30 was possible; it overbalanced and fell.

Jali leaned breathless over the balustrade, and saw and heard the falling body strike upon a small flat roof fifty feet below. There the creature began to writhe in agony; it could do no more than twist and turn upon the self-same spot.   35

Jali was trembling, but beneath his agitation there was a deep, troubled wonder. Here was the little plant now waving with a kind of jaunty cynicism. And there was the writhing snake. The world, unquestionably, was a place of mystery and horror. This was revealed in the writhing of the crippled 40 snake, in the jaunty waving of the innocent plant in the wind.

In answering the questions below, you must use your own words as far as possible:

a. Give, each in a single word or *short* phrase, the exact meaning of *four* of the following words as they are used in the above passage: betrayed (l. 6); perplexity (l. 11); vent (l. 14); sway (l. 20); sluggish (l. 22); lunge (l. 28); writhe (l. 34).

b. i. In what ways do you think the snake's body seemed to the writer to be glistening 'like a stream of flowing metal' (l. 4).

   ii. What is the meaning of 'flickering' (l. 21), and to what is it usually applied?

c. Explain the metaphor in 'the dull red anger waiting to explode' (ll. 22–23), and show how the adjectives heighten the effect.

d. i. Why does the writer describe the snake's action as a 'fatal act' (l. 28)?

ii. Why do you think the snake 'could do no more than twist and turn upon the self-same spot' (ll. 34–35)?

e. 'Jali was trembling, but beneath his agitation there was a deep, troubled wonder' (ll. 36–37). What were the reasons for (i) Jali's trembling, and (ii) his wonder?

(University of London, G.C.E. for overseas candidates)

5. Read the passage below carefully, and then answer the questions that follow, **using your own words as far as possible:**

As a rule the Boran are very brave indeed, and are among the few African tribes who still hunt lions with a spear. They also kill elephants, not for food but for spear blooding, or to prove their manhood. When elephants are located there is great excitement and fierce competition among the young 5 men. Each tries to be the first to blood his spear; the one who does so claims the trophy. No young man is looked upon with favour by the girls until he has won his spurs by killing some dangerous animal.

But brave as the Boran are, two fierce man-eaters com- 10 pletely overawed them. This was partly due to the cunning and boldness of the lions, partly to the fact that, when hunted, they would always retreat into dense riverine undergrowth, where it was impossible for a man to poise and throw a spear. Superstition had also added its quota to the fear with which 15 they were regarded. It was said that before starting off on a raid the lions would repair to an open sandy place and there make two rows of depressions in the sand with their paws. Then, using twigs as counters, they would play the ancient game of 'bau' (a game of unknown antiquity, which resembles 20 draughts and is played all over Africa). If the omens were good they would raid a village and claim a victim; if not they would wait. Another story had it that the lions were the spirits of two 'holy men' who had been murdered, long ago, by the Boran and who had now come back in this shape to 25 seek their revenge. So strongly was this view held that the local Boran had petitioned a practising 'holy man' to come from a great distance to exorcize the spirits. He came with book, bell and candle and charged a fee of sixty goats, but the lions continued their depredations. To add to the legend 30 of the lions' invulnerability, many famous hunters had tried on previous occasions to kill them and had failed owing to lack of time. This confirmed the Boran's opinion that the lions were supernatural beings and that it was useless to hunt them.

a. Give, each in a single word or a **short** phrase, the exact meaning of **four** of the following words as they are used in the above passage:

blooding (l. 3); trophy (l. 7); overawed (l. 11); quota (l. 15); antiquity (l. 20); petitioned (l. 27); depredations (l. 30).

b. Give THREE distinct reasons why the young men of the Boran hunt elephants.

c. Re-write the following sentences, substituting words or phrases of your own for the words italicized, to prove that you have understood their meaning: 'They would always *retreat* into *dense riverine* undergrowth, where it was impossible for a man to *poise* and throw a spear' (ll. 13–14).

d. i. For what purpose, according to Boran superstition, did the lions play 'bau'?

    ii. What service did the 'holy man' claim to perform in return for his fee of sixty goats? What effect did his efforts have?

e. Give the meaning of the following figurative expressions as they occur in the passage:

    i. won his spurs (l. 8);

    ii. with book, bell and candle (ll. 28–29).

        (University of London, G.C.E. for overseas candidates)

6. Read the following passage carefully, and then answer the questions below, *using your own words as far as possible:*

Never shall I forget the night we decided to spend on the edge of the crater of Santiago. During the day the heat had been intense, but, at first slowly and then more rapidly, this changed to extreme cold. Lying full-length we peered, fascinated, over the edge into the depths below, and watched a 5 sight which is ineffaceably stamped on my mind for ever.

The great crater dropped perpendicularly for fifteen hundred feet. Only gigantic volumes of smoke were visible by day, but at night it was an inferno. The whole of this dreadful place—the sheer cliffs, even the great boulders which jutted 10 out from the rocky strata—were illuminated by fire. We could see to the extreme bottom, where flames streamed up two hundred and fifty feet towards the sky, lighting the columns of smoke to an immense height. Realizing the overwhelming

forces of nature lying under the surface of the earth directly 15
beneath us, we shuddered. Spell-bound, we lay there for
hours; we wanted to leave, but something mesmeric, irresistible, impelled us to remain.

Within the crater a raging whirlwind was continuous;
even where we lay the ground shivered incessantly. Several 20
times masses of rock broke from the sides of the crater and
boomed away below, and the echoes flung back from the walls
added to the roaring which circled the yawning mouth of this
nerve-shattering Hades.

The air grew colder until at last it was frigid. Finally, at 25
about two o'clock in the morning, in a numbed condition, we
tore ourselves away. It was only then I seemed able to think
clearly, and could analyse the reason for the abnormally low
temperature. The burning gases and the super-heated air from
the subterranean fires shoot up with immense velocity for 30
thousands of feet; a corresponding amount of air which is icy
cold is sucked down from a great height, and envelops the bare
ground around.

The hours of darkness, which seemed interminable, passed
at last. Fortunately the sun rose in a cloudless sky, and never 35
was warmth more welcome. During the night we had both
experienced a sinister influence—a morbid depression, a
distaste for, and longing to escape from, the world—almost
a loathing of life. The crater, although repellent, lured, and
an awful desire to drop over the edge into the warmth of the 40
seething furnace below possessed us. But as the sun rose
higher this unhealthy state of mind rolled from us like the
mists in the valleys.

a. Give, each in a single word or *short* phrase, the exact meaning
   of *five* of the following words as they are used in the passage:
   peered (l. 4); perpendicularly (l. 7); gigantic (l. 8); visible
   (l. 8); illuminated (l. 11); incessantly (l. 20); frigid (l. 25);
   abnormally (l. 28).
b. This account does not actually state what Santiago was. Say
   what you think it is, and quote from the passage *four* phrases
   (each phrase to be not more than four words) supplying
   evidence for your answer.
c. By expressing the following in simple words of your own
   bring out their meaning clearly:
   i. ineffaceably stamped on my mind (l. 6).

ii. something mesmeric, irresistible, impelled us to remain. (ll. 17–18).

d. Explain briefly why the adjectives are so appropriate to the nouns in the following expressions:
   i. raging whirlwind (l. 19).
   ii. yawning mouth (l. 23).
   iii. seething furnace (l. 41).

e. In simple words of your own explain why the author and his companion could be 'numbed' with cold when so near a crater giving forth flames and heat.

7. Read the following passage carefully, and then answer the questions below, *using your own words as far as possible:*

The shallow basin in which the lake lay might have been hundreds of miles away from the town, so completely shrouded was it by a thick wide belt of evergreens: tall firs, cypresses, cedars and pines entwined closely with a thicket of lower trees and bushes, and were so interwoven as to form an im- 5
penetrable screen, a dense lofty rampart which followed the curves of the shoreline, towering above the water in a gloomy unbroken wall as far as the eye could reach. In addition to this barrier of dark leaves, the fall of the land helped to seclude the sunken lake, which was at a considerably lower level than 10
the town, and to exclude any street noise.

The place did not appear to be very popular, for it was completely deserted, and, in any case, inaccessible to traffic, only a footpath skirting the forest of last year's canes, sere and brown, that stood, with a few tattered leaves clinging 15
to them, in the shallows. The total effect could not be called unimpressive, but it was distinctly sad. The melancholy aspect of black trees and forsaken water was increased by the curious flat level light, which cast no shadows and seemed to dissolve all colours. The tremendous grey arch of the sky 20
mirrored itself exactly in the glassy expanse of the lake, into which it merged with no trace of horizon line, the other shore being hidden behind the low clouds.

What struck me most forcibly in the scene was the absence of life; not a single living thing—not a fly, not an insect 25
between the stones—moved in all this vista upon which the very light seemed to fall dead.

a. Give, each in a single word or *short* phrase, the exact meaning of *four* of the following words as they are used in the above passage:

shrouded (l. 2); impenetrable (l. 5); seclude (l. 9); unimpressive (l. 17); melancholy (l. 17); forcibly (l. 24); vista (l. 26).

b. i. What is the proper term (other than 'evergreens') for trees such as are mentioned in lines 3 and 4?

ii. What picture of the 'canes' in the lake do you obtain from the expression 'sere and brown' (ll. 14–15)?

c. i. What different characteristics of the barrier presented by the trees are emphasized by comparing it first to a 'screen', and then to a 'rampart' (l. 6)?

ii. Give *two* reasons put forward by the author for the silence in the area described in the passage.

d. Give *four* details in this scene which help to create an atmosphere of sadness.

e. Explain clearly in your own words what you understand by the following:

i. 'inaccessible to traffic' (l. 13).

ii. 'a footpath skirting the forest of last year's canes' (l. 14).

(University of London G.C.E. for overseas candidates)

8. Read the following passage carefully, and then answer the questions below, using your own words as far as possible:

The Near and the Far

Little Prince Jali stepped out on to the balcony, and looked down upon the plain in awe. It was true that from the tower of his father's palace at home there was an even wider view; but that one was familiar, this one was full of mystery. The wall of this strange palace went down and down, until it 5 merged into the sweeping side of the fort; the fort itself crowned the summit of a hill; and the bare rock of the hill continued a precipitous descent down into the River Jumna. The red glitter of sunset lay upon the river; across the water shady groves alternated with sun-swept patches of millet 10 and corn; beyond stretched the desert.

For the last two years of his life—and he was now twelve —the desert had held Jali under a spell. Nearly every evening at home he would climb up into the tower to gaze upon it. Beyond the roofs, beyond the green and irrigated fields, 15 beyond the glistening palms and the dark clumps of citron, cypress, and mango—beyond the little world that he knew, there stretched that other world which his eye alone could

reach. There it lay, a playground for the winds, a floor for
the light of evening to flow along, the home of mirage and 20
coloured airs.

It was a region that seemed to promise him a disembodied
nimbleness, an unearthly freedom. Its very boundaries were
unsubstantial—lines of hills pencilled so lightly along the
horizon that noonday melted them into the white-hot sky. 25
Only at sunset did those hills become real. Then it was that
they emerged serenely, yet with melancholy, out of nothing-
ness into beauty. Cliffs, battlements, ranges then took on a
substance just solid enough to catch the tints of gold and
rose that streamed through the air. But this lasted for a few 30
minutes only. Swiftly rising, the dusk submerged them, and
what had been hidden day-long under the glare from above
was now drowned in a darkness from underneath. Night
rolled across the plain; sharp stars pricked the blue; in a
moment nothing was left but the twin darkness of earth and 35
sky.

a. Give, each in a single word or *short* phrase, the exact meaning
   of *four* of the following words as they are used in the passage:
   precipitous (l. 8); alternated (l. 10); irrigated (l. 15); serenely
   (l. 27); melancholy (l. 27); submerged (l. 31).
b. Give the exact meaning of 'desert' and 'spell' as used in l. 13
   of the passage, and write sentences, one for each word, in
   which they are used as parts of speech different from those
   in l. 13.
c. Give *two* short expressions, *one* from the first paragraph and
   one from the second, which show Jali's feelings of awe when
   he looked down upon the plain.
d. Explain clearly how the following expressions are used
   figuratively in the passage:
   'crowned the summit of a hill' (l. 7),
   'sharp stars pricked the blue' (l. 34).
e. Explain clearly what you think the writer meant by 'a playground for the winds, a floor for the light of evening to flow
   along' (ll. 19-20).
f. Express very briefly, in your own words, the great difference
   that took place in the scene after sunset.

   (University of London G.C.E. for overseas candidates)

9. *Vocabulary*
In each case explain the meaning of the word in italics.

85

Comprehension

a.
1. It was an art *exhibition*.
2. He *retracted* his statement.
3. They were both *exiled*.
4. The ore was *exported*.
5. The car was *imported*.
6. He *imitated* his friend.
7. The meat was *contaminated*.
8. He was a *spendthrift*.
9. He *extinguished* the fire.
10. The dog was *infested* with fleas.
11. a *heretic*
12. an *atheist*
13. an *agnostic*
14. an *infectious* disease
15. a *contagious* disease
16. a *council* meeting
17. *counsel* for the defence
18. a *human* being
19. a *humane* act
20. in *mortal* combat

b.
1. His manner is very *plausible*.
2. He *deceived* me.
3. Cars *depreciate* in value.
4. I *deprecate* his action.
5. This glass is *transparent*.
6. That curtain is *translucent*.
7. He is a *casual* labourer.
8. at *infrequent* intervals
9. He will *collaborate* with you.
10. That is an *inefficient* way.
11. one of my *prime* aims
12. a rich *abundance* of assistants
13. *secular* affairs
14. a *divine* right
15. an *established* reputation
16. of *social* importance
17. an *authoritative* view
18. an *infallible* remedy
19. an *obsolete* method
20. a *technological* era

10. *Vocabulary*

In each case explain the meaning of the word (or word group) in italics.

a.
1. Stained glass windows have an *eloquence* of their own.
2. He has kept his savings *intact* despite the *hard* times.
3. The two men arrived *simultaneously*.
4. Let *bygones* be bygones.
5. It will disturb the most *blissful* sleeper.
6. He sat there watching us *placidly*.
7. The dog suddenly *emitted* a dismal *wail*.
8. The film was *unutterably* boring.
9. His *provocative* attitude will cause trouble.
10. The fact that he has *made restitution* of the money will *count* a lot when the magistrate *pronounces* the sentence.

b.
1. *unpredictable* behaviour
2. a *self-indulgent* person
3. a childish *pastime*
4. a *persuasive* manner
5. an *inflexible* air
6. a *voluntary* effort
7. an *unmitigated* fool
8. a *precarious* existence
9. a *harmonious* family
10. a universal *catastrophe*

11. a *materialistic* aim
12. *intellectual integrity*
13. *mental* torment
14. a *repulsive* idea
15. a *speculative* affair

16. to be *inclined* to agree
17. a *sagacious* look
18. a *beseeching* look
19. a *lucid* explanation
20. in *divers* ways

11. *Vocabulary*

Write sentences, one for each word, to show that you know the difference in meaning between the words in each pair:

1. desert, dessert
2. stationary, stationery
3. compliment, complement
4. illegible, ineligible
5. illusion, allusion
6. elude, allude
7. effect, affect
8. honorary, honourable
9. imminent, eminent
10. immigrate, emigrate

11. ingenious, ingenuous
12. industrial, industrious
13. stimulant, stimulus
14. astronomy, astrology
15. continuous, continual
16. incredulous, incredible
17. consecutive, alternate
18. diluted, dilated
19. luxurious, luxuriant
20. voracious, veracious

12. *Vocabulary*

Write sentences, one for each word, to show that you know the difference in meaning between the words in each pair:

1. accountable to, accountable for
2. imaginary, imaginative
3. alternately, alternatively
4. postpone, cancel
5. adjourn, postpone
6. suspicious, suspected
7. disinterested, uninterested
8. dominate, domineer
9. partake, participate
10. pedal, peddle

11. imply, infer
12. licence, license
13. practice, practise
14. advice, advise
15. famous, infamous
16. conscious, conscience
17. restrain, refrain
18. defer, differ
19. entrance, entranced
20. extinct, extant

13. *Vocabulary*

In each case below, explain:

i. what idea the words both express
ii. the exact way in which the words differ in meaning

1. hedge, fence
2. clock, calendar
3. rude, discourteous
4. precocious, immature
5. quarrel, argument

6. uneducated, unintelligent
7. obsolete, old-fashioned
8. woman, lady
9. unique, rare
10. modern, efficient

Comprehension

(For further exercises on vocabulary, see Chapter 9 on page 175.)

14. Read the following passage and answer the questions below. Answer as far as possible in complete sentences and in your own words to show that you understand.

Sales—Opportunity or Racket?

Without question there are plenty of bargains to be had at sales time—particularly at the top-quality shops whose reputation depends on having only the best and newest goods in stock each season. It tends, for obvious reasons, to be the fashion or seasonal goods which in due course become the 5 biggest bargains.

It is true that some goods are specially brought in for the sales but these too can provide exceptional value. A manufacturer may have the end of a range left on his hands and be glad to sell the lot off cheaply to one shop; or he may have a 10 surplus of a certain material which he is glad to make up and get rid of cheaply; or he may be prepared to produce a special line at low cost merely to keep his employees busy during a slack period. He is likely to have a good many 'seconds' available and if their defects are trifling these may be particularly 15 good bargains.

Nevertheless, sales do offer a special opportunity for sharp practices and shoppers need to be extra critical. For example the 'seconds' should be clearly marked as such and not sold as if they were perfect. (The term 'substandard', incidentally, 20 usually indicates a more serious defect than 'seconds'.) More serious is the habit of marking the price down from an alleged previous price which is in fact fictitious. Misdescription of this and all other kinds is much practised by the men who run one-day sales of carpets in church halls and the like. As 25 the vendors leave the district the day after the sale there is little possibility of redress. In advertising sales, shops may say 'only 100 left' when in fact they have plenty more; conversely they may say '10,000 at half-price' when only a few are available at such a drastic reduction. If ever the warning 'let the 30 buyer beware' were necessary it is during sales.

(Adapted from *Your Money's Worth* by Elizabeth Gundrey)

i. In what sort of shop, according to the passage, would you probably get the best bargains during a sale? Why should this be so?

ii. What are 'seasonal goods'? What is the 'obvious reason' why they should be among the best bargains?

iii. What is the writer telling us about and giving examples of in the second paragraph? Write down as (a), (b), (c) and (d) the four *types* of goods she is dealing with.

iv. What are 'seconds'? Which would probably be best value for money, 'seconds' or 'substandard goods'? Why?

v. Write a sentence of your own with the same meaning as 'There is little possibility of redress.'

vi. What reason would a shop have for advertising '10,000 at half-price' when it had only a few such items?

vii. Consider the title again. Is the writer attacking sales, defending them or what? What is her general advice to us?

(Metropolitan Regional Examinations Board)

15. *Read carefully the following extract from a story and answer the questions below. Answer as fully as you can to show that you understand the passage.*

They spoke of the future: 'Wonder what it's like out there?'

'Well, the pitchers sure look nice. I seen one where it's hot an' fine, an' walnut trees an' berries; an' right behind, they's a tall up mountain covered with snow. That was a pretty thing to see.'   5

'If we can get work it'll be fine. Won't have no cold in the winter. Kids won't freeze on the way to school. I'm gonna take care my kids don't miss no more school. I can read good, but it ain't no pleasure to me like with a fella that's used to it.'

And perhaps a man brought out his guitar to the front of   10
his tent. And he sat on a box to play, and everyone in the camp moved slowly towards him, drawn in towards him. Many men can chord a guitar, but perhaps this man was a picker. There you have something—the deep chords beating, beating, while the melody runs on the strings like little foot- 15
steps. Heavy, hard fingers marching on the frets. The man played and the people moved slowly in on him until the circle was closed and tight, and then he sang 'Ten-Cent Cotton and Forty-Cent Meat'. And the circle sang softly with him. And he sang 'Why do You Cut Your Hair, Girls?' And the circle   20
sang. He wailed the song, 'I'm Leaving Old Texas', that eerie song that was sung before the Spaniards came, only the words were Indian then.

And now the group was welded to one thing, one unit, so

89

that in the dark the eyes of the people were inward, and their 25
minds played in other times, and their sadness was like rest,
like sleep. He sang 'McAlester Blues' and then, to make up
for it to the older people, he sang 'Jesus Calls Me to His Side'.
The children drowsed with the music and went into the tents
to sleep, and the singing came into their dreams. 30

And after a while the man with the guitar stood up and
yawned. 'Good night, folks,' he said.

And they murmured, 'Good night to you.'

And each wished he could pick a guitar, because it is a
gracious thing. Then the people went to their beds, and the 35
camp was quiet. And the owls coasted overhead, and the
coyotes gabbled in the distance, and into the camp skunks
walked, looking for bits of food—waddling, arrogant skunks,
afraid of nothing.

The night passed, and with the first streak of dawn the 40
women came out of tents, built up the fires, and put the coffee
to boil. And the men came out and talked softly in the
dawn.

'When you cross the Colorado river, there's the desert,
they say. Look out for the desert. See you don't get hung up. 45
Take plenty of water, case you get hung up.'

'I'm gonna take her at night.'

'Me too.'

The families ate quickly, and the dishes were dipped and
wiped. The tents came down. There was a rush to go. And 50
when the sun arose, the camping place was vacant, only a
little litter left by the people. And the camping place was
ready for a new world in a new night.

But along the highway the cars of the migrant people
crawled out like bugs, and the narrow concrete miles stretched 55
ahead.

(*The Grapes of Wrath* by John Steinbeck)

   i. What country are these people travelling in? What indica-
tions of this can you find in the passage?

  ii. What do you think was the purpose of their journey?

 iii. Can you tell from the extract whether these people were
happy or sad? Write a simple reason for your answer.

 iv. What does the passage tell you about the possible future of
the children?

  v. What kinds of songs were the people singing? (There were

several kinds.) Do you think they were appropriate? Give
your reasons for thinking so.

vi. Why do you think the author called the guitar 'a gracious
thing' (ll. 34–35)?

vii. Why do you think someone in the party suggested that he
was going to cross the desert at night? What difficulties would
the desert present to these people?

viii. Would you say from the passage that there was a spirit of
adventure abroad among these people? Give reasons for your
answer.

ix. Imagine you were one of the party. What would you like and
what would you dislike about the trip?

(Metropolitan Regional Examining Board)

16. Read the following passage and answer the questions below
it.

In the Atlantic some 574 ships were sunk between 3rd
September 1939 and 9th May 1945: High though this figure
is, together with the complementary loss of over twenty
thousand seamen, it must be seen in relation to the fact that
merchant ships made seventy-five thousand crossings, sailing   5
in two thousand two hundred convoys. Indeed at peak periods
on the Atlantic, there were no less than seven hundred ships
at sea at the same time. To visualize such a heterogeneous
fleet of steamships in transit at any given monent across the
great ocean is a succinct way of appreciating how the picture 10
had changed in the century since the *Britannia* thrashed her
lonely course over three thousand empty miles. Now on the
great steamship lanes no ship is likely to be alone for long.
Radio and radar have both 'shortened in' the world. The
sense of wonder has, generally speaking, left the Atlantic and 15
gone elsewhere—perhaps into space.

(*Atlantic Conquest* by Warren Tute)

a. Explain *five* of the following expressions as they are used in
the passage. In your answer do not use the words in italics.

i. the *complementary* loss (l. 3); ii. at *peak periods* on the
Atlantic (ll. 6–7); iii. such a *heterogeneous fleet* (ll. 8–9); iv.
steamships *in transit* (l. 9); v. at any *given* moment (l. 9);
vi. a *succinct* way (l. 10); vii. the great steamship *lanes*
(ll. 12–13).

b. To what do the two dates in the first sentence refer?

Comprehension

c. For what purpose does the author find it necessary to mention the number of crossings made?

d. For what purpose is the *Britannia* introduced into the argument?

e. Why is the word *Britannia* in italics in the passage?

f. Why is 'space' (l. 16) brought into a passage dealing with ships?

g. Explain why 'shortened in' is in inverted commas.

h. Do you think this passage came at the start or at the end of an account of the conquest of the Atlantic? Give your reasons for your answer.

i. In Chapter 1 we considered various ways of ending a composition. Which of these ways is used at the end of this passage?

j. The following statements refer to the passage. Some are true but some are false. Say which statements are false and explain briefly why you think they are not true.

   i. About 100 ships were sunk each year in the Atlantic during the period 1939 to 1945.

   ii. In considering the number of ships sunk during this period, we also have to bear in mind the large number of crossings made and the number of ships at sea at any one moment.

   iii. At the busiest times there were 2,200 convoys at sea on the Atlantic at the same time.

   iv. It is likely that the *Britannia* crossed the Atlantic in the first half of the nineteenth century, judging from the evidence in the passage.

   v. Now men no longer cross the Atlantic in ships but spend their time exploring space.

   vi. This passage deals with the conquest of Man by the Atlantic.

17. Read this news report and then answer the questions about it.

Newcastle, N.S.W., Australia, *Friday*. Thirty firemen worked desperately for four hours today to break up a dangerous petrol slick on the surface of Newcastle harbour. The petrol spread more than a quarter of a mile along the harbour foreshore, after it was accidentally discharged from the 12,000 ton tanker *R. W. Miller*. Shortly after dawn this morning crew members aboard the tanker began pumping the petrol into storage tanks at the inflammable liquids wharf. Hundreds

92

of gallons were pumped into the harbour during a four-minute period before crew men realized that the hoses to the 10 storage tanks had not been connected. Firemen and police immediately sealed off the area and barred the lighting of fires. By then the petrol had spread around a number of other vessels, and an oil fuelling lighter, moored near the tanker. Firemen worked desperately with maximum pressure hoses to 15 break up the slick before the outgoing tide carried it further down the already busy harbour. Using the water jets they washed it towards a less busy side of the harbour, where it soaked into foreshore sand.

a. At about what time were the firemen summoned to the harbour?

b. What task were they summoned to do?

c. From your reading of the passage what do you think a 'slick' is?

d. A news report often starts with a summary of the report, followed by a more detailed account of the incident. At what point in this report does the detailed account start?

e. About how long did the danger to shipping in the harbour last? Give a reason for your answer.

f. Explain what danger did or did not exist for shipping entering the harbour at (i) 3 a.m. and (ii) 8 a.m.

g. Imagine that you are a newspaper reporter and that you were sent to the harbour soon after the incident to write it up from the 'human interest' point of view. You interview various people on the ship and on shore. Now write the first 3 to 5 sentences of your report which will eventually be in considerable detail for a local paper. Start with an eye-witness's account in his own words.

h. Imagine that you are the officer in charge of the firemen. After the petrol has been successfully dealt with, you have to write up your report on the incident. Write the first two sentences of your report. Start with precise details of the time and place.

i. These statements refer to the news report. Say which are false and explain briefly why you think they are false.

   i. The firemen had probably finished their work by about noon.

   ii. As far as can be seen from the report, this incident seems to have been caused by sabotage.

   iii. The petrol got on to the water when a ship was being refuelled in the harbour at Newcastle in New South Wales, Australia.

iv. It took the crew four minutes to discover that the firemen's hoses had not been properly connected.

v. There was some danger until the firemen and police barred the oil fuelling lighter from the area.

vi. In the end the petrol was washed out to sea by the outgoing tide.

vii. There was really no need to summon the police to the scene of the incident since no crime was involved.

viii. If anybody had thrown a lighted match into part of the harbour, it is possible that the *R. W. Miller* would have exploded.

18. Two teachers wrote these reports on a boy named Peter:

a. Peter has shown commendable initiative this term and has taken an active part in class discussions and seminars. He has shown originality of thought and approach. He is a natural leader and has spurred others on to greater efforts.

b. Peter has been almost impertinent this term and has shown insufficient respect for the opinions of those in authority. He can be critical and argumentative at times and has displayed a stubborn trait. He is beginning to have a bad influence on his fellow pupils.

i. Both reports say rather similar things but in different ways. Can you think of any reasons for this?

ii. From these reports what kind of boy do **you** think Peter is?

iii. Make a list of favourable words or expressions in *a* and unfavourable ones in *b* which create the impression desired by the writer and which really describe the same traits of character in Peter.

iv. What attitude do you think each of these teachers would display in his own home towards a daughter who is beginning to show signs of developing an independent spirit? Give reasons for your answers.

(Welsh Joint Education Committee—adapted)

19. A man working abroad wanted to buy a house in his own country, return to it and settle down. He was sent details of a number of houses, including the following advertisement:

Charming modern bungalow for sale. Near railway but not in densely crowded area. All modern conveniences, sanitation, facilities. 2 reception rooms, 3 bedrooms, novel kitchen, natural garden, car space, electricity buses nearby. Interior in immaculate order.

a. Does the adjective 'modern' also apply to the word 'sanitation' in your opinion?

b. What sort of kitchen is conjured up in your mind by the expression 'novel kitchen'?

c. What sort of garden would you expect to find at the house? Give some details.

d. What provision is there for a garage?

e. What significance, if any, is there in the fact that there is no comma after *electricity*?

f. In what condition would you expect to find the outside of the house?

The man who read this advertisement wrote to a friend in his own country and asked him to visit the bungalow and send him a report on it. This is part of the report:

> Frankly, this place is little better than a dump. It must be at least thirty years old and is charming only if you have a passion for living with rats and cockroaches.
>
> For a start, it is miles from anywhere—about 12 miles from the nearest town (on a road not made up yet) and about 3 miles from the nearest village. A railway line passes about half a mile from the property but the nearest station is 11 miles away. There is not another building within half a mile— and that is a hut used by farm-workers for storing their tools.
>
> The water comes from a well sited too near the drainage slope of the provision made for sanitary arrangements—a hole in the ground. There are 2 reception rooms and 3 bedrooms. Although they have been freshly painted, they are small and hot. The 'garden' is entirely wild and has never been cultivated. Cooking and lighting are by paraffin. There are termites in the wood-work of the house and the outside is very shabby.
>
> The house is isolated and in a bad state of repair. I'm sure you wouldn't like it.

g. From this report what can you conclude about the man who drew up the advertisement?

h. Point out *two* expressions in the advertisement which are deliberately misleading.

i. Point out two expressions in the advertisement which are true.

j. Point out two unfavourable points which have not been mentioned at all in the advertisement.

k. Explain how the bungalow might be a danger to the health of its occupants. Give at least two reasons.

20. Read this review of a book and then answer the questions about it.

To condense Australia into 282 small pages is no small feat, but in the paper-back, *Australia: Her Story* (Pan Books, 5s.) author Kylie Tennant does much more.

In this handy book, invaluable to students, prospective migrants, visitors and the ordinary reader, Miss Tennant 5 plunges straight into the story of Australia from the very beginnings to the present day, and keeps up a rattling good tale all the way through.

History would never be dull if all textbooks were like this, where the dates and titles, facts and figures are never more 10 than two sentences away from the flesh and blood people with whom they were concerned. Thus, while firmly and efficiently progressing through her chronological account, Miss Tennant, Sydney author and journalist, manages to enclose in her small space a host of no less important tales. 15 There is plenty of colour in the stories of old Australia and of the new, where safety signs in industrial projects have to be written in 12 languages because of the diversity of settlers, and where a radio telescope in Canberra has a mile-long movable arm to seek the farthest stars known to man. 20

Australia: Her Story has a map of the settlement of Australia, a list of ,important dates and an index.

                           (*Australia and New Zealand Weekly*)

a. Explain the meaning of the following as they are used in the passage:
   i. to condense Australia (l. 1)
   ii. no small feat (ll. 1–2)
   iii. prospective migrants (ll. 4–5)
   iv. a rattling good tale (ll. 7–8)
   v. the diversity of settlers (l. 18.)
b. What purpose is served by the use of *very* in line 6?
c. What quality would the reviewer like to find in textbooks dealing with history?
d. What impression of the book is created in your mind by the use of *firmly* in line 12?
e. How is the expression 'plenty of colour' (l. 16) related to the ideas expressed at the beginning of the third paragraph?
f. What point is the reviewer trying to make by referring to the radio telescope?

4. Exercises with objective-type questions

Exercise 21

Read this passage and then answer the questions on it.

Land of the ancient Phoenicians, Lebanon lies like a sharp stone between the square toe of the Eastern Mediterranean and the huge almost *encompassing* fist of Syria. Only 30–35 miles wide and 120 miles long, this is a capsule country (with the advantage to the holidaymaker that it can be *swallowed* 5 and enjoyed whole!) but one rich in history, legend and scenic splendour. A narrow but fertile coastal plain is wedged between the sea and the towering Lebanon limestone mountain range, which rises to over 10,000 feet and is veined with deep valleys where slopes support *picturesque* villages and 10 cultivated terraces, the product of centuries of toil. To the east again lies the rift valley of the Bekaa; and beyond, the second mountain range, the Anti-Lebanon, soars between Lebanon and Syria. The mountains were once thickly forested, not only with the famous cedars but with *innumerable* pines. 15 Today there are woods but no great forests, a fact not surprising *in the light of* the massive exports of timber made over a period of five thousand years.

Under the hot sun and an *intense* blue sky, however, *starkness*, with its reminder of the nearby vast Syrian desert, has a 20 burning beauty of its own. The ancient past is everywhere. On the road from Beirut, the capital, to Byblos, the oldest continuously inhabited city in the world, the mountain juts out in a stern promontory, making the road almost impassable. Traditionally, it has always been a great achievement 25 for armies to penetrate as far as this point.

(From B.O.A.C.'s *Traveller's Digest*)

a. For each of the words or expressions taken from the passage and given below, choose the word or expression which best explains the meaning shown in the passage. Write down only the number of the word or expression and the letter which appears immediately in front of the meaning you choose.

Example:

    8. *land* (l. 1): (A) earth; (B) soil; (C) country; (D) the farm; (E) continent. ......8C......

    1. *encompassing* (l. 3): (A) adjacent to; (B) near to; (C) surrounded; (D) surrounding.

2. *swallowed* (l. 5): (A) rejected; (B) drunk; (C) passed through; (D) thoroughly explored; (E) ignored.
3. *picturesque* (l. 10): (A) very pretty; (B) grotesque; (C) unusual; (D) mountainous; (E) rural.
4. *innumerable* (l. 15): (A) very few; (B) quite a lot; (C) countless; (D) hardly any.
5. *in the light of* (l. 17): (A) in the sun; (B) open to the view; (C) in view of; (D) in the opinion of.
6. *intense* (l. 19): (A) earnest; (B) very; (C) pale; (D) broad.
7. *starkness* (ll. 19–20): (A) barrenness; (B) brightness; (C) sand; (D) fear.

b. In each case write the letter which appears in front of the most suitable answer.

1. What name is given to the people who live in Lebanon?
   (A) The Phoenicians   (D) The Syrians
   (B) The Lebanese   (E) The Bekaa
   (C) The Lebanonese
2. To what does the reference to 'capsule' in l. 4 refer?
   (A) Food for holidaymakers.
   (B) Something to do with space rockets.
   (C) The Government of the country.
   (D) The size and shape of the country.
   (E) The mountainous nature of Lebanon.
3. In which direction does the sea lie from the Anti-Lebanon range?
   (A) To the east.   (C) To the north.
   (B) To the west.   (D) To the south.
4. To what does 'a fact' refer in l. 16?
   (A) The great forests.
   (B) The woods.
   (C) The considerable export trade in the past.
   (D) The absence of the great forests which once existed in the mountains.
   (E) The presence of innumerable pines.
5. To what does 'its' refer in l. 21?
   (A) Beauty.   (D) The blue sky.
   (B) The desert.   (E) The starkness.
   (C) The hot sun.
6. If we judge only by the first sentence in this passage, what aspect of the country is expected to appeal to travellers?
   (A) Its scenic beauty.   (B) Its antiquity.

Exercise 22

Read this passage and then answer the questions on it.

The political and religious institutions of the Bome Valley villages are best introduced in relation to their physical manifestations. The villages are set close together. Compounds are small by comparison with those of some places, housing, as a rule, only a man, his wives and unmarried children. Larger compounds with more wives' huts mark the residences of hamlet-heads and village-chiefs but do not include the hut-clusters of married men. The centre of each village is the chief's compound and dancing-yard, and we shall describe one such complex.

Fronting the dancing-yard is the *utsham* or audience hall of the chief, a two-doored house, one door of which is the chief's entry. It contains log benches for lesser men, those without the privilege of bringing their own stools to assemblies and placing them on the left of the chief's door. The chief's own stool, to the right of his door, will be placed on a leopard-skin. The *utsham* contains the slit-drums played for two of the societies owned by the chief, *kwen* and *tshibi*. The *utsham* is the venue for discussions between the chief and his *mekum*, and for convivial meetings of *tshibi*, a mask-society open to any man of substance. A bigger signal-drum is placed on the verandah facing the dancing-yard, for relaying assembly calls and alarms by means of the drum-names borne by local patrilineages, villages and societies. The dancing-yard centres round the oathing altar, a flat stone backed by an upright marker-stone. Disputes over property including theft were brought here until recently; formerly witchcraft cases were also submitted to the ordeal of the oath. First the chief would pour wine or water over the *eshum*. The man desiring to exculpate himself would walk round the *eshum* four times proclaiming his innocence, touch the *eshum* with both hands and then strike his own belly. A false oath on the *eshum* led to a perjurer's death within a year from a swollen belly, and his heir paid a fine to the chief. But if the accusation proved groundless, the accuser paid a goat or goats to the chief, their number depending on the seriousness of the accusation. (The passing of the *eshum* is lamented and regarded as the direct cause of the growth of perjury and bribery in the customary courts first established by the British.)

Comprehension

In each case below, write down the letter which appears in the front of the most suitable answer.

1. What is the purpose of the description, in the first paragraph, of the size and nature of the compounds?
   (A) As an introduction to an account of traditional dances.
   (B) As part of a Government census.
   (C) As a preliminary to an account of political and religious institutions in the area.
   (D) There is insufficient information in the passage to answer this question.

2. 'Complex', at the end of the first paragraph, refers to
   (A) the *utsham*
   (B) some unknown problem
   (C) the dancing-yard
   (D) the chief's compound and dancing-yard
   (E) a hut-cluster of married men

3. The chief meets his *mekum* in
   (A) the audience hall
   (B) the dancing-yard
   (C) his own house
   (D) the open air
   (E) none of the places mentioned above

4. The *eshum* referred to in l. 29 is probably
   (A) kept in the *utsham*
   (B) the property of the *kwen*
   (C) an upright marker-stone
   (D) the oathing altar
   (E) some kind of ceremony

5. In l. 37 'passing' means
   (A) giving from one person to another
   (B) walking past
   (C) walking round and round the stone
   (D) not using (this ceremony) any more
   (E) success

6. The last sentence suggests that in earlier times the attitude to the *eshum* was
   (A) rather frivolous
   (B) essentially serious
   (C) one of indifference
   (D) something to be lamented
   (E) something that could not be helped

Exercise 23

Read this passage and then answer the questions about it.

The present state of things on the planet earth would be rather a puzzle to an observer from another planet. If he landed in the United States, the most conspicuous animals in sight would be automobiles, and if he examined these vigorous hard-shelled creatures, he would find that each contains one or 5 more soft, feeble organisms that appear notably helpless when removed from their shells. He would decide, after talking with these defenceless creatures, that they had no independent existence. Few of them have anything to do with the production or transportation of food. They need 10 clothing and shelter, but do not provide them for themselves. They are dependent on their distant fellows in thousands of complex ways. When isolated, they usually die—just like worker ants that wander helplessly and hopelessly if separated from their colony. 15

If the observer were intelligent (and extraterrestrial observers are always presumed to be intelligent) he would conclude that the earth is inhabited by a few very large organisms whose individual parts are subordinate to a central directing force. He might not be able to find any central 20 brain or other controlling unit, but human biologists have the same difficulty when they try to analyse an ant hill. The individual ants are not impressive objects—in fact they are rather stupid, even for insects—but the colony as a whole behaves with striking intelligence. 25

When human observers descend on a foreign planet, they may find it inhabited by organisms in an even more advanced stage of social co-operation. Perhaps its moving and visible parts will be entirely secondary, like the machines of man. Perhaps the parts that are really alive will be even more help- 30 less: mere clots of nerve tissue lying motionless and sedentary far underground. Perhaps this organic stuff, having served its creative purpose, will have withered away, leaving the machines that it has created in possession of the planet.

In each case below, write down the letter which appears in front of the most suitable answer.

1. What is the writer's purpose in bringing into the passage the reference to motor-cars in America?

(A) Each one contains a helpless creature.

(B) By analogy, he wishes to show that when men from earth visit another planet they may meet similar machines which, despite their numbers, are not the dominant species on the planet.

(C) He is trying to show that these hard-shelled creatures do not have anything to do with the production or transportation of food.

(D) He is demonstrating that they would puzzle an observer from the planet earth because he would assume that they are the most conspicuous animals.

(E) He is particularly interested in crustaceans.

2. Why are the 'creatures' in l. 5 referred to as *hard-shelled* but the 'creatures' in l. 8 referred to as *defenceless*.

(A) Although a motor-car is made of metal, it is incapable of defending itself.

(B) Motor-cars are helpless without a human being to guide or direct them.

(C) In l. 5, 'creatures' refers to cars. In l. 8 it refers to the feeble human beings inside them.

(D) The writer seems to have become muddled in his thinking.

(E) In l. 5 the writer is thinking about the exterior of the cars and the metal they are made of. In l. 8 he is thinking of their mental or reasoning powers, and we know that they cannot reason for themselves.

3. In l. 11, 'them' refers to

(A) clothing and shelter
(B) the automobiles
(C) the soft, feeble organisms
(D) different types of food
(E) none of the things mentioned above

4. In l. 12 the use of 'distant' implies

(A) that the planets are far apart
(B) that men landing on earth would have to obtain supplies from their own planet
(C) that the inhabitants of earth use and require raw materials and other things brought from distant places
(D) that the inhabitants of earth usually live some distance from each other
(E) that worker ants are helpless when separated from their colony

5. Why might an observer from another planet look for a central brain on earth?

(A) Because he would conclude that the earth is inhabited by very few organisms.

(B) Because he would realize that the hard-shelled creatures were incapable of thinking for themselves and needed somebody to make them move.

(C) Because he would conclude that the defenceless creatures inside the hard-shelled creatures had no independent existence and were controlled by some central brain.

(D) Because he would assume that the organization on earth was similar to that on his own planet.

(E) The reason is not given in the passage.

Exercise 24

Read this passage and then answer the questions on it.

Change—or the ability to adapt oneself to a changing environment—is essential to evolution. The farmer whose land is required for housing or industry must adapt himself: he can move to another place and master the problems peculiar to it; he can change his occupation, perhaps after a period of training; or he can starve to death. A nation which cannot adapt its trade or defence requirements to meet world conditions faces economic or military disaster. Nothing is fixed and permanently stable. There must be movement forward, which is progress of a sort, or movement backwards, which is decay and deterioration.

In this context, tradition can be a force for good or for evil. As long as it offers a guide (without insisting that its path is the only one), it helps the ignorant and the uninformed to take a step forward and, thereby, to adapt themselves to changed circumstances. Tradition, or custom, can guide the hunter as effectively as it can influence the nervous hostess. But if we make an idol of tradition, it ceases to become a guide and becomes an obstacle lying athwart the path of change and progress. If we insist on trying to plot the future by the past, we clearly handicap ourselves and invite failure. The better course is to accept the help which tradition can give but, realizing that it necessarily has its roots in the past, to be well aware of its limitations in a changing world.

Comprehension

In each case, write down the letter which appears in front of the most suitable answer.

1. How is the incident of the farmer, in ll. 2–6, relevant to the writer's comments on tradition?
    (A) Farmers are generally influenced by tradition, particularly in the way in which they sow and harvest their crops.
    (B) There is nothing in the passage to show the relevance.
    (C) The farmer is mentioned as an example of the need for people to be adaptable. One criticism of tradition is that it may prevent people from becoming adaptable.
    (D) The farmer may have to undergo a period of training, and tradition is something which concerns training.
    (E) If the farmer does not pay due regard to tradition, he will starve to death.

2. Why is change said to be essential to evolution?
    (A) The world changes as it progresses and evolves. Hence we must be able to change too, and adjust ourselves to new conditions.
    (B) It would be boring to have things always in exactly the same condition.
    (C) The use of force often leads to a change of some kind.
    (D) The best way to achieve progress is to preserve things as they are now, and not to make unnecessary changes.

3. In l. 5, 'it' refers to
    (A) evolution   (D) master
    (B) change   (E) another place
    (C) the farmer

4. In l. 12, 'this context' refers to
    (A) decay and deterioration
    (B) movement forward
    (C) tradition
    (D) a world which is fixed and permanently stable
    (E) a changing world

5. In l. 19, the obstacle 'lying athwart the path of change' is
    (A) the attitude of accepting tradition as a guide only
    (B) excessive devotion to tradition without realizing its limitations
    (C) future events
    (D) an excessive desire for change without considering the possible consequences
    (E) progress

6. The writer concludes by offering the following advice:

(A) Since tradition necessarily has its roots in the past, and we are concerned primarily with the future, it would be better to take no notice of tradition.

(B) Although we must face the future, we can learn how to deal with new events by studying the traditions of the past. The best thing to do, therefore, is to keep firmly to tradition when facing a new problem, and not to break with tradition under any circumstances.

(C) We should realize the limitations of a changing world and not invite failure by trying to plot the future.

(D) We should neither worship nor reject tradition but take from it whatever it can offer in any particular instance.

(E) He does not make his meaning clear.

Chapter 6

Making a Summary

more and more people will want to escape

1. Making a summary

In an examination you may be asked to do one of the following:

a. Make a summary using not more than a certain number of words, lines or sentences.

b. Make notes on a passage so as to bring out the main ideas or arguments in it.

c. Make a summary or notes dealing with only part of the passage or some of the points in it.

(*Note:* The question should tell you whether the 'notes' must be complete sentences or can be in normal note-form, i.e. not in complete sentences.)

Making a summary is a task which nobody can avoid in life. When you pass on news at home, at school or at work, you often make a very good summary. You don't count up words or underline statements with a worried look on your face. You just grasp the main points and pass them on to your listener. This is the ideal method.

The method suggested here for making a summary is as follows:

a. Understand the passage and find its theme.

b. Make rough notes on each 3–8 lines.

c. Arrange the notes in the right order and join them up so that they read smoothly.

d. If necessary, check for length; shorten or lengthen as required, taking care that the continuity is maintained.

e. Write down the final summary.

If you are not told to keep to a given number of words, you may be able to omit *d*. You are advised NOT to rule columns on your paper. Under no circumstances should *b* be omitted. Underlining the essential points in the passage can be dangerous because it may lead you to copy expressions from the passage. However, if you do want to underline a few points, make sure that you make adequate rough notes as you read through the passage. Let us now consider the various tasks in detail.

i. *Finding the theme*

From the chapter on composition, you know that the theme is the central idea which dominates the whole passage—the main argument being put forward by the author. When you have found the theme, write it down in rough after your first reading of the passage.

Exercise 1

Say which of the following is the theme of the passage in Exercise 15 on page 117. Say why you reject the alternatives.

a. There is a need for more car parks in parts of Africa.

b. The national parks of Africa are important because they are expensive to maintain and are often over-crowded.

c. The national parks and wild-life reserves in African countries are financially important because they attract tourists who spend money. It would be a good idea to develop these and more parks.

Exercise 2

Say which of the following seems to you to be the theme of the passage in Exercise 16 on page 120. Explain why you would reject each of the alternatives.

Making a Summary

a. Englishmen dislike the work of the Forestry Commission but private landlords like it.
b. An attack on the formal forestry methods of the Forestry Commission in England, and an explanation of the virtues of the 'natural' system of growing them.
c. How forests help us.
d. The need for more trees in the industrial parts of England, France and Germany.

Exercise 3

Say which of the following seems to be the theme of the passage on page 56. Explain why you would reject the others.

a. All about sharks.
b. Undersea exploration.
c. The sea.
d. Heroic supermen.

Exercise 4

Say which of the following seems to be the theme of the passage on page 61. Explain why you would reject the others.

a. A meeting with dolphins at sea.
b. Fishing for dolphins with rockets.
c. A day in the life of a school of dolphins.

Exercise 5

Give the themes of each of the following passages:

a. Exercise 7 on page 67.
b. Exercise 8 on page 68.
c. Exercise 3 on page 77.
d. Exercise 4 on page 78.
e. Exercise 5 on page 80.
f. Exercise 6 on page 81.

Exercise 6

Give the themes of each of the following passages:

a. Exercise 14 on page 88.
b. Exercise 15 on page 89.
c. Exercise 17 on page 92.

Exercise 7

Give the themes of passages 1, 2 and 3 in section 4 of this chapter, starting on page 128.

Exercise 8

Give the themes of passages 4, 5 and 6 in section 4 of this chapter.

ii. *Making notes of the key ideas; what to omit; continuity.*

You find the theme of a passage when you read it for the first time. When you read it the second time, make rough notes (in pencil) of the key ideas. This will usually mean that you must make a note for every 3–8 lines. You can use any abbreviations you like in your notes, which you must eventually cross out when the final summary has been made.

Do not include any questions in your notes. Change them into indirect questions in some way. Do not bring in new matter or put in any comments.

When you are making your rough notes, leave out these things:

a. unnecessary detail or illustrative examples

b. negative statements which do not convey any useful information

c. repetitive statements

d. irrelevant topics or comments (especially in the opening sentences of a passage)

Make the rough notes in your own words as far as is reasonable. Use words and short expressions from the passage when necessary but don't copy sentences or longer expressions from it.

Exercise 9

Read the following passage and then answer the questions about it.

It is estimated that some seven hundred million people—about half the world's adult population—are unable to read or write, and there are probably two hundred and fifty million more whose level of attainment is so slight that it barely qualifies as literacy. 5

Recently the attack on illiteracy has been stepped up. A world plan has been drawn up by a committee of Unesco experts in Paris, as part of the United Nations Development Decade, and an international conference on the subject has also been held. Unesco stresses that functional literacy is the aim. 10 People must learn the basic skills of responsible citizenship:

the ability to read notices, newspapers, time-tables, letters, price-lists: to keep simple records and accounts, to sort out the significance of the information gathered—and to fill in forms.   15

The major areas of illiteracy are in Asia, Africa, and Central and South America. In Africa there are at least one hundred million illiterates, comprising eighty to eighty-five per cent of the total population. In Europe the figure is about twenty-four millions, most of them in Southern Europe, with 20 Spain, Italy, Portugal, and Jugoslavia heading the list (the United Kingdom has about seven hundred thousand).

In India the problem is still staggering. The 1951 census revealed that of a total population of three hundred and fifty millions, eighty-two per cent were illiterate. In 1947 the 25 target was set to reduce illiteracy by half within five years. This was hopelessly unrealistic, and led to short cuts and lowering of standards. The familiar 'each one teach one' formula was expanded to 'each one teach two', and there was much talk about laws to make learning and teaching com- 30 pulsory. Since 1952 campaigns have been smaller, usually in blocks of about one hundred villages. Village camps lasting four to six weeks are the favourite method; the camp atmosphere helps to create the psychological ferment necessary to overcome the inertia of centuries.   35

In Northern Nigeria, just after the war, ninety per cent of the population had never been to school, and literacy was regarded as the preserve of a small, often despised, minority of clerks, teachers and officials. There was no popular hankering after literacy, and local rulers were indifferent, even hostile, so 40 that progress was slow, and still is today.

In Morocco, on the other hand, where a national campaign was launched in 1956, the response was immediate and overwhelming. Adults fought to get into crowded schools; inexperienced teachers ran into difficulties, and had to be given 45 emergency courses.

It is generally agreed that extension and improvement of primary education is the best single weapon against illiteracy. But there is equally no doubt that adults—even very old ones —can learn if they want to, and if they are imaginatively 50 taught. A constant danger is that of a relapse into illiteracy through lack of practice. Continuation schools for adults are badly needed; the hope is that, having explored the pleasures and the usefulness of literacy, they will demand that their children are thoroughly educated, and become a positive 55 force for progress.

a. Express the theme of this passage in not more than two sentences.

b. These are points of examination technique:

   i. If you have to make a summary of about 160–180 words, about how many lines will your final summary contain? (The answer will differ slightly from one person to another, depending on handwriting.)

  ii. The passage contains about 55 lines in 7 paragraphs. How many rough notes are you going to make?

 iii. About how long will each rough note be?

 iv. How many words do you expect to have in all your rough notes together? (Remember to leave room for linking expressions.)

c. Read the first paragraph of the passage again. Then make a rough note which sums it up.

d. Point out some illustrative examples or details in the second paragraph which you would NOT include in your rough notes or summary.

e. Make a rough note summing up the second paragraph.

f. In the third paragraph which names of countries and continents (if any) would you *include* in your summary? Why? Would you mention the United Kingdom or not? Why?

g. Make a rough note on the third paragraph.

h. In the fourth paragraph:

   i. Which dates would you mention in your summary and why?

  ii. What idea is repeated by being contained in the first two sentences?

 iii. Is it necessary to include 'each one teach one' or 'each one teach two' in your summary? Why?

i. Make a rough note summing up the fourth paragraph.

j. What idea is repeated within the fifth paragraph (about Northern Nigeria)?

k. If you happened to live in Northern Nigeria and disagreed with this paragraph, could you add your own comments when making a summary?

l. Make rough notes on the fifth, sixth and last paragraphs.

Keep the rough notes you have made. You will need them in Exercise 11.

Making a Summary

Exercise 10

Join up each pair of sentences in any sensible way.

a. Illiteracy is widespread. It is a serious problem.

b. People must be literate. Then they can become responsible citizens.

c. Unesco experts are attacking illiteracy. They want to help people to become responsible citizens.

d. The problem is most serious in Asia, Africa, and Central and South America. It is also present in Europe.

e. At one time literacy was not popular in Northern Nigeria. It was greatly desired in Morocco.

f. (*Use a method different from that used in e.*)
Literacy programmes have met with indifference in some places. The campaign has been most successful in Morocco.

g. Primary and adult education are essential. They must be followed up by adequate practice.

Exercise 11

Join up the rough notes you made in Exercise 9, making a summary of the passage dealing with illiteracy. Do NOT bother about the final length of your summary. Concentrate on accuracy of language and on making it read fluently with adequate links between ideas and sentences.

Exercise 12

In each case below, change the start of the second sentence to establish a link with the previous sentence—by similarity, contrast, modification or in any other suitable way. Do NOT combine the two sentences. Add or alter words.

Example: Unesco experts are attacking illiteracy. It is essential to produce responsible and literate citizens.

Unesco experts are attacking illiteracy. *They believe that* it is essential (or *Their aim is*) to produce responsible and literate citizens.

1. In Africa the problem is serious and much remains to be done. In India the task is staggering.

2. In Northern Nigeria there was some hostility to literacy. In Morocco the response was immediate and overwhelming.

3. Primary and adult education are essential. There must be adequate practice.

4. Illiteracy is widespread in parts of Asia, Africa and the Americas. We shall eventually obtain a fully educated electorate.
5. Most people have a desire to learn and to take their place in an educated community. A few may be too shy or too lazy to seek education.

Exercise 13

Read the following passage and then answer the questions below it.

In 1798 the political economist Malthus predicted that in time mankind would face starvation, having outgrown the available food supplies. Today, a century and a half later, there are still experts who forecast the same global disaster—unless urgent measures are taken to avert it.   5

By the end of the present century there may well be over four thousand million people living on this globe, an increase of over fifty per cent on today's figure. In order to keep pace with this increase in mankind the farmers of the world would have to step up their production of food by at least two per 10 cent every year. Such a rate of increase has never been maintained in any country by conventional methods of agriculture, despite modern mechanization and the widespread use of fertilizers. There are no large worth-while reserves of potential farmland remaining, and good fertile land is continually 15 being diverted to industrial use. Moreover, erosion of the soil takes a constant toll.

Intensive research, carried out over many years in all manner of climatic conditions, has produced a revolutionary method of growing crops without using any soil at all. Hydro- 20 ponics, as this technique is called, may well be the answer to all our food worries. Already it has accomplished wonders in producing huge crops where not a blade of grass has grown since time immemorial. Hydroponics was once a complicated and expensive business; now it is well out of the experimental 25 stage. Labour costs are far lower than when normal methods of agriculture are employed. In fact, it is a completely automatic system. There is no hard manual work, no digging or ploughing, and no weeding to speak of. Yields can be far higher than they are in soil.   30

Making a Summary

The system itself is quite simple, provided a few straight-forward rules are carefully followed. The plants are grown in troughs or beds, about a yard wide and of any convenient length. These may be made from wood, concrete, asbestos sheets, painted metal, or some other suitable material. The 35 troughs are fitted with drainage systems, and filled to a depth of eight inches with a mixture of stones, sand, or even cinders. This 'aggregate', as the growing-medium is called, holds moisture, and anchors the plants' roots in position. It has to be kept constantly damp with ordinary water. At periodic 40 intervals special mixtures of nutrient chemicals are applied to the troughs. These contain all the vital elements essential for healthy growth. During the past year some important advances have been made in the matter of nutrient application, and the latest chemicals last for up to six months after 45 one application. Apart from keeping the aggregate in the beds moist, which can be done by fitting up sets of irrigation pipes, there is no other work to do on the hydroponic 'farm' except the usual general attention to plants. It is, in fact, complete automation, based on factory lines, and although 50 old-fashioned gardeners may shudder at such a word, the plants love it, and respond by giving bumper crops.

a. Which of the following best sums up the whole passage?

    i. In 1798 Malthus predicted that we should all starve eventually.

    ii. The science of hydroponics.

    iii. Modern developments in agriculture.

    iv. Technical progress in horticulture.

    v. Hydroponics may prevent a future shortage of food.

    vi. The world will become increasingly short of food. Hydroponics may be the answer to this problem.

b. What information, if any, is there in the first paragraph which cannot be found in the next one?

c. Is it necessary to know what a political economist is to have a good grasp of the meaning of the whole passage?

d. How much of the first sentence, if any, MUST be included in a summary of the whole passage?

e. In a summary you would have to make the point that the natural resources of the world will eventually be unable to support a greatly increased population (unless something like hydroponics is used). Do you consider that the following points

should be used in your summary? In each case give a reason
why you would or would not include the information.

   i. by the end of the present century
   ii. over four thousand million people on this globe
  iii. an increase of over 50 per cent
   iv. 2 per cent annual increase in production of food cannot be
      achieved by normal methods of agriculture
   v. no large worth-while reserves of potential farmland left
  vi. land is lost through erosion and industrialization

f. Without looking back at the passage, briefly explain the advantages of hydroponics.

g. Imagine that you have seen this article in a scientific or horti-
cultural journal. You are a reporter working for a newspaper.
Convert the article into a news report amounting to 60 to 120
words. Give it a factual headline.

h. You are a sub-editor working for the same newspaper as in *g*
above. A reporter submits a report of 60 to 120 words on the
topic dealt with in *g*. Unfortunately, there is not much space
available in the paper. Cut the reporter's account (done in *g*
above) down to 20 to 30 words.

Exercise 14

Read the following passage and then answer the questions
based on it.

While the intelligence of ants is limited—for example,
they have no proper language, cannot be said to reason (to
think things out), and do not, except in one case, use tools—
their mental powers should not be underrated. Experiments
have shown that they can learn the correct route in simple   5
mazes which have six blind alleys, and individual ants vary
in their ability to do this and in the speed (or number of runs
through the maze) with which they learn their lesson. Just as
in the maze, so it is in the world of work; some individuals
learn to do jobs better and more quickly than other ants in   10
the nest.

These quicker learners are the primitive leaders of the
community, the 'excitement centres'. They are called 'excitement centres' because, although they determine what activities are carried out and when, they do not do so by sitting   15
down and thinking about it and then giving directions to the
other ants, but they excite the ants into doing the different

jobs by starting to do them themselves. The excitement centre ants are in effect the first individuals in each colony to respond to the stimulus of jobs needing to be done. The 20 settling down to work of the twenty or thirty excitement centre ants soon arouses in the other ants feelings of their own hunger and need to go out foraging, or of their own instincts to repair a broken part of the nest or to build new chambers to provide accommodation for a rapidly expanding 25 brood.

Thanks to this leadership, the seemingly complex round of jobs of the ant community is fairly economically and successfully achieved. Food-getting is the most important task. It is no light one to get in food enough for from 40,000 to half- 30 a-million individuals each day. A colony of 40,000 carnivorous ants will eat a quart of insect food (equivalent to over 20,000 insects) every day during the active summer months. Yet there are always several times more ants in the nest than there are out foraging. Inside the nest, the queens must be 35 carefully tended and guarded, and the eggs they lay carried off to the appropriate chamber. The brood require constant attention, for the larvae (grubs) must be fed and unceasingly licked, so that their skins are kept moist, and the cocoons must be watched so that ants ready to hatch out can be helped to 40 emerge. Few ants can escape from their cocoons or pupal skins unaided. The nest structure also requires continual care and must be kept scrupulously clean, properly drained and proof against enemy invasion. Then there are the aphid cows (greenflies, blackflies and whiteflies), both inside and 45 outside the nest, to be milked, or other guests to be tended or kept from prowling too near the queens or brood. For in each ants' nest there are many such insect guests, especially of the beetle kind. Some five thousand species of insects and spiders are found only in the nests of ants, living there per- 50 manently as either welcome or tolerated lodgers.

a. What is the theme of this passage?
b. Which of the following, if any, would you include in your
summary?
   i. a quart of insect food
  ii. their skins are kept moist
  iii. greenflies, blackflies and whiteflies
  iv. the beetle kind

c. Who or what are the 'individuals' referred to at the end of the first paragraph?

d. Find, in the first paragraph, illustrative examples which will not occur in the final summary or in the rough notes.

e. Will it be necessary to mention the maze (first paragraph) in your summary? If not, how can you summarize the point exemplified by the maze?

f. Point out details in the second paragraph which will be omitted in a summary of about 150 words.

g. Make rough notes on the passage.

h. Working only from your rough notes, and without referring to the original passage again, make a summary of 150 to 200 words.

2. Examination techniques

Exercise 15

Summarize, *in your own words as far as possible*, the following passage (which contains about 490 words), reducing it to between 150 and 170 words. State at the end the *exact* number of words you have used.

The national parks of Africa are an important economic asset of the territories in which they lie, for they attract tourists (our tiresome word for modern pilgrims and travellers); and tourists bring in a substantial revenue, not merely through disbursements in the national parks themselves, but chiefly 5 through what they spend in the country at large, on transport, accommodation, equipment, photography and souvenirs.

The national parks and wild-life reserves are now the main reasons why they come to East Africa, and one of the main reasons why they come to South Africa and Mozambique; 10 and the same could soon hold for Central Africa. Tourism is increasing in volume throughout Africa's wild-life area, and in Kenya, for instance, has already become the second largest source of national revenue, to the tune of over £8 million. What is more, it is capable of a very large further increase in 15 the near future (of course, always provided that there is no World War, and no major political trouble in eastern Africa).

So long as Western prosperity continues, with populations increasing and industrialization being intensified, more and more people will want to escape farther and farther from its 20 results, in the shape of over-large and over-crowded cities, smoke, noise, boring routine, and the over-mechanization of life. Air travel will certainly become cheaper and more popular, and will take more people farther afield.

I would prophesy that the revenue to be derived from 25 tourism in East Africa (which already runs to well over £10 million) could be certainly increased five-fold, and probably ten-fold, in the next ten years, provided that the business is properly organized. It will be necessary to improve access to the national parks and accommodation within them, catering 30 both for those who like comfort and for those who prefer a more do-it-yourself holiday; to provide museums and guides; to maintain a really adequate staff of wardens, scientists and game scouts, good fencing and anti-poaching measures; and to produce the right sort of publicity. 35

It will be necessary to work in with travel and tourist agencies in arranging good holidays, efficient itineraries and so-called package tours, to set up new national parks, and to open up new areas, such as parts of the coast and the uplands, for the enjoyment of visitors. And all this without over- 40 crowding the national parks, which would spell their ruination (already at some seasons some of the roads in the Kruger Park are overcrowded with cars full of tourists).

This will cost money—quite a lot of money. So far, game departments and national parks have been among the most 45 neglected of government departments in Africa: how can they be provided with this extra finance? I would hazard the guess that if the African territories could co-operate in the latter, and make reasoned application to some United Nations agency for a loan to develop their tourist trade, they 50 would have a good chance of getting it.

(University of London, G.C.E. for Overseas Candidates)

Do not read any farther until you have finished your summary of the passage above.

This is what the examiners said in their report addressed to intending candidates and those who had failed already:

In writing a good summary, you must first prove that you have understood the original passage, and you can do this only by using your own words wherever possible.* You must be careful not to introduce facts or ideas of your own into your answer. You must reduce the length of your answer to the required number of words*; and this means that you have space for only the most important points. You cannot afford to waste words, but on the other hand your sentences must be in good, natural English, so do not try to save words by leaving out *the* or *a*. Many weak candidates use most of their allowance of words on the first half of the original, so that, in the later stages, their summaries are incomplete. This lack of balance is a bad fault. The better candidates proved that the passages set this year (*including the Alternative paper*) were not at all difficult, but most answers were bad. In the passage about national parks, few took the many chances to save words by summing up a long list of details in a short phrase. For instance, the money spent on transport, accommodation, equipment, photography and souvenirs could be grouped together as 'indirect profits'; and a phrase like the 'evils of industrialism' would include many of the facts listed in the third paragraph. The writer says that probably, in the future, far more Europeans will spend their holidays in Africa, but many candidates thought he meant that these Europeans would come as permanent settlers. This is a serious misunderstanding. The weakest candidates thought that national parks were car-parks; their answers, of course, were worthless.

Note: The examiners' remarks about 'using your own words' and the number of words used were made in the light of the syllabus and examining methods then prevailing. It is possible that there will be some change in due course but we will consider that point on page 127.

In marking a summary, the examiners look for three main points:

a. Within the limits of the number of words, have all the *main points* of the original passage been included?

b. Are they linked up smoothly in the summary so that it reads fluently?

c. Is the summary technically correct, i.e. are the punctuation marks, grammar etc. corrrect?

Now compare your summary with the one given below. It has not been provided by the examiners but it is an example of what is expected from candidates.

Rough notes

i. National parks important in economic life of some African countries. Attract tourists and bring direct and indirect revenue to countries.

  ii. Particularly so in East and South Africa. Could be in Central.

 iii. Increasing no. of people from West will take advantage of cheaper air fares to travel more widely to avoid industr.

 iv. Revenue could probably be incr. 10-fold in next decade if facilities in and out of parks improved.

  v. Good org. and new parks needed to avoid over-crowding. Loan could perhaps be obt. from a UN agency if concerned Afr. countries prod. cooperative plan of devel.

(*Note:* These are merely rough notes made in pencil on the examination paper. **They must be crossed out when finished with.**)

Final summary

National parks and wild-life reserves play an important part in the economic life of some African countries, particularly in East and South Africa. They attract tourists and thus bring substantial direct and indirect revenue. In Kenya, for example, tourists are the second largest source of revenue, and there are potentialities in Central Africa.

With the rise in population in the West and with continued prosperity there, an increasing number of people will take advantage of cheaper air fares to travel more widely, seeking to avoid the unpleasantness of their industrialized environment.

If there were improved facilities in and out of the parks, the revenue from tourism could probably be increased as much as ten-fold in the next decade. To achieve this, it is vital to have good organization and new national parks to avoid over-crowding. One way of financing this work would be by way of a loan which could perhaps be obtained from a United Nations agency if the interested African countries produced a co-operative plan for development.   (169 words)

Exercise 16

Summarize, *in your own words as far as possible*, the following passage (which contains about 500 words), reducing it to between 150 and 170 words. State at the end the *exact* number of words you have used.

Much of the work done by the Forestry Commission in

England during the last fifty years is disliked by the man in the street. From what he sees on holiday he complains that it is unnatural, with straight lines of little trees all alike, of the same species and the same age, with too many conifers, and 5 not enough variety and colour. The Commission is impenitent, and talks of the dangerous concept of the natural forest. Most of the popular grumbles are easily answered. Bluntly, the non-foresters are interested in the look of things, but for the forester handsome is as handsome does. 10

There is, however, another point of view. A serious school of forestry exists, little known in England, but estimated to command the allegiance of seventy-five per cent of French and Swiss foresters and of a large body of Germans, which teaches that more natural or more natural-looking forestry 15 is the best. Species of trees should be mixed, natural regeneration (from fallen seed) should be encouraged, and felling should be on a selection system. That is, individual trees should be felled as they mature or as space is needed for others to grow, but there should not be wholesale felling, as when 20 fifty acres or more of trees are all cut down at once, this operation being followed by 'industrial-type' planting, specifically for future clearing.

The essential idea of this system has long been known in Germany, under the name *Dauerwald* (perpetual forest). It 25 has its supporters in England also, and one well-known landowner who practises this type of forestry on a large scale is emphatic that woodlands or forests managed in the natural way are much healthier and less subject to disease. Also they are certainly less liable to storm damage and frost and drought. 30 Costs and yields are more even. A distinction should perhaps be made between State forest and private woodland. The latter still comprises more than seventy-five per cent of England's woodlands and forests. State forests are more modern, established since 1920 on poor land, whereas private 35 woodlands are mostly old-established and on better land, where a more natural and less industrial system of growing trees may seem more fitting and be more easily practised.

But 'natural' forestry is emphatically not so natural that mere common sense will suffice. Experience, skill, judgment 40 and sustained attention are needed—some say more skill than in 'industrial' forestry. Disputable and highly contentious issues are legion, and many of them are difficult and

technical. But the development of nuclear energy has un- 45
doubtedly weakened one of the older arguments for the cultiva-
tion of trees to provide timber supports in mines, namely, that
we must have a three years' standing store of essential timber
against an emergency. The curse of rabbits, long a major
obstacle to 'natural' forestry, has declined in recent years.
It might also be argued that the amenity aspects of forestry 50
become more important, relatively, to a nation at once increasingly urbanized and increasingly affluent.

    (University of London, G.C.E. for Overseas Candidates)

(*Note:* Some Englishmen might say that the subject-matter of
this passage is open to objection and to criticism of the way in
which the point is argued. It is extremely doubtful, for example,
whether the bland assumption in the first sentence is true. I do
not think the man in the street dislikes much of the work done
by the Forestry Commission. The writer makes this rather rash
claim in order to give the impression that he is pressing a popular
view instead of a personal one. However, **the summary of this
passage must not contain any ideas or views not in the
original passage**. The person who makes the summary may
not criticize the content of the original passage, or add to it in
any way. Some candidates do not seem to understand this point.)

This is what the examiners said in their report addressed to
intending candidates and those who had failed already:

    It is in the summary question that the majority of candidates
show that they have not had adequate preparation for the
examination. Most candidates seem to have only one method
of tackling this question—to select snippets from the original
passage and string them together. That they have not really
understood the argument of the passage is clear from the fact
that many use the wrong conjunctions in joining up these
snippets, by, for example, using 'but' instead of 'and', thereby
making nonsense of the argument. Another fault arising from
this method is that frequently candidates have used up the
given numbers of words before reaching the end of the
passage, so that often the latter part, which may be even more
important than the first one or two paragraphs, has to be
squeezed into a line or two at the end. Unless the general
drift of the argument has been seized before an attempt is
made to summarize, the candidate is bound to fail.

    In the passage set in this paper many candidates failed to

see the contrast made between beauty and function, or between natural and industrial forestry, the purpose of the comparison between State and private woodlands. All these were basic to the argument of the passage. Another common fault is the failure to generalize, and to remove illustrative detail; for example, the following should be omitted, or generalized: in the first paragraph fifty years, the detail about the trees; in the second paragraph the reference to seventy-five per cent, details of the nationalities, fifty acres, and in the third paragraph reference to seventy-five per cent and 1920. In the second, third and fourth paragraphs there is also opportunity for generalization about planting, felling and management.

There was frequently too much copying of whole passages or sentences, including unnecessary detail, and this was most apparent in parts of the passage which had obviously not been understood, particularly in the last paragraph, which candidates seemed to find most difficult, the argument about the effect of nuclear developments being frequently misunderstood. One or two points of idiom were also not grasped. Many candidates did not know the meaning of 'handsome is as handsome does', or see its connection with the relative importance of beauty and function. The special meaning of 'school' in the passage defeated most candidates, and there were many references to pupils from France, Germany and Switzerland being taught forestry in English schools. The 'man in the street' was interpreted as, among other things, a low class individual, a street walker and a scavenger. The complete lack of comprehension may perhaps be illustrated by one example, summarizing the first two sentences of the passage: 'Street walkers on holiday complain that too many trees in England are in uniform.'

Now compare your summary with the one given below. It has not been provided by the examiners but it is the type of work expected from candidates.

Rough notes

i. Average Englishman complains For. Comm. creates unnatural forests of formal shape and uniform content. Commission believes in utility and declines to change.
ii. Consid. support in some Europ. countries for method of

  growing trees similar to that in natural forest with selective
  (as opposed to wholesale) felling.
iii. This system has some support in England and one landowner
  thinks it is more suitable and prod. trees less prone to disease
  and damage from climate. However, private landowners have
  better land than that of State forests.
iv. Consid. skill needed for natural forestry. Rabbits no longer
  a great nuisance. Visual appeal important.
 v. No longer need for 3 years' standing store of pit-props.

(*Note:* The ideas in the original passage seem poorly developed
and poorly arranged so some rearrangement may be necessary
to put continuity into a passage which lacks it.)

Final summary

  The English Forestry Commission is criticized for creating
forests formal in shape and too uniform in content. An alternative is available in the 'natural' system of forestry which has
considerable support in some European countries. There, many
experts favour forests of mixed trees, as in nature, and selective,
not wholesale, felling. This system has some support in England
and one private landowner thinks it produces trees less prone to
disease and damage from the climate. It must be observed,
however, that most private estates are on better land than that of
State forests and their trees are usually old-established. 'Natural'
forestry requires great skill and has its problems but the rabbit
nuisance has declined and the visual appeal of natural forests
is becoming increasingly important in an industrialized country.
  Nevertheless, the Forestry Commission prefers utility and
declines to change to 'natural' forestry although nuclear power
has made it less vital for a three years' standing store of pit-
props to be maintained. (161 words)

(*Note:* I found this summary much more difficult to make than
the one in Exercise 15, partly because of the need to introduce
some kind of *evident* theme and order into a passage in which
the points are not too well arranged or made.)

  Notice that in this summary the consecutive points are linked
by the use of these words:

  An alternative is available . . . – There . . . – This system . . .
  – It must be observed, however, that . . . – Nevertheless . . .

  Notice also that while I have almost never copied from the

passage, I have not hesitated to use words and expressions from it when I could not find anything better in the time available. The final summary was made with only a casual glance at the original passage; most of it came from the rough notes and my memory of **the basic ideas** of the original.

The examiners' views

The extracts from the examiners' reports on the previous pages will have shown you what the examiners expect. Here are a few more vital points taken from past reports:

i. 'Almost invariably candidates failed to find the simple theme of the passage.' 'Most failed because they did not try to grasp the passage as a whole.'

ii. 'Few had been taught that details have no place in a summary.' 'Many candidates do not seem to know that illustrative detail and examples should be removed.'

iii. 'Many good candidates had evidently been advised to cast their answers in reported speech; this is not asked for, and should be avoided, since it leads to word-wasting formulas such as "The author went on to point out that . . .", and causes difficulty in the management of tenses.'

iv. 'Some candidates do not seem to know that they must not add material or give their comments on the subject-matter.' 'Candidates are frequently penalized for the addition of . . . material, or their own comments on the argument.'

v. 'Candidates are required to use their own words as far as possible. This does not mean that no words from the passage are to be used. It always happens that certain words cannot be advantageously replaced, and the use of such words is not penalized, but when the candidate offers merely a string of short passages, all exactly copied from the original, or even, as often happens, whole sentences without alteration, such work cannot be given much credit.'

It may be helpful to you to understand how a summary is marked in an examination. As mentioned on page 119, the examiners look for three things:

a. Have all the main points been given within the number of words allowed?—Make sure that nothing has been added or twisted. Make sure that all details and examples have been reduced to generalizations.

b. Does the whole summary read smoothly?—Make sure that the sentences are properly linked and not just a succession of jerky statements

c. Is the language correct?—Make sure that the summary does not contain errors of tenses, prepositions, pronouns, agreement, spelling, punctuation etc.

3. A summary of the advice

Here is a summary of the advice given in this chapter:

a. The method of making a summary

1. *Study the passage until you can find its theme. Write it down.*
2. *Make rough notes on each 3–8 lines.*
3. *Link up your notes properly so that they do not read in a jerky or unconnected way.*
4. *Check for length and amend when necessary; write out the final summary.*

b. Points which require attention

1. *Always cross out your rough work.*
2. *Do not turn the whole passage into reported speech. If the passage contains dialogue, any summary of the conversation may be in reported speech.*
3. *Your summary should not normally contain direct questions.*
4. *Omit details, examples, repetition and irrelevant remarks.*
5. *Do not add to or comment on the subject-matter of the original passage.*
6. *Obviously your summary must be of the required length if any limits are given.*
7. *Develop the art of generalizing a mass of details to sum them up in one or two sentences.*
8. *Don't copy passages from the original unless there is no better way of expressing an idea. In any case, keep your borrowings to the minimum.*
9. *In your concern for the facts of the passage, never let your language deteriorate. Check your work for accuracy of language, punctuation etc. before you hand it in.*

Note

a. Using the correct number of words.
b. Avoiding copying from the original.

Fashions change in life and in examinations. On page 119 we

referred to the problems mentioned in *a* and *b* above. It is advisable to say something further about these two matters.

The golden rule is to follow the instructions given by the examiner even if they come as a surprise to you.

a. Using the correct number of words

In life there are times when the length of a summary does not much matter. There are times when it has to fall within certain rough limits, and there are times (particularly in newspapers, on the radio and on television) when it has to come within very rigid limits. If your examination follows the practices of daily life, therefore, you may expect to find that you are given (i) no guide as to length, or (ii) a very general guide as to length, e.g. '100 to 200 words', 'about 10 to 20 lines' or 'reducing it to about a half of it present length', or (iii) very rigid limits as to length, e.g. 150 to 170 words.

At the moment of preparing this book, certain examination syllabuses are under review, and it may be that for YOUR particular examination there is a change in the instructions. Partly for this reason, the instructions in the exercises in section 4 of this chapter vary considerably. They will give you practice in working to different lengths and under different conditions. Do not avoid the exercises which now seem unusual to you. They may become routine exercises in the future.

b. Avoiding copying from the original

Here, too, changes are likely. In adult life there is normally no bar to using the words of an original when making, for example, a digest of news or a summary of an article or a report of a speech or incident.

To be sure that you have the right attitude to this matter, you must patiently consider the problems of the examiners and the history of summary work in examinations.

i. Once upon a time instructions to candidates did not warn them to use their own words. The result was that some candidates just extracted sentences from the original, put in 'and' or 'but' here and there and tried to pass this off as a summary. It wasn't. It was merely a series of extracts which frequently made little sense and did not cover the main points.

ii. To stop this, the examiners began to introduce a warning to candidates to use their own words. However, some very conscientious candidates wrongly assumed that this meant that they could not use any word from the original. They then began to get into difficulties finding other words for 'man', 'science', 'hydroponics' etc. The result was often rather pathetic and not very sensible.

iii. In desperation, at least one examining board has now dropped the instruction to candidates telling them to use their own words. This may lead bad candidates back to (i) above—but they will fail. Instead of putting in an instruction to candidates, the examining authorities have made it clear in their reports, instructions to schools, circulars etc. that they want the attitude explained on page 125 of this book. It is repeated here because it shows exactly what is expected:

> *This does not mean that no words from the passages are to be used. It always happens that certain words cannot be advantageously replaced, and the use of such words is not penalized, but when the candidate offers merely a string of short passages, all exactly copied from the original, or even, as often happens, whole sentences without alteration, such work cannot be given much credit.*

iv. Nevertheless, you may one day face an exercise in which you are required merely to make notes of a passage and may have more freedom to use key expressions in it. Watch your instructions and follow them precisely.

4. *Further exercises

1. Make a summary of the whole passage, which contains 342 words, in **not more than 115 words.** Take care to give a continuous connexion of ideas. Failure to keep within the limit of 115 words will be penalized.

One of the many things we take for granted in the twentieth century is the speedy collection and delivery of letters to and from all parts of the world at astonishingly cheap rates. A husband away on a business trip can write home to his wife 2,000 miles away knowing that the letter will reach her in a few days. His special air-letter may cost him less than a loaf of bread or his own bus fare to work.

This service, however, is a boon of comparatively recent origin. Until modern times the cost of sending letters privately

* If necessary, the rubric of some of the following exercises can be altered to provide further practice in note-taking or to require pupils to find a predetermined number of points in any given passage.

was so great that the arrival of a letter was a considerable 10
event and might even cause financial hardship to the receiver,
who had to bear the charges. There were, indeed, from the
Middle Ages onwards, special messengers who carried State
correspondence, and other messengers employed to travel
with news between the great monasteries or the great mer- 15
chants' houses, but for centuries there was no official post
service by which private letters could be sent. It was not until
1840 that the official organization known as the Penny Post
was established in Great Britain and gave ordinary people
cheap and efficient postal deliveries. 20

The Penny Post and the development of world-wide postal
services since have given us many obvious advantages, but
there has been one result which makes us sometimes regret the
passing of the bad old days. In the seventeenth and eighteenth
centuries the arrival of a letter was a great occasion, and the 25
letter-writer knew it. He did not confine himself to brief information about his own health and enquiries about his
correspondent's, or to the bare mention of visits and expeditions. A letter was a journal of his life, a little piece of himself
through which his family could enter into all his feelings, 30
experiences and thoughts. Letters written by famous men
and women of the past to their families and friends tell us
more about the writers than any biographer can hope to do,
and for this reason they are still treasured.

(University of Cambridge)

2. Make a summary of the whole passage, which contains 346
   words, in **not more than 120 words**. Take care to give a
   continuous connexion of ideas, and use your own words **as
   far as possible.** Failure to keep within the limit of 120 words
   will be penalized.

How much pain do animals feel? This is a question which
has caused endless controversy. Opponents of big-game
shooting, for example, arouse our pity by describing the
agonies of a badly-wounded beast that has crawled into a
corner to die. In countries where the fox, the hare and the 5
deer are hunted, animal-lovers paint harrowing pictures of
the pursued animal suffering not only the physical distress of
the chase but the mental anguish of anticipated death.

The usual answer to these criticisms is that animals do not
suffer in the same way, or to the same extent, as we do. Man 10

was created with a delicate nervous system and has never lost his acute sensitiveness to pain; animals, on the other hand, had less sensitive systems to begin with and, in the course of millions of years, have developed a capacity for ignoring injuries and disorders which human beings would find in- 15 tolerable. For example, a dog will continue to play with a ball even after a serious injury to his foot; he may be unable to run without limping, but he will go on trying long after a human child would have had to stop because of the pain. We are told, moreover, that even when animals appear to us 20 to be suffering acutely, this is not so; what seem to us to be agonized contortions caused by pain are in fact no more than muscular contractions over which they have no control.

These arguments are unsatisfactory because something about which we know a great deal is being compared with 25 something we can only conjecture. We know what we feel; we have no means of knowing what animals feel. Some creatures with a less delicate nervous system than ours may be incapable of feeling pain to the same extent as we do: that is as far as we are entitled to go. The most humane attitude, 30 surely, is to assume that no animals are entirely exempt from physical pain and that we ought, therefore, wherever possible, to avoid causing suffering even to the least of them.

(University of Cambridge)

3. Make a summary of the whole passage, which contains 344 words, in **not more than 120 words.** Take care to give a continuous connexion of ideas. Failure to keep within the limit of 120 words will be penalized.

It would be difficult to find a more striking illustration of the efficiency of the world's postal services than that provided by the Cambridge School Certificate Examination. Question papers are posted to scores of countries, and answers written by tens of thousands of boys and girls are despatched by post 5 to Cambridge. Some are transported across the sea in ships, others across land and sea in aeroplanes. All of them travel a part of their journey on railways, and some on the special underground railway that takes letters and postal packets across London. 10

Year after year, this feat of organization is carried to a successful conclusion. It is always possible that a ship, an aircraft or a train may suffer an accident and its mail be des-

troyed; but such catastrophes are mercifully rare Occasion- 15
ally an examiner finds that the edges of some answer-papers
are frayed, perhaps eaten away by a famished rat in the hold
of a steamer, or that some handwriting has been damped and
blurred, perhaps because a wave broke over a surf-boat.
Sometimes a mail-bag lies unnoticed for days or weeks in a
corner of a post office; but delays in delivery are commend- 20
ably infrequent. The normal expectation is that all the answer-
papers will reach their destination, undamaged and with
reasonable punctuality.

The postal service in every country where the Examination
is taken is organized by its government. Each government 25
gets revenue from the sale of stamps, but has agreed not to
collect postal revenue from the others. For example, the
Government of Jamaica will deliver anywhere in that island,
without fee, packets bearing United Kingdon stamps. Similarly the British Government will deliver at Cambridge, free 30
of charge, packets that bear Jamaican stamps. Such co-
operation, practised as it is by every government, is a good
augury for the future. Since international co-operation
enables one and the same examination to be taken by young
people in areas as far apart as, for example, Africa and the 35
Caribbean, can it not do more and safeguard their lives from
the dangers of international war?

(University of Cambridge)

4. Summarize, *in your own words as far as possible*, the following
   passage (which contains about 520 words), reducing it to
   between 160 and 180 words. State at the end the *exact*
   number of words you have used.

The existence of an abundant deep-sea fauna was discovered, probably millions of years ago, by certain whales
and also, it now appears, by seals. The ancestors of all whales,
we know by fossil remains, were land mammals. They must
have been predatory beasts, if we are to judge by their power- 5
ful jaws and teeth. Perhaps in their foragings about the deltas
of great rivers or around the edges of shallow seas, they discovered the abundance of fish and other marine life and over
the centuries formed the habit of following them farther and
farther into the sea. Little by little their bodies took on a form 10
more suitable for aquatic life; their hind limbs were reduced
to rudiments, which may be discovered in a modern whale

by dissection, and the forelimbs were modified into organs for steering and balancing.

Eventually the whales, as though to divide the sea's food 15 resources among them, became separated into three groups: the plankton-eaters, the fish-eaters and the squid-eaters. The plankton-eating whales can exist only where there are dense masses of small shrimps to supply their enormous food requirements. This limits them, except for scattered areas, to 20 Arctic and Antarctic waters and the high temperate latitudes. Fish-eating whales may find food over a somewhat wider range of ocean, but they are restricted to places where there are enormous populations of schooling fish. The blue water of the tropics and of the open ocean basins offers little to either of 25 these groups. But that immense, square-headed, formidably toothed whale known as the cachalot or sperm whale discovered long ago what men have known for only a short time —that hundreds of fathoms below the almost untenanted surface waters of these regions there is an abundant animal 30 life. The sperm whale has taken these deep waters for his hunting grounds; his quarry is the deep-water population of squids, including the giant squid Architeuthis, which lives in mid-ocean at depths of 1,500 feet or more. The head of a sperm whale is often marked with long stripes, which con- 35 sist of a great number of circular scars made by the suckers of the squid. From this evidence we can imagine the battles that go on, in the darkness of the deep water, between these two huge creatures—the sperm whale with its seventy-ton bulk, the squid with a body as long as thirty feet, and writh- 40 ing, grasping arms extending the total length of the animal to perhaps fifty feet.

The greatest depth at which the giant squid lives is not definitely known, but there is one instructive piece of evidence about the depth to which sperm whales descend, presumably 45 in search of the squids. In April 1932, off the coast of Colombia, a cable was brought to the surface for repair. Entangled in it was a dead forty-five-foot male sperm whale. The submarine cable was twisted around the lower jaw and was wrapped around one flipper, the body and the tail flukes. The 50 cable was raised from a depth of 540 fathoms, or 3,240 feet.

(University of London G.C.E. for Overseas Candidates)

5. Summarize, *in your own words as far as possible*, the following

passage (which contains about 515 words), reducing it to between 150 and 170 words. State at the end the *exact* number of words you have used.

The significance of all earlier attempts to scale Mount Everest is that, regardless of the height they reached, each added to the mounting sum of experience. The building of this pyramid of experience was vital to the whole issue; only when it had attained a certain height was it within the power 5 of any mountaineering team to succeed. Seen in this light, other expeditions did not fail; they made progress. We were inspired by their example, their persistence, their spirit of quest, their determination that there should be no surrender.

Thus inspired, we gave ourselves to sound, thorough, meti- 10 culously detailed planning. On Everest, the problems of organization assume the proportions of a military campaign, and we planned the ascent on these lines. It was thanks to this that we were able not only to foresee our needs in every detail but also to have constantly before us a clear programme 15 to carry out at every stage.

The chance of success of big Himalayan expeditions has often been adversely affected by ill-health among the climbers. The number in our party, though sufficient to execute our predetermined plan, left no large margin to allow for any 20 handicap of sickness. The plan adopted was an ambitious one in that it depended on the active participation high on the mountain of almost the entire team; if several us had been sick when the opportunity for the Assault occurred, it is very doubtful if we should have reached the top. That we were 25 so fit was due initially to careful selection of the party. In the field, the training and acclimatization carried out in the period allotted for this purpose was an astounding success. We have also to thank those who furnished our sound and sufficient diet and emphasized the need for drinking large 30 quantities of liquid daily throughout our time on the mountain, and especially at high altitudes. Nor must we forget the care we received from our doctors.

Our unity as a party was undoubtedly the biggest single factor in the final result, for the ascent of Everest demanded 35 a very high degree of selfless co-operation; no amount of equipment or food could have compensated for any weakness in this respect. It would be difficult to find a more closely knit team than ours. It is a remarkable fact that throughout

the whole four months that we were together, often in trying 40
circumstances, I never heard an impatient or angry word
passed between any members of my party. This made my
task infinitely easier, and most particularly when the time
came to decide the individual tasks to be undertaken during
the period leading up to and during the Assault. It could not 45
fall to everyone to attempt the summit, and for some there
must have been disappointment made greater by their fitness
to go higher. But everyone rightly believed that he had a
vital part to play in getting at least two members of the team
to the top, and it was in this spirit that each man carried out 50
his job. In this lay the immediate secret of our success.
(University of London G.C.E. for Overseas Candidates)

6. Summarize, **in your own words as far as possible**, the
following passage (which contains about 485 words), reducing
it to between 150 and 170 words. State at the end the **exact**
number of words you have used.

The most famous case of an animal said to be capable of
counting is that of a horse in Germany called Clever Hans.
The episode occurred at the beginning of the present century.
The horse's owner believed that animals can think and reason
as we can and that this faculty can be brought out by training 5
the animals. He trained Clever Hans to give the answers to
problems of arithmetic; the horse gave the correct answer by
tapping the right number of times with its forefoot. Clever
Hans was taught to tap units with one forefoot and tens with
the other. The animal gave the correct answers not only to 10
additions but to other processes of arithmetic, including
converting fractions to decimals. It gave the right answers
too when the questions were not spoken but shown to it
written on a card.

This case was so much talked about in the newspapers that 15
a committee of scientists was formed to investigate the astonishing powers of the horse. The committee, after a careful
investigation, found that the owner and trainer of Hans was
an honest man, that he had not purposely trained his horse
to stop tapping, and so to give a correct answer, by giving 20
it a slight clue as is done with performing circus animals.
The absence of such trickery was proved by the fact that
members of the committee themselves got the right answers
from Hans even when the owner was not present.

It looked as if the horse really could think and count. But 25
soon after this another scientist discovered what really was
the truth of the matter. He found that if the horse was asked
questions to which none of the people present knew the
answers, then the animal never gave a correct answer. It
could not even answer the simplest question. The questions 30
were asked by showing the horse a card which the questioner
himself had not read. The biologist soon discovered that,
when the horse gave the correct answers, what really occurred
was this: the horse responded to almost imperceptible movements of head or body made by a questioner who knew the 35
answer. These movements were quite unconscious, and the
questioner did not know that he made them. But the questioner was aware, of course, of the number of taps that the
horse should make. He counted the taps to himself, and
when the horse arrived at the right number, the questioner's 40
tension would be relieved by a very slight unconscious head
or body movement. It was to this movement that the horse
responded by stopping the tapping of its foot. Questioners
who did not know the answer made no such movements; so
the horse was confused. The horse had really taught itself to 45
answer these very small movements during its training: it
was always induced to try its best by rewards of corn or sugar.
          (University of London G.C.E. for Overseas Candidates)

7. Read the following passage in which a nineteenth-century
   Englishman lays down the principles by which he thought
   the new Cunard Steamship Company should be guided when
   sending ships from England to North America. In not more
   than five sentences give the five principles which he suggests.

In an undertaking of such magnitude, it is of the greatest
importance that the whole be reviewed in a broad and liberal
manner at the outset and everything that can be brought to
bear either for or against the interest of the speculation, fairly
weighed and balanced before anything is decided upon. . . . 5
I am aware that in getting up the first of these vessels great
care and attention will be necessary to gain the different
objects in view and in doing this an extra expense may be
incurred, but which may be avoided in all the other vessels.
    If the practical difficulties etc. are fairly surmounted in 10
the first vessels—and which I have no doubt but they may—
the first cost and sailing expenses of the two first vessels ought

not so much to be taken into account. In fact, I consider it
as nothing compared with seeing them so efficient as to set
all opposition at defiance and to give entire confidence to 15
the public in all their arrangements and appointments, cost
what it may at first, for upon this depends entirely the
success, nay, the very existence of the Company.

I wish therefore to be impressed upon the minds of your
friends, the great necessity of using every precaution that 20
can be thought of to guard against accidents on such a long
passage and if accidents shall happen, to be prepared with a
remedy to meet any common one that may occur, as far as
possible. By attending to this you will give confidence to
the public and comfort to yourselves, and in the end I am 25
certain it will more than repay you.

The plan I would propose with regard to the whole of the
engineer department is: I would endeavour to get a very
respectable man and one thoroughly conversant with his
business as an engineer; I would appoint this man to be 30
master engineer, his duty to superintend and direct all the
men and operations about the engines and boilers etc. to be
accountable to the Captain for his conduct—viz. to be under
the Captain.

All the other men for working the engines should be regular 35
bred tradesmen, and all the firemen boiler-makers. A work-
shop, with a complete set of tools and duplicates of all the
parts of the engines that are most likely to go wrong, should
be on board.

In a word I would have everything connected with the 40
machinery very strong and of the best materials, it being of
the utmost importance to give confidence at first, for should
the slightest accident happen so as to prevent the vessel
making her passage by steam, it would be magnified by the
opposition and thus, for a time at least, mar the progress of 45
the Company.

But if, on the other hand, the steam vessels are successful
in making a few quick trips at first and beating the sailing
vessels very decidedly, then you may consider the battle won
and the field your own. . . .   50

(Robert Napier cited in *Alantic Conquest* by Warren Tute)

8. This exercise is designed to test your ability to differentiate
between relevant and irrelevant material. Read the following

account of the Cocos-Keeling Islands in the Indian Ocean. Then use it (and no other source) to write a short account of the history (and of nothing else) of the islands.

Your account must be given in a tabulated form; this means that you must make a series of numbered notes in strict chronological order, dealing with the history of the islands. Your notes will not be in rough so they must be complete sentences. You may decide the total length yourself but be sure to include all the important facts, summarized in your own words when possible.

The Cocos-Keeling Islands

The Cocos-Keeling Islands, a small group of coral formation, lie in the Indian Ocean, on the direct route from Colombo to Fremantle and about half-way between them.

The southern group consists of 24 named islands varying in size from the six-mile long and half-mile wide Pulo Pan- 5
jang to mere detached banks. Fifteen miles to the northward lies the atoll of Keeling, and it seems that this was the land first sighted in 1608 by Captain William Keeling of the East India Company.

The modern history of the atoll may be said to have begun 10
in 1825 when it was visited by John Clunies Ross, who found the islands uninhabited. In the same year, Alexander Hare settled there, bringing with him settlers of mixed oriental origin. In 1827 Ross returned from Scotland with his wife and children in the ship *Borneo* and settled on Pulo Selma, 15
or Home Island. After some ten years, Hare, his influence having grown less, left the islands. In 1854, Ross died and was succeeded by his son, John George Clunies Ross, who married S'pia Dupong, a Malay lady of Royal Sulu blood. In 1857, the islands were formally annexed to Great Britain, 20
and Ross was appointed Governor at Her Majesty's pleasure. He died in 1872 and was succeeded by his son, George Ross, under whose governorship considerable prosperity was enjoyed and much was done to improve the domestic amenities of the people. In 1884, Ross made a voyage to England in his 25
Cocos-built schooner of 178 tons and, during his absence, a Commission visited the group to grant letters patent to him and to place the islands under the Government of the Straits Settlements. This was not formally done, however, until 1903.

George Ross, in ill health, sailed for England in 1910. He 30

137

died the same year in the Isle of Wight, where he was buried
at Bonchurch. In 1915 his remains were disinterred for re-
burial at Cocos.

John Sydney Clunies Ross succeeded his father and ruled
through the difficult years succeeding the first world war, 35
when the islands shared the world-wide depression from general loss of trade. He died in 1944 and left his son John, the
fifth in the direct line, to carry on with the family tradition.

In 1901 a violent cyclone caused enormous damage, destroy-
ing 800,000 coconut trees and in the same year the seclusion 40
of the islands was broken more permanently by the coming of
the cable and its attendant staff. At the present day the cables
run from Pulo Tikus, or Direction Island, to Perth, Mauritius and Java. A small Australian staff is maintained there by
the Overseas Telecommunications Commission (Australia). 45
For accommodation they have a range of bungalow type
buildings, which include cable office, living quarters, billiards
rooms, library and mess. Recreation mainly consists of tennis,
fishing and sailing. All the boats are island built. During the
rainy season a fairly good supply of vegetables is produced but 50
at other times tinned varieties are resorted to; a large freezer
now provides an ample supply of fresh meat. The staff are
dependent on visits two or three times a year of a ship chartered
to bring food, clothing and other stores, which are supplemented by air-freighted fresh vegetables. 55

Numerous sea birds make their home on Keeling and other
islands of the group. Land crabs abound; turtle and fish are
plentiful in the lagoon, where, it is said, giant clams up to six
feet in diameter are to be found. Imported pests such as
mice, rats, cockroaches etc., are all too numerous. 60

The small population are, on the whole, well trained and
there are some highly-skilled craftsmen, particularly in woodwork. The general labour conditions are good and the people
are housed in a model settlement. The Clunies Ross Estate is
responsible for their employment and welfare, and no one has 65
ever wanted for food or employment. Sickness and crime are
unknown. There are no police and the court has to deal only
with breaches of local rules such as sailing at night without
permission.

The cable station has been an enemy target in two wars. On 70
9th November, 1914, the German cruiser *Emden* landed a demolition party to destroy the installation. They had only partly

138

succeeded in their aim when H.M.A.S. *Sydney* came into sight and *Emden* abandoned her party. After a brisk action, Emden was forced ashore on North Keeling Atoll, where she 75 became a total wreck. The German demolition party seized the island schooner *Ayesha* and made their escape and after an adventurous voyage arrived at Jeddah. The cable staff having hidden spare instruments were speedily able to restore communications. 80

On 3rd March, 1942, during the second world war, a Japanese warship shelled the station and although the cable office was destroyed, communications were resumed within a few hours. A plain language radio message from Head Office to Batavia intimating that Cocos was permanently out of action 85 presumably deceived the Japanese, who never again interfered with the island.

In mid-1944, with Malaya in enemy hands and air communications with Australia extremely difficult, it was decided to develop an Air Staging Post at Cocos, and West Island was 90 chosen for the site. The island was well vegetated and presented a formidable task to the airfield engineers. Despite difficulties, by April, 1945, a runway over 2,000 yards long had been completed and two radar stations were in operation. In May, the first Liberator, en route for Australia, landed, refuelled 95 and made a night take-off for Guildford, Perth. Spitfire and Beaufighter squadrons also operated from the island until the cessation of hostilities in the Far East. In February, 1946, it was decided to close down the station.

On 22nd June, 1951, another link was forged in the islands'100 history when it was announced that Cocos-Keeling was to be transferred to Australia. This agreement was ratified in 1956.

(By courtesy of P. and O.–Orient Lines)

9. Assume that you are an Investigating Officer working in the Traffic Department of a police force. Traffic in your country keeps to the left-hand side of the road. One of your tasks is to read reports of traffic accidents, collect further evidence if necessary, make a précis of each accident, and forward the whole file to a superior officer who will study the report and decide whether or not to prosecute. The space for the précis of each accident is on the front of the file and will permit you to write about 80 to 120 words only.

Making a Summary

Read the following statements and then make a précis of the incident.

a. Statement by Sgt. Lloyd (Traffic Department)

Acting on instructions, at 9.15 p.m. on Wednesday, 5.1.1966, I proceeded to a point in River Road about fifty yards south of the Gala cinema. There I interviewed Mr. George Williams of 127 River Road, Mr. John Williams of the same address, and Mr. David Lee of 57 Market Lane. Mr. George Williams claimed that he had been knocked down by a motor-car, registration number GXB 731, driven by a Mr. Frederick Cole of 62 Government Road.

I took statements from Mr. George Williams, Mr. John Williams, Mr. David Lee, Mr. Frederick Cole and Mrs. Mary Cole. (These are attached.)

I inspected Mr. George Williams and found that he had minor bruises on his right calf, and a slight cut on his left arm. He declined to have these treated so I allowed him to go. When I had taken statements from Mr. and Mrs. Cole, I allowed them to go.

There was no street light at this point and visibility was bad. It was a dark evening with no moon. The weather was fine and the road was dry. I have carried out experiments with regard to Mr. Cole's contention about being dazzled at this point in the road and confirm what he says.

b. Statement by by Mr. George Williams of 127 River Road

At about ten past nine on Wednesday, 5.1.1966, I was walking along River Road in a northerly direction, proceeding from my home to the Gala cinema. I was walking on the left-hand side of the road, accompanied by my brother (Mr. John Williams) and a friend, Mr. David Lee. We were walking three abreast and I was on the outside. I agree that I was wearing a dark blue shirt and black trousers.

When I was about fifty yards from the cinema, I saw the lights of a car coming towards us. Then I suddenly became aware of the lights of a car coming from behind us and proceeding in the same direction as that in which we were going. Before I could do anything, something hit my right leg and knocked me into my friends. I fell down and cut my left arm.

When I got up, I saw that the car which had hit me had stopped. Its registration number was GXB 731 and a man got out of it and came to speak to me. I have since learnt that the man is Mr. Frederick Cole of 62 Government Road.

Mr. Cole said, 'I'm very sorry. I just didn't see you. The lights of the other car dazzled me. Are you all right?'

I told him I was not badly hurt. My brother telephoned for the Traffic Police. (*This statement is confirmed by his companions.*)

c. *Statement by Mr. Frederick Cole of 62 Government Road*

At about ten past nine on Wednesday, 5.1.1966, I was driving along River Road in a northerly direction. I was accompanied by my wife. I was driving slowly because of the darkness and estimate my speed to have been about twenty miles an hour.

As I approached a point about fifty or sixty yards south of the Gala cinema, I was dazzled by the lights of an oncoming car which was then coming round a bend in the road. I started to slow down even further and pulled in a little to my left. As I did so, I suddenly saw some vague shapes on my near side and was aware that the near side wing of my car had touched something. I stopped immediately and went back to see what had happened. I saw three men, all wearing clothes so dark that they were almost impossible to see at night. I saw one of the men get off the ground so I spoke to him.

I said, 'I'm very sorry. I didn't see you. The lights of that other car were dazzling me. Are you all right?'

The man said that he was all right. Then he noticed a slight scratch on his left arm. I gave him my name and address.

No, I do not know whether the men were walking abreast or in single file. I did not see them until after I had stopped the car and got out.

(*This statement is confirmed by Mrs. Cole who was sitting at the front, on the near side, beside her husband who was driving. She states that she saw the men just as the car touched Mr. George Williams. She is certain that they were walking three abreast.*)

10. In not more than **five** lines give a summary of any experiment you have recently done in any science lesson OR of any work done in a practical subject such as Domestic Science.

11. In not more than **ten** lines give a summary of any recent visit you have paid to a dentist, doctor or optician.

12. Give an oral summary of any recent important speech which you have heard on the radio or television or which you have read in a newspaper.

13. Give an oral summary, lasting not longer than ten seconds, on the position of women in your country.

14. Give an oral summary, lasting not longer than thirty seconds, of any recent game (e.g. football, hockey, basketball etc.) which you have watched.

15. Give an oral summary, lasting not longer than thirty seconds, of any film you have seen recently OR of any book you have read.

16. Give an oral summary, lasting not longer than two minutes, of the history of the land in which you live.

17. Give an oral summary, lasting not longer than a minute, of any accident you have seen. It can be an accident in your home or a traffic accident.

18. Give an oral summary of any important event at your school, such as a Speech Day, a concert, a school play, a sports meeting etc.

19. Give an oral summary of the festivities in your home OR in your town OR in your country on any day which has a special significance in your land, e.g. for religious, political or other reasons.

20. Give an oral summary, lasting not longer than thirty seconds, of your views on the treatment of criminals.

21. Make a written summary, from five to ten lines in length, of the following extracts from *The Examining of English Language*, the Eighth Report of the Secondary School Examinations Council, Department of Education and Science, U.K., 1964. Combine the material from the two extracts so that you treat them as a whole.

i. Our eighth criticism is directed to that part of the present papers which consist of questions on grammatical and other minutiae. Some of the most eloquently critical comments we received from the schools were directed against these questions; we share the view that they are of 5
doubtful utility in any examination of English language and that in their present form they do great harm. Such questions are often based on a few usages which are appropriate enough in some styles of the language, but which have come to be traditionally condemned as in- 10
correct in all. Other exercises in the same class are based on traditionally prescribed rules of grammar which have

been artificially imposed upon the language. They have
had little relevance to usage at any past time and they
have even less to contemporary usage. No examination is 15
serving a useful purpose for schools, candidates, em-
ployers or the outside world generally if it encourages
pupils to adopt a form of examination room English instead of seeking to express appropriately what they have
to say.   20

ii. The first improvement we recommend is that the trivial
questions referred to above should be excluded from the
papers. They serve no useful educational purpose and
indeed have a bad effect upon teaching. It is said that they
provide an objective method of differentiating candidates 25
but any such differentiation is really between perform-
ances in skills which are largely artificial and which bear
little relation to the candidates' ability to write or understand English. We therefore recommend that the ordinary
level English language papers, if retained should be con- 30
fined to questions testing the candidates' power to express
themselves in the English language and to questions
testing their power to read English with understanding.
Within these wide limits examining bodies should find
ample freedom for setting a variety of different kinds of 35
question.

(Slightly adapted)

22. Summarize, **in your own words as far as possible**, the
following passage (which contains about 515 words), reducing
it to between 150 and 175 words. State at the end the **exact**
number of words you have used.

The discovery of the Antarctic not only proved one of the
most interesting of all geographical adventures, but created
what might be called the heroic age of Antarctic exploration.
By their tremendous heroism, men such as Shackleton, Scott,
and Amundsen caused a new continent to emerge from the 5
shadows, and yet that heroic age, little more than a century
old, is already passing. Modern science and inventions are
revolutionizing the techniques of former explorers, and,
although still calling for courage and feats of endurance,
future journeys into these icy wastes will probably depend on 10
motor vehicles equipped with caterpillar traction rather than
on the dogs that earlier discoverers found so invaluable.

Making a Summary

Few realize that this Antarctic continent is almost equal in size to South America, and an enormous field of work awaits geographers and prospectors. The coasts of this continent 15 remain to be accurately charted, and the mapping of the whole of the interior presents a formidable task to the cartographers who undertake the work. Once their labours are completed, it will be possible to prospect the vast natural resources which scientists believe will furnish one of the largest treasure 20 hoards of metals and minerals the world has yet known, and almost inexhaustible sources of copper, coal, uranium, and many other ores will become available to man. Such discoveries will usher in an era of practical exploitation of the Antarctic wastes. 25

The polar darkness which hides this continent for the six winter months will be defeated by huge batteries of light, and make possible the establishing of air-fields for the future inter-continental air services by making these areas as light as day. Present flying routes will be completely changed, for 30 the Antarctic refuelling bases will make flights from Australia to South America comparatively easy over the 5,000 miles journey.

The climate is not likely to offer an insuperable problem, for the explorer Admiral Byrd has shown that the climate is 35 possible even for men completely untrained for expeditions into those frozen wastes. Some of his party were men who had never seen snow before, and yet he records that they survived the rigours of the Antarctic climate comfortably, so that, provided that the appropriate installations are made, 40 we may assume that human beings from all countries could live there safely. Byrd even affirms that it is probably the most healthy climate in the world, for the intense cold of thousands of years has sterilized this continent, and rendered it absolutely germfree, with the consequences that ordinary and extra- 45 ordinary sicknesses and diseases from which man suffers in other zones with different climates are here utterly unknown. There exist no problems of conservation and preservation of food supplies, for the latter keep indefinitely without any signs of deterioration; it may even be that later generations 50 will come to regard the Antarctic as the natural storehouse for the whole world.

Plans are already on foot to set up permanent bases on the shores of this continent, and what so few years ago was

regarded as a 'dead continent' now promises to be a most 55
active centre of human life and endeavour.

(University of London G.C.E. for Overseas Candidates)

23. Summarize, *in your own words as far as possible*, the following
passage (which contains about 520 words), reducing it to
about 170 words. Give your summary a suitable title, and
state at the end the *exact* number of words you have used.
(*You should spend about forty-five minutes on this question.*)

The first thing to realize in studying the English language
is that it is primarily something that is spoken, not written.
The introduction of a system of recording thought and speech
by writing (and later by printing) was a very important step
forward, and without it we should be very largely ignorant of   5
the ways of life and the modes of thought of our ancestors. We
should be completely shut off from the great minds of the past,
and it would be quite impossible for us to undertake such a
study, since we should have no means of knowing anything
about the language of the people who lived in this country   10
five hundred or a thousand years ago, and still less should we
be in a position to relate that language to the tongues spoken
in other countries. The only means we have of knowing the
kind of language used by Julius Caesar or by King Alfred the
Great—the words they employed and the grammar of their   15
speech—is by studying such written documents as have
survived; and in the main that will be the method employed
by future generations when they wish to investigate the
language of our own age. Now because of this necessity of
relying on written documents for learning about language,   20
and because reading and writing have come to occupy so large
a place in our daily lives, there has grown up a tendency to
think of language in terms of the written or printed word.
But printing and writing are only substitutes for speech. In
its primary sense language, as its name implies, is oral. Print-   25
ing and writing have certainly had an influence on the development of language—usually displaying a conservative tendency,
opposed to too rapid change or innovation; but in the last
resort what is written is determined by what is said.

Secondly we must realize that in language change is con-   30
stantly going on. If we look at a passage from Chaucer (who
was writing towards the end of the fourteenth century), and
compare it with the English that is spoken and written today,

it is obvious that the language has altered considerably in the intervening five hundred years or more; and, if we go even 35 further back, we find an even greater difference. These facts are really too self-evident to need pointing out. But though this evolutionary factor is obvious and generally recognized, there is frequently a tendency to assume that it is a thing of the past, and that, in all 'civilized countries' at least, language 40 has now become more or less fixed and set, so that the English, the French and the German of today will be the English, the French and the German of two centuries hence. This is far from the truth.

In the third place, it should be realized that speech or 45 language is the distinguishing characteristic of man as such, and is one of the chief attributes which differentiate him from the other animal species. Why? The answer is probably to be found in the development of mind. The species which developed mind and personality also developed speech.   50
(University of London G.C.E. for Overseas Candidates)

24. Summarize, *in your own words as far as possible*, the following passage (which contains about 480 words), reducing it to 150–170 words. State at the end the *exact* number of words you have used. (*You should spend about forty-five minutes on this question.*)

No reference book, perhaps no book of any kind except the Bible, is so widely used as 'the dictionary'. Even houses that have few books or none at all beside 'the Scriptures' possess at least one dictionary; most business offices have dictionaries, and most typists keep a copy on their desks; at one time or   5 another most girls and boys are required by their teachers to obtain and use a dictionary.

Admittedly, the dictionary is often used merely to determine the correct spelling of words, or to find out the accepted pronunciation, and such a use is perhaps not the most im-   10 portant from an intellectual point of view. Dictionaries may, however, have social importance, for it is often a matter of some concern to the person using the dictionary for such purposes that he should not suggest to others, by mis-spelling a word in a letter, or mispronouncing it in conversation, that 15 he is not 'well-bred', and has not been well educated.

Yet, despite this familiarity with the dictionary, the average person is likely to have many wrong ideas about it, and little

idea of how to use it profitably, or interpret it rightly. For
example, it is often believed that the mere presence of a word 20
in a dictionary is evidence that it is acceptable in good
writing. Though most dictionaries have a system of marking words as obsolete, or in use only as slang, many
people, more especially if their use of a particuar word has
been challenged, are likely to conclude, if they find it in a 25
dictionary, that it is accepted as being used by writers of
established reputation. This would certainly have been true
of dictionaries a hundred years or so ago. For a long time
after they were first firmly established in the eighteenth
century, their aim was to include only what was used by the 30
best writers, and all else was suppressed, and the compiler
frequently claimed that his dictionary contained no 'low'
words. Apparently this aspect of the dictionary achieved
such importance in the mind of the average person that most
people today are unaware of the great change which has taken 35
place in the compilation of present-day dictionaries.

Similarly, the ordinary man invariably supposes that one
dictionary is as good and authoritative as another, and, moreover, believes that 'the dictionary' has absolute authority, and
quotes it to clinch arguments. Although this is an advantage, 40
in that the dictionary presents a definition the basic meaning
of which cannot be altered by the speaker, yet it could be
accepted only if all dictionaries agreed on the particular
point in question. But ultimately the authority of the dictionary rests only on the authority of the man who compiled it, 45
and, however careful he may be, a dictionary-maker is fallible:
reputable dictionaries may disagree in their judgements, and
indeed different sections of the same dictionary may differ.

(University of London G.C.E. for Overseas Candidates)

25. Given below is an annual report of the Jos Branch of the
    Nigerian Field Society. Assume that this report is sub-
    mitted to you for publication in *The Nigerian Field* but that
    you find it necessary to summarize the report in about 100 to
    200 words because of shortage of space. Make a summary
    of the report.

The Jos Branch membership continues to rise in spite of the
departure of about ten Fellows, including some of the stal-
warts who gave full and unstinting support to our activities.
Mr. M. T. Horwood, our chairman, retired from Nigeria to

take up a post in the U.K. One of the Plateau's most illus- 5
trious figures, Mr. J. L. Farrington, General Manager of
A.T.M.N. Ltd., a fellow of this branch, retired in September
of this year. Our membership figures have shown an increase
of about 50 per cent during the last two years.

The following lectures were given to the Branch throughout 10
the year, the approximate attendance being given in brackets.

January: 'Miniature Wild Flowers of the Plateau' by the
Rev. P. London of the Sudan Interior Mission,
Jos. (35)

February: 'The Snakes of Jos and its Environs' by Dr. G. T. 15
Dunger, F.Z.S., illustrated with coloured slides.
(105)

March: 'The Birds of Zaria' and 'A Naturalist at Lake
Chad' by Mr. C. H. Fry of Zaria University. (50)

April: 'Egyptology' by Mr. E. Hodgetts with coloured 20
slides. (50) 'The Elephants of Lake Chad' by Mr
Roger Harrison with a coloured cine film on this
subject. (58)

May: 'Wase Rock Revisited' by Dr. G. T. Dunger,
F.Z.S., with an illustrated account of the fauna, 25
particularly the colony of Rosy Pelicans that
reside on the summit. (60)

June: 'A Fellows' Exhibition' given by Fellows of the
Branch, including 'Molybdenite Mining on the
Plateau' by K. Paulo, with exhibits; 'Rare Birds on 30
the Plateau', a series of coloured slides by V. Smith
and 'The Capture, Ringing and Release of Wag-
tails on the Plateau', an 8 mm. cine film by the
same exhibitor; 'Local Bird Calls', a sound quiz
on tape by M. T. Horwood; 'Nigerian Animal 35
Travelogue', a coloured cine film by F. Lawrence;
a miscellany of coloured slides by Dr. G. T.
Dunger on 'The Mating and Reproduction of the
toad, *Bufo regularis*, the Straw Coloured Fruit
Bats of Barakin Ladi, a phenomenal hailstorm on 40
the Plateau in April etc.' Owing to a breakdown
in postal facilities, the notices did not reach
Fellows in time and only eleven attended this
meeting.

July: 'Family, Community and Agricultural Cycle in 45

the Irigwe (Miango Tribe)' by Walter Sangree, Ass. Prof. of Anthropology at the University of Rochester. (40)

August: 'The Lizards of Northern Nigeria' by Dr. G. T. Dunger, F.Z.S., with illustrations by coloured 50 slides. (55)

September: 'Plateau Tribal Life', a 16 mm. coloured cine film by Mr. Charles Paris. (60)

October: 'A Fellows' Exhibition'—this was virtually a repeat of the June meeting. (40) 55

November: 'Perses . . . 560 B.C. to 300 B.C.' by Mr. E. Hodgetts, illustrated with coloured slides. (45)

December: 'Sericulture—an Experiment in Nigeria' by Mr. L. Cronje, Veterinary Entomologist from Zonkwa. Annual General Meeting. 60

(Adapted from a report in *The Nigerian Field*, Vol. XXX, No. 1)

26. Make notes on the following passage in such a way as to bring out the main points. Your notes should be numbered and arranged in the order necessary to present a logical development of ideas. Each note must consist of one or two complete sentences which summarize part of the original passage. The total length of your notes should be from about 10 to 20 lines but this is merely a guide to you and it is not essential for you to keep strictly within these limits.

There are two sorts of obscurity that you find in writers. One is due to negligence and the other to wilfulness. People often write obscurely because they have never taken the trouble to learn to write clearly. This sort of obscurity you find too often in modern philosophers, in men of science, and 5 even in literary critics. Here it is indeed strange. You would have thought that men who passed their lives in the study of the great masters of literature would be sufficiently sensitive to the beauty of language to write if not beautifully at least with perspicuity. Yet you will find in their works sen- 10 tence after sentence that you must read twice to discover the sense. Often you can only guess at it, for the writers have evidently not said what they intended.

Another cause of obscurity is that the writer is himself not quite sure of his meaning. He has a vague impression of what 15 he wants to say, but has not, either from lack of mental power or from laziness, exactly formulated it in his mind and it is

natural enough that he should not find a precise expression
for a confused idea. This is due largely to the fact that many
writers think, not before, but as they write. The pen origi- 20
nates the thought. The disadvantage of this, and indeed it is
a danger against which the author must be always on his
guard, is that there is a sort of magic in the written word.
The idea acquires substance by taking on a visible nature,
and then stands in the way of its own clarification. But this 25
sort of obscurity merges very easily into the wilful. Some
writers who do not think clearly are inclined to suppose
that their thoughts have a significance greater than at first
sight appears. It is flattering to believe that they are too
profound to be expressed so clearly that all who run may read, 30
and very naturally it does not occur to such writers that the
fault is with their own minds which have not the faculty of
precise reflection. Here again the magic of the written word
obtains. It is very easy to persuade oneself that a phrase that
one does not quite understand may mean a great deal more 35
than one realizes. From this there is only a little way to go to
fall into the habit of setting down one's impressions in all
their original vagueness. Fools can always be found to discover a hidden sense in them. There is another form of wilful
obscurity that masquerades as aristocratic exclusiveness. The 40
author wraps his meaning in mystery so that the vulgar shall
not participate in it. His soul is a secret garden into which
the elect may penetrate only after overcoming a number of
perilous obstacles. But this kind of obscurity is not only
pretentious; it is short-sighted. For time plays it an odd trick. 45
If the sense is meagre, time reduces it to a meaningless verbi-
age that no one thinks of reading. But occasionally it throws
a sharp cold light on what had seemed profound and thus
discloses the fact that these contortions of language disguised
very commonplace notions. 50

(*The Summing Up* by W. Somerset Maugham)

27. Read again the passage on page 56. Then write four sentences
which summarize the author's statement of the attractions of
diving for amusement.

28. Read again passage 5 on page 80. Then in four sentences
give four reasons why the Boran were afraid of the man-
eating lions.

29. Read the passage in Exercise 21 on page 97. Then, in three

sentences, give three things which might attract tourists to
Lebanon.

30. The following account of a conversation contains three
points in favour of co-education and three arguments against
it. Summarize the six points in six sentences which are
arranged under the headings 'For' and 'Against'.

I entered the room just in time to hear Mrs. Jordan snort
with disgust. She was a lady who held strong views.

'Co-education!' she exclaimed with some bitterness. 'I'm
completely against it. It makes tomboys out of the girls. You
never know what they're going to get up to next!'   5

'Yes,' agreed her husband. 'And it makes the boys soft and
effeminate. It works both ways you know.' He was proud of
the fact that he had gone to a boys' school.

'Ah, but it teaches the boys and girls how to get on with
each other,' commented Mr. Smith, an old friend of the   10
family. 'It makes them more at ease with each other so that
they don't feel shy and embarrassed when dealing with a
member of the opposite sex.'

Mrs. Jordan was quick to take her chance. She had evidently
been waiting for the point to arise.   15

'Get on with each other,' she repeated. 'That's just the
trouble. Some of them get to know each other a little too well.
I don't believe in friendships of that sort at an immature age.
You never know the trouble it can cause. Why, there was
that girl——' She stopped suddenly and glanced around in   20
an embarrassed way.

'Yes?' said Mrs. Smith encouragingly. 'What girl?'

'Oh, never mind,' said Mrs. Jordan. 'Girls should be
brought up to be ladies, and boys should be——.'

'Men,' added her husband quickly.   25

'I don't know,' started Mr. Smith. 'You're exaggerating. I
don't think that sort of trouble is any worse in co-educational
schools that it is anywhere else. You must admit that there is
usually better discipline in a co-educational school. The boys
are too anxious to impress the girls to cause much trouble.'   30

'That's a matter of opinion,' retorted Mrs. Jordan. 'There's
nothing wrong with the discipline in the girls' schools I
know.'

Mr. Smith did not take up the challenge. 'And co-educational schools are more convenient from an administrative   35

point of view,' he commented. 'Particularly in a small town. In many cases it would be impossible to build two separate schools so one school seems to be the sensible answer. It's just common sense.'

'Well, if you're talking about administrative problems,' 40 said Mr. Jordan, 'what about P.E. lessons, games, and lessons such as Domestic Science and Woodwork. They're easy in a single-sex school. But in a co-educational school the class has got to split in half each time.'

'There are ways round that,' said Mr. Smith. 'You can 45 always combine two classes. It's done in quite a few schools.' He turned to me and asked, 'What do you think about this, Frank?'

I wasn't going to be drawn into the argument. 'If you want my candid opinion,' I said, 'it's time for lunch. Come on. 50 Let's stop arguing and start eating.'

Chapter 7

Letters

Dear Mary

1. Friendly or informal letters

Here is an example of a friendly letter:

> 171 Any Road,
> Ibadan
> 2nd February 1966
>
> Dear George,
>
> Many thanks for your letter. We were all delighted to hear from you again and to know that you had returned from the U.K.
>
> Is there any chance that you will be in Ibadan in the next few months? If so, you will be most welcome to come and stay with us as long as you like.
>
> When I last heard from her, Bunmi was living in Idera Street but I don't know what the number of her house is. I'll find out and let you know as soon as possible.
>
> That's all for the moment. I'm in a hurry to catch the post and welcome you back. Bayo sends his best wishes— as do Iyabo and Muyiwa. They are all anxious to see you again and hear about your travels.
>
> With the very best wishes,
> Yours,
> *Deji*

As you can see, this letter is really only a hurried note: the type of letter we often have to write.

Notice these things about friendly letters:

i. **The address** is usually put in the top right-hand corner.

In England we do not put the name of the writer above the address but some people in other countries like to do this and it is sometimes a good idea. When you write your address, there is no need to put the name of the country unless you are writing to somebody abroad.

Exercise 1

On the blackboard, write these addresses as if you were writing a letter from them:
a. Your own address.
b. An address in any foreign country (in which you must pretend to be staying).
c. Your school address.
d. The address of any relative who does not live with you.

ii. **The date** can be written beneath your address or anywhere convenient at the top of the letter. It can be written in any of these ways: 2nd February 1966; February 2nd 1966; 2.2.1966; 2.2.'66. When you are working, you may find that your employer (e.g. a business firm, a government department, one of the armed services) insists that you write the date in a particular way.

iii. **The greeting** in a friendly letter depends upon many factors, e.g. the relationship between the writer and the person to whom the letter is addressed; racial and family customs; the purpose of the letter etc.

In England we normally start with *Dear* and the given (or Christian) name of the person to whom we are writing. However, if this person is older than the writer, in a much higher position in life, or not on terms of close friendship, we might start *Dear Mr. Brown* or *Dear Miss Smith* or *Dear Mrs. Green.* Later on, when the two people know each other better, *Dear Mr. Brown* might be changed to *Dear David*, and *Dear Miss Smith* might become *Dear Mary.*

Sometimes you must be very careful with the type of greeting you use at the start of your letter. For example, it may happen that I have a girl-friend called Margaret Smith. I may have been

writing *Dear Margaret* for several months. If I then start a letter
with *Dear Miss Smith*, there will be trouble for me. Why?

Exercise 2

Discuss with your teacher the opening greeting to be used
when writing a friendly letter to each of the following:
a. Your brother.
b. A sister.
c. Your father.
d. Your mother.
e. A school friend.
f. A cousin of about the same age.
g. An uncle whose name is George Williams.
h. An aunt whose name is Mary Cole.
i. A man named Deji Adenubi. He is a friend of your father and
   much older than you are. You have met him once, when he
   came to visit your father.
j. The headmaster, headmistress or principal of your school.
k. Your form teacher. (Assume that you have left school.)

iv. In **the body of the letter** try to follow two rules:
   1. Write for your reader and not for yourself—unless you feel
like being selfish. Try to decide what things your reader wants
to know, or is interested in, and then write about those topics.
Remember that the things which interest you may bore your
reader.
   2. Once you have decided what you are going to write about,
try to get to the point quickly and then express yourself clearly.

v. **The ending** in a friendly letter can cause as much trouble as
the opening greeting. Most of the remarks in (iii) above also apply
to this section. We can cover most possibilities in this way:
a. In letters to close friends you can end with *Yours sincerely*,
   Yours, Your affectionate friend or any other suitable ending. You
   should NOT end with *Yours faithfully* or *Yours truly* because
   these are used to end business letters.
b. In letters to acquaintances and to friends who are rather older
   than you, the ending *Yours sincerely* can be used.

Exercise 3

Say how you would end the eleven letters mentioned in
Exercise 2.

Exercise 4

Write one of these letters, spending about 40 minutes on the task:

a. *Write a letter to a friend in a distant country, giving an account of your daily life.

b. *Write a letter to a friend describing a journey you have made by boat, pointing out what made it particularly interesting.

c. *Write a letter to a friend in hospital who has been prevented from joining you on a holiday which you had planned together, but on which you have had to go alone.

d. Write to a friend or relative whom you have not seen for about a year. Give details of your family, yourself and anything of interest to your friend.

(*Note:* Topics marked with an asterisk are taken from past examination papers of the University of London.)

Exercise 5

Write one of these letters:

a. To a friend or relative describing a wedding in which you are both interested and which you attended.

b. A relative has written to you to enquire about your future career. He has offered to finance any further studies which may be required. Write your reply.

c. Write to a friend to ask him or her to do something for you.

d. Write to apologize to a friend for being unable to meet him or her as previously arranged.

Exercise 6

Write one of these letters:

a. To a relative to invite him or her to stay with you.

b. To a relative who has written to enquire about your progress at school or in a job.

c. To a friend to ask him or her if he would like to join you in a holiday or trip which you are planning.

d. An adult friend of your mother or father has written to them from another district to enquire about the secondary schools in your district. Draft a possible reply which your parents can use in their own letter.

Exercise 7

Write one of these letters:

a. Write to the principal of your school, or to a teacher in it, asking for a testimonial which you can use in obtaining a job. Assume that you have already left school and give brief details of yourself to act as a reminder.

b. Write a letter full of family and local news to a friend in another town.

c. A friend has written to you to ask you to lend him or her some money. Write a reply.

2. Business letters

Here is a short business letter:

---

171 Any Road,
Ibadan
2nd February 1966

The Manager,
Riskall Insurance Co. Ltd.,
P.O. Box 99A71,
Anytown

Dear Sir,

Endowment Assurance

Thank you for your letter of 28th January and for the proposal form which I now return, duly completed.

I attach a copy of my birth certificate and should be grateful if you would kindly return it in due course.

Yours faithfully,
George Williams

There are many different kinds of business letters. You will probably find that different commercial firms and government departments have their own way of setting out a business or formal letter. When you get a job, be guided by the advice of your superiors and by the layout shown in copies of letters in the files.

The main ways in which the layout of a business letter differs from that of a friendly letter are:

a. The name and address of the addressee are given at the start of the letter, as in the example, OR are put on the left-hand side of the page after the body of the letter.

b. After his signature, the person who writes the letter often prints his name or has it typed.

c. The letter starts *Dear Sir* or *Dear Madam* (to an individual) or *Dear Sirs* (to a firm).

d. There is often (but not always) a subject heading, as in the example. This is to make sure that the letter quickly finds its way to the right man or department in a large firm.

e. The letter usually ends *Yours faithfully* or *Yours truly* (the latter is slightly less formal). Unless you are ordered to do so, do not use the ending 'I am, Sir, Your obedient servant'.

f. The language is more formal and does not include colloquialisms and such contractions as *I'll, didn't* etc.

Exercise 8

You have received a bill from any shop, firm or public utility. Write to query an item on the bill.

Exercise 9

You have received an invoice from a firm in respect of goods supplied (or services rendered) three months ago. When you check your own records, you find that you have already paid the bill. Return the invoice, explaining that you have already paid the amount. If possible, give details of the date and method of payment.

Exercise 10

Assume that you have bought something from a firm by post but that you now find it to be unsatisfactory. Write a suitable letter to the firm concerned.

Exercise 11

Write ONE of these letters:

a. To a shop or firm to order some goods.

b. To a garage or firm to order a spare part for a car or scooter. Give full details.

c. To a firm of hauliers to ask them to call at your house to collect some crates or furniture for delivery elsewhere.

Exercise 12

Write to a hotel to book accommodation for yourself or for members of your family. Give details of (a) the dates concerned and (b) the type of accommodation you want.

Exercise 13

Write *one* of these letters:
a. To a hotel to cancel accommodation which you had booked earlier.
b. To a firm to return some goods which were sent to you. Assume that you have found that the goods are not what you ordered.
c. To a travel agency to enquire about the cost of a holiday which you have been thinking about.
d. To a firm to ask them for an estimate for repairs to your house.

Exercise 14

Write *one of these letters:*
a. To a bus or coach company to enquire about the cost of an outing which you have been thinking about. Ask how much it would cost to hire a coach. Give full details of the date, distances involved, the size of the coach required etc.
b. A firm has offered you an interview in connection with a job for which you have applied. Write to accept or decline the interview.

Exercise 15

Write a letter to the editor of any newspaper. You can comment on an earlier letter or on any item of news, or you can make a complaint or offer a suggestion.

Exercise 16

Assume that you are working for a commercial firm. Write ONE of these letters:
a. To a customer who is behind with hire-purchase payments for his car. Threaten to re-possess the car.
b. To a customer who has not paid a bill. Threaten to take legal action.
c. To an angry customer who has returned a bill with the comment that he paid it several weeks ago. When you check

the records you find that the customer is right. Write a letter of apology and explanation.

Exercise 17

Write ONE of these letters:

a. To a firm which has not yet supplied goods which you ordered more than three weeks previously. (In your first letter you sent full details and the necessary money.)

b. To a bus company OR to the station-master of a railway station in another town, enquiring about some lost property.

Exercise 18

Write ONE of these letters:

a. You have been asked to interview a well-known person for your school magazine. Write to him or her to ask for an interview. Explain why you want the interview.

b. Write to your local radio station criticizing any programme which you have listened to.

c. There has been a mistake in a bill which has been sent to you. The bill is too high OR it contains an error in addition. Return the bill with your comments.

d. Write to any government department on any topic you like.

3. Invitations and replies

An invitation (and its reply) can be formal or informal.

i. Informal invitations

Here is an informal invitation and a possible reply:

---

46 Any Road,
Lagos
14th March 1966

Dear Mary,

You will probably be pleased to hear that John has passed his examination and will return from London tomorrow afternoon.

To celebrate his success we are planning to have a dinner at the Jubilee restaurant, in Market Street, at 8 p.m. next Saturday, 20th March. We shall be delighted to hear that you can come. Please do say you can.

With best wishes,
Yours,
Peju

> 141 Any Street,
> Lagos
> 16th March 1966
>
> Dear Peju,
>   Many thanks for your letter. We were all very happy indeed to hear about John's success and his return.
>   Yes, thank you, I shall be delighted to come to the dinner on Saturday. This time I'll make sure I'm punctual!
>   See you on Saturday.
> > With best wishes to all,
> > Yours,
> > *Mary*

There are no special problems in an informal invitation or reply. It is written in the same way as a friendly letter and can be worded in many different ways. The important thing in the invitation is to remember to give the place, time and date. If such an invitation has to be declined, it is courteous to give a good excuse to avoid hurting the feelings of the other person.

ii. Formal invitations

These can vary in their wording, according to the traditions of the people, ceremony etc. concerned.

Here are a formal invitation to an English wedding and two formal replies:

> Mr. and Mrs. J. K. Smith
> request the pleasure of the company of
> Miss Joan Brown
> at the marriage of their daughter,
> Annette, to Mr. Brian Wilkinson,
> at the Parish Church, Dawlish,
> on Saturday, July 3rd, 1966, at 2 p.m.,
> and afterwards at The Langstone Cliff Hotel, Dawlish.
>
> Littleham,
>   41 Any Road,
>   Dawlish   R.S.V.P.

an acceptance

> Miss Joan Brown thanks Mr. and Mrs. J. K. Smith for their kind invitation to the wedding of their daughter, Annette, on July 3rd, 1966, and has much pleasure in accepting the invitation.
>
> 782 The Drive,
>   Dawlish

a refusal

> Miss Joan Brown thanks Mr. and Mrs. J. K. Smith for their kind invitation to the wedding of their daughter, Annette, on July 3rd, 1966, but deeply regrets to say that she will be unable to be present because of the illness of her mother.
>
> 782 The Drive,
>   Dawlish

It is not necessary for the person accepting or refusing the invitation to give his own address and some people prefer to leave it out.

Notice that the invitation, acceptance and refusal are not signed. They can be printed, typed or written by hand but no signature appears on them. The word 'I' never appears on a formal invitation or reply; they are both written impersonally.

It is usual to give a formal reply to a formal invitation but this is not always essential. Particularly if you are a close friend of the person who issues the invitation, you can send an informal reply like this:

> 782 The Drive,
>   18th June 1966   Dawlish
>
> Dear Mrs. Smith,
>   It was kind of you and your husband to invite me to Annettte's wedding. Of course I shall be delighted to come. I hope the weather keeps fine for her.
>   Best wishes,
>   Yours sincerely,
>   *Joan Brown*

Exercise 19

a. Write a formal invitation from the principal, staff and pupils of your school, inviting somebody to the annual Speech Day OR to a sports meeting.

b. Write a formal acceptance of the above invitation.

c. Write a formal refusal of the invitation in *a.*

Exercise 20

Write an informal invitation to a friend to a party at your house.

Exercise 21

You have received a formal invitation to be present at the public opening of a new shop or building. Write a formal refusal.

Exercise 22

Write a formal invitation to a friend, inviting him or her to your own wedding. The invitation will have to be written in the name(s) of your parent(s) or guardian(s).

4. An application for a job

i. Forwarding a completed application form

In some cases it is necessary to complete an application form when applying for a job. All the information about the applicant has to be written (or typed) on the form, and only a covering letter is required:

---

23 Any Road,
Any Town
14.11.1966

The Personnel Manager,
Newtown Motor Co. Ltd.,
P.O. Box 47, Newtown

Dear Sir,

<u>Vacancy for audit clerk</u>

I have much pleasure in enclosing a completed application form in respect of the above vacancy, and I attach copies of two recent testimonials.

I shall be happy to attend for an interview at any time convenient to you.

Yours faithfully,
G. Williams

---

ii. *Without an application form*

Applications which are made in the form of a letter can vary considerably. The more an applicant wants a job, the more he will be careful in setting out his application. An application for such a senior post as city surveyor or engineer may be a very elaborate one. It can consist of several typed sheets, bound or stapled together, with several appendices which include copies of testimonials and descriptions of the past work of the applicant. On the front there may be a cover-sheet which gives an index to the various headings in the application.

A person who is applying for his first job will not make such an elaborate application but it is wise to try as hard as you can if you really want to get the job. Here is an application by somebody who already has a job. The items marked with an asterisk would be left out by somebody seeking his first position.

---

22 Any Road,
Any Town
13th November, 1966

The Manager,
Any Insurance Co. Ltd.,
62 Main Street, Any Town

Dear Sir,

<u>Vacancy for accounts clerk</u>

With reference to your advertisement in the 'Daily News', I have much pleasure in applying for the position of accounts clerk. I give below details of myself and shall be happy to attend for an interview at any time convenient to you.

<u>Name</u>:	George Williams
<u>Address</u>:	22 Any Road, Any Town (Telephone: 41772)
<u>Age</u>:	20½. Born 9.5.46 in Any Town.
<u>*Marital state</u>:	Single
<u>Education</u>:	1952–1958: Any Town Primary School
	1958–1963: Any Town Secondary School
<u>Qualifications</u>:	1963, a Grade 2 School Certificate with Credit in English, Mathematics, Geography, History, General Science and Art.

	1965, by private study I obtained Cambridge H.S.C. passes at principal level in Economics and History.
*Experience:	1963–65: Junior Clerk in Wide-World Export Co. Ltd. In this post I was in charge of the Petty Cash account and did some ledger posting.
	1965–present date: Accounts clerk in New Radio Co., 581 Any Street, Any Town. Details of my work are explained in the testimonial from this firm.
*Reason for wishing to leave:	In my present post opportunities for gaining further experience and promotion are very limited.
Sport:	At school I played for the school first teams in Soccer and Hockey. I was also school cross-country champion.
General:	I was a sub-prefect at school and an active member of various school societies. At the moment I am studying for a U.K. accountancy qualification and am taking a correspondence course.
Testimonials:	I enclose copies of testimonials from the following:

a. The Headmaster, Any Town Secondary School.
b. The Manager, Wide-World Export Co. Ltd.
c. The Manager, New Radio Company.
d. John Cole Esq., 475 Any Road, Any Town.

Referees:	You are invited to refer to any of the above gentlemen concerning my character and capabilities.

In addition, you are invited to refer to the undermentioned:
a. F. J. Lee Esq., 14 Market Street, Any Town.
b. Dr. L. T. Brown, 131 River Road, Any Town.

Yours faithfully,
G. Williams

If possible it is better to type an application for a job. Any enclosures should be fastened to the back of the letter, and arranged in the order in which they are mentioned in the application.

Notes:

i. If it is not possible to tell your sex by looking at your name, put (*Miss*) or (*Mr.*) after your name in the letter and at the end.

ii. In your country it may also be necessary to add another heading, after *Age*, giving your race and/or citizenship.

iii. Under *Experience* or *General*, you could add any special experience which you have had and which is relevant to the post for which you are applying.

iv. Before you give a person's name as a referee, make sure you have obtained his permission.

Exercise 23

Look in the advertisement columns of a local newspaper until you find a job in which you might be interested. Copy the advertisement into your exercise book, and then write out an application for the post.

Chapter 8

Reports

The higher you rise in life

The higher you rise in life, the more likely it is that you will one day have to make out reports on various subjects.

A report can be verbal or in writing; it can be formal or informal; it can consist of one or two words only or it can run to several hundred pages. Here are some examples:

a. A simple verbal report

You are the foreman in charge of some men who have recently put up a new iron gate in front of a school. After a few days the manager of the firm sends you to inspect the gate and to see if it is satisfactory. You bring back your report: 'Yes, it's working fine. The headmaster is quite satisfied with it.'

b. A simple formal report

You are the foreman in charge of some men who are repairing a large wooden hut. One of the men has broken his left leg in an accident. You make a written report to the manager of the firm:

27 Any Street,
Any Town
27th September 1966

The Manager,
Building Construction Co. Ltd.,
27 Any Street, Any Town

Dear Sir,
Accident to Mr. D. Williams (labourer)
at 143 Market Street on 27.9.1966

I wish to report that one of our labourers, Mr. D. Williams, broke his left leg in an accident at a building site today. The circumstances are set out below.

At ten o'clock this morning I was in charge of a gang of men repairing a wooden store at the rear of the Modern Furniture Company of 143 Market Street, Any Town.

While the men were working on this hut, the manager of the Modern Furniture Company asked me to send a man to inspect the roof of a nearby store in the same compound. Our ladders were not long enough for the task so the manager supplied one. I looked at the ladder and it seemed to be sound and in good order. I then told a labourer, Mr. D. Williams, to climb up the ladder and look at the roof. When Williams reached the top of the ladder, a rung broke and he fell down from a height of about twelve feet.

Williams fell on his left side and seemed to have injured his left leg. The manager of the Modern Furniture Company lent us his car. We put Willliams in it and took him to the General Hospital where he was detained. I have since learnt from the hospital that he has broken his left leg and will be in hospital for some weeks. I have informed Williams's family that he is in hospital.

I have since examined the ladder and find that the rung which broke (the second from the top) had been partly eaten away by a boring beetle. This damage is not visible from the outside.

Yours faithfully,
C. K. Lee

c. Formal reports which must follow a definite pattern

In many cases the form or layout of a report must follow a pattern decided by somebody in authority. This happens with school reports, for example, and with many reports made in the armed forces, the government and some large business firms.

Here is an example of an annual report made by an army officer on a sergeant in his unit:

ANNUAL CONFIDENTIAL REPORT

Rank: Sergeant
Name: L. T. Smith
Number: 79145872

	Very Good	Good	Satis- factory	Weak	Unsatis- factory
Initiative		√			
Loyalty		√			
Honesty			√		
Punctuality				√	
Reliability			√		
Leadership		√			
Sense of Responsibility		√			
Tact				√	
Intelligence			√		
Personal Appearance	√				
Stability			√		
Health and Vitality	√				
Co-operation		√			

RECOMMENDATION FOR PROMOTION:

i. Accelerated promotion: No

ii. Normal eligibility: Yes

iii. Unfit for present rank: No

2.12.1966   *J. Brown*, O.C. 'A' Company, REA

d. A more detailed business report

You work in the sales department of a firm which makes good quality shirts and other articles of clothing. A new newspaper has recently been established in your country. The manager asks you whether the firm should advertise in it. He asks you for a written report. You type it on a sheet of office notepaper.

To: The Manager
From: Mr. R. K. Lee,
         Sales and Advertising Dept.   1.6.66

      1. Advertising
      2. 'The New Morning News'

I do not recommend that we advertise in 'The New Morning News' for the following reasons:

1. Circulation	The estimated circulation of this paper is about 15,000 copies daily—considerably less than its rivals.
2. Readers	As far as we can judge at the moment, the paper appeals mainly to people in the lower income groups whereas our products are aimed primarily at people with higher incomes.
3. Policy of the newspaper	The policy of the newspaper is not yet clear but it has shown itself unusually critical of the Government and has aroused the resentment of highly placed politicians. I am therefore doubtful as to its future. Further, I suggest that if we advertise in it we may be suspected of supporting the (rather radical) views of the paper. This could be damaging to our interests.
4. Advertising rates	The charge per column inch is only 20 per cent less than that of established newspapers with a circulation some 500 per cent greater than that of 'The New Morning News'. Advertisements would not be good value for money.

I suggest that we keep the position under review and reconsider the matter in, say, six months' time. Unless I hear from you to the contrary, I will automatically submit a further report on 1.12.66.

R. K. Lee

Note: Since this is an inter-office memorandum there is no need for the usual greeting and ending.

e. A difficult business report

You are the managing director of a big firm. Your annual salary is about £6,000 (sterling) and you are expected to earn it. The board of directors sends you to a neighbouring country to see whether it is possible to set up a factory and sales organization there. You are asked to spend a month in the country and then bring back a detailed report on a project which may involve well over a million pounds. If you make a serious mistake, the money may be wasted and your career may be finished.

In the aeroplane on your way to the foreign country, you look over the following draft sub-headings, knowing that you may have to write several pages about each of them:

1. The political scene   ? stability   ? investment risk.
2. Market potential:
    a. Population figures and trends.
    b. Rival products and likely developments.
    c. Consumer trends.
    d. Export potential.
    e. ? Tariff protection.
3. Possible sites for the factory.
4. Construction.
5. Distribution.
6. Agencies.
7. Finance; local participation.
8. Advertising.
9. Staffing:
    a. Administrative.
    b. Clerical and manual.

Such a report, with appendices, maps and reports from consultants, might run into hundreds of pages. It would clearly be a difficult thing to make—but somebody has to do this sort of work and to prepare for it.

Points to remember when making a report

In making a report you may have to remember some or all of these points:

1. Be quite certain of the aims of your report and the subject(s) you are supposed to deal with.
2. The report should have a title, or heading, and the date.
3. It should show to whom the report is addressed and by whom it is made.
4. Give *all* the information and put it in the right order.
5. Written reports are usually set out in formal English (without colloquialisms and contracted forms).
6. You can use sub-headings and tabulate your work so that the information is clearly set out and easy to find. The sub-headings should be arranged in a logical order.
7. A long report (consisting of many pages) may require a list of contents and/or an index. It may also need maps, sketches,

evidence, statements etc. and these can sometimes be put in separate appendices at the end.

8. Make a recommendation if you are asked to do so.

9. The layout of the report will depend very much on the circumstances under which it is made. The police, the armed forces, government departments and commercial firms each have their own way of setting out reports. Look at existing reports on the files or seek the assistance of your superior, if in doubt.

10. Type or write the report as neatly as possible, underlining subheadings etc. so that the report is visually attractive.

Exercise 1

Make ONE of these reports:

a. To the principal of your school on the suitability of the school canteen. In your report you should include the following subheadings as well as any others which seem desirable: Size (for the number of pupils who use it); Food served (amount, value, suitability, variety etc.); Cleanliness (of food, utensils, building and staff); Prices charged; Staffing (enough to handle the rush hours?); Finances (is the rent, if any, enough?). Make any recommendations which you find necessary to improve facilities.

b. It is suggested that a new primary OR secondary school should be built in your district. You are asked to make a report to your Chief Education Officer as to the most suitable site. Bear in mind the cost and availability of land, the suitability of existing roads, the areas from which the pupils will come etc. Then make your report.

c. You are employed by the Town (or City) Council in a busy place. You are asked to make a report suggesting ways of improving facilities for parking cars in your area. Consider such points as the growth of the town, the need for people to be able to reach shops, the need of shops to have customers, the need for more car parks—and where to put them, the desirability of using parking meters etc. Make your report.

d. You are working in a government department or for a commercial firm. You are asked to write a report to show whether an employee is suitable for promotion or not. Consider such points as his sense of initiative, ability to accept responsibility, intelligence, loyalty, punctuality, experience and qualifications, tact, personal appearance and whether or not he works hard. Write your report.

Exercise 2

Make ONE of these reports:

a. To the principal of your school on the work of any existing school society.

b. To the police on the way in which you were involved in an accident.

c. To your local Football Association, Hockey Association (or any other sports organization) on the circumstances which led you, as the referee, to send a player off the field. Give exact details.

Exercise 3

Make ONE of these reports:

a. To the police on the circumstances which led you and members of your family to detain a man and take him to the police station.

b. To the principal of your school on the cleanliness and sanitary condition of the school building and its grounds.

c. To the managing director of an imaginary company on the best site for a new cinema in your district.

Exercise 4

Make ONE of these reports:

a. On a new car which you have been testing.

b. On a new scooter which you have been testing.

c. On any home appliance (such as a refrigerator, cooker, clothes-washer, vacuum cleaner etc.) which you have been trying out.

Exercise 5

Make ONE of these reports:

a. On a new type of crop or vegetable which you have been trying to grow to see whether it is suitable for farmers in your district.

b. On a book which you have been asked to read to see whether you consider it suitable for use in your school. (Do not write about a book already in use at school.)

c. On the traffic conditions in your district and on ways of improving them.

d. On the causes of accidents in homes in your area and on ways of preventing them.

Chapter 9

Vocabulary Exercises

ideas borrowed from Latin and Greek

A reminder

Please remember that exercises of the type in this chapter are of limited value. Because of limitations of space, in this chapter we shall be forced to consider many words in isolation, i.e. not in sentences which show how they are used. When you meet a new word, you have two tasks to perform: you must find out what meanings it can have, and you must learn how to use it, e.g. what preposition or other word usually comes before or after it.

Make a point of learning from your teacher (a) the meaning of each word and (b) its usage in sentences. It is no good knowing the meaning of a word if you cannot use it in a sentence.

As we saw in an earlier chapter, your best way of increasing your vocabulary is to read as many interesting books as possible. This is far more important than any amount of vocabulary exercises.

1. Prefixes and suffixes

Modern English is derived from an early form of the German language and there is a strong similarity between many English and German words. However, in the last thousand years or so English has been influenced by other languages and has borrowed words and parts of words from them. In particular, modern English contains many words and ideas borrowed from Latin and Greek. We shall see some of these when we consider prefixes and suffixes.

i. Prefixes

extra = *beyond* extraordinary = beyond the ordinary state of affairs

When you consider the prefixes and examples given below,
a. Note the meaning or effect of the prefix.
b. Notice the example given. Find out its meaning and then use it in a sentence.
c. When possible, find at least one further example and use it in a sentence. Use a dictionary.

ab	*from*	absent
ad	*to*	adhesive
ambi	*on both sides*	ambidextrous
ante	*before*	antecedent
anti	*against*	antiseptic
arch	*chief*	archangel
auto	*self*	autobiography
bene	*well*	benefactor
bi	*twice, two*	biped
circum	*around*	circumstances
com	*with*	comparison
contra.	*against*	contradict
de	*down*	descend
demi	*half*	demigod
dia	*across*	diameter
dis	*not, away from*	discontented
em } **en** }	*in, on*	enclose
equi	*equal*	equidistant
ex	*out*	expire

ex-	*formerly, used to be*	ex-captain
extra	*outside, beyond*	extraordinary
fore	*before*	foretell
for	(*with a negative effect*)	forbid
hemi	*half*	hemisphere
hexa	*six*	hexagon
homo	*similar*	homonym
hyper	*over, above*	hypercritical
hypo	*below, under*	hypodermic
in	*in, into,*	invade
im	*against, on,*	imprint
il	*towards*	illegal
ir		irrelevant
inter	*between, among*	intermarriage
intro	*inwards*	introspective
mal	*bad(ly)*	maladjusted
male	*not*	malevolent
mali		malignant
met	*after,*	
meta	*with change*	metamorphic
meth		
mis	*badly, wrongly*	misbehave
mono	*one, single*	monosyllable
non	(*with a negative sense*)	non-intervention
		nonsense
oct		
octa	*eight*	octopus
octo		
omni	*all*	omniscient
out	*beyond*	outlaw
	too much,	overdose
over	*beyond,*	overseas
	above	overhanging
pan	*all, united*	pan-African
penta	*five*	pentagon
per	*through*	perforate
peri	*around*	perimeter
phil(o)	*loving*	philosophy
poly	*many*	polygamous
post	*after*	postscript
pre	*before*	precaution
pro	*for, forward, before*	proclaim

proto	first	prototype
pseudo ⎱ pseud ⎰	false	pseudo-classical pseudonym
quadr ⎫ quadri ⎬ quadru ⎭	four	quadrant
re ⎰	again, back, down	readdress recede repress
retro	back	retrospective
se	without, apart	secure
semi	half	semicircle
sine	without	sinecure
sub ⎫ sup ⎬ sus ⎭	under	submarine
super	more than	superhuman
tele	far, at a distance	telescope
tra(ns)	across	transatlantic
tri	three	triangle
ultra	extremely	ultra-modern
un	(with a sense contrary to that of the word to which it is added)	unfasten undo unreel unveil
un	not	uneducated untrue
un(i)	one	unanimous
under	below, too little	under-charge undergraduate
vice	capable of taking the place of, next in position to	vice-chairman vice-president
with	against	withstand

ii. Suffixes

Try to find further examples of words which have the suffixes shown in bold type:

a. Suffixes denoting a person

| captain | scrutineer | inspector |
| artisan | citizen | saviour |

beg**gar**	box**er**	spin**ster**
secret**ary**	amat**eur**	daugh**ter**
enthusi**ast**	attorn**ey**	fa**ther**
advo**cate**	financi**er**	bab**y**
employ**ee**	motor**ist**	law**yer**

b. Suffixes denoting a place

dispens**ary**	fact**ory**	thea**tre**
nurs**ery**	treasur**y**	

c. Suffixes denoting a state or condition or forming an abstract noun

leak**age**	boy**hood**	govern**ment**	dep**th**
ignor**ance**	serv**ice**	matri**mony**	cruel**ty**
bankrupt**cy**	swimm**ing**	soft**ness**	lati**tude**
wis**dom**	translat**ion**	hat**red**	pleas**ure**
promin**ence**	social**ism**	friend**ship**	jealous**y**

d. Suffixes which make diminutives

kit**ten**	part**icle**	book**let**	duck**ling**	hill**ock**

e. Suffixes which make adjectives or are found on adjectives

loy**al**	moder**ate**	stead**fast**	derogat**ory**
residen**tial**	rep**lete**	care**ful**	omin**ous**
habit**ual**	fin**ite**	acroba**tic**	infec**tious**
Elizabeth**an**	horr**ible**	un**ique**	hand**some**
Austral**ian**	excus**able**	viv**id**	back**ward**
regul**ar**	finish**ed**	gent**le**	filth**y**
honor**ary**	wood**en**	mascul**ine**	
resist**ant**	Japan**ese**	Engl**ish**	
obedi**ent**	grot**esque**	act**ive**	

f. Suffixes which make verbs

enumer**ate**	wand**er**	advert**ise**	establi**sh**
deep**en**	magni**fy**	American**ize**	dazz**le**

The following exercises deal with the roots of words as well as with affixes (prefixes and suffixes). Use a good dictionary which explains the origin of words.

Exercise 1

Examine each of the following words, and then for **nine** of them give the meaning of the part in bold type, and the exact meaning of the whole word. The following example shows how you are to set out your answer:

Example: **manu**script: by hand; original copy written by hand.

audible; sui**cide**; **contra**dict; **bene**factor; **im**migrant; **aque**-duct; **super**human; duck**ling**; sub**terra**nean; **arch**bishop; **uni**que.

(University of London G.C.E.)

Exercise 2

Choose *five* of the following dictionary definitions, and for each write down a single word of equivalent meaning, beginning with *ex*. For example, for *trained by practice, skilled*, you would write *expert*.

   i. developed in detail; clear, definite
  ii. lay bare by digging; unearth
 iii. excessive prodigality in expenditure
 iv. put out, quench
  v. send out (commodities) from one country to another
 vi. banish from one's native land
vii. a public display (of works of art, etc.)

(University of London G.C.E.)

Exercise 3

For each of the dictionary definitions listed below write down a single word of equivalent meaning, beginning with *in*. For example, for *not characteristic of normal civilized behaviour, brutal, barbarous*, you would write **in***human*.

   i. to blow out or distend with wind or water
  ii. an unbeliever, a disbeliever in religion
 iii. to affect with a disease
 iv. frail, feeble, unsound, not strong
  v. liquid forced into the body for medicinal purposes

(University of London G.C.E.)

Exercise 4

In each case give the meaning of the part of the word in bold type, and then use the word correctly in a sentence.

a. **circum**ference	*f.* **omni**vorous
b. **dis**satisfied	*g.* **vice**-chancellor
c. **hyper**sensitive	*h.* **contra**vene
d. **equi**lateral	*i.* **extra**-mural
e. **anti**-aircraft	*j.* **poly**theism

Exercise 5

In each case give the meaning of the part of the word in bold type, and then use the word correctly in a sentence.

a. **ultra**-smart
b. **en**close
c. **dia**gonal
d. **mal**formation
e. **il**legible

f. **mono**poly
g. **fore**see
h. **retro**grade
i. **phil**anthropist
j. **pan**-American

Exercise 6

Use a dictionary to find out (a) the meaning of the part of the word in bold type and (b) the meaning and usage of the whole word.

a. **mono**rail
b. **bi**ennial
c. **trans**port
d. **ana**chronism

e. **ortho**dox
f. **loco**motive
g. **co**-operate
h. **bio**chemistry

i. **auto**mation
j. **under**estimate
k. **hydro**electric
l. **pre**fabricated

Exercise 7

Use a dictionary to find out (a) the meaning of the part of the word in bold type and (b) the meaning and usage of the whole word.

a. **ex**-serviceman
b. **non**-intervention
c. **pseudo**-antique
d. **polio**myelitis

e. **equi**valent
f. quadri**lateral**
g. **octa**gonal
h. **sus**pended

i. **tri**cycle
j. **luna**tic
k. **inter**com
l. **kilo**cycle

Exercise 8

Use a dictionary to find out (a) the meaning of the part of the word in bold type and (b) the meaning and usage of the whole word.

a. **pen**ultimate
b. **atmo**sphere
c. **metro**politan
d. **audit**orium

e. **ig**noble
f. **ego**tist
g. **geo**graphy
h. **in**operable

i. **physio**therapy
j. un**con**scious
k. **carto**grapher
l. Anglo**phil**

Exercise 9

Use a dictionary to find out (a) the meaning of the part of the word in bold type and (b) the meaning and usage of the whole word.

a. **hetero**dox   e. techn**ology**   i. education
b. **ac**celerate   f. **micro**phone   j. **pan**chromatic
c. **super**sonic   g. **con**vent   k. **bene**volent
d. **de**contaminate   h. **phil**ately   l. **psych**ology

2. Making words

When you do the exercises in this section make sure that you know the meaning of each word **and** how to use it in a sentence. Ask your teacher if you are in doubt.

Exercise 10

Make nouns showing the quality or characteristic shown by each of these adjectives:

a. deep   e. broad   i. healthy
b. warm   f. wide   j. high
c. long   g. true   k. dead
d. strong   h. young

Exercise 11

Make nouns corresponding to these adjectives:

a. punctual   f. odd   k. legal   p. dense
b. reliable   g. generous   l. noble   q. ferocious
c. sincere   h. peculiar   m. stupid   r. sensitive
d. similar   i. scarce   n. sparse   s. precocious
e. curious   j. special   o. hostile   t. facile

Exercise 12

Make nouns corresponding to these adjectives:

a. necessary   f. persistent   k. hot   p. vacant
b. keen   g. negligent   l. fat   q. proud
c. alert   h. resentful   m. cruel   r. lenient
d. difficult   i. speculative n. new   s. foolish
e. suspicious   j. anxious   o. red   t. free

Exercise 13

Make nouns from the following words. Alternatives are possible in some cases.

a. defend	*f.* create	*k.* pose	*p.* ignore
b. arrive	*g.* magnify	*l.* obey	*q.* grieve
c. silent	*h.* complex	*m.* sober	*r.* fail
d. err	*i.* argue	*n.* destroy	*s.* gather
e. hinder	*j.* laugh	*o.* slack	*t.* rebel

Exercise 14

Make nouns from the following words. Alternatives are possible in some cases.

a. believe	*f.* object	*k.* deceive	*p.* behave
b. withdraw	*g.* approve	*l.* receive	*q.* act
c. propel	*h.* lose	*m.* confess	*r.* permit
d. oppose	*i.* refuse	*n.* relieve	*s.* rely
e. exhibit	*j.* complain	*o.* improve	*t.* criticize

Exercise 15

Make nouns from the following words.

a. pronounce	*f.* perplex	*k.* accompany	*p.* applaud
b. exclaim	*g.* bewilder	*l.* depart	*q.* ascend
c. fly	*h.* reprove	*m.* choose	*r.* depart
d. see	*i.* construct	*n.* survive	*s.* comply
e. coarse	*i.* constrict	*o.* satisfy	*t.* fail

Exercise 16

Make adjectives from the following words:

a. vice	*f.* nonsense	*k.* sauce	*p.* despise
b. misery	*g.* brute	*l.* part	*q.* knowledge
c. envy	*h.* comedy	*m.* station	*r.* fantasy
d. gas	*i.* virtue	*n.* omen	*s.* circle
e. decide	*j.* licence	*o.* freeze	*t.* express

Exercise 17

Make adjectives from the following words:

a. form	*f.* slave	*k.* hypothesis	*p.* climate
b. contempt	*g.* problem	*l.* benefit	*q.* obtrude
c. persuade	*h.* preference	*m.* provoke	*r.* fraud
d. comfort	*i.* conjecture	*n.* presume	*s.* nose
e. tribe	*j.* medicine	*o.* grace	*t.* dogma

Exercise 18

Make verbs which end in **en**:

a. cheap	*f.* soft	*k.* loose	*p.* fright
b. strong	*g.* sweet	*l.* wide	*q.* tough
c. bright	*h.* haste	*m.* long	*r.* weak
d. hard	*i.* light	*n.* tight	*s.* fast
e. dark	*j.* fat	*o.* short	*t.* slack

Exercise 19

Make verbs which start with *en*, *im* or *in*:

a. habit	*d.* prison	*g.* fold	*j.* close
b. pose	*e.* noble	*h.* snare	*k.* danger
c. rage	*f.* flame	*i.* plant	*l.* press

Exercise 20

Make adverbs from these words:

a. success	*f.* courage	*k.* enthusiasm
b. noisy	*g.* plenty	*l.* temporary
c. ease	*h.* occasion	*m.* event
d. humour	*i.* necessary	*n.* danger
e. affection	*j.* skill	*o.* positive

3. Synonyms

When you find the synonyms required by the exercises below, you may use a single word or a short expression but make sure that you know how to use it in a sentence. It sometimes happens that words which are similar in meaning are rather different in usage and that one of them CANNOT be substituted for another without some further change being made to the sentence. When you are doubtful, ask your teacher to help you.

Exercise 21

Find synonyms for the words in bold type, altering *a* and *an* when necessary:

a. an **agile** movement	*e.* the evidence was **untrue**
b. **reply to** the letter	*f.* an **enormous** ant-hill
c. considerable **peril**	*g.* an **enthusiastic** player
d. quite an **assembly**	*h.* he took his **chance**

e. a dull **ache**   *k.* I tried to **hide** it
f. it has been **finished**   *l.* it stopped **suddenly**

Exercise 22

Find synonyms for the words in bold type, altering *a* and *an* when necessary.

a. two **enemies**   *g.* it **ripped** easily
b. **'Halt!'** he said   *h.* a **strange** noise
c. speak **truthfully**   *i.* the two **voyagers**
d. quite a **marsh**   *j.* a **stubborn** person
e. he is the **proprietor**   *k.* it is **superfluous**
f. I have **mended** it   *l.* he is rather **reticent**

Exercise 23

Find synonyms for the words in the left-hand list by choosing the most suitable word from the right-hand list:

a. avaricious: meek, nasty, greedy, grasping
b. blame: censure, argue, dislike, shame
c. implacable: immovable, relentless, fixed, firm
d. courteously: polite, pleasant, rude, politely
e. obvious: noticeable, vague, clear, apparent
f. emancipate: set free, set off, avoid, come from
g. customary: usual, usually, use, habitually
h. lucidly: melting, obscure, clear, clearly
i. veracious: hungry, ravenous, truthful, untrue
j. poor: indigent, weak, hungry, uneducated

Exercise 24

Find synonyms for the words in the left-hand list by choosing the most suitable word from the right-hand list.

a. vexation: revenge, dislike, annoyance, angry
b. width: wide, broad, depth, breadth, length
c. skilful: dextrous, cunning, careful, old
d. adversary: opposite, enemies, foes, opponent
e. symmetry: beauty of shape, geometry, grave, dead
f. superfluity: current, fluid, excess, abundance
g. gullible: a creek, easily deceived, guilty, rare
h. remainder: quotient, waste, residue, resident
i. innocent: unusual, harmless, sinless, childish
j. obstacle: objection, fence, obstruction, delay

Exercise 25

Discuss in class the differences in meaning and **usage** of the following, *some* of which are synonyms:

1. serene, calm, placid, peaceful, uneventful
2. rich, powerful, wealthy, affluent, influential
3. cautious, careful, apprehensive, worried, shrewd
4. to decline to, to refuse to, to object to
5. innocuous, safe, harmless, inoffensive
6. rumour, belief, fact, opinion, news
7. hearsay, evidence, gossip, testimony
8. cancel, postpone, adjourn, defer, delay
9. heckle, harass, jeer at, scoff at, deride
10. finesse, craft, cunning, artistry, competence

Exercise 26

Discuss in class the differences in meaning and usage of the following:

1. abuse, insults, calumny, slander, libel
2. daring, bold, rash, impetuous, brave, stupid
3. to hamper, prevent, discourage, encourage, interfere with
4. indefinite, indeterminate, vaguely, undecided
5. hasty, speedy, rapid, agile, lively, quick
6. bored, uninterested, disinterested, uninteresting
7. spacious, specious, spatial, spate
8. destroy, raze, annihilate, obliterate, wipe out
9. civilized, educated, intelligent, wealthy, polite
10. lady, woman, girl, lass, female, spinster, widow

Exercise 27

Discuss in class the differences in meaning and usage of the following:

1. man, boy, youth, gentleman, lad, bachelor, widower
2. well-behaved, bland, courteous, obsequious, servile
3. humble, ill-mannered, modest, weak, gentle
4. zealous, prejudiced, keen, eager, enthusiastic
5. reconciliation, truce, friendship, treaty
6. alter, amend, rectify, correct, change
7. dismay, concern, worry, fear, horror, panic

8. summary, précis, digest, synopsis, paraphrase
9. payment, fee, salary, stipend, honorarium, reward
10. impeccable, guilty, faultless, correct, blameless

Exercise 28

Find possible synonyms (single words or short expressions) for these words:

1. irate
2. perplexed
3. reciprocal
4. crucial
5. defective
6. arduous
7. impetuous

8. allege
9. exhausted
10. endeavour
11. ludicrous
12. warmer
13. warmed
14. disastrous

15. radiant
16. auspicious
17. tranquil
18. amiable
19. manifestly
20. isolated

Exercise 29

Find possible synonyms for these words:

1. tyrannical
2. deferential
3. naïve
4. mean (adj.)
5. requite
6. dispute
7. authentic

8. repudiate
9. arduous
10. abstain from
11. elated
12. ingenuous
13. biased
14. dissipated

15. coercion
16. equivocal
17. turbulent
18. a travesty
19. expedient
20. disparage

Exercise 30

Make lists of words which are fairly similar to each of the following:

1. fear
2. glad
3. annoyed
4. clear

5. say
6. praise
7. dislike
8. useful

9. old
10. new
11. strong
12. calm

4. Antonyms

When you consider antonyms for the words given below, remember that you are concerned not merely with the meaning of the words but with the way they are used in sentences.

Exercise 31

Give antonyms (or words of opposite meaning) for the following:

1. complicated
2. rash (adj.)
3. talkative
4. concave
5. rarely
6. a decrease
7. to prosper
8. overweight
9. to pacify
10. arrogantly
11. the zenith
12. antagonistic
13. objective (adj.)
14. to export
15. abstract (adj.)

Exercise 32

Give antonyms for the following:

1. enmity
2. disparage
3. adversity
4. immune from
5. sophisticated
6. failed
7. antonym
8. doubtful
9. depth
10. age (n.)
11. wisdom
12. melt
13. contradict
14. to lament
15. sour
16. lean (adj.)
17. foreigner
18. deny
19. reluctant to
20. nonchalant

Exercise 33

For the following words give antonyms OR short expressions which convey an opposite meaning.

1. a subordinate
2. prohibit
3. alleviate
4. progress (n.)
5. hasten
6. erroneous
7. accidentally
8. cantankerous
9. leniency
10. lenient
11. spurious
12. candidly
13. rejection
14. penchant
15. compulsorily
16. industrious
17. altruistic
18. omega
19. misanthrope
20. hospitable

Exercise 34

For the following words give antonyms OR short expressions which convey an opposite meaning.

1. diffident
2. meagre
3. responsible
4. onerous
5. discordant
6. moderately
7. propitious
8. vivacious
9. relax
10. provoke
11. momentous
12. ambiguous
13. paucity
14. mutinous
15. termination

Exercise 35

For the following words give antonyms OR short expressions which convey an opposite meaning.

1. conspicuous	8. sterile	15. repel
2. unique	9. timid	16. slovenly
3. beneficial	10. an enigma	17. squeamish
4. miserly	11. to shun	18. portable
5. censure (n.)	12. temporarily	19. jaded
6. mercenary (adj.)	13. sober (adj.)	20. drastic
7. impromptu (adj.)	14. artificial	

5. Homonyms (and words pronounced in the same way)

Homonyms are words which have the same form as each other and are pronounced in the same way but which have different meanings, e.g. *race* (of people) and *race* (at a sports meeting). It is convenient to consider in this section words which differ in form but which are pronounced in the same way, e.g. *wait* and *weight*.

Exercise 36

Use each of the following words in two separate sentences (which can be spoken or written) so that it is used in two different senses:

1. tender	8. temple	15. scale	22. base
2. file	9. arm	16. air	23. plot
3. yard	10. left	17. mail	24. ear
4. league	11. date	18. case	25. desert
5. pound	12. lime	19. match	26. stern
6. die	13. own	20. sound	27. cricket
7. graze	14. ring	21. bark	28. mean

Exercise 37

Use each of the following words in two separate sentences so that it is used in two different senses:

1. seal	6. jar	11. fit	16. swallow
2. bale	7. row	12. well	17. page
3. quarry	8. light	13. soil	18. grave
4. hawk	9. sole	14. cape	19. van
5. corporal	10. lie	15. fair	20. pawn

Vocabulary Exercises

Exercise 38

For each word find another word which is pronounced in a similar way but which is spelt differently and has a different meaning:

1. wait	6. heel	11. herd	16. flees
2. mind	7. buy	12. born	17. pail
3. meat	8. sale	13. coarse	18. pane
4. soul	9. quay	14. write	19. weigh
5. team	10. dear	15. grate	20. hail

Exercise 39

For each word find another which is pronounced similarly but which is spelt differently and has a different meaning:

1. through	6. night	11. sew	16. whale
2. fought	7. taught	12. know	17. due
3. nose	8. been	13. sort	18. rouse
4. reign	9. faint	14. bow	19. break
5. hue	10. crews	15. queue	20. wrap

Exercise 40

For each word find another which is pronounced similarly but which is spelt differently and has a different meaning:

1. two	5. main	9. roar	13. stare	17. bare
2. tail	6. where	10. here	14. there	18. whole
3. road	7. bread	11. soar	15. boy	19. Dane
4. toad	8. tare	12. veil	16. beer	20. fain

6. What is the difference?

Exercise 41

Answer these questions which are taken from past papers of the University of London G.C.E. examination for overseas candidates.

a. Write sentences, one for each word, to show that you know the difference in meaning between the words in THREE of the following pairs:

ingenious, ingenuous; industrial, industrious; imaginary, imaginative; imply, infer; council, counsel.

b. Write sentences, one for each word, to show that you know the difference in meaning between the words in THREE of the following pairs:

affect, effect; advice, advise; dominate, domineer; illegible, ineligible; partake, participate.

c. Write sentences, one for each word, to show the difference in meaning between the words in FIVE of the following pairs:

stimulant, stimulus; incredulous, incredible;
diluted, dilated;   voracious, veracious;
continuous, continual; alternately, alternatively;
luxurious, luxuriant

d. Explain the exact difference in meaning between the terms in each of the following pairs:

  i. postpone a meeting *and* adjourn a meeting
  ii. suspicious character *and* suspected character
 iii. a reasoned dislike *and* an instinctive dislike
 iv. astronomy   *and* astrology
  v. continual rain   *and* continuous rain

e. Explain carefully the exact difference in meaning between the two sentences in each of the following pairs:

  i. Six year-old motor cars will be in the race.
   Six-year-old motor cars will be in the race.
  ii. On the landing you will find a dirty clothes-basket.
   On the landing you will find a dirty-clothes basket.
 iii. The reporter interviewed a cross section of the public.
   The reporter interviewed a cross-section of the public.

f. Choose TWO of the following groups of words, and explain the exact differences in meaning between the words:

  i. crowd, mob, audience
  ii. difficult, perilous, treacherous
 iii. erase, exterminate, devastate

g. Compose sentences to illustrate the difference in meaning between the words in pairs given below. Write TEN sentences, one for each word. You must make no change in the form of the words you have chosen.

council, counsel; deprecate, depreciate; transparent, translucent; desert, dessert; human, humane.

h. Explain the difference in meaning between the sentences in each of the following pairs:

Vocabulary Exercises

    i. The performance will be given on three consecutive days.
      The performance will be given on three alternate days.
   ii. Our honourable treasurer deserves our warmest thanks.
      Our honorary treasurer deserves our warmest thanks.
  iii. I am not accountable to Miss Jones.
      I am not accountable for Miss Jones.

i. Write sentences, *one for each word*, to bring out the difference in meaning between the two words in each of THREE of the following pairs: imminent, eminent; imaginary, imaginative; stationary, stationery; emigrant, immigrant.

Exercise 42

First discuss in class the differences in meaning between the following words; then use each word in a sentence.

1. avenge, revenge
2. famous, infamous
3. adapt, adopt
4. interested, interesting
5. persecute, prosecute
6. priceless, worthless
7. inflammable, inflammatory
8. elusive, illusive
9. bath, bathe
10. literally, literary

Exercise 43

Discuss the differences in meaning between the following words and then use them in sentences.

1. principle, principal
2. allusion, illusion
3. exhausting, exhaustive
4. negligible, negligent
5. credible, credulous
6. respectable, respectful
7. compliment, complement
8. scene, scenery
9. hoard, horde
10. contemptible, contemptuous

Exercise 44

Discuss the difference in meaning between the following words and then use them in sentences.

1. oral, aural
2. confidant, confident
3. infectious, contagious
4. uncomfortable, discomfiting
5. ascetic, aesthetic
6. beneficent, beneficial
7. ceremonial, ceremonious
8. elicit, illicit
9. exhausted, exhausting
10. intricate, extricate

Exercise 45

Discuss the difference in meaning between the following words and then use them in sentences.

1. fictitious, factitious	6. popular, populous
2. official, officious	7. pertinent, impertinent
3. strategic, tactical	8. irreverent, irrelevant
4. suit, suite	9. momentous, momentary
5. irreparable, irreplaceable	10. sanguine, sanguinary

Exercise 46

Discuss the difference in meaning and/or usage between the following words and expressions and then use them in sentences.
1. to consist of, to be composed of
2. to refrain from doing something, to restrain somebody from doing something
3. to bring something to me, to take something from me
4. to be angry with somebody, to be angry at something
5. some time, sometimes
6. any body, anybody
7. all ready, already

7. Definitions (and explanations)

Exercise 47

Answer the following questions which are taken from past papers of the University of London G.C.E. examination for overseas candidates.

a. Describe as exactly as you can, using *not more* than 30 words for each, TWO of the following:

a bicycle pump, a banana, an electric torch, a mouse-trap, a thermometer.

b. Write clear, concise definitions (one sentence for each) of THREE of the following: a mirror, a safety razor, a vacuum cleaner, a rainbow, a propelling-pencil, a fountain-pen.

c. For each of the italicized parts of the following sentences give a single word with the same meaning. The word you supply must not be formed from any word used in the sentence you are dealing with.

Vocabulary Exercises

     i. His behaviour in class is *not able to be prophesied beforehand*.

    ii. It is time he grew up, and stopped being *inclined to indulge in practices fit only for a youngster*.

  iii. We tried *the action of arguing a person out of doing something*, but he still persisted in his futile attempts.

  iv. All the donations of the members were *of their own free-will*, and no attempt was made to force them to give.

    v. The two authors decided to *work together in a joint effort* in preparing a new history book.

d. Re-write the sentences listed below, replacing each italicized expression by a single word, but making no other changes.

Example:

   Question: The waiter *took away* the empty dish.

   Answer: The waiter *removed* the empty dish.

     i. The actor amused the company by *taking off* the famous statesman.

    ii. The innkeeper was easily *taken in* by the plausible rogue.

  iii. The journalist, faced with a charge of libel, *took back* his wild statement.

  iv. In character, the boy *took after* his mother.

    v. He had such charm that I *took to* him immediately.

e. Choose SIX of the following words, and for each of the six write a sentence introducing the word so as to show its meaning clearly:

    casual, infrequent, collaborate, inefficient, impersonal, distraction, inevitable, familiarize.

Exercise 48

Give single words which express the sense of the words given in italics:

1. It is best not to write examination answers in handwriting *that cannot be read*.

2. The candidate had to withdraw when he heard that he was *one who could not, according to the rules, be elected*.

3. Every man is *liable to be called upon to account* for his own actions.

4. One does not like to see men whose behaviour and manners are *more like those of a woman than a man*.

5. The problem we had for homework last night seemed to be *one that was never likely to be solved*.

6. The two players tried to kick the ball *at one and the same time.*
7. Some writers are fond of using words *that are no longer in use.*
8. It is to be feared that doctors will never find a *remedy for all diseases.*
9. The scheme for draining the marshes was *one that could not be put into practice.*
10. Lord Nuffield was famous as a *man who was generous to his fellow-men.*
11. The secretary's proposal was adopted *with the full agreement of all the members.*
12. We asked for an explanation, as some of his remarks were *capable of bearing more than one meaning.*
13. I am afraid he must be regarded as *pretending to be better than he is.*
14. It was a *practice bound up with the life* of the school that every new boy shook hands with the headmaster.
15. Old English poetry was remarkable for *the recurrence of the same initial sound in words in close succession.*
16. The equipment used by mountaineers must be *easily carried from place to place.*
17. The committee *suspended proceedings and dispersed* until the following Thursday.
18. That man is *too ready to believe anything.*
19. She wastes a lot of time because she is *over-attentive to minor details.*
20. He has never settled down and is *a person who leads a wandering life* at heart.

Exercise 49

Give a single word exactly equivalent to each of the following expressions:

1. that can be easily broken
2. inclined to be fat
3. contrary to law
4. a person who chooses to live in a country other than his own
5. having the ability or qualifications required to do something
6. full of sorrow for something which you have done wrong
7. in a way suggesting an unwillingness
8. to repay somebody who has paid out money on your behalf
9. in a condition between childhood and manhood
10. a person who assumes a false character or personality

Vocabulary Exercises

Exercise 50

In the following sentences, replace the words in italics by a single word having the same meaning.

1. His speech in the debate contained much sound argument, but his delivery was *on one and the same note* and barely audible.
2. The scout was commended for his courage, leadership and *power to use all means available* in directing the rescue operations.
3. The second time a holiday was granted to celebrate the gaining of a State Scholarship, the boys hoped that a *rule for future cases* had been established.
4. *Rendered amazed and silent* by the accusation, he could offer no adequate defence.
5. The officials of the mining company decided to consult a *scientist trained to investigate the earth's crust.*
6. *Medicines to cause vomiting* should not be taken by a patient who has swallowed a corrosive poison.
7. When the successful architect and sculptor won a £500 prize in a play-writing competition, his friends admired his *many-sided talent.*
8. They continued to make hopeful plans although their prospects of making money were *vague and hazy as the clouds.*
9. We *took it for granted* that you had missed the train.
10. Our forwards attacked *from time to time* during the second half of the game.

8. Marking the stress

Some dictionaries mark a stressed syllable by putting a mark after it; some put the mark before it. In this section we will put the mark before the syllable which is stressed:

'prefect	'expert	're'born
pre'fer	ex'plain	re'fer
'preference	expla'nation	refe'ree
prefe'rential	ex'planatory	'reference

The pronunciation of some words depends upon whether they are used as nouns (with emphasis on the first syllable) or as verbs (with emphasis on the second syllable):

nouns	*verbs*
'convict	con'victed

ˈtransfer   transˈfer
ˈinsult   inˈsulted

Exercise 51

Mark the syllables which are emphasized when the following words are spoken. Put a mark *before* each stressed syllable.

1. away	6. habitual	11. hasten	16. naïve
2. sadly	7. delightful	12. glisten	17. enter
3. humble	8. calamity	13. sergeant	18. coerce
4. unique	9. furniture	14. valuable	19. aloof
5. guardian	10. missionary	15. river-bed	20. usual

Exercise 52

Mark the stressed syllables on the words in bold type.

1. The **rebels** were soon captured.
2. I don't think they will **rebel** now.
3. The number of supporters has **decreased** considerably.
4. There will be a **decrease** during the month.
5. He hopes to have an **increase** in his salary.
6. It was **increased** at the end of the year.
7. There is an **escort** waiting for him outside.
8. I will **escort** you to the office.
9. There has been an increase in **exports.**
10. We **export** machinery to many countries.
11. You will need a **permit** to enter that country.
12. Do you think she will **permit** us to go?
13. We must **protest** against his decision.
14. They will take our **protest** seriously.
15. His **contract** is a particularly favourable one.
16. They have **contracted** to finish it within six months.
17. He always **conducts** himself in a mature way.
18. His **conduct** has not been a source of worry to us.
19. Four candidates are going to **contest** that seat.
20. The **contest** was an extremely interesting one.

9. Objective exercises

Exercise 53

In each case, choose the right word to go in the blank space. Write down the letter which appears immediately before the word you choose.

1. Don't worry. It won't burn. It's . . .
   A. inextinguishable   B. inflammable   C. inflammatory
   D. non-inflammable

2. Their team is . . . of ex-internationals
   A. composed   B. consisted   C. comprises   D. compromised

3. It is my . . . that he has lost the money.
   A. believe   B. belief   C. believed   C. beliefs

4. We must get to the root of the matter and find out the . . .
   cause of his troubles.
   A. secondary   B. post-secondary   C. primary   D. elementary

5. He . . . the charge and denied that he had had anything to do
   with the money.
   A. protested   B. protected   C. repealed   D. repudiated

6. If he tells anybody, he will put the success of the whole
   project in . . .
   A. insecurity   B. jealousy   C. jeopardy   D. exposure

7. I . . . the doctor at the hospital until he agreed to release me.
   A. badgered   B. festered   C. persecute   D. prosecuted

8. I know he doesn't like the house but I think he is . . . to
   the fact that he will have to stay there for some time.
   A. reconciled   B. satisfied   C. contented   D. aggrieved

9. Your handwriting is practically . . . I can hardly read it.
   A. illegitimate   B. ineligible   C. eligible   D. illegible

10. In the . . . for gallantry the sergeant's bravery and disregard
    of personal danger were highly praised.
    A. accusation   B. citation   C. quotation   D. impeachment

Exercise 54

Choose the right word to go in each blank space. Write down
the letter which appears immediately before the word you choose.

1. A man who likes his fellow human beings is a . . .
   A. philatelist   B. philanderer   C. philanthropist
   D. misanthropist

2. A doctor who treats mental diseases is called a . . .
   A. psychologist   B. psychotic   C. neurotic   D. psychiatrist

3. A *paediatrician* specializes in the diseases of . . .
   A. feet   B. children   C. eyes   D. ears   E. old people

4. In a civil court of law, the *plaintiff* is the person who . . .
   A. brings the suit   B. defends the suit   C. tries the suit
   D. maintains silence in the court

5. To *exonerate* a person means . . .
   A. to throw him out   B. to hurry him up   C. to banish him
   D. to free him from blame

6. *Adversary* is similar in meaning to . . .
   A. birthday   B. hostile   C. rival   D. opponent

7. In the word *Anglophile, phile* means . . .
   A. an enemy of   B. a lover of   C. smaller
   D. relating to the mind

8. If you are caught trying to smuggle that watch through the Customs, it will be . . .
   A. compensated   B. confiscated   C. castigated
   D. consolidated

9. If you are *put off* by the sight of something you feel . . .
   A. anxious   B. repelled   C. disinterested   D. disenchanted

10. If a person is *put out* by something he will be . . .
    A. removed from the place   B. forcibly ejected   C. disconcerted
    D. condemned

Exercise 55

From the four choices after each sentence, choose the one which is nearest in meaning to the word or expression in italics. Write down the letter which appears immediately before the word or expression you choose.

1. His ideas are rather *unorthodox* at times.
   A. aggravating   B. contrary to accepted opinions   C. atheistic
   D. provocative

2. The *prototype* of this machine was produced in Japan.
   A. copy   B. replica   C. duplicate   D. original

3. I feel that his action is definitely *retrograde*.
   A. progressive   B. going back to a former condition
   C. unusual   D. foolish because it is too rash

4. The scientist wanted to *see* the experiment *through*.
   A. find out the secret of   B. stay and finish   C. watch
   D. observe carefully

5. I think you're *dead* right, you know.
   A. exactly   B. nearly   C. not   D. not alive

6. He asked me to lend him some money but I sent him away
   with a flea in his ear.
   A. with more than he had asked me to lend him   B. with less
   than he had wanted to borrow   C. discomfited by my refusal
   and reproof   D. highly delighted at my kindness

7. It would be *premature* to make a decision at this point.
   A. foolish   B. stupid   C. sensible   D. too hasty

8. She is inclined to be *impetuous* at times.
   A. discourteous   B. unthoughtful   C. rash in her actions
   D. aloof

9. His attitude is much too *complacent.*
   A. self-satisfied   B. self-centred   C. self-absorbed
   D. self-critical

10. He was *hoist with his own petard* when he tried to trap Peter.
    A. deceived by his own greed   B. most successful
    C. caught by his own trick   D. held back by his own modesty

10. Topic vocabularies

It is sometimes an advantage to consider a particular topic,
such as 'Air Travel', and words commonly used in connection
with it. Notice, however, that:

i. We are concerned only with words and expressions in common
   usage and *not* with unusual words.

ii. When you meet a new word, you must find out how to use it
    in a sentence or in several different contexts if this is possible.

Exercise 56

Discuss in class the meaning and usage of the following words.
Air Travel

1. travel documents	11. a boarding gate
2. an international certificate of vaccination/inoculation	12. the boarding point
	13. foreign currency
3. a passport	14. local currency
4. a visa	15. flight number
5. an immigration permit	16. the traffic office
6. a flight coupon	17. the town terminal
7. a reservation	18. check-in time
8. an onward reservation	19. economy class
9. to reconfirm a reservation	20. tourist class
10. a boarding card/pass	

21. the captain	31. pressurized
22. the first officer	32. a fuelling truck
23. the cabin staff	33. a hydraulic pump
24. a steward(ess)	34. a transit stop
25. no gratuities	35. the undercarriage
26. the galley	36. en route to London
27. a sedative	37. the outward journey
28. a call button	38. stopover passengers
29. a seat-belt	39. an overnight bag
30. air-conditioned	40. personal luggage
41. the scheduled departure time	46. a lady's vanity case
42. the liability of the carrier	47. a baggage check
43. at the option of the carrier	48. the free baggage allowance
44. a refund	49. the excess baggage charge
45. the point of embarkation	50. a window blind

Exercise 57

Discuss each of the following topics in class, and try to compile a list of useful words and expressions related to it.

1. Travel by sea
2. The railway
3. Building
4. Road transport
5. Agriculture

Exercise 58

Discuss each of the following topics in class, and try to compile a list of useful words and expressions related to it.

1. Commerce and office work
2. Insurance
3. The postal services, including the telephone
4. Fishing
5. Sports

Exercise 59

Discuss each of the following topics in class, and try to compile a list of useful words and expressions related to it.

Vocabulary Exercises

1. Entertainment, including the cinema, radio and television
2. Photography
3. Common manufacturing industries in your country
4. The police and the law courts
5. Newspapers, magazines and advertising

Exercise 60

Discuss each of the following topics in class, and try to compile a list of useful words and expressions related to it.

1. Religion
2. Central and local government
3. Mining
4. Simple maintenance in the house
5. The public utilities: electricity, gas, water etc.

'Sudden a thought came'

Chapter 10

Figures of Speech

In the expression 'Figures of Speech', the word *Figures* means *devices* or *attractive methods*. Centuries ago men used to study a subject called *Rhetoric* which is the art of expressing yourself well in speech or in writing. In the early books on Rhetoric, the ancient teachers listed many 'Figures of Speech' which potential orators and lawyers could use to make their speeches more interesting or impressive. The study of figurative language has continued since that time.

In this chapter we shall deal in detail with similes and metaphors, and with the difference between figurative and literal expressions. We shall then briefly consider eleven other figures of speech. At this level a student should learn to recognize, understand and use similes and metaphors. However, the figures of speech in section 2 are of less importance at this stage except to students who have a particular interest in (any) language or literature.

1. Similes and metaphors

i. Similes and metaphors are used to try to make an account or a description more vivid and interesting. They bring into a passage words which create a mental picture and thus enable the reader to visualize the scene more effectively.

ii. A simile makes a comparison between two things or persons and is often introduced by *as* or *like*. The two things are of different kinds and are said to be similar in one respect only and not in all ways.

Examples:

a.   Feebly she laugheth in the languid moon,
While Porphyro upon her face doth look,
Like puzzled urchin on an aged crone,
Who keepeth clos'd a wond'rous riddle-book
As spectacled she sits in chimney nook.

b.   Sudden a thought came *like a full-blown rose,*
Flushing his brow, and in his pained heart
Made purple riot . . .
        (both from 'The Eve of St. Agnes' by Keats)

c. In this sustained simile Keats compares the way in which a lonely man spoke to the sound of a solitary gust of wind blowing through mighty trees:

As when upon a trancèd summer night,
Forests, branch-charmèd by the earnest stars,
Dream, and so dream all night, without a noise,
Save from one gradual solitary gust,
Swelling upon the silence; dying off;
As if the ebbing air had but one wave;
So came these words, and went;
            ('The Fall of Hyperion' by Keats)

d. We can of course have similes in prose but there they are usually rather less striking:

It was a big decision to make. He stood there silently for a moment, *like a man on the edge of a precipice.*

The centre-forward charged down the field *like some mad elephant hurtling through a clump of bamboo.*

All these similes are examples of figurative speech (or writing). In the last example, for instance, we do not mean that the player was an elephant or that he was as big as one. His impetuous rush is likened to the rush of a mad elephant in the jungle. The image of a mad elephant is brought in to try to help the reader to visualize the scene during the game. The picture created in the reader's mind is more effective than the word *wildly* in this sentence: 'The centre-forward charged wildly down the field.'

iii. A metaphor takes the comparison a stage further by saying that a person is something which he is not OR that he is doing something which, in fact, he is not doing.

For example, there is a metaphor in the saying 'People who live in glass houses shouldn't throw stones.' We mean that people in a vulnerable position should not attack others. A man who has been convicted of fraud is hardly in a position to criticize anybody who travels on the railway or a bus without paying for his ticket. We do not imply that this man actually lives in a glass house.

Examples:

a. He is apt *to ride roughshod over* everyone's feelings.
b. Their party had a *landslide* victory during the election.
c. I think you ought to pay the bill. You are *standing on rather slippery ground* at the moment and he may sue you if you don't pay.
d. That discovery was a real *milestone* in the history of science.
e. When he advertised for a wife he was nearly overcome by the *avalanche* of replies.

The words in italics are used figuratively and not literally. In *e*, for example, if *avalanche* were literally true we would expect to find the man lying underneath an enormous pile of letters.

Exercise 1

Answer these questions which are taken from past examination papers:

a. Choose FIVE of the following words, and for each word chosen write a sentence using the word in a metaphorical sense: summit, cream, armed, milestone, avenue, avalanche, fruit.
b. Choose FIVE of the following sentences, which contain metaphors, and express their meaning in your own words without using any figures of speech:

   i. The beleaguered fortress was relieved at the eleventh hour.
  ii. It is easy to be swept along by the current of popular opinion.
 iii. He was too apt to ride roughshod over everyone's feelings.
 iv. We must not be surprised if young people tug at their moorings.
  v. He was almost at the end of his tether when he stumbled on the solution of his difficulty.

vi. After the failure of his last novel his reputation stands on slippery ground.

vii. It is most unlikely that the unsuccessful party will suffer a landslide at the forthcoming election.

Exercise 2

Answer these questions which are taken from past examination papers:

a. Choose THREE of the following words, and use each one in a separate sentence, in a figurative sense, and explain clearly the figurative usage: heart, tower, sea, harvest, veil, spirit.

b. Explain clearly in your own words the meaning of any FOUR of the following figurative expressions: to bury the hatchet; to turn the tables; to face the music; to let the cat out of the bag; to be at loggerheads; a titanic struggle; to be on tenterhooks.

c. Use THREE of the following expressions figuratively in separate sentences so as to bring out clearly the meaning of each: i. a dog in the manger; ii. a fly in the ointment; iii. a pig in a poke; iv. a wolf in sheep's clothing; v. a bull in a china-shop; vi. a snake in the grass.

d. Choose FIVE of the following sentences, and express *in a single word or a short phrase* the meaning of each figurative expression in italics. Do NOT write out the whole sentence.

i. His industry, perseverance and determination ultimately brought him *a rich harvest*.

ii. All his ambitions *came to dust*.

iii. It is difficult to insult such a *thick-skinned* person.

iv. This may teach the young man not to *play with fire*.

v. There is no *armour* against fate.

vi. He *turned a blind eye* to the miseries of his companions.

vii. It was not until comparatively late in life that he *entered the political lists*.

Exercise 3

Answer the following questions, which are taken from past examination papers:

a. Choose THREE of the following words and write sentences, one for each word, to illustrate their use in a figurative sense. Explain clearly the difference between your use of the word and its use in a literal sense.

heart, tower, crown, rain, herald.

b. Express the full meaning of each of the following passages in simple English, using no metaphors:

   i. All human things are subject to decay,
     And when fate summons, monarchs must obey.
   ii. People who live in glass houses should not throw stones.
   iii. As the twig's bent the tree's inclined.

c. Each of the following adjectives can be used metaphorically with an appropriate noun: sharp; fiery; icy; bald; hungry; small; blind.

Write down these adjectives and opposite each of them write ONE noun with which it is used metaphorically. Do not use any noun more than once.

Examples:	*Adjective*	*Noun*
	warm	welcome
	cold	shoulder

d. Give briefly the meanings of the following expressions, as used figuratively:

   i. to give chapter and verse;
   ii. to turn over a new leaf;
   iii. to take a leaf out of someone's book;
   iv. to talk like a book;
   v. to read between the lines;
   vi. a chapter of accidents.

Exercise 4

Answer the following questions:

a. Choose SIX of the following words and construct sentences in which each word is used (a) in its literal sense, and (b) metaphorically (12 sentences in all): hound, crown, comb, vice, root, wealth, anchor, jungle.

b. Choose FOUR of the following metaphorical expressions.

Give the meaning of each and suggest circumstances in which each might be used:

   i. read between the lines,
   ii. working in the dark,
   iii. a catspaw,
   iv. to be wise after the event,
   v. face the music,
   vi. beat about the bush,
   vii. putting the clock back.

c. Choose three of the following words, and show how each can be used as a metaphor by including it in a sentence of your own composition: veil, harvest, poison, path, smile.

2. Other figures of speech

i. *Rhetorical questions* are questions used purely for effect in a speech. In most cases, the speaker does not want a reply or expect that one will be given. For example, a speaker who wishes to impress his audience with his honesty may say, 'Can anyone say that I am a liar?' Similarly, in a debate a speaker may ask, rhetorically, 'Do we really want to see our country enslaved by a foreign power?' In some cases the speaker asks his question and then answers it himself (before an enthusiastic heckler can do so).

ii. *Hyperbole* is the name given to a gross exaggeration of the facts, e.g. 'Come and look at the orchids. There are *thousands* of new shoots on them.' (In fact, there are only eighteen new shoots on the plants.) Hyperbole is fairly common and is used to heighten the effect of whatever we wish to say.

iii. *Oxymoron* is the use of two contrasting words or ideas to create a rather unusual or startling effect, e.g. 'He played in a *crudely skilful* sort of way.' 'His air was one of *friendly hostility*.' You can sometimes find examples of oxymoron in magazines which print items called 'Picturesque Speech'.

iv. *Litotes* consists of deliberately understating the condition of something and it is therefore the opposite of hyperbole. For example, an explorer may have struggled through a very difficult and dangerous journey in which he escaped from death several times. On his return to his own country, he may be interviewed by a reporter who asks, 'What sort of a trip did you have?' If he replies, 'It wasn't without incident,' we shall have an example of litotes.

Similarly, if we call a serious riot 'a slight disturbance' the understatement is an example of litotes.

v. *Paronomasia* is a play or pun on words. There is a pun on the meaning of *dear* in this brief conversation between a young man and his girl-friend. They have been out for a walk and the girl is rather bored. She sighs and says, 'Oh dear.' Quick to seize an opportunity, the young man says, 'Who? Me?' There is a well-known example early in *Julius Caesar* when a cobbler says he is 'a mender of soles', playing on the words *soles* and *souls*.

vi. *Anastrophe* is a change in the normal order of words and it is used to emphasize a particular word, e.g. 'Smoking he absolutely loathes' and 'In rushed my mother-in-law . . .'

vii. *Alliteration* is the repetition in successive words of the same letter or sound. The repetition can be in words which are next to each other or in words near each other.

    a. *B*lack is the *b*eauty of the *b*rightest day (b)

    b. I gave him a *sh*ort, *sh*arp *sh*ock   (sh)

viii. *Euphemism* consists of using a mild or inoffensive expression in place of one which might be objectionable in some way, e.g.

    a. She *passed away* last night. = She died.

    b. He *gave me some advice* concerning my conduct. = He scolded me.

    c. He is *not quite his normal self.* = He is insane.

ix. *Syllepsis* is the use of one word to govern two others but with a change in its sense, e.g. 'He *lost* the game and his temper.'

x. *Aposiopesis* consists of leaving a statement unfinished. This is often done to increase suspense or to leave the reader to form his own conclusions.

    a. You'd better do it or else . . .

    b. After a short chase, the angry villagers caught up with the murderer. Two burly young men jumped on the criminal and brought him to the ground. Waving their sticks, the rest of the villagers closed in on the helpless man . . .

xi. *Antithesis* is the use of two neatly balanced and contrasting statements, e.g.

    a. To err is human; to forgive, divine.

    b. He is a jack of all trades and master of none.

Note: There are also about twenty other figures of speech but they do not concern us at this stage.

Chapter 11

Proverbs and Idiomatic Sayings

A bird in the hand is worth two in the bush

Warning

Most of the proverbs and sayings in this chapter are used in speech rather than in formal writing. It often happens in schools that after a lesson on proverbs some of the pupils fill their essays with them. This is quite wrong. If you feel tempted to do this, don't study the chapter at all!

This chapter is included in the book (a) because you will want to understand the sayings when somebody uses them in conversation with you, (b) because you may sometimes want to use them yourself in conversation and (c) because examiners occasionally ask you about them. Remember, however, that we do NOT normally use them in written work. Notice that these are figurative expressions and most of them should not be used in their literal sense.

Note: Brief explanations of the following proverbs and idioms are given at the end of the chapter.

Exercise 1

Briefly explain what each of the following means and when it could be used in conversation. If possible, find a parallel saying in another language.

1. Once bitten, twice shy.
2. Nothing venture, nothing gain.
3. Wise men think alike.

4. Fools seldom differ.
5. Absence makes the heart grow fonder.
6. Out of sight, out of mind.
7. Every cloud has a silver lining.
8. It never rains but it pours.
9. Look before you leap.
10. A bird in the hand is worth two in the bush.
11. Opportunity knocks but once.
12. People who live in glass houses should not throw stones.
13. Don't meet trouble half way.
14. He has burnt his boats behind him.
15. Too many cooks spoil the broth (soup).
16. Many hands make light work.
17. Still waters run deep.
18. Walls have ears.
19. He who rides on a tiger can never get off.
20. He took his pitcher to the well once too often.

Exercise 2

Briefly explain what each of the following means and when it is used. If possible, find a parallel saying in another language.

1. Empty vessels (*pots*) make most noise.
2. That's a case of the pot calling the kettle black.
3. He bit the hand that fed him.
4. There are as good fish in the sea as ever came out of it.
5. When in Rome, do as the Romans do.
6. More haste, less speed.
7. There is no smoke without fire.
8. A friend in need is a friend indeed.
9. Set a thief to catch a thief.
10. Lightning never strikes twice in the same place.
11. Don't fish in troubled waters.
12. He is pouring oil on troubled waters.
13. Don't cross the bridge until you come to it.
14. There's many a slip between cup and lip.
15. Don't count your chickens until they are hatched.
16. To jump out of the frying pan into the fire.
17. To close the stable door after the horse has gone.
18. To be caught between the devil and the deep blue sea.
19. You can't make a silk purse out of a sow's ear.
20. A leopard doesn't change its spots.

Exercise 3

Briefly explain what each of the following means and when it could be used. If possible, find a parallel saying in another language.

1. Every dog has its day.
2. Don't be a dog in a manger.
3. Give a dog a bad name.
4. The road to Hell is paved with good intentions.
5. The early bird catches the worm.
6. First come, first served.
7. You can't get blood out of a stone.
8. He who hesitates is lost.
9. Easy come, easy go.
10. You are sitting on the fence.
11. You are trying to run with the hare and hunt with the hounds.
12. Fools rush in where angels fear to tread.
13. Charity begins at home.
14. You will reap what you sow.
15. If you sow the wind, you will reap the whirlwind.
16. He is sowing his wild oats.
17. He was hoist with his own petard (i.e. caught by his own attempted trick).
18. He who pays the piper calls the tune.
19. Don't carry coal to Newcastle (a place where there is a lot of coal).
20. By hook or by crook.

Exercise 4

Briefly explain what each of the followng means and when it could be used. If possible, find a parallel saying in another language.

1. Don't try to teach your grandmother how to suck eggs.
2. Like father, like son.
3. A chip off the old block.
4. There's a skeleton in his cupboard somewhere.
5. That present is a real white elephant.
6. His success is only a flash in the pan.
7. He has taken French leave and disappeared.
8. To take a busman's holiday.

9. One man's meat is another man's poison.
10. A new broom sweeps clean.
11. Rome was not built in a day.
12. Birds of a feather flock together.
13. You can't see the wood for the trees.
14. Don't look a gift-horse in the mouth.
15. It is no good crying over spilt milk.
16. You can't have your cake *and* eat it.
17. He wants his bread buttered on both sides.
18. Familiarity breeds contempt.
19. Don't burn your candle at both ends.
20. The cobbler's children are always the worst shod.

Exercise 5

Briefly explain what the following mean and when they can be used. If possible, find a similar saying in another language.

1. Let the cobbler stick to his last. (A *last* is a wooden model used for making shoes.)
2. All is grist that comes to the mill.
3. A bad workman blames his tools.
4. Necessity is the mother of invention.
5. A stitch in time saves nine.
6. What is bred in the bone will come out in the flesh.
7. You may as well be hanged for a sheep as a lamb.
8. As you make your bed so you must lie in it.
9. Let sleeping dogs lie.
10. If the cap fits you, put it on.
11. Time and tide wait for no man.
12. Good wine needs no bush.
13. You must cut your coat according to your cloth.
14. Pride goes before a fall.
15. The least said, the soonest mended.
16. Half a loaf is better than none.
17. Don't nurse your grievance.
18. Don't spoil the ship for a halfpennyworth of tar.
19. As the twig is bent so the tree is inclined.
20. Don't play to the gallery.

Exercise 6

Briefly explain what the following mean and when they are used. If possible, find a similar saying in another language.

1. He nailed his colours to the mast.
2. You must paddle your own canoe.
3. Forewarned is forearmed.
4. If wishes were horses, beggars would ride.
5. To escape scot-free.
6. To take the wind out of somebody's sails.
7. To live in a fool's paradise.
8. To tell a white lie.
9. To be a rough diamond.
10. A wild-cat scheme.
11. To do a Quixotic act.
12. To catch a Tartar.
13. To put the clock back.
14. To attempt a Herculean task.
15. To strike while the iron is hot.
16. To keep a stiff upper lip.
17. To read between the lines.
18. To face the music.
19. To make short work of something.
20. To turn over a new leaf.

Exercise 7

Explain what the following mean and when they are used:

1. A square peg in a round hole.
2. On the horns of a dilemma.
3. Hobson's choice.
4. To mind one's P's and Q's.
5. To live from hand to mouth.
6. To lend an ear.
7. To be out of the wood.
8. To have too many irons in the fire.
9. To twist somebody round one's little finger.
10. To turn a deaf ear to.
11. To turn a blind eye to.
12. To keep abreast of your work.
13. To keep in step with the times.
14. To be called to account.
15. To clear the air.
16. To leave no stone unturned.
17. To make an ass of yourself.
18. To make a pig of yourself.

19. To be tied to somebody's apron strings.
20. To give yourself airs.

Exercise 8

Explain what the following mean and when they are used:
1. Practice makes perfect.
2. Waste not, want not.
3. Make hay while the sun shines.
4. Where there's a will, there's a way.
5. Cowards die many times before their deaths.
6. The pen is mightier than the sword.
7. A little learning is a dangerous thing.
8. Spare the rod and spoil the child.
9. Procrastination is the thief of time.
10. A miss is as good as a mile.
11. Don't let the right hand know what the left hand is doing.
12. The burnt child fears the fire.
13. Even a cat may look at a king.
14. A fool and his money are soon parted.
15. He's not the only fish in the sea.

Exercise 9

Explain what the following mean and when they are used:
1. to keep up appearances
2. to give yourself away
3. to get your back up
4. to back out of something
5. to go back on your word
6. to have your back to the wall
7. to jump at the bait
8. to bank on something happening·
9. to get more than you have bargained for
10. to make the best of a bad bargain
11. to find your bearings
12. to be at everybody's beck and call
13. to get out of bed on the wrong side
14. to have a bee in your bonnet
15. to have bats in your belfry
16. to make a bee-line for a place

17. two miles as the crow flies
18. to tighten your belt
19. to give somebody a wide berth
20. to kill two birds with one stone

Exercise 10

Explain what the following mean and when they are used:

1. to be a stumbling-block
2. to do something in cold blood
3. a blot on the landscape
4. a fly in the ointment
5. to be in the same boat
6. to have a bone to pick with somebody
7. to be in somebody's good or bad books
8. to be out of bounds
9. A lot of water has flowed under the bridge since then.
10. to be tarred with the same brush
11. to bear the brunt of an attack
12. to nip a plan in the bud
13. to take the bull by the horns
14. to hit the nail on the head
15. This player can't hold a candle to that one.
16. to have a card up your sleeve
17. to have the trump card
18. to trump somebody's ace
19. to put (or lay) all your cards on the table
20. It is quite on the cards that she may come.

Exercise 11

Explain what the following mean and when they are used:

1. to have somebody on the carpet (or to be on it)
2. to call somebody over the coals (or to be called over them)
3. to be like a cat on hot bricks
4. to turn the other cheek
5. to give somebody a blank cheque to do something
6. *a.* to be under a cloud; *b.* to be in clover
7. *a.* to be a turncoat; *b.* to be cocksure
8. to pay somebody back in his own coin
9. *a.* to be off colour; *b.* to show your true colours

10. *a.* to come a cropper; *b.* cupboard love
11. to have everything all cut and dried
12. *a.* dead right; *b.* dead on time
13. *a.* the under dog; *b.* dog tired; *c.* a dog's life
14. It is only a drop in the ocean.
15. *a.* a red letter day; *b.* a dead letter
16. to get hold of the wrong end of the stick
17. to put the cart before the horse
18. to manage to make both ends meet
19. to see eye to eye with somebody
20. Now the fat is really in the fire.

Exercise 12

Explain what the following mean and when they are used:

1. to pass the buck
2. to have a feather in your cap
3. to feather your own nest
4. to get cold feet
5. to have a finger in too many pies
6. *a.* to play second fiddle; *b.* to be light-fingered
7. *a.* to be hand in glove with; *b.* to fall foul of
8. to have the ball at your feet
9. to have the ball in your court
10. to put your foot in something
11. Two can play at that game.
12. The game is not worth the candle (*or* risk).
13. to run the gauntlet
14. an iron hand (*or* fist) in a velvet glove
15. to go against the grain
16. to get the upper hand
17. to keep harping on the same string
18. to talk through your hat
19. to bury the hatchet
20. to have a swelled (*or* swollen) head

Exercise 13

Explain what these mean and when they are used:

1. He can't make head or tail of it.
2. *a.* down-hearted; *b.* half-hearted; *c* whole-hearted

3. to skate on thin ice
4. to take the law into your own hands
5. He hasn't got a leg to stand on.
6. to stand on your own two feet
7. *a.* on the mark; *b.* off the mark; *c.* wide of the mark
8. *a.* not to mince matters; *b.* to be on your mettle
9. That sort of thing happens once in a blue moon.
10. to put words into somebody's mouth
11. to take the words out of somebody's mouth
12. to be out of sorts
13. to look for a needle in a haystack
14. to keep an open mind on a subject
15. to take pains to do something
16. to grease somebody's palms
17. a hard nut to crack
18. to rob Peter to pay Paul
19. He bought a pig in a poke.
20. to put your shoulder to the wheel

Exercise 14

Explain what these mean and when they are used:

1. *a.* to put up with something; *b.* to put a game off
2. to smell a rat (in some plan)
3. to catch somebody red-handed
4. to be on the rocks
5. to give somebody a run for his money
6. to give somebody the cold shoulder
7. to be at sixes and sevens
8. *a.* to be thick-skinned; *b.* to be thin-skinned
9. to call a spade a spade
10. to use a sprat to catch a mackerel
11. to pull up the ladder
12. to turn the tables on somebody
13. to get your teeth into something
14. to be at the end of your tether
15. to be under somebody's thumb
16. *a.* to toe the line; *b.* to hold your tongue
17. to have your back to the wall
18. to sail near the wind
19. to pull the wool over somebody's eyes
20. to clutch at a straw

Exercise 15

Explain what the following mean and when they can be used:

1. His bark is worse than his bite.
2. You can't make bricks without straw.
3. Necessity knows no law.
4. He is laughing up his sleeve.
5. Butter wouldn't melt in his mouth.
6. Don't put all your eggs in one basket.
7. Don't let the grass grow under your feet.
8. Don't wash your dirty linen in public.
9. He had to pocket his pride.
10. You ought to use more elbow-grease.

Exercise 16

Explain what the following are or what they mean when they are used in a figurative sense. Say when they might be used.

1. an open secret	11. the sheet-anchor
2. a red herring	12. a mare's nest
3. a bad egg	13. a hornets' nest
4. a nest-egg	14. double Dutch
5. a bad penny	15. at loggerheads
6. soft soap	16. a red rag to a bull
7. a close shave	17. a makeshift
8. a slowcoach	18. a rough and ready method
9. a deadlock	19. a mouthpiece
10. a dressing-down	20. eyewash

Explanations

Here are brief explanations of the proverbs and idiomatic sayings in this chapter. To save space, the explanations are as brief as possible and alternative answers are not given.

Exercise 1

1. Once you have been hurt, you avoid the same source of danger.
2. If you don't take a risk, you won't make a profit.
3. Wise men come to the same (obvious) conclusion.
4. Foolish men come to the same (obvious) conclusion.
5. When you are separated from somebody you grow more fond of him.

6. When you are separated from somebody you soon forget him.
7. There is something good for you in every trouble or problem.
8. Troubles never come one at a time; if one comes, many come.
9. Look ahead before you take any (drastic) action.
10. Something which you have already got is better than a bigger possible advantage which is not yet within your grasp.
11. You may not get this chance again.
12. People who are in a vulnerable position should not attack or criticize others lest they be hurt themselves.
13. Don't anticipate trouble; wait until it comes.
14. He has made it impossible for himself to retreat or change his mind.
15. Too many people on one job will get in each other's way and spoil the job in some way.
16. The more people there are, the easier the job will be.
17. You can't tell what a quiet person may do or be thinking about. Sometimes they may surprise you.
18. Somebody may hear even when you think you are speaking in secret.
19. If you start on a dangerous job you may be unable to stop.
20. He was greedy and tried to get something for himself once too often. This time he was caught.

Exercise 2

1. Uninformed or foolish persons talk too much or make the most fuss.
2. A guilty person is accusing another one of a similar sin.
3. He attacked (or was ungrateful to) somebody who helped him.
4. There are plenty of other similar opportunities.
5. When in a strange place, act as the local people do.
6. If you go too quickly you won't achieve much because you will make a mess of things in some way.
7. Rumours and other signs of trouble usually have a basis in fact.
8. A friend who helps you when you really need help is a true friend.
9. If you want to catch a thief, send another one to trap him.
10. You never get exactly the same sort of trouble twice.
11. Don't try to make a personal profit out of other people's troubles.
12. He is trying to calm down a troubled situation.
13. Don't anticipate the event; wait until it happens.
14. Nothing is certain until it is achieved.
15. Don't assume that you have got an advantage or some gain until it has actually come to pass.
16. To go from one difficulty to another.
17. To take precautions (against theft or anything else) too late.
18. To be faced with two equally unpleasant alternatives.
19. You can't make something good out of bad material.
20. An unpleasant character never reforms.

Exercise 3

1. Everybody has a chance of being on top eventually.
2. Don't be selfish by preventing others from using something which you don't need yourself.
3. To give somebody a bad reputation (whether deserved or not), or to assume that a man is always bad merely because he has made one mistake.
4. It's no good merely having good intentions; you must carry them out as well.
5. The person who arrives first or sees an opportunity first gains an advantage.
6. The person who gets there first is served first or has the first chance.
7. You can't get something out of a person (especially a good quality) if he doesn't possess it in the first place.
8. If you don't take your chance when it comes you may never have a similar opportunity again.
9. Money which is earned easily is soon spent.
10. You are trying to avoid making a decision.
11. You are trying to join both sides.
12. Foolish people rush to do what wise people keep away from.
13. You should start your kind deeds and charity in your own house.
14. What you get in the future will depend on what you do now or how you behave.
15. If you act foolishly you will face unpleasant consequences.
16. He is enjoying himself but making the mistakes and doing the wrong things which one expects of a young man.
17. He was caught by his own trick.
18. The person who finances a project has the right to say how it will be carried out.
19. Don't take something to a place where there is already enough.
20. By any method—legal or illegal.

Exercise 4

1. Don't try to teach a very experienced person how to do something.
2. The son is like his father.
3. The child is like its parent(s).
4. He is concealing some unpleasant fact about his past.
5. That present is an awkward one: I have to keep it but it is of no value or use to me.
6. His success is an unusual and isolated event. He is not always as successful as that.
7. He is absent without permission.
8. To spend your time on holiday doing the same sort of thing as you normally do at work.

9. One man may violently dislike what another person likes.
10. A person who is new to a job always works enthusiastically at first.
11. You cannot accomplish a big or difficult task quickly.
12. People with similar tastes or interests associate with each other.
13. There are so many similar things or problems that I can't find the important one with which I want to deal.
    OR
    There are so many similar things or problems that I can't make a reliable judgement of the matter as a whole.
14. Don't query the motives of a person who gives you a present.
15. Once you have made a mistake it is useless to waste time by bemoaning your error.
16. You can eat a cake or keep it but you can't do both things. Similarly, in many cases you can't expect to have two advantages: one from taking action and one from not taking action.
17. He wants a greater advantage than he is entitled to.
18. When you know somebody too well you may become contemptuous of them. Similarly, if you do something too often you may become careless of the dangers involved.
19. Don't try to gain a double advantage.
20. The children of a specialist are always those who receive the least benefit from his knowledge or craft. (In this case charity does not begin at home.)

Exercise 5

1. Let each specialist keep to his own trade or business.
2. I can make use of anything: it doesn't matter what comes along.
3. A bad workman blames his tools instead of himself.
4. Things are invented when the need is great enough.
5. An action taken at the right time (especially to repair something) will save more drastic action later on.
6. Children will inherit the qualities of their parents.
7. You are going to be punished (severely) for a small sin anyway so you may as well commit a worse one.
8. You must put up with the situation you have created.
9. Don't rouse somebody who could harm you but who is not aware of you at the moment or not bothering with you.
10. If you think the description or accusation applies to you, you are welcome to think so.
11. The opportunity is there. You will lose your chance if you delay and don't take any action.
12. Something which is good does not need to be advertised.
13. You must live or act according to your income or circumstances.
14. If you continue to be proud you may bring down some misfortune on your head.

15. The less you say, the less there will be to apologize for or to deal with.
16. A small advantage is better than none.
17. Don't brood over your troubles.
18. Don't spoil a good plan because you are too mean to spend a little extra money on it or make a small extra effort.
19. The child shows the characteristics of its parents.
20. Don't curry favour with the section of the audience (*or* with people) who are easily impressed.

Exercise 6

1. He made his intentions clear, despite the risk involved.
2. You must do it yourself without help from others.
3. If you know what is coming you can prepare for it.
4. If you could accomplish a thing merely by wishing it, beggars would ride on horses.
5. To escape completely and without injury.
6. To prevent somebody from doing something (impressive).
7. To think you are much better off than you really are and to ignore the sober facts of life.
8. To tell a lie for a good cause.
9. A person who is rather rough in some ways but essentially a fine person as far as personal characteristics go.
10. A speculative scheme which is rather far-fetched.
11. To act in such a way as to uphold the honour or interests of another person without regard for your own interests. It *nearly* means 'foolishly unselfish'.
12. To catch somebody who proves unexpectedly difficult to deal with.
13. To take a retrograde step.
14. To attempt an almost impossible task.
15. To seize an opportunity at the best possible moment.
16. To put up with difficulties without complaining.
17. To look into circumstances and find a hidden meaning. To draw a deduction from the apparent facts.
18. To face up to (unpleasant) consequences.
19. To do something quickly.
20. To reform.

Exercise 7

1. Somebody in a job or position which does not suit him.
2. Faced with two unpleasant alternatives.
3. No real choice at all; forced to do something.
4. To be very careful.
5. To exist under difficult conditions, e.g. those of poverty.
6. To listen.

7. To escape from difficulties.
8. To be involved in too many projects.
9. To gain power over somebody and to make them do what you want.
10. To ignore.
11. To pretend not to see.
12. To keep up with your work.
13. To keep in touch with modern developments and changes.
14. To be required to explain your conduct.
15. To explain.
16. To make the maximum effort in an enquiry.
17. To act foolishly (in front of other people).
18. To be greedy.
19. To be unduly reliant on, or influenced by, another person.
20. To behave in a conceited manner.

Exercise 8

1. The more you practice, the better you will become.
2. If you don't waste your resources, you will not be in need.
3. Make the most of your chance while it is there.
4. If you want to do a thing sufficiently, you will eventually find a way of doing it.
5. The thought of death frightens a coward so that he imagines himself to be faced with death many times before it comes.
6. The influence of the intellect (as represented by the written word) is greater than that of physical force (as represented by the sword).
7. Insufficient knowledge can cause harm.
8. The absence of discipline will spoil a child's character.
9. Putting off things continually will lead to a waste of time and opportunity.
10. As far as success is concerned, the failure by a slight margin to achieve something is just as serious as failing by a very wide margin.
11. Keep something a secret.
12. We avoid a source of danger which has hurt us once before.
13. Even a lowly person may have ambitions.
14. A foolish person gets rid of his money rashly.
15. He is not the only suitable person who is available.

Exercise 9

1. to make it look as if you are richer or better off than you are
2. to betray your thoughts
3. to become annoyed
4. to withdraw
5. to break a promise
6. to be cornered or in difficulties
7. to be quick to be attracted by something intended to deceive

8. to rely on something happening
9. to meet more opposition (etc.) than you had expected
10. to adjust yourself as well as you can to an unpleasant situation
11. to settle down or find out what you want to do
12. to be available to do what anybody wants you to do
13. to get up in the morning in a bad temper
14. to have an unreasonable conviction or desire in your mind
15. to be mad (or abnormal)
16. to go straight to a place
17. two miles in a straight line
18. to make economies in your expenditure
19. to avoid somebody; to keep well out of his way
20. to accomplish two things with one action

Exercise 10

1. to be an obstacle
2. to act without the heat of passion
3. an obstacle or an eyesore
4. an obstacle or hindrance
5. to be in the same predicament or situation
6. to have something about which to quarrel with somebody
7. to be in or out of favour
8. to be in a forbidden place
9. Things have changed a lot since then.
10. to have the same faults
11. to endure the main attack by being the principal target
12. to frustrate a plan before it can be started
13. to face up to a threat or to deal openly with some danger
14. to get to the root of something by disclosing the cause of some trouble or by disclosing exactly what is the centre of the matter
15. This one is not nearly as good as that one.
16. to have some device or trick ready to be used
17. to have the ability to take the decisive action which will bring victory
18. to defeat a move which another person had supposed would bring him victory
19. to disclose exactly what your intentions are and what resources etc. you have
20. It is quite possible that she may come.

Exercise 11

1. to scold somebody or summon them to be scolded (or to be scolded yourself)
2. to reprove somebody (or to be reproved)
3. to be extremely apprehensive, nervous or uncomfortable

4. in a dispute, to refuse to defend yourself and to invite further attack
5. to allow him to act as he wishes
6. *a.* to be under suspicion; *b.* to be in an extremely favourable position
7. *a.* to change your mind and join the opposition; *b.* to be (too) confident of your position
8. to obtain revenge by doing what somebody has done to you
9. *a.* to feel ill or below one's normal standard
   b. to show your real nature
10. *a.* to suffer misfortune; *b.* love or affection for the purpose of gain
11. to have everything prepared
12. *a.* quite right; *b.* exactly on time
13. *a.* the inferior; *b.* very tired; *c.* a poor sort of life
14. It is only an insignificant amount.
15. *a.* a very special day of some significance
    b. something, often a rule or law, no longer observed
16. to interpret a position wrongly and to misunderstand the facts
17. to have things in their wrong order
18. to manage to survive financially
19. to agree
20. Now we are really in trouble.

Exercise 12

1. to pass the responsibility to somebody else
2. to have done something worthy of honour
3. to look after your own interests (selfishly)
4. to be afraid
5. to be involved in too many undertakings
6. *a.* to have an inferior role; *b.* to be inclined towards theft
7. *a.* to be working (surreptitiously) with somebody
   b. to get into trouble with
8 and 9. to be in the position of having to make the next move
10. to do something wrong
11. Two can do that sort of thing.
12. It is not worth taking the risk.
13. to have to face successive risks or dangers
14. a hardness concealed by a gentle exterior
15. to be against a person's inclinations
16. to gain control
17. to keep talking about the same thing or making the same complaint
18. to talk nonsense
19. to make peace
20. to be conceited

Exercise 13

1. He can't understand it.

2. *a.* depressed; *b.* not enthusiastic; *c.* keen
3. to do something which may easily cause you trouble
4. to act in accordance with your own opinions and not in accordance with the law
5. He has no excuse, reason or justification.
6. to be independent of others and manage your own affairs
7. *a.* accurate or relevant; *b.* and *c.* inaccurate or irrelevant
8. *a.* to speak bluntly or frankly; *b.* to be alert and prepared
9. It happens extremely rarely, if at all.
10. to accuse somebody of having said something which they did not say
11. to say something which another person was about to say
12. to feel unwell
13. to look for something which it is almost impossible to find
14. to be unprejudiced
15. to be very careful about doing something and to try hard
16. to bribe
17. a person difficult to deal with or a problem which is hard to solve
18. to take from one deserving person to give to another
19. He did something without foreseeing the consequences *or* he bought something without first having examined it and then found out that it was no good.
20. to make an effort

Exercise 14

1. *a.* to tolerate it; *b.* to postpone it
2. to suspect evil
3. to catch somebody in the middle of doing something wrong
4. to be destitute or in great difficulty
5. to make somebody work hard to catch you *or* generally to extend a person in some way
6. to snub or ignore a person
7. to be confused or muddled
8. *a.* insensitive; *b.* unduly sensitive
9. to speak bluntly
10. to use some small bait to catch a more substantial victim
11. to cut off help from a person
12. to reverse the position so that you are on top
13. to attack something in a determined way
14. to be at the end of your resources
15. to be under somebody's control
16. *a.* to do as you are ordered; *b.* to be silent
17. to be cornered or in a difficult position
18. to act in a way which is nearly illegal or in which you risk being caught
19. to deceive
20. to seize any slender chance of getting out of difficulties

Proverbs and Idiomatic Sayings

Exercise 15

1. He threatens but is not very likely to take action.
2. You can't do it unless you have the necessary materials.
3. If the need is sufficiently great, the law is disregarded.
4. He is laughing at us without letting us see that he is doing so.
5. He is very innocent and naïve. (Often used in a derogatory way.)
6. Don't rely too much on one thing. Don't put all your resources into one undertaking.
7. Be active; don't be idle.
8. Don't let the public know about your private troubles.
9. He had to forget about his pride.
10. You ought to try harder. (elbow-grease = effort)

Exercise 16

1. a supposed secret about which everybody knows
2. a device to throw you off the track of something by leading you astray
3. something useless or bad
4. anything saved up
5. a useless person or a bad one
6. flattery
7. a narrow escape
8. somebody who works or moves slowly
9. an impasse or a position in which two sides have failed to agree and further progress appears impossible
10 a scolding
11. the thing or person on whom we rely
12. something which at first appears to be interesting, quite a discovery or the cause of controversy but which eventually turns out to be of no interest at all
13. something which, if stirred up, can bring trouble
14. incomprehensible
15. in dispute with
16. that which arouses and antagonizes
17. a substitute of an inferior nature
18. a method thought of quite quickly or capable of being applied quickly and one which will suffice although it is not perfect
19. somebody under the control of another person so that he says what he is told to say
20. pretence meant to deceive (particularly a false story)

Chapter 12

Punctuation

*learn to diagnose their own par-
ticular weaknesses*

It is assumed that the student already has a working knowledge of punctuation. The aim of this chapter, therefore, is not to provide a catalogue of all the uses of all punctuation marks. Instead, it is to give students an opportunity for practice (and correction) and to enable them to become familiar with the types of questions which can be set in examinations. It is hoped that individual students will learn to diagnose their own parti-cular weaknesses and to overcome them. However, a few general observations are called for:

i. Textbooks and dictionaries do not always agree on the use of a particular punctuation mark and this is very obvious in their treatment of the hyphen.[1] In other cases, the disagreement

---

[1] It is probably more correct to regard the hyphen and the apostrophe as matters of spelling but it is convenient to discuss them in a chapter on punctuation.

is understandable because, for example, the use or omission of a comma may be merely a matter of opinion. In punctuating a passage, therefore, we must often be prepared to choose between correct alternative solutions.

ii. The standard of punctuation in some novels, newspaper reports and magazine articles is surprisingly poor. Some writers have little idea about when to start a new sentence. You should thus be wary of regarding any particular writer or book as a model to follow.

iii. In general (but NOT in all cases) students tend to use too many punctuation marks in their essays—particularly after they have had a lesson on punctuation. It is better to use too few commas than too many.

iv. The greatest weaknesses in School Certificate and G.C.E. scripts are:

> *a.* A failure to put in a full stop and to start a new sentence when required.
>
> *b.* The insertion of a full stop in the wrong place so that it separates a main statement and a dependent one and leaves the latter standing nervously by itself.

1. The full stop

We use a full stop (also called a *period*):

i. To mark the end of a sentence.

ii. At the end of a statement which makes complete sense by itself, e.g. *Yes.*

iii. After abbreviations.

Some people think that it is not necessary to put a full stop after an abbreviation if the first and last letters of the abbreviation are the same as those of the full word, e.g. Mr, Sgt, Messrs and Mrs as compared with Mr., Sgt., Messrs. and Mrs. You can put a full stop after abbreviations like these or leave it out.

Exercise 1

Correct the punctuation in these two sentences which illustrate the common errors mentioned at (iv) above:

1. There were several pictures hanging on the wall, one of them was mine.

2. It is difficult to provide free education for everybody up to university level. Because of the expense involved.

Exercise 2

Insert one full stop and one capital letter in each case:

1. There is another problem which we must consider it is the question of suitability.
2. This type of car is very popular as a taxi there are many reasons for this.
3. My brother pointed out that it has several advantages for example it is very economical to run.
4. There is plenty of room in the boot the spare tyre is in a separate compartment under the boot.
5. The car may not suit everybody it is really a family car.
6. Those people are probably descended from a race who lived in the mountains many centuries ago their ancestors probably arrived in this district in recent times.
7. They are extremely skilful farmers we can learn a great deal from them, if we can persuade them to co-operate with us.
8. Through the centuries they have improved many of their techniques one very useful device is that used for irrigation.

Exercise 3

Make one correction to the punctuation of each of the following passages, which are taken from published books and are wrongly punctuated:

1. In modern times the Chinese are to be found mainly in the towns where they excel in the world of business and commerce, they provide most of the professional classes and contractors.
2. Many Indians work on the great rubber estates but they are known primarily as tradesmen and shopkeepers, like the Chinese the majority of Indians entered Malaysia as indentured labourers during the nineteenth and early twentieth centuries. (Two corrections are possible but one will suffice.)
3. As one of the world's five greatest ports Singapore derives much of its wealth from its entrepôt trade, it is also being developed into an industrial city with modern industries providing employment opportunities for its growing popula-ation.
4. Our ship lay at anchor off Freetown for several hours, the sea was like a sheet of glass and a haze hung over the water.
5. After a great deal of haggling we finally agreed on a price,

it was a little more than I had expected to pay but it was not unreasonable.

2. The use of capital letters

i. As you already know, we must use a capital letter at the start of a sentence and with proper nouns, e.g. Mary, Lagos Jamaica, Monday, July etc. We also use capital letters for titles and ranks, e.g. Sir Winston Churchill, Captain Lee, and for the major words in the titles of books, films etc.

ii. In the past there was some confusion concerning the use of capital letters. Some writers used a capital letter every time they wished to emphasize a word or when they thought the word was important. You can see something of this in the works of Charles Dickens and occasionally in modern books. However, such usages are now disappearing and should not be imitated. Be careful not to use capital letters for such words as *education, gold, transport, patriotism* and *war* when they are used in essays.

iii. There is a tendency to use capital letters for such places as Post Office, Police Station, Railway Station etc. when you are referring to one particular place but to use small letters when you are not referring to one special place. However, some writers almost always give them small letters so both usages must be accepted.

iv. When a rank is not followed by a name we use small letters. Compare the following:

a. I asked Sgt. Lee where the other men were.

b. I noticed two police sergeants talking by the car.

Exercise 4

Write out the following titles of books, films etc., putting in capital letters when necessary:

1. the old man and the sea
2. fair stood the wind for france
3. mirror of the sea
4. a high wind in jamaica
5. where angels fear to tread
6. brother to the ox
7. a joker for your buttonhole
8. the men on the dolman islands

9. the daughter of the sun
10. the man who came to dinner

Exercise 5

Find the ten words which would normally start with a capital letter when used in a sentence in an essay: april, vital, foreign, imports, murder, detective, road, climate, temperature, television, dictionary, city, lagos, captain, friday, ice, refrigerator, postman, david, river, september, africa, school, university, chinese, french, hedge, historical, biological, medicine, doctor, scientist, palace, jupiter, july.

Exercise 6

Find the ten words which would normally start with a capital letter when used in a sentence in an essay: kitchen, feast, civilization, politics, oil, citizens, freedom, unity, football, nigerian, museum, saturday, tuesday, concert, club, hospital, rent, garage, polygamy, literature, language, ambition, infinitive, english, australia, italian, composition, chapters, ghana, benefit, trinidad, music, domestic, industry, agriculture, ethiopia, boundary, border, gold, electricity, coal, tin, examination, candidate, mauritius, stream, island.

Exercise 7

Insert capital letters where necessary. Deal with the italicized book titles by using inverted commas to enclose your ordinary handwriting:

1. Write a geographical account of the nile basin OR of the congo basin. Describe the effect of the canary current on the sahara desert.
2. Study this extract from the ordnance survey map of england and wales.
3. Question 1 was popular, but little was known about the levant company, nova scotia, the south sea bubble or admiral rodney. The royal africa company was confused with the royal niger company.
4. This book has been approved by the igbo literature advisory sub-committee for use in schools.
5. They are going to play mozart's symphony in d major at the concert next tuesday evening.

6. We arrived at kai tak airport on thursday morning and went to the miramar hotel in kowloon where I changed some australian pounds into hong kong dollars.
7. Give the substance of st. paul's speech in the synagogue at antioch of pisidia and explain why he left the city.
8. Answer questions on dickens's *great expectations* or on shaw's *arms and the man.*
9. The visit to his highness lasted about an hour. The oba's wife is an attractive lady who accompanied her husband on a trip to rome, milan, zurich, paris and london last year.
10. After buying a few provisions at the stall of a yoruba trader we proceeded northwards along dahomey's fine main road towards the town of tashi. On the michelin road map of west africa, from which we were planning our route, this town bears the name of malanville.
11. I have just read an article called 'meta village chiefdoms of the bome valley in the bamenda prefecture of west cameroon' by e.m. chilver. It appeared in the january issue of *the nigerian field.*
12. The income tax act no. 4 of 1963 brought in a system of p.a.y.e. Under this act husband and wife are assessed separately.

3. The comma

The comma is NOT a substitute for a full stop and should NOT be used in place of one. Glance back at Exercise 3 and notice the type of error shown there. It is common in the work of some candidates (and a few professional writers) and must be avoided. In general terms, a full stop separates expressions which make complete sense by themselves whereas a comma marks a shorter pause and is used with ideas which are dependent on each other and cannot be separated by a full stop.

Exercise 8

In each case insert a comma OR a full stop and a capital letter (whichever is correct).

1. There is something wrong with the door it won't shut properly.
2. I left the windows of the car open not thinking that anybody would steal anything from it.

3. I discussed several problems with him one being that of the layout of the kitchen.

4. From a tremendous range of dishes here are a few samples picked because they have proved to be popular with travellers for many years.

5. Winter is dry, sunny and clear typhoons pay an occasional visit between July and October.

6. There is some high forest mostly in the south-east.

7. Nigeria's climate has an undeservedly bad reputation mainly due to the lack of adequate medical facilities and other amenities in the past.

8. The university site at Ife consists of about 16,000 acres it is planned to start building operations as soon as possible.

9. There is a profusion of cloth imported from all parts of the world the range of furnishing fabrics is rather limited but there is a wide selection of dress materials.

10. I discussed several problems with her one of them was that of the layout of the lounge.

The following examples illustrate most of the uses of the comma. In each case try to explain why a comma is used. Discuss each case and try to evolve the best possible explanation.

a. The captain of the team, Peter Lee, was injured in the second half, leaving only ten fit players on the field.

b. Having agreed to accompany him, I felt that I could not withdraw at the last moment.

c. 'Your car,' he informed us, 'is obstructing the road.'

d. 'Are you ready, John?' I asked.

e. We saw sampans, tugs, destroyers and ferries in the harbour.

f. If he arrives in time, he can certainly go with us.

g. The inspector interrogated the prisoner, and John took down his statement.

h. His confession, as a matter of fact, came as quite a surprise.

i. Take this one to Mary, John, and ask her what she thinks of it.

j. These are ours; those over there, yours.

k. I will inquire into, and deal with, both of those matters.

l. I gave him a pen, which he promptly lost.

Exercise 9

Insert the number of commas shown in brackets.

a. (2) This the man explained was a great relief to him.

235

b. (2) He works in London an unhealthy and dirty city and lives in the countryside.

c. *(3) 'If you would prefer not to tell us about it well that's your affair and we won't interfere.'

d. (2) 'It's a bit awkward you see' he admitted at last.

e. *(4) The sound on the television set ceased abruptly. Almost immediately there was a brief vivid flash on the screen and it too stopped working.

f. (2) In April 1932 off the coast of Colombia a cable was brought to the surface for repair.

g. (3) Literacy was once regarded as the preserve of a small often despised minority of clerks teachers and officials.

*Note:** In *c* and *e* it is possible to use fewer commas than the number shown in brackets.

Problems with commas

Because punctuation is a matter of usage and not a question of following unchanging rules, there are several problems connected with the use of the comma:

i. Some writers use a comma between two adjectives but others do not, so that both of these forms must be accepted as correct:

> *small red dots* or *small, red dots*

When the first adjecive refers to the second one (rather than to the noun), no comma is used, e.g. *a dark red dress.* A comma can be put in when it is felt that the two adjectives are not closely related, e.g. *a huge, black-maned beast.*

ii. When three or more adjectives or nouns are used, two methods of punctuation are possible:

> *clerks, teachers, and officials* (two commas)
> or
> *clerks, teachers and officials* (one comma)

You can please yourself which method you follow; both are acceptable.

iii. The use of a comma with *and* and *but* depends on the sense of the particular sentence. If there is any danger that the meaning may be confused by the omission of a comma, put one in. If the first statement is long, there is a tendency to use a comma to denote a pause:

> *The greatest depth at which the giant squid lives is not*

definitely known, but there is one piece of evidence about the depth to which whales descend.

iv. A comma must be used in front of *or* when the statement after *or* is an explanation and not an alternative. Compare these sentences:

   a. explanation: The cable was raised from a depth of 540 fathoms, or 3,240 feet.

   b. alternative: He was told to buy some sugar or some saccharin.

v. Do not be guided too much by one particular writer or book. These two examples are taken from passages in examination papers in the same year. (The passages were set for summary or for comprehension.)

   a. that immense, square-headed, formidably toothed whale

   b. He made the air vibrate with a deep short throaty roar.

It is only fair to add that (*b*) is most unusual and not a model to be followed.

4. The colon and the dash

i. the colon

The colon can be used to introduce a list of items or examples but only when the statement before it is complete in itself. Compare these sentences:

a. In the bag there are some bananas, a pineapple, a lettuce and a cucumber.

b. In the bag you will find these things: some bananas, a pineapple, a lettuce and a cucumber.

Why is a colon *not* used in *a*? Remember these two sentences and the guidance given above them.

When the list is set out in a tabulated form or starts on the next line, a dash is sometimes put after the colon but this is not essential.

When a colon introduces a list, it often happens that the items in the list are an explanation of a word earlier in the sentence, as in this example:

c. People must learn the basic *skills* of responsible citizenship: the ability to read notices, newspapers, timetables, letters, price-lists; to keep simple records, to sort out the significance of the information gathered—and to fill in forms.

A colon is often used after such expressions as *What really happened was this* and *What I suggest is this*, e.g.

d. What really occurred was this: the horse responded to movements made by the questioner.

We can also use a colon to introduce a cause or explanation which is closely linked to the preceding statement:

e. I knew I could not escape: the men were watching me too closely.

A colon can be used to introduce a quotation in this way:

f. Pope shows his wit and mastery of language in this type of line: 'To err is human; to forgive, divine.'

Note: Some writers also use a colon in place of a comma to introduce direct speech.

ii. **the dash**

A single dash marks a break in the flow of a sentence. A full stop marks the end of an idea but a dash shows an interruption in the expression of an idea. See the example at *c* above. Here are two further examples:

a. Something was moving slowly and cautiously along the gutter —a snake.

b. In 'natural' forestry experience, skill, judgement and sustained attention are needed—some say more skill than in 'industrial' forestry.

Warning: Do not use a dash together with a comma.

We can also use a single dash in these ways:

c. To repeat, emphasize or explain an idea:

He stared at the face—a face which he would never forget.

In this type of sentence be particularly careful not to punctuate the two statements as separate sentences. This type of error is quite common:

wrong: I saw an unusual sight when I was in Lagos. A sight which impressed me a great deal.

right: I saw an unusual sight when I was in Lagos—a sight which impressed me a great deal.

d. In place of a colon before a list of things which explain or give examples of a previous word:

He abandoned them all—his family, his relatives, his friends and the traditions of a lifetime.

e. To indicate hesitation in dialogue:

    'Well,' he said, 'I—I—can't tell you any more.'

f. To show that something has been left out or that a statement is incomplete:

    'I didn't know Mr. B—— lived at—' he started to say.

Two dashes can be used in place of parentheses or brackets: Some seven million people—about half the world's adult population—are unable to read or write.

5. The semi-colon

The semi-colon is used instead of a full stop when the writer feels that the two statements are so closely related that the break marked by a full stop would be too long. In this usage the semi-colon could be replaced by a full stop without altering the sense of the passage.

  i. The sperm whale has taken these deep waters for his hunting grounds; his quarry is the deep-water population of squids which live at depths of 1,500 feet or more.

  ii. I was reluctant to leave; Mary was still staring at me as if she was expecting me to explain about the robbery.

    Notice that when the semi-colon is used in this way the statements before and after it make complete sense by themselves.

The semi-colon can also be used in lists when it is felt that a comma might cause confusion. This would be the case if one of the items in the list already included a comma:

    'Give the meaning of the following: diligently; grotesque; signed, sealed and delivered; disintegrate into sections; ill-defined.'

Exercise 10

Punctuate the following statements correctly by putting in a semi-colon in each case.

  1. Seen in this light, other expeditions did not fail they made progress.

  2. If the omens were good, the men would raid a village and plunder it if not they would wait.

  3. At one time only the rich could afford variety in their food

now modern methods of transport and packing bring fruit and imported food within the reach of many.

4. Spell-bound, we lay there for hours we wanted to leave, but something mesmeric impelled us to remain.

5. Within the crater a raging whirlwind was continuous even where we lay the ground shivered incessantly.

6. The burning gases shoot up with immense velocity for thousands of feet a corresponding amount of air is sucked down from a great height.

7. Slowly men ceased to live in a haphazard, unplanned way they settled down, and grew together, establishing communities.

8. What struck me most forcibly in the scene was the absence of life not a single living thing—not a fly, not an insect between the stones—moved in all this vista.

Exercise 11

The following passages are shown with their original punctuation. In each case say whether alternative methods of punctuation are possible and, if so, what you would suggest.

1. The national parks of Africa are an important economic asset for they attract tourists (our tiresome word for modern pilgrims and travellers).

2. The beginning followed an invariable routine; they would lead and we would follow.

3. Jali was trembling, but beneath his agitation there was a deep, troubled wonder.

4. Even houses that have few books or none at all beside 'the Scriptures' possess at least one dictionary; most business offices have dictionaries, and most typists keep a copy on their desks; at one time or another most girls and boys are required by their teachers to obtain and use a dictionary.

5. He picked his way to the seaward edge of the platform and stood looking down into the water. It was clear to the bottom and bright with the efflorescence of tropical weed and coral.

6. In Europe the number of illiterates is about twenty-four millions, most of them in Southern Europe, with Spain, Italy, Portugal, and Jugoslavia heading the list (the United Kingdom has about seven hundred thousand).

7. There is no doubt that adults—even very old ones—can learn if they want to, and if they are imaginatively taught.

8. Ker stopped the car at once. 'Now watch,' he said; 'he's hunting.'

6. Inverted commas or quotation marks

We use inverted commas for direct speech, and quotation marks for quotations. They are the same in appearance and both are sometimes called 'speech marks'.

i. Notice that at the end of a speech the other punctuation marks usually come inside the quotation marks and not under them or outside them:

'When you are ready,' he said, 'we can both start.'

ii. This is not necessarily the case when a quotation is used at the end of a sentence:

His conduct reminded me of the saying: 'Don't do as I do; do as I say'.

Note: Influenced by the punctuation of direct speech, as in (i), some people would prefer to put the full stop inside the quotation marks at the end of the quotation; it does not matter which method is used.

iii. Inverted commas are also used for titles when writing by hand. Here are three methods in common use:

handwriting: It is called "Who killed Jordan?"
in a writer's manuscript: It is called Who killed Jordan?
(In this case the underlining is a way of telling the printer to use italics.)
in a book: It is called *Who killed Jordan?*

iv. Inverted commas are used when we wish to single out a word or expression, especially if it is a foreign word or one used in a way different from its normal usage:

a. Rabbits are a curse in "natural" forestry.
b. They play the ancient African game of "bau".
c. Many years ago gamblers used to organize "farms" or centres to which people flocked as soon as their work was done.

v. We sometimes have speech or a quotation occurring within direct speech. This involves the use of double *and* single inverted commas. In writing we tend to use double inverted commas for the original speech, and single ones for any quotation or second speech:

He said, "I heard John say, 'I won't go'."

Punctuation

In most novels the use of inverted commas is similar to this:

He said, 'I heard John say, "I won't go".'

You can use either method in your work but keep to the same system right through one piece of work.

Exercise 12

Punctuate the following passages correctly, putting in capital letters and new paragraphs when necessary:

1. do you want to go to the cinema tonight john i asked my brother er im not sure he replied then he thought for a moment and added yes i think itll make a change
2. mary what was the title of that book you were reading last night asked david mary looked up the kraken wakes she said you mean the one about those things in the sea dont you yes replied david thats the one where is it now
3. how long do you think itll take to repair the car i asked the mechanic cant say he replied a little mournfully dont know whats wrong with it yet i lifted the bonnet and we peered hopefully into the greasy depths well i asked him broken fan belt he said half an hour at the most if weve got one in stock
4. youre wrong david mary said to me remember that youre in a difficult position she added yes i know i told her what you really mean is people in glass houses shouldnt throw gravel about thats right she said with a smile
5. morning the stranger said good morning i replied curious to know what he wanted your father in he asked jerking his head towards the house why do you want to know i asked he frowned and stared at me suspiciously

7. The question mark

The question mark is used after a *direct* question:

He asked me, 'What's your name?'

Be careful not to put question mark after an indirect question:

He asked me what my name was.

In punctuating dialogue, you must expect to find some direct questions in a rather unusual form:

i. 'Tired?' he asked me after a little while.
ii. 'Anybody there?' she said.

iii. 'Found anything?' he asked.
iv. 'Pass me that book, please,' I said to Mary.
'The one with the red cover?' she asked.
'Yes, please,' I said.

Exercise 13

In the following exercise, direct and indirect questions are mixed together. Find the direct questions which should finish with a question mark. Put in the question marks.

1. Is it time to go.
2. He asked whether it was time to go.
3. Ask them to tell you how to do it.
4. I wanted to know where they had gone.
5. Do you think they will both come, John.
6. I wonder what she will say to that.
7. Pass the sugar, please.
8. I am trying to find out where she bought that dress.
9. I'm not sure who did it.
10. May we go now.
11. When shall we tell them about the accident.
12. Are you sure that this is the right way to open it.
13. We must try to find out how we can help them.
14. I have forgotten to ask him to post those letters.
15. You can't do it by yourself, can you.
16. They won't arrive until after dark, will they.
17. I can't make out what he's talking about.
18. Those aren't flowers, are they.
19. I don't know when the aeroplane will arrive.
20. He asked me where you had hidden it.

Notice the position of the question mark in these examples:

i. "Did he say, 'I won't'?" I asked Mary.
ii. (In a composition) Is it right for us to be guided by the adage: "Absence makes the heart grow fonder"?

8. The exclamation mark

This is used after exclamations and when we particularly wish to convey the idea of emphasis or strong emotion:

'Oh!' he exclaimed. 'So that's your game!'

It is not considered correct to use two or three exclamation marks to stress a remark but this is sometimes done in letters to friends and other informal writing. Guard against any temptation to use too many exclamation marks in formal work.

9. The apostrophe for contractions and for possession

a. for contractions

In a contraction, an apostrophe shows that one or more letters are missing.

Exercise 14

Give the full form of each of these contractions:

1. I'd	6. I won't	11. didn't	16. you're
2. it's	7. they've	12. can't	17. you'd
3. he'll	8. they're	13. I'll	18. you'll
4. he'd	9. there'll	14. aren't	19. she's
5. I shan't	10. there's	15. isn't	20. where's

b. for possession

The apostrophe is used to show possession or that one thing is part of another. It is normally used only with human beings, some common animals and in a few expressions such as *a day's delay, an hour's time, a week's holiday, the sun's rays, in two years' time* etc. In other cases we use *of* or *of the*, e.g. *the roof of the house.*

To form the possessive of a noun:

i. if the word does not already end in 's', **add 's**

   David—book becomes *David's* book

ii. if the word already ends with an 's', **add an apostrophe only**

   ladies—voices becomes *ladies'* voices

However, we can add *'s* to any surname or given name, whether it ends in 's' or not, e.g. *Bayo's* book, Mr. *Lee's* car, *Aris's* uncle. If the name already ends in 's' some people prefer not to say or write the extra 's' and use *Aris'* uncle instead. Both forms are correct. We also add *'s* to singular nouns ending in 'ss' e.g. the *heiress's* jewels.

Exercise 15

Use an apostrophe or *'s* to combine the following words as in the examples:

the girls—shoes:	the girls' shoes
the man—voice:	the man's voice

1. Peter—hands
2. my friend—father
3. two weeks—time
4. the women—dresses
5. my sister—school
6. the policeman—hat
7. the babies—food
8. the lady—car
9. Adeniyi—relatives
10. James—brother
11. Mr. Smith—car
12. the actor—hair
13. a month—delay
14. my brothers—shoes
15. my brother—radio
16. the players—boots
17. the employees—pay
18. the moon—rays
19. the tiger—paws
20. Mrs. Lim—sister

Exercise 16

Combine the following by using an apostrophe *or 's* or *of:*

1. the ruler—the end
2. the announcer—voice
3. the soldiers—weapons
4. my cousin—house
5. my cousins—bicycles
6. the bus—the back
7. the path—the width
8. the fight—the noise
9. Miss Williams—bag
10. Miss Cole—basket
11. the team—the strength
12. the fishermen—boats
13. the fire—the scene
14. the captain—decision
15. my parents—opinions
16. the workers—union
17. George—excuse
18. two minutes—time
19. the nation—strength
20. Madam Oni—car

10. The hyphen

There is only one certain way of learning which words contain a hyphen, which are written as two separate words and which are written as one word only: you must learn and remember each word as you meet it. Even dictionaries disagree very considerably on this point. The reason for this disagreement is that English is still a living language and some words are still in the process of change. As far as hyphens are concerned, the stages of development are:

a. two words come to be used next to each other, e.g. *to morrow, half crown, class room.*

b. A hyphen is introduced to make them into one word, e.g. *to-morrow, half-crown, class-room.*

c. Some people leave out the hyphen and make them into one word, e.g. *tomorrow, classroom.*

The change from *a* to *c* may take fifty to five hundred years, and the authorities who compile dictionaries cannot always agree on the stage at which a particular word is.

Nevertheless, there are some principles which may help you:

1. If you want to be very careful (as, for example, in preparing an article for publication) check doubtful words with *The Concise Oxford Dictionary* or one of similar merit.

2. If the omission of a hyphen would cause confusion, put one in. This is necessary, for example, to show the difference between *recover* and *re-cover.*

3. We tend to put a hyphen in such expressions as *do-it-yourself* and *up-to-date* when three or more words are meant to be considered as one unit.

4. A hyphen is used in expressions like the following:

   a black-maned lion   some bottle-nosed dolphins
   a square-headed whale   a barbed-wired fence
   a pitch-dark room   the wild-life reserves

   In the expression *a pitch-dark room* it would be wrong to leave out the hyphen. We do not mean 'a pitch room'; the word *pitch* describes *dark* rather than *room.*

5. As you would expect, there are a number of words which can be written with or without a hyphen, e.g. *cooperate (co-operate), today (to-day)* etc.

6. In some cases a hyphen is not used with a prefix in a word in common use, e.g. *anticyclone, anticlimax, international* but one is often used when the same prefix is employed to form a less common word, e.g. *anti-poaching, anti-sports, intercontinental, inter-departmental.*

11. The use of italics

Roman type: This is Roman type.
Bold type: **This is bold type.**
Italics: *These are italics.*

Italics are used in print. As we saw earlier, in a manuscript we show a printer that italics are needed by underlining a word, e.g. His strong point is his savoir faire. (French; it means 'the ability to know what to do in various circumstances'.)

Italics are used:

   i. for words taken from another language, as above
  ii. to emphasize a word
 iii. for the titles of books, articles, films etc.
 iv. to make headings stand out or to draw the attention of the reader to instructions etc.
  v. when words or expressions are quoted from a passage
 vi. for any other reason which makes it necessary for the words to be singled out from their context

Exercise 17

Explain why italics are used in each case below:

1. Answer *one* of the five questions given below.
2. Describe the climate of the south-west of England *or* that of the north-west coast of France.
3. At the end of the corridor he saw a notice on a door: *Danger-Radiation.*
4. *When in doubt, don't do it,* his father had always told him.
5. The *Rover III* was successfully launched at eight o'clock this morning and is now on its target course.
6. 'What do *you* want, Mr. Brown?' my father said.
7. 'Why don't you admit that you stole the money?' 'Because I *didn't.*'
8. I was furious that the accident had to happen at *this* stage.
9. I read about it in the *Daily Screech* last week.
10. Here on the Plateau, the snakes *Telescopus variegatus* and *Dromophis praeornatus* are common under rock flakes.
11. A Skaapsteker (*Psammophylax sp.*) has turned up at Bauchi, the first in West Africa; Thollon's Water Snake (*Grayia tholloni*), unmentioned in Villier's *Les Serpents de l'Ouest Africain*, is very common in the rivers and streams of the Plateau.
12. *The Transfer of Privileges and Duties*
    A *mban* and *usami* may go together. When the *usami* is opened the 'father' will pour wine or water in the new *eghwum.*

Exercise 18

In the following passages indicate which words should be printed in italics. If you were writing or typing each passage for publication, how you would show the printer that italics were needed?

Punctuation

1. **Suggested Reading:** Village in the Jungle (by Leonard Woolf); Lost World of the East (by S. Wavell).
2. The dancing-yard is also the scene of the assembly called ukwiri, summoned when epidemics have been reported.
3. The meaning of sinister today is quite different from what it used to mean.
4. A policy of laissez-faire may seem attractive but it may do us harm.
5. The notice on his door, Knock and Wait, did not seem very encouraging. I would have preferred to see the single word Welcome.
6. You made quite a faux pas when you told them about the accident.
7. Remember to use to after reply.
8. In his Travels, Derek Johnson describes some very unusual incidents.

12. Miscellaneous exercises

In the following exercises those marked with an asterisk have been taken from past examination papers.

*1. *One* rule of punctuation has been ignored in each of the sentences listed below. Re-write each sentence, correcting the punctuation but making no other changes; and, in each case, add a note stating the rule you have applied.

Example:
Question: The legacy was used to found a dogs home.
Answer: The legacy was used to found a dogs' home.
The apostrophe is needed to show the plural possessive.

a. 'Will you be coming with us Timothy?' asked Uncle Tom.
b. The dog retired contentedly to it's kennel.
c. The corporal asked the sentries why they had not reported the incident?
d. Doctors, who are negligent, endanger their patients' lives.
e. The house contained the following furniture; floor-mats, string beds, six bentwood chairs and a dining-room table.

*2. i. Punctuate the following passages and
     ii. Give the reasons for the marks of punctuation you use.

a. Theyre not going to tell me which is ours which is theirs and which is my fathers.

248

b. I wont listen to you she exclaimed who do you think you are youre not going to force your ideas or anyone elses on me.

*3. Look at the passage on page 61 and then explain why the following are used in it:

    a. the hyphen (l. 1)
    b. the capital C (l. 2)
    c. the apostrophe (l. 18)
    d. the apostrophe (l. 22)
    e. the italics (l. 23)
    f. the pair of dashes (l. 32)

*4. Introduce each of the following into a short sentence of its own, correctly punctuated:

    a. a list consisting of three items
    b. the name of a person who is being addressed in direct speech
    c. the possessive plural of the noun 'mouse'
    d. a personal possessive pronoun ending in *s*
    e. the title of a book.

(*Note:* the pronouns referred to in *d.* are *hers, his, ours, yours* and *theirs.*)

*5. One rule of punctuation has been ignored in each of the sentences listed below. Re-write each sentence, correcting the punctuation but making no other changes; and in each case add a note stating the rule you have applied

    Example:
    Question: 'Its a shell!' cried Jack.
    Answer: 'It's a shell!' cried Jack.
            An apostrophe is needed to mark the omission of the letter *i.*

    a. One tablet of the opiate gave twenty-four hours sleep.
    b. 'I was only telling him where he' Bertrand was beginning when Charles rudely interrupted him.
    c. At Waterloo, General William Stewart he was called 'Old Grog Willie' by his troops had every member of his staff struck down.
    d. The car was travelling at 60 mph.
    e. 'I climbed a rock, said Ralph slowly, and I found out that this is an island.'

*6. Explain the use of the commas in the following sentences:

    a. Mary, you are not paying attention.

    b. Montgomery, the late Commander-in-Chief, is writing his life story.

    c. He is, to put it mildly, not the worst player.

*7.   i. Write two separate sentences each illustrating a different use of the comma.

  ii. Write two separate sentences each illustrating a different use of the apostrophe.

 iii. Write two separate sentences, one to illustrate a use of the semi-colon, the other to illustrate a use of the colon. Add a short note to each sentence, explaining why you have used each particular stop. (*Note:* This instruction applies to (iii) only.)

*8. Write notes to explain the reasons for the punctuation of lines 7–14 of the following passage:

> When a train draws up in a railway station those who are already seated in it are subjected to the inquisition of a hundred anxious eyes. Intending passengers, doubtful which compartment to choose, hurry up and down the platform, hesitate, seize the handle of a door and release it,   5
> consult among themselves, and finally take the plunge.
> What reasons prompted such a traveller, after so much mental debate, so to choose his travelling companions? There was as much room elsewhere; there was a corner to be had next door; the air in that compartment was not   10
> more fresh than that in a dozen other compartments. If, then, it were not superior comfort that drew him to that particular compartment, the cause of his coming into it must rest in the occupants themselves.

*9. Read this passage which is an extract from a novel. The scene is India, and Douglas is the Principal of a Mission College.

> Before the heats of later spring deepen into the intolerable fierceness of May, there is a brief interlude of storm— the season of Rudra, the Terrible God. Waiting for that cleansing outburst, the earth was tremulous with little gusts of wind, sudden panting tongues of sand. Finished   5
> was the magnificence of the simul tree; its red bowls were tumbled everywhere, and the ground was covered with

the white cotton that wrapped the seeds. To Douglas, viewing all things according to their utility, the tree was an unmitigated nuisance; it 'made the compound 10 untidy'. All its crimson grandeur—there was one tree in the college grounds which made a vast pool of brightness on the sky, a full hundred feet above the beholder's head, splashing and staining the blue above into an incredible glory—was as nothing beside the trouble that it gave to 15 sweep up the seeds. That other loveliness of the Indian spring, the palas, was a similar curse; caterpillars ate its leaves into unsightliness, and then these strewed the floor. This year annoyance was intensified by a wonderful flowering. He loved tree-cutting; nothing so gave him 20 the feeling that the College was progressing as the sight of axe-wielding men beside a row of logs.

Say why the following punctuation marks are used in the passage:

    a. the comma after 'Rudra' (l. 3)
    b. the comma after 'Douglas' (l. 8)
    c. the quotation marks in ll. 10 and 11
    d. the dashes in ll. 11 and 15
    e. the semicolon after 'tree-cutting' (l. 20)

*10. i. Write out all the parts of a letter, other than the actual body of the letter, so as to show the required punctuation.

    ii. Write a sentence to illustrate *four* different uses of capital letters, explaining in each instance why they are used, and a second sentence to show how single and double quotation marks are used.

*11. Punctuate and paragraph the following passage, supplying the necessary capitals:

    presently i chanced to see a pasteboard sign lying upon a desk and bearing these words take care of him he bites i hurriedly climbed upon the desk fearful of a dog underneath but saw none what are you doing there asked mr moll i beg your pardon sir i replied if you please im looking for a dog dog what dog i pointed to the sign no copperfield he said gravely thats not a dog thats a boy my instructions are to put this sign on your back im sorry to do so but must do it.

12. Add one punctuation mark to each of the following sentences and then say why you have added it.

a. We stopped for a rest under a convenient tree it seemed to have been made for tired travellers.

b. The colour of that car is quite nice. Its almost the same colour as Uncle's car.

c. The contents of the case came as quite a surprise a large bunch of keys, a pair of gloves and nearly ten thousand pounds in notes.

d. Opposite our house there is a childrens playground which is quite noisy at times.

e. 'What's wrong David?' I asked.

f. The rumours suggested that there were hundreds, or even thousands, of armed men in the vicinity numbers that made us think that something serious was about to happen.

g. 'Peter where did you put the keys?' she asked.

h. I got up and went to the door there was nobody outside.

i. The truth indeed, was that there had been no change in his condition.

j. There we waited, huddled together as a protection against the cold and wondered whether anybody would come to look for us.

13. In each case insert one punctuation mark, or a pair of punctuation marks, and then say why you have made the insertion.

a. His brother whom I think you met last month has suggested that we should all go to visit him.

b. He has found Peter's book and now he wants to know where Davids is.

c. If they are interested in shopping, there are other places they can visit Lagos, for example. (*Alternative answers are possible.*)

d. Above the din the voice of a woman protesting angrily rose in fury.

e. The wire made a T shaped tear in the back of his shirt.

f. He has come to give a lecture on soil erosion a particular problem in this district.

g. He said that it was somebody elses bicycle.

h. There are ten members on the Board the President, the Hon. Secretary and eight others.

i. The solution to the problem is simply this much more money must be found to develop the facilities of the area.

14. From the four alternatives given below, choose the correct punctuation mark which should be put in the sentence at the point shown by the brackets. Write down the letter which appears immediately in front of the one you choose. Notice that when you choose a full stop it is assumed that the next word will start with a capital letter.

1. Some passers-by took pity on the injured man ( ) they stopped to help him out of the car.
   A (,) B (.) C (') D (:)
2. He showed me the contents of the purse ( ) a few coins, a bunch of keys and a crumpled photograph.
   A (,) B (.) C (;) D (:)
3. She wants to know where you live ( )
   A (.) B (?) C (!) D (,)
4. 'I've got something to tell you,' John said to me.
   'Yes ( )'
   'Mary has managed to get a job at last.'
   A (,) B (?) C (.) D (!)
5. 'Be quiet ( ) The baby is asleep.'
   A (') B (?) C (!) D (,)
6. We had to stop just before the bridge ( ) there had been an accident and the road was blocked.
   A (.) B (,) C (:) D (!)
7. Give the meaning of the following words ( ) *meretricious, flamboyant* and *consternation*.
   A (;) B (,) C (—) D (:)
8. He said, 'Did John remember to post those letters for me on his way to work this morning ( )'
   A (.) B (?) C (') D (,)

Chapter 13

The accused man maintained

Spelling and Usage

1. Different or Difference?

Different is an adjective; *difference* is a noun.
   adjective: I know a *different* way to the river.
   noun: What is the *difference* between them?

Exercise 1

Choose the right word from the brackets and put it in the
blank space.

(different; difference)
1. The . . . was more than I had expected. He had changed a lot.
2. Those shoes are . . . from these. They are bigger.

(patient; patience)
3. . . . is a virtue so you must learn to be . . .
4. He lost his . . . and became extremely im. . .

(independent; independence)
5. Ghana is an . . . nation. The people value their . . .
6. He wanted to stand as an . . . candidate.

(innocent; innocence)
7. The accused man maintained that he was . . . and soon most
   of us were convinced of his . . .
8. Unfortunately, it sometimes happens that . . . men suffer with
   the guilty.

(negligent; negligence)
9. He was charged with . . . driving.
10. Your . . . nearly cost me my life.

Exercise 2

Make up sentences in which you use the following adjectives and, in separate sentences, the nouns ending in *ence* which can be formed from them:

1. confident	6. obedient	11. absent
2. excellent	7. disobedient	12. silent
3. convenient	8. patient	13. impertinent
4. violent	9. present	14. impatient
5. indifferent	10. negligent	15. innocent

2. Self or Selves

Notice the spelling of these reflexive or emphasizing pronouns:

singular	*plural*
myself	ourselves
himself, herself, itself	themselves
yourself	yourselves

Only the **plural** *forms end in* **selves**.

Exercise 3

Put in any suitable reflexive or emphasizing pronoun:
1. She made the dress all by . . .
2. We enjoyed . . . Did you enjoy . . ., Peter?
3. I hope you didn't hurt . . ., boys.
4. I scratched . . . on that piece of wire.
5. There's nothing wrong with the engine . . . but the body of the car looks shabby.
6. Surely you two can repair those socks . . .
7. The cow injured . . . when it tried to get across the ditch.
8. I think those silly goats have lost . . .
9. There's nothing wrong with those words . . . but I don't like the way you use them.
10. He excused . . . from the cocktail party, thinking that it was a waste of time and money.
11. I must learn to protect . . . against that kind of trick.
12. The plan . . . is quite sound but Mr. Lee has convinced . . . that it is too expensive.

3. Interesting or Interested?

Adjectives which end in **ed** *often show that something has already happened to the noun or pronoun to which they refer.*

255

Spelling

Adjectives which end in **ing** show that something is still going on or show how something affects us.

Exercise 4

Choose the right word from the brackets and put it in the blank space.

(interesting; interested)

1. I thought the book was very . . . but my brother was not . . . in it.
2. The scientists have just made a most . . . discovery. I am sure you were . . . when you heard about it.

(exciting; excited)

3. She was very . . . when she heard about Peter's success.
4. The film was very . . . and well worth seeing.

(damaging; damaged)

5. He made a . . . statement when he admitted that he had been drinking with a friend.
6. The . . . car was towed to a garage.

(amazing; amazed)

7. That was really an . . . coincidence.
8. We were . . . to hear that he had arrived already.

(annoying; annoyed)

9. She felt very . . . when she saw what had happened.
10. It is . . . to miss a bus or a train by a minute or so.

Exercise 5

Use each of the following words in a sentence:

1. drowned	9. tired	17. disappointed
2. drowning	10. tiring	18. disappointing
3. exhausted	11. worried	19. decayed
4. exhausting	12. worrying	20. decaying
5. increased	13. amused	21. astonished
6. increasing	14. amusing	22. astonishing
7. boiled	15. puzzled	23. startled
8. boiling	16. puzzling	24. startling

4. Numbers

Notice the spelling of the words given below, and make sure

that you know how to pronounce them. If you are studying by yourself, use Daniel Jones' *English Pronouncing Dictionary* (or a similar book) to check your pronunciation.

four	five	nine
fourth	*fifth*	*ninth*
fourteen	fifteenth	ninety
forty	eight	eleventh
fortieth	*eighth*	twelve
forty-three	eighteen	*twelfth*

5. Practice or Practise?

ce: *Practice*, *licence* and *advice* are **nouns**.

se: *Practise*, *license* and *advise* are **verbs**.

With these and similar pairs of words, the noun contains a 'c' but the verb contains an 's'.

Exercise 6

Put the right word in each blank space:

(*licence; license*)

1. You must get a . . . for your radio.
2. He regards freedom as a . . . to do what he likes.
3. The manufacturers have agreed to . . . us so that we can produce it in our country.

(*practice; practise; practised*)

4. In future I will . . . as hard as I can.
5. Did they manage to get in any . . . last night?
6. Where did they . . . yesterday?
7. It is said that . . . makes perfect.
8. We all . . . as well as we could last week.

(*prophecy; prophesy*)

9. I think I can . . . what will happen to him.
10. My . . . will probably be fulfilled, alas.
11. The witches' first . . . soon came true.

(*device; devise; devised*)

12. He has invented a . . . for ploughing more efficiently.
13. He has . . . a method whereby we can all go.
14. We must try to . . . some alternative plan.

(*advice; advise*)

15. We may . . . him not to buy the house.

257

16. He did not give us any . . .
17. She did not . . . us at all.

Note: The *ing* form of the verbs in this section always ends in *sing* and never in *cing*, e.g. *practising, advising.*

6. Stop and Stopping

We double the final consonant when we add *ing* or *ed* to a word of one syllable which ends in a consonant preceded by a short vowel, e.g.

stop: stopping	grab: grabbing	lob: lobbed
hit: hitting	get: getting	clap: clapped
cut: cutting	skip: skipped	run: running

7. Awkward pairs

Exercise 7

Notice the spelling of the following words and then use them in separate sentences:

1. *a.* there	5. *a.* choose	9. *a.* pedal
b. their	*b.* chose	*b.* paddle
2. *a.* hear	6. *a.* till	10. *a.* diary
b. here	*b.* until	*b.* dairy
3. *a.* knew	7. *a.* loose	11. *a.* piece
b. new	*b.* lose	*b.* peace
4. *a.* affect	8. *a.* compliment	12. *a.* beliefs
b. effect	*b.* complement	*b.* believes

8. Thief and Receive

When *ie* and *ei* are pronounced with the sound of *ee* (as in *thief* and *receive*), we usually put 'i' before 'e' except after 'c'. The principal exception is *seize.*
ie: relief, believe, achieve, fiend, field.
ei: receipt, perceive, deceive, conceit, ceiling.

9. Realise or Realize?

There are a number of words which end in *ise* or *ize*. We can divide them into three groups:

a. Words which must end in *ise*: e.g. *surprise, rise, revise, compromise, comprise(d)* of, etc.

b. Words which must end in *ize*: e.g. *prize.*

c. Words which can be spelt with *ise* or *ize*: e.g. *realise/realize; equalise/equalize; monopolise/monopolize* etc.

In the past there used to be a preference for the spelling with *ise* but many authorities now prefer to use *ize*; both forms are acceptable and in widespread use.

10. 'e' or no 'e'?

When a suffix beginning with a vowel (e.g. *ing, able*) is added to a word which ends with 'e', the 'e' is omitted *unless*: (i) the word ends in *ce* or *ge* and the suffix begins with *a, o* or *u*, e.g. *changeable, courageous*; (ii) the word ends in *ee, oe* or *ye*, e.g. *agreeing.*

Thus we have:

love: loving, lovable   write: writing
fascinate: fascinating   sense: sensible

11. Disagree and Dissolve

When the prefixes *dis, mis, un* and *in* are added to a word there will NOT be a double 's' or 'n' unless the word already starts with one of these letters.

dis + agree = disagree.
dis + solve = dissolve
un + kind = unkind
un + necessary = unnecessary

In particular, notice the spelling of *disappear* which has two *p*'s and one *s*.

12. Refer and Referred

We double the final consonant of a word when its last syllable bears stress and ends in a consonant preceded by a single vowel, and the suffix added to it is unstressed and begins with a vowel.

refer: referring, referred
occur: occurred, occurring
permit: permitted, permitting

In a rather similar way, we double the final 'l' of many words of more than one syllable even though the stress may not fall on the last syllable, e.g. *travel: travelled, traveller.*

13. Spelling lists

When you study the following lists, do these things:

(i) Make sure that you know the meaning of each word.
(ii) Make sure that you can use it in a sentence.
(iii) Learn how to spell it.

List 1	*List 2*	*List 3*	*List 4*
careful	encourage	occasion	privilege
skilful	definitely	occasionally	ledge
fulfil	barbed-wire	mathematics	pigeon
fulfilled	bell-shaped	Tuesday	atmosphere
business	honour	Wednesday	acquaintance
contented	honourable	February	aquarium
describe	honorary	library	beginning
humour	interested	envelope	lightning
humorous	juvenile	develop	separately
benefit	adolescent	development	surprised

List 5	*List 6*	*List 7*	*List 8*
argue	tragedy	behaviour	helpful
argument	tragic	saviour	helpfully
reference	contemptuous	receive	hopeful
criticism	continuous	receipt	hopefully
neighbour	pathetic	recipe	embarrassing
reasonably	intended	disappoint	climb
usually	relatives	disappear	climbing
miniature	theatre	dissimilar	description
scenery	explanation	distrust	rhyme
achieve	explain	dissect	rhythm

List 9	*List 10*	*List 11*	*List 12*
profession	successful	habits	veranda(h)
professor	necessary	surrounding	bungalow
preferred	implements	drawer	toilet
referred	subscription	later	lavatory
allotment	imagination	latter	latrine
allotted	cooperation	complexion	laboratory
vehicle	musicians	connexion	competition
physical	brilliant	connection	upstairs
physique	thief	dining-room	sitting-room
unique	thieves	dinner	pleasant

List 13	*List 14*	*List 15*	*List 16*
unnecessarily	excursion	ammunition	sumptuous
temporarily	promising	accommodation	extravagant
customarily	widened	arriving	inaugurate
transferred	particular	snacks	corrugated
transfer	truly	academically	convenient
research	career	intellectual	favourite
writer	accustomed	literature	arctic
sacrifice	contemplating	preceded	antarctic
sacrificed	insult	proceeded	harass
illiterate	modern	journey	campaign

List 17	*List 18*	*List 19*	*List 20*
altogether	grotesque	besiege	solemnly
medicine	picturesque	interrupt	vegetable
pronounce	conscious	ridiculous	paralyse
pronunciation	conscience	jeopardy	prejudiced
mischievous	manoeuvre	secretary	principal
mischief	phenomenon	appendix	principle
hygiene	curious	anxiety	exaggerate
refrigerator	curiosity	reservoir	tongue
persuasion	vicious	courteous	pretentious
influential	eccentric	picnic	guardian

Chapter 14

Synthesis and Sentence Construction

I saw him walking to school this morning

Synthesis is the opposite of *analysis*; applied to sentences, it means 'the joining together of parts so as to form a whole'. It involves joining a number of short sentences or expressions together to form one or more longer sentences.

Please notice and remember the following warning. Synthesis is useful when it (a) stops you from writing too many very short sentences, (b) gives you an opportunity to learn about and practise ways of joining shorter statements, and (c) gives you practice in the use of conjunctions and other joining words. However, it can be harmful if it gives you the (misleading) impression that a good sentence is a long one. This is not the case. As mentioned in the chapter on composition, unduly lengthy sentences should be avoided. A good average length is about two lines.

When you do the following exercises, therefore, bear in mind (a), (b) and (c) above but do not allow yourself to be forced into writing lengthy sentences as a habit.

1. Simple, Compound and Complex sentences

We must glance at the meaning of the terms *Simple*, *Compound* and *Complex* in case you meet them in an examination; otherwise they are of little value.

a. **A Simple sentence** contains only one finite verb, e.g.

I **saw** him walking to school this morning and looking keen to get there and start work.

Exhausted by the climb, Peter sat down to rest.

262

Note: The words *walking, looking, to get, start, exhausted* and *to reach* are not finite verbs.

b. **A Compound sentence** consists of two or more main clauses or statements, each containing a finite verb and neither being dependent on the other. Taken separately, each should make complete sense by itself, e.g.

> *I saw him walking to school* but *he did not notice me.*
> *Peter helped me,* and *David helped John.*

c. **A Complex sentence** consists of any number of main clauses but it also contains one or more dependent (or subordinate) clauses which will not make complete sense by themselves, e.g.

> The car *which he borrowed from his uncle* was badly damaged *when he ran off the road* and *hit a tree.* (The three dependent statements are in italics; the main one is *The car was badly damaged.*)

Note: If you find it impossible to remember the meaning of *Simple, Compound, Complex, finite* and *clause,* do not worry. You will be able to speak and write good English without knowing about these terms although a knowledge of them *may* be helpful in an examination.

2. Joining main clauses or statements

The words in bold type below show ways of joining main clauses:

  i. I went to the market **and** bought several things.
  ii. I went to the market **but** didn't buy anything.
 iii. He was **both** surprised **and** pleased.
 iv. That camera was **neither** cheap **nor** very useful.
  v. You can stay here **or** come with us.
 vi. You can **either** stay here **or** come with us.

Exercise 1

Join the following sentences by using one of the methods shown above and by making any necessary changes to the sentences.

  1. He was tired. He didn't want to go to bed.
  2. He was very tired. He wanted to go to bed.
  3. She wasn't hungry. She wasn't thirsty.
  4. Peter hasn't heard from the University yet. David hasn't heard either.

5. You can get to the station this way. It will take you a long time. The path is rather muddy.
6. Her temperature is high. She appears to have a fever.
7. He is hard-working. He is intelligent.
8. He is not lazy. He is not stupid.
9. There was no chance to escape. There was no opportunity to explain what was wrong.
10. He may come by train He may come by taxi.

3. Relative Pronouns

Please see the separate chapter on Relative Pronouns (*who, which, that, whose* and *whom*) for their use in combining statements. You should study that chapter, and work through the exercises, before attempting the exercises at the end of this chapter.

4. Although and Though

a. Although the bus was full, I managed to get on it.
b. He agreed to play *although* his ankle still hurt him.
c. Although new universities are being established in England, existing ones improved and many new places being provided for able students, (yet) it remains true that—per head of population—facilities are not as good as in certain other countries.

Normally, we do NOT use another linking word with *although*. As in *a* and *b*, it is usually the only link between two statements and it is wrong to use *but* as an additional link. However, some writers occasionally use *yet* (as in *c*) but only if the expression after *although* is unusually long.

d. He agreed to come *though* he is a very busy man.
e. I left the clothes out *though* it was raining.
f. We ought to invite her *even though* she may decline to come.
g. It looks *as though* they are not going to come after all.
h. He behaves *as though* he owns the whole town.
i. I'm sure he won't sell it—*though* you never know.

When it is used by itself, *though* is used in a way similar to that of *although*. However, it cannot be replaced by *although* in the expressions *even though* and *as though*.

Exercise 2

Complete the following in any sensible way:

1. Although I wanted to watch the film, . . .

2. Although it was raining, . . .
3. Although I hadn't much money left, . . .
4. We managed to arrive in time although . . .
5. I was not really cross with her although . . .
6. He did not succeed even though . . .
7. It looks as though . . .
8. It seems as though . . .

Exercise 3

a. Use each of the following in two sentences, making a total of eight sentences: *although, though, as though, even though.*
b. Join the following sentences by using *although* and any of the conjunctions already mentioned in section 2 on page 263.

1. The current was strong. I was tired. I managed to swim across the river.
2. The dress was rather expensive. She could hardly afford it. She decided to buy it.
3. Peter had hurt his ankle. He managed to score a goal. His left boot hurt his foot.
4. Mr. Lee was not pleased. He was not apparently surprised. He had not seen David for several years.
5. The road was very bumpy. We drove along it We drove less quickly than usual.
6. The road is flooded. You can get there by rail. You can get there by boat.
7. We could not lift it. We could not move it. We tried our hardest.
8. He was sorry. He was disillusioned. He would not admit it.

5. Because

In conversation we often use a statement which begins with *because*:

David: Why didn't you get one for me?
Peter: Because I was in a hurry and didn't have time to look round the town.

In formal written work, *because* introduces a dependent clause which should not be punctuated as a separate sentence. It must be accompanied by the main statement:

I did not get one because I was in a hurry.

Synthesis and Sentence Construction

The expression *because of* is very useful:

> *Because of* the floods, we decided not to go.
> He was annoyed *because of* the lengthy delay.

Exercise 4

Combine these sentences by using *because* or *because of* and by making any necessary changes:

1. The weather was bad. The game was cancelled.
2. The price was high. We decided not to buy it.
3. He sold his car. It was getting rather old.
4. A considerable amount of rain falls in that district. There is a range of mountains there.
5. We could not go to school. There was a curfew.
6. He switched off the television set. He wanted to do some work.
7. There was a drought. The crop was not very good.
8. He could not attend the interview. His father was very ill.

6. Since and For

Since is followed by a definite date or point in time which answers the question 'When?'

For is followed by a length of time which answers the question 'For how long?'

since	last Monday	**for**	a few days
	March the first		two minutes
	1965		ten years
	yesterday		half an hour

Exercise 5

Put in *since* or *for*:

1. He has not been here (a) . . . last week; (b) . . . some time
2. She has been working here (a) . . . more than a year; (b) . . . the time when your brother came.
3. It hasn't rained (a) . . . the last six weeks; (b) . . . early in March.
4. (a) . . . you decided not to speak to him; (b) . . . the last few days, he has not been his usual self.
5. (a) . . . as long as I can remember; (b) . . . the time when we left Ibadan, those trees have been there.

6. I have been waiting (*a*) . . . half an hour; (*b*) . . . two o'clock.
7. We have made considerable progress . . . the country became independent.
8. . . . most of his life he has been a farmer and . . . he started to use tractors his profits have increased considerably.
9. I have been looking for that key . . . the last half an hour. I haven't seen it. . . . I lent it to Peter.
10. . . . his operation, he has not been so bad-tempered.

7. So that

We can use *so that* to show the purpose of an action:

a. I shut the window *so that* the rain would not get in.
b. He lent me some money *so that* I could buy the book.
In most cases, we can express the same idea by using an infinitive:
c. I shut the window to keep the rain out.
d. I shut the window to prevent the rain from getting in.
e. He lent me some money to buy the book.

8. So

So often shows the consequence of an action or situation:

a. It was late *so* we decided not to play any more.
b. The Minister needed more money for developments *so* he raised the income tax.

9. Before, After and Until

These three words can be used to introduce a time expression:

a. I want to get there *before* the film starts.
b. *After* I had finished my work, I went to see Margaret.
c. We must wait here *until* the others come.

10. If and Unless

As you know, it is necessary to be careful with the sequence of tenses when using *if* and *unless*:

possible: If they come, we shall be able to go out.
less possible: If they came, we should be able to go out.
impossible: If they had come, we should have been able to go out.

a. They will grow well *unless* the sun is too hot for them.

b. He said they would arrive at eight o'clock *unless* there was some delay on the road.

c. I wouldn't have done it if he had not promised to help me.

Exercise 6

a. Complete the following in any sensible way:

1. She brought in the dry clothes so that . . .
2. He bought a film so that . . .
3. I had to stand on a chair so that . . .
4. He sprained his wrist so . . .
5. When I got home there was nobody there so . . .
6. The first few pages of the book were boring so . . .
7. I hope we get there before . . .
8. Before you eat the fruit . . .
9. We went for a drive after . . .
10. After I had sown the seeds, . . .
11. Don't tell anybody anything until . . .
12. I'm afraid we'll have to wait until . . .
13. If you happen to see a pen exactly like Peter's, . . .
14. If that music is disturbing you, . . .
15. If I knew where it was, . . .
16. If I knew how to do it, . . .
17. If the train stopped at his village, . . .
18. If you had been more careful, . . .
19. If you had saved two shillings a week for the past year, . . .
20. If you had tested the brakes before you went out, . . .

b. Combine the *ideas* in the following statements to make one sentence. You may omit or alter words but must retain the same ideas. There are alternative methods of making one sentence.

1. I shortened one of the legs of the table. I did not want it to wobble any more.
2. I shut the door. I did not want to hear the noise outside.
3. It was very hot. We decided to go for a swim.
4. There were several applicants for the job. Peter knew he did not have much chance of getting it.
5. I cleaned the car. We went for a drive.
6. We made a raft. We took the luggage across the river.
7. The road may be flooded. Then we shall not be able to go.
8. He might have come to see us yesterday. Then we should have been able to discuss the scheme with him.

9. The rope might have broken. Then you would have hurt yourself.
10. He may not go. Then I don't want to go.

11. During and While

During is usually followed by a noun or pronoun with which it makes a phrase. This does not contain a verb.

While usually starts a clause, which contains a finite verb.

During ⎰ the game
⎱ the storm
⎩ it

While ⎰ we were playing
⎱ they were arguing
⎩ he was standing there

a. I lost some money during my visit to Kingston.
b. The phone rang while we were watching television.

12. Miscellaneous exercises

Exercise 7

Using infinitives, join each of the following pairs of sentences into *one* sentence, making changes in order and wording only when necessary.

Example: He is very lazy. He will not revise his work.
Answer: He is too lazy to revise his work.

1. He is very rich. He will not feel the expense.
2. She has a large family. She must provide for them.
3. He could not recognize me. He was very ill.
4. We could not drink the coffee. It was too hot.
5. He has a lot of problems. He must think about them.
6. There are two more shirts. They must be repaired.
7. There is another invoice. It must be checked.
8. It is very late. We cannot go there now.
9. This log is extremely heavy. We can't pick it up.
10. There are some more invitations. They must be sent out.

Exercise 8

Find different ways of combining each pair of sentences:

1. It started to rain. I was watching the game.
2. He turned off the television set. He was not interested in the programme.

3. Part of the cliff fell down. It had been considerably eroded by wind and rain.
4. He will come with us. He wants us to pay for him.
5. You must send a copy of your birth certificate. Then we can verify the date of your birth.
6. He was able to relax. He could consider the new problem. It had arisen during the last few days.
7. He came back. Then we took him out to dinner. We asked him about the rumours. He had mentioned them before.
8. I took Peter's watch by mistake. I thought it was mine.
9. He went to see Mary. He had not realized that she was on holiday.
10. I had finished with the book. I took it back to Peter. I thanked him for lending it to me.

Exercise 9

Complete these sentences in any sensible way, taking care to use a suitable tense or form of any verbs you use.

1. He looked at me as if . . .
2. It is quite possible that . . .
3. It is impossible for us . . .
4. It is unlikely that . . .
5. We will wait as long as . . .
6. They told me that they walked as far as . . .
7. As long as he is working there . . .
8. I'll come as soon as . . .
9. I promised to go round to David's house as soon as . . .
10. I asked them where. . . .
11. He told me what . . .
12. I don't know who . . .
13. I can't understand why . . .
14. I wonder whether . . .
15. She wants to know when . . .
16. While we were waiting for a bus, . . .
17. During half-time . . .
18. Unless he agrees to reduce the price . . .
19. Off the record, I can tell you that . . .
20. As far as I can make out, . . .

Exercise 10

Combine the facts of the following sentences so as to form one sentence. You may omit or change words as necessary but must retain the facts of the original sentences.

1. Mauritius is an island. It is in the Indian Ocean. It lies just north of the Tropic of Capricorn.
2. Kingston is in Jamaica. Jamaica is an island. It is south of Cuba. It is east of Haiti.
3. We ran to the quay. The ferry was due to arrive there. We hoped to be the first to greet Mary.
4. He drove carefully. The road was wet. It was slippery. There was a danger. The car might skid.
5. The bell rang. I looked at my watch. I was surprised. It was not time for the lesson to end.
6. He agreed with me about the plan. It was a lot of nonsense. It would certainly fail.
7. I left the office. Mr. Coles was still working. It was nearly seven o'clock.
8. This is the camera. I bought it last week. It cost nearly twenty pounds.
9. He took the car to the garage. He needed some petrol. He wanted to buy a can of oil.
10. He managed to repair the lorry. It took him a long time. It cost him a lot of money.

Chapter 15

Indirect Questions

where she lives

direct question: '**Where has she gone?**' he asked me.	*(a)*
indirect questions: He asked me **where she had gone.**	*(b)*
I want to know **where she has gone.**	*(c)*
'Do you know **where she has gone?**'	*(d)*

When we change a direct question into an indirect one, we make the following changes:

a. **Punctuation**

    i. We do not use inverted commas unless the indirect question occurs inside a direct question as in *(d)* above.

    ii. We do not use a question mark unless the indirect question occurs inside a direct question as in *(d)* above. Notice that no question mark is used in *(b)* and *(c)*.

    iii. We do not use a comma after such introductory verbs as *said, asked* etc.

Exercise 1

Punctuate the following correctly. Some are direct questions; some are indirect questions.

1. We must try to find out how to increase exports.
2. How can we increase exports he asked me.
3. I want to know where she lives.
4. He said to me where does she live now.
5. He asked why we were so late.

272

6. He asked why are you so late.
7. Do you know when they are due to arrive he said.
8. He said that he did not know what she had bought.
9. Where did you buy that transistor radio my father asked.
10. He wanted to know where I had bought it.
11. See if you can find out how much she paid my father told me.
12. Do you know why Peter is absent today David the teacher said.

b. **Word Order**

The order of words in an indirect question is the same as in a statement with the subject *before* the verb. In a direct question the subject comes after the verb or in the middle of it. Compare these examples:

> *direct:* 'What *is* **she** *doing?*'
> *indirect:* I want to know what **she** *is doing*.

c. **Pronouns, Place and Time**

It is usually necessary to alter any pronouns (e.g. *he, she, you*), possessive adjectives (*her, our, your*) and words which show place or time. The changes are similar to those made when we change direct speech into reported speech. In some cases, of course, the sense is such that no change is needed.

d. **Tenses of verbs**

Sometimes (but NOT always) we put the tense of the verb in the direct question back into a past tense. If the action is unfinished, the same tense can be used, as in (i) below. If the action has been completed or is no longer being considered, a past tense is often used as in (ii).

> i. *direct:* He asked me, 'How much do you weigh?'
> *indirect:* He asked me how much I **weigh**.

In (i) both references are to the same point in time—now.

> ii. *direct:* When we were on holiday last year he asked me, 'How much do you weigh?'
> *indirect:* When we were on holiday last year he asked me how much I **weighed**.

In the indirect question the time is different from that of the direct question. Presumably, the speaker's weight has changed since the original question was asked.

As you can see from these examples, whether or not to change the tense will depend upon many factors including the passage

273

of time (if any) and the idea you wish to express. Here is another example:

iii.　*direct: 3 p.m.* My father said, 'Where's Peter gone?'

　　indirect: 3.10 p.m. My father asked me where Peter **has** gone.

　　8 p.m. (Peter has returned.) Not long after Peter had gone out my father asked me where he **had** gone.

Exercise 2

Put *He wants to know* in front of the questions below and change them into indirect questions. Make any changes which are essential.

1. Where is she now?
2. What is it?
3. Who are they?
4. What is he using?
5. How is she today?
6. When are they coming?
7. How much is there left?
8. How many are there left?
9. What is her name?
10. Where are the keys?
11. What is she looking for?
12. Where is my book?

Exercise 3

Put *I don't know* in front of the questions below and change them into indirect questions. Make any necessary changes.

1. How does it open?
2. When does it start?
3. Where do they live?
4. How much does it cost?
5. How long does it take?
6. How often do they come?
7. What do they want?
8. How does it work?
9. Why do they do that?
10. Why do they wait there?
11. When does she arrive?
12. Where does he work?

Exercise 4

Change these questions into indirect questions. Put *He asked me* in front of each question and make any necessary changes. This time change the tense of the verb in the direct question. Use the Simple Past tense as in the example:

direct: 'Why is David absent?'

indirect: He asked me why David **was** absent.

1. Why are you late?
2. Why is it locked?
3. Why are your shoes dirty?
4. When is her birthday?

5. What's the matter?
6. Where's my brother?
7. Why is Mary angry?
8. Who's there?
9. When does it start?
10. What does she want?

11. What do they make?
12. When can you come?
13. What may happen?
14. Where do you live?
15. Where does it lead?
16. Why does it stop?

Exercise 5

Change these questions into indirect questions which start
with *He asked me*, as in the example. Use *whether* or *if* and change
the tense of the verb in the direct question.

direct: Is the ferry still running?
indirect: He asked me whether the ferry was still running.

1. Is Peter ready yet?
2. Are you certain?
3. Is the iron hot?
4. Are you thirsty?
5. Is the radio on?
6. Are they yours?
7. Is it mine?
8. Is it an old one?

9. Are there any letters?
10. Are the shops still open?
11. Is David still working there?
12. Are you going out?
13. Is it raining now?
14. Are you waiting for me?
15. Is the fan working properly?
16. Are the men asleep?

Exercise 6

Change these questions into indirect questions which start
with *He asked me*, as in the example. Use *whether* or *if* and change
the tense of the verb in the direct question.

direct: Will it rain tonight?
indirect: He asked me whether it would rain last/that night.

1. Will Mary come in time?
2. Will you buy one for me?
3. Will it break?
4. Will they stop long?
5. Will the fire spread?

6. Will it arrive on time?
7. Will she remember me?
8. Will you write to me?
9. Will anybody find out?
10. Will anything happen?

Exercise 7

Change these questions into indirect questions which start
with *I don't know.* Do not change the tense of the verb in the
direct question.

Indirect Questions

1. What will he say?	6. Where has he gone?
2. When will she come?	7. What have they found?
3. Why will it die?	8. Why has Peter come?
4. How will it finish?	9. How has he done it?
5. Who(m)* will they catch?	10. Why have they resigned?

Note: *In (5) conventional grammarians would prefer us to use *Whom* but, despite their efforts, *whom* is fast disappearing in this context.

Exercise 8

Change these questions into indirect questions which are prefaced by *He asked me*. In some (but not all) cases, use *whether* or *if*. In each case, retain the tense of the verb in the direct question.

1. Was your answer right?	7. Were they yours?
2. Were they both there?	8. Was it mine?
3. Was she playing netball?	9. What was Mary doing?
4. Were the windows open?	10. Where were they going?
5. Was the train on time?	11. Who was coming?
6. Were any goals scored?	12. Who was there?

Exercise 9

When reporting a question, it is sometimes necessary to make it clear that the action of the indirect question refers to a point of time further back in the past.

Change these questions into indirect questions which are prefaced by *He asked me*. Change the tense of the verb in the direct question, as in the examples.

direct: 'When were you working there?'
indirect: He asked me when I had been working there.

direct: 'Was Peter waiting for you?'
indirect: He asked me whether Peter had been waiting for me.

1. Was it raining?
2. Were you at the concert?
3. Where were you working then?
4. Who was driving the car at the time?
5. When were you last in Lagos?
6. Where were the two men hiding for so long?
7. What kind of work were you doing at school then?
8. Were the escaped prisoners ever caught?

276

9. Who was refereeing the game?
10. What were you doing at that time of the year?

When the verb in a direct question is in the Present Perfect tense (he *has gone*; *I have finished*) and we wish to make an indirect question, we can take this action:

a. retain the Present Perfect tense, or

b. change it to the Past Perfect tense (he *had gone*).

The action we take will depend upon the circumstances, as these examples show:

3 p.m. Peter is working in the garden. His father says to David (Peter's brother), 'Has Peter finished yet?' David goes out into the garden and says to his brother, 'Dad wants to know *whether you have finished yet.*' Peter replies, 'No, not yet. I shan't be long.'

3.30 p.m. Peter has finished his work and gone out. Everybody in the house knows this except Peter's father who happens to ask David again, 'Has Peter finished yet?' Before David can reply, his mother enters the room and asks, 'What did Father ask you then?' David replies, 'He asked me *whether Peter had finished yet.*' David uses *had finished* because he knows that Peter has finished his work already.

Exercise 10

Change these into indirect questions after *He wants to know*. Retain the tense of the verb in the direct question.

1. Have you seen anything of Peter today?
2. Have the men repaired the refrigerator yet?
3. Has the flood gone down yet?
4. Has anybody lost any money today?
5. What has happened to my bicycle?
6. Where has everybody gone?
7. Why have those two boys over there been excused from the cross-country race?
8. Where has Mary put my camera?
9. Has anybody scored a goal yet?
10. Has there been any change in the patient's condition?

Exercise 11

Change the following into indirect questions after *He asked me*. Change the tense of the verb in the direct question so that it is in the Past Perfect tense (e.g. *had kicked*) OR the passive form of that tense (e.g. *had been kicked*) OR the continuous form of that tense (e.g. *had been kicking*).

1. Has anybody been looking for me?
2. Has the bridge been repaired yet?
3. Have two men been to the house?
4. How much have you spent?
5. How many people have been injured?
6. Has a solution been found to the problem yet?
7. What has Margaret lost?
8. How badly has the scooter been damaged?
9. Which one of them has borrowed my bicycle?
10. Which man has offered to sell you a smuggled watch?
11. Who has discovered the entrance to the cave?
12. Where have the boys left the table-tennis balls?
13. What has happened to make you change your mind?
14. Who has been trying to cut down the tree over there?
15. Why has David been looking so miserable lately?

When the verb in a direct question is in the Simple Past tense (he *found*; I *left*) and we wish to make an indirect question, we can retain the Simple Past tense OR use the Past Perfect tense, according to the context. If we particularly wish to refer to a point farther back in time, we use the Past Perfect tense. However, in modern English speech many people do not bother to use the Past Perfect tense very much so you may often hear the Simple Past tense instead.

Exercise 12

Change these direct questions into indirect questions after *He wants to know*. Retain the Simple Past tense of the verb in the direct question.

1. Who did it?
2. Who found it?
3. Did Peter catch them?
4. Did the bus stop?
5. Did you win?
6. When did she arrive?
7. How did they come?
8. Where did you buy it?
9. Where did Emman go?
10. What did Lolu say?
11. Who spoke to her?
12. Where did the fire start?
13. How many refused to go?
14. How much did it cost?
15. What did they say?
16. What did George take?

Exercise 13

Change the following into indirect questions but this time alter the tense of the verb to the Past Perfect tense. Start with *He wanted to know.*

1. Did you tell anybody else about the scheme?
2. Did you see Muyiwa or his brother?
3. Which country was the first to resign from the United Nations Organization?
4. How often did you travel along that road last week?
5. When did you last see them alive?
6. What did the men come to do?
7. Did the mechanic finish repairing my car?
8. Did the fishermen have much luck? (Use *had had.*)
9. Why were the boys so long?
10. Why wasn't the house sold earlier?

Questions with 'shall'

There are three kinds of questions which start with 'Shall I . . .' or 'Shall we . . .'

i. **Pure Future** (Will something happen in the future?)
   direct: 'Shall we reach Sekondi in time?' I wondered.
   indirect: I wondered whether we **would** reach Sekondi in time.

ii. **Obligation** (Do you think we *ought* to do something?)
   direct: 'Shall we clean out this room?' they asked me.
   indirect: They asked me whether they **should** (or **ought to**) clean out the/this/that room.

iii. **Desire** (Does somebody want to do something?)
   direct: 'Shall we go to the cinema?' I asked him.
   indirect: I asked him whether he wanted (or *would like*) to go to the cinema.

As you can see from these examples, when questions like these are changed into indirect questions great care must be taken to use the correct form.

Exercise 14

Change the following into indirect questions:

1. 'Shall we go and visit Uncle?' George asked his brother.
2. 'Shall I injure my ankle again if I play?' I wondered.
3. 'Shall we be in time to meet Peju's train?' I asked my father.

4. 'Shall I send the letter by airmail or by surface mail?' my sister asked me.
5. 'Shall I lock the door when I come to bed?' my brother asked.
6. Carolyn asked, 'Shall I leave my hair in curlers all night?'
7. 'Shall we leave the sacks by the tree?' the workmen asked.
8. 'Shall we manage to see Mr. Lee in Kowloon?' I asked.
9. 'Shall I tell Mother about the accident?' my sister asked me.
10. 'Shall Peter and I pay for the damage we have caused?' George asked his father.
11. 'Shall I switch off the radio now?' I asked.
12. 'Shall we go to the sports stadium and watch the semi-final?' my friend asked me.

The indirect form of questions with tags

There are alternative ways of making an indirect question out of a direct question which uses question tags:

i.   *direct:* 'You are going to the cinema, aren't you?'
     indirect: He asked me whether I was going to the cinema.
     OR
     He asked me whether I was going to the cinema and seemed to assume that I was.
     OR
     He asked me whether it was true that I was going to the cinema.

The difficulty in making the indirect question is to decide whether or not to show the affirmative or negative assumption made by the person who asks the question. There is no definite rule. The exact form of the indirect question must depend upon the situation.

ii. *direct:* 'You didn't break this mirror, did you?'
     indirect: He asked me whether I had broken the mirror.
     OR
     He just wanted me to confirm that I had not broken the mirror.
     OR
     He asked me whether I had broken the mirror and assumed that I had not.

Exercise 15

Change the following into indirect questions, using any suitable method:

1. 'There weren't any letters this morning, were there?' Mary asked her mother.
2. 'The road is still flooded, isn't it?' my brother said to me.
3. 'That door won't open properly, will it?' my mother said to me.
4. I asked my sister, 'You haven't seen my camera, have you?'
5. 'She didn't cause much damage to the car, did she?' my brother said to me.
6. 'You can't come tomorrow evening, can you?' George asked his friend.
7. 'That new hotel isn't open yet, is it?' my uncle asked me.
8. 'There's a good film on the television tonight, isn't there?' David said to his sister.
9. 'Peter is going to play football this evening, isn't he?' John asked me.
10. 'Mary would have come if she could have, wouldn't she?' my sister said to me.
11. 'That fan won't work, will it?' I said to George.
12. Mr. Lee asked me, 'You will tell Mary, won't you?'

Chapter 16

Indirect Speech

Be more careful

We study indirect speech not merely to be able to report a speech or prepare for an examination question. There are many expressions which use the same type of pattern as we find in indirect speech and it is important that you should practise these and be able to use them confidently. For example, all the following expressions (and their negative forms) can begin sentences with a pattern similar to that found in indirect speech:

It is (un)likely that . . .   I know (that) . . .
It is possible that . . .   Everybody knows (that) . . .
It appears that . . .   I am sure . . .
It seems that . . .   We are all agreed that . . .
Are you sure that . . .?   Nobody will deny that . . .
I am convinced that . . .   Tell him that . . .

At the same time, it often happens in life that we are faced with the question 'What did he say?' and a knowledge of the techniques of indirect (*or* reported) speech is necessary to enable us to reply.

1. Orders and Requests

We can change an order or a request into indirect speech by using an infinitive, e.g.

    direct: Hurry up!
  indirect: He told me *to hurry up.*
    direct: Don't forget to tell her.
 indirect: He told/asked/reminded me *not to forget* to tell her.
    direct: Don't be silly!
  indirect: He told me *not to be* silly.

Exercise 1

Change the following into indirect speech by using an infinitive (with *not* when necessary). Make up your own introductory words, e.g. *He told me . . .*

1. Don't be long!	8. Tell me the truth.
2. Give her it.	9. Switch on the fans.
3. Put it here.	10. Don't worry about me.
4. Give me them.	11. Don't strain yourself.
5. Don't tell anybody.	12. Help me to do it.
6. Be quiet!	13. Be more careful.
7. Let it go!	14. Enjoy yourself.

2. Changes to make

When we change direct speech to indirect speech the following changes are made:

a. Punctuation

We do not use inverted commas with the indirect statement and we do NOT put a comma after such introductory verbs as *said* and *told*.

> *direct:* He said, 'I'm coming tomorrow.'
> *indirect:* He said (that) he was coming the next day.
> > OR
> He said he is coming tomorrow.
> > OR
> He said that he would come tomorrow/the next day.

Notice that in the indirect statements there is no comma after *said*. The alternative forms given here are all correct. Which form we would use depends entirely on the situation, e.g. how soon after the original speech the indirect statement is made.

b. Pronouns etc.

We must change some pronouns and possessive adjectives to make the meaning quite clear, e.g.

> *direct:* She said, '*I*'ve lost *my* key. Can *I* borrow *yours*?'
> *indirect:* She said *she* had lost *her* key, and asked me whether *she* could borrow *mine*.

c. Words showing place and time

It is often necessary to change words showing place and

283

time so that the meaning is quite clear. In most cases, the changes are a matter of common sense; the choice of words depends entirely on the situation involved. For example, sometimes we must change *tomorrow* to *the next day* but if the speech is reported on the same day, it may be better to retain *tomorrow*.

> *direct:* (6 p.m. A boy is leaving a group of friends.)
> 'Cheerio. See you tomorrow evening.'
> *indirect:* (Ten seconds later. One of the boys did not hear the speech above so he asks a friend what the boy said.)
> 'He said *he would see us tomorrow*.'
> OR
> 'He said *he'll see us tomorrow*.'

Here the indirect statements are inside direct speech—as is usually the case in conversation. The situation is such that it is better to retain *tomorrow*.

3. Changing the tense

In many cases it is NOT necessary to change the tense of verbs when reporting a speech or message. Everything depends on the situation involved; the following points are merely guides, not rules.

i. If the direct speech contains a statement which is always true, we do not change the tense of the verb, e.g.

> *direct:* He said, 'Rain *causes* erosion in the mountains.'
> *indirect:* He said rain *causes* erosion in the mountains.

ii. If the original message or speech refers to something which is still happening when it is reported OR has not yet happened, we often retain the original tense of the verb, e.g.

> *a.* *direct:* He said, 'I'm trying to repair my watch.' (5.15 p.m.)
> *indirect:* He said he is trying to repair his watch. (5.16 p.m.)

> *b.* *direct:* He said, 'It will probably rain tomorrow.' (5 p.m.)
> *indirect:* He said it will probably rain tomorrow. (8 p.m.)

In (*a*) the use of *was* in place of *is* might mislead the listener by making him think that the person concerned had finished repairing his watch. In (*b*) *would* can be used in place of *will* without changing the meaning.

iii. We do not usually change the tense of a verb when the reporting or introductory verb is in the Simple Present tense or in the Present Perfect or Simple Future, e.g.

> *direct:* 'The current is too strong for swimming,' said Peter.
>
> *indirect:* Peter says the current is too strong for swimming.

If it is necessary to change the tense of a verb, this is the type of change which you will have to make:

in direct speech	*in indirect speech*
he is	he was
he can	he could
he may	he might
he is making	he was making
he makes	he made
he was playing	he had been playing
he has found	he had found
he found	*he had found
he will write	he would write
he will have finished	he would have finished
he would help	he would have helped
he was injured	*he had been injured

*In these cases, the Simple Past is sometimes retained (in place of the Past Perfect), particularly in speech.

Exercise 2

Assume that you receive the telephone messages shown below. In each case, write down the message in reported speech, putting at the top the name of the person to whom the person is addressed

Example:

> *direct:* 'Please ask your father if it will be convenient for me to come and see him this evening. I understand that he wants to sell his car and I might be interested in buying it. Ask him to phone 22146 to let me know if it is O.K. My name is Williams.'
>
> *indirect:* Father,
>
> A man called Williams phoned this morning. He says he understands that you want to sell your car and he may be interested in buying it. He wants to know if it is convenient for him to come to see you this

285

evening. Will you please phone 22146 to let him know if it is all right.

Peter

You can put your own name at the end of each message or you can make up one. Make up any other names which may be necessary.

1. 'Please ask Peter to phone me as soon as he comes in. Tell him it's urgent,' said Margaret.
2. 'Please tell your brother that his scooter is ready for collection. We've finished the repairs. You'd better remind him that we close at half past five,' the man from the Central Garage said to me.
3. 'Ask your mother not to come for her appointment tomorrow morning. The dentist, Mr. Coles, has got the flu and won't be able to work for at least a week. I'll let her know when Mr. Coles is back at work again,' the receptionist at the dentist's said to me.
4. 'There are two crates addressed to your father here at the railway station. Does he want us to deliver them or will he pick them up? No, they're not very big—about 2 feet by one foot by one foot. Get him to ring me at 3155,' the man in the Goods Department of the railway said to me.
5. 'Ask your brother to come to the police station as soon as possible,' the police sergeant said on the phone. 'Tell him to bring his driving licence and certificate of insurance with him.'
6. 'Please ask Susan whether she would like to come on a picnic with us tomorrow. We're leaving at eight o'clock in the morning and returning in the evening. My uncle's taking us in his car. Ask her to phone me when she gets home,' Margaret said to me.
7. 'Is Peter there?'
'No, I'm afraid he's not. He's gone out but he'll probably be back in about an hour's time.'
'Oh. Do you know if he's going to watch the football match this evening?'
'No, I'm not sure. I heard him talking about it but I don't know whether he's made up his mind about going. Shall I get him to phone you when he comes in, George?'
'No, thanks. Don't bother. I'll ring again at about four o'-clock.'
8. 'This is Mrs. Williams. Will you please tell your mother that

I can't meet the children when they come out of school? My car's broken down. Tell her not to worry though. My husband is going to collect them in a taxi. They may be a few minutes late. Many thanks.'

Exercise 3

Deliver each of these messages as instructed, using indirect speech.

1. Your father says, 'If anybody phones say that I have gone out but will be back about half past five. Get the name and number of anybody who phones.' A few minutes later, somebody phones. Deliver your father's message.
2. You have just started work in an insurance office. A customer phones and says, 'Please tell Mr. Olude that I've had an accident. I've reversed into a tree. Nobody's been hurt and I don't intend to claim for the damage to the car. Does he want me to report it officially? Get him to give me a ring at my office—87748. The name's Dawodu.' Deliver the message.
3. You expect your brother to return to the house within the next half an hour. Meanwhile, a friend calls and says, 'Please ask John to come and referee our football match at the Jubilee Park at five thirty tonight. Tell him I'm sorry to give him such short notice but somebody else has let us down at the last minute. Now we're relying on him. If he doesn't come, the match will be off. Many thanks.' Shortly afterwards, your brother returns. Pass on the message. You do not know the name of the person who delivered the message but you know he works in the same office as your brother.
4. You work for an electrical firm. You receive the following message on the telephone: 'This is Williams here. I want somebody to come and look at my fridge. It isn't working. I don't know what is wrong with the darned thing. Please send somebody as soon as you can. The address is 48 Gordon Street. Thank you.' Pass on the message to an electrician.

Exercise 4

Change the following into indirect speech:

1. 'I shall not wait here for more than five minutes,' she said.
2. 'Put this book back in the cupboard, Elsie,' the teacher said.

3. 'If Jack wants to be considered for the post,' said the Secretary, 'he must let the Committee know immediately, as entries ought really to have been in yesterday.'

4. 'The bus should come in a minute or two,' David said. 'I don't think it's worth walking into town.'

5. 'Have you booked accommodation at any hotel?' I asked my friend. 'I'm sure Mother will be glad to let you stay with us for a few days.'

6. 'What have you got in that case?' the policeman asked me. 'What are you doing walking about town at this time of the night?'

7. 'I've lost my way,' the stranger told us. 'Am I on the right road to Kabala? How long will it take me to get there?'

8. 'I think the Government is absolutely right to ban the advertising of cigarettes,' my uncle said to me. 'What do you think about it?'

9. 'I'm sorry,' the manager said. 'There seems to have been a mistake. We shouldn't have sent that bill to you at all. It should have gone to somebody else. Please accept our apologies, Mr. Lee.'

10. 'Turn that radio off!' my father ordered. 'I'm fed up with that rubbishy sort of music. It's not really music at all.'

Exercise 5

Change the following into indirect speech:

1. 'I went to a sale this morning,' Margaret said to her sister. 'It was pretty crowded but there were some good bargains there. I managed to get a couple of dresses quite cheaply.'

2. 'Send him off, ref!' the spectator shouted at the referee. 'Chuck 'im off. 'e's not a centre-forward. 'e's a blinking all-in wrestler!'

3. 'I'm very sorry,' the driver of the lorry said to me. 'I had to brake suddenly to avoid a dog. I didn't have time to give you a warning. Is your car badly damaged?'

4. 'How's your brother?' Mary asked me. 'Has he recovered from his operation yet? Margaret and I want to visit him as soon as he is well enough to receive visitors.'

5. 'I don't think this is your pen,' Peter said to me. 'It looks more like Father's. Yours has got a finer nib than this one.'

6. 'When you reach the river,' the man said to us, 'you'll

probably find the ferry waiting for you. The trip across won't
take very long—ten minutes at the most.'

7. 'Hey! Don't pull that out!' I shouted to my younger brother.
'That's not a weed; it's a flower.'

8. 'The fire probably started in that cable up there,' the fireman
said to my father, pointing at a hole in the ceiling. 'It looks to
me as if somebody has been overloading the wire. Look at that
black mark in the corner.'

9. 'I'll probably see you next Monday,' Peter told me. 'I'm
coming to Accra to see about buying a house so I'll give you a
ring and see if we can fix up a meeting. I'd like to meet your
brother, too, if it can be arranged. He knows a lot about
property there.'

10. The policeman told the magistrate, 'I was walking along
Market Street in an easterly direction when I heard shouts
coming from the entrance to the Plaza Hotel. I went there
and saw two men fighting. I attempted to stop them but was
knocked down. With the aid of two passers-by, I separated
the men.'

Exercise 6

Change the following passages from indirect to direct speech:

1. Replying on behalf of the guests, Sir Thomas Roberts said
that it gave him great pleasure to be there then, among so
many friends. He had been delighted when he had received
their invitation, and he could promise them that that party
would linger long in his memory. They knew that he had
spent many years away from that town, his birthplace; but
let them be assured that he had often recalled the days of his
youth. Many of them had been at school with him, and he was
proud that they had become leaders in the life of the town.
He doubted whether any other town had achieved prosperity
more rapidly.

2. Giving evidence, Det. Constable H. R. Smith said that at
5.15 a.m. on the 27th he saw Johnson at the police station and
told him that he was making enquiries into the breaking and
entering of a jeweller's shop earlier that night, and that he
(witness) understood that he had been found in possession of
a stolen van. Johnson said that he did not know anything
about the robbery. He said that he had only taken the van and
was returning it when he was caught. Informed that he was

being arrested on suspicion of breaking into the shop, he said that that was up to the police and it was their job to prove it.

Exercise 7

Change the following into indirect speech:
1. He said, 'I'll come as soon as I can.'
2. She told me, 'I went to visit my uncle on Saturday.'
3. Peter said, 'I may come when I've finished my work.'
4. The other driver claimed, 'My car was stationary at the time of the accident. Yours was travelling at quite a high speed.'
5. He always says, 'I can look after myself.'
6. My uncle told me, 'Learn to defend yourself against bullies. They'll keep away from you if they think you can beat them.'
7. Mr. Williams said, 'Please excuse me from the dinner party. I have to stay at home and look after my mother. She is ill.'
8. I warned Mary, 'Be careful with that razor-blade. It's very sharp. You can cut yourself easily with it.'
9. 'Yes,' he said. 'I think it will rain soon.'
10. 'No,' I told the shopkeeper. 'I don't want that camera. It's too expensive. I can't afford it.'

Part II

Revision Exercises

Chapter 17

Adverbs

her visit to Japan

1. Making Adverbs

Most adverbs end in *ly*, *ily* or *ically* although there are many which do not, e.g. *here, there, seldom, almost, sometimes, very, well, worse, often* etc.

Exercise 1

Form adverbs from the words given below and make sure that you know (i) what they mean and (ii) how to use them in a sentence.

1. punctual	6. efficient	11. skilful	16. tragic
2. entire	7. anxious	12. week	17. competent
3. wise	8. monotonous	13. day	18. absolute
4. rough	9. courteous	14. annual	19. rare
5. eventual	10. cautious	15. part	20. regular

Exercise 2

Form adverbs from these words and make sure that you know what they mean and how to use them in a sentence.

1. logic	6. theory	11. specific	16. able
2. biology	7. history	12. noisy	17. horrible
3. pathetic	8. geometry	13. ordinary	18. terrible
4. democracy	9. geography	14. temporary	19. hospitable
5. grammar	10. physique	15. greedy	20. unanimous

Exercise 3

Form adverbs from these words and make sure that you know what they mean and how to use them in a sentence.

1. pretentious	6. body	11. custom	16. prime
2. noticeable	7. weary	12. honour	17. luck
3. unmistakable	8. clumsy	13. casual	18. fever
4. irretrievable	9. angry	14. brief	19. dogma
5. invisible	10. odd	15. lazy	20. architect

2. The function of adverbs

An adverb can modify, or add to the meaning of, a verb, an adjective or another adverb.

with a verb

He spoke *angrily*. She tried *hard*. He is coming *soon*.

with an adjective

It is *unusually* heavy. I saw a *very* old lorry.

with another adverb

She walks *rather* slowly. He drove *extremely* carefully.

When an adverb modifies an adjective or another adverb it normally comes immediately before it, as in the examples above. An important exception is the adverb *enough* which comes after the adjective or adverb which it modifies, e.g.

Is it cool *enough* in here?

He drove carefully *enough* to satisfy the examiner.

In constructing a sentence we can use a phrase or clause in place of an adverb:

an adverb: We can start *soon*.
an adverb phrase: We can start *in a minute or two*.
an adverb clause: We can start *when you are ready*.

A clause contains a finite verb but a phrase does not.

Exercise 4

Use an adverb of similar meaning in place of the words in italics.

1. He always arrives *at the right time*.

2. She spoke *for a few moments* about her visit to Japan.

294

3. *For a few moments* he felt dazed by the collision.

4. He gave his opinions *in a way which suggested that he would not tolerate any argument or contradiction.*

5. When they had considered his plan, they agreed *and everybody was of the same opinion.*

6. He opened the door *in a cautious manner.*

7. He behaved *in a reckless way.*

8. That was a most unusual story. *In the normal way,* I would not believe it.

9. He was *very much* surprised at the result.

10. They come to see us *from time to time.*

Exercise 5

The sentences below illustrate the use of different types of adverbial clauses. Make sure that you can imitate the pattern of each sentence. In each case, make up three more sentences which contain the words in bold type, used in a similar way to introduce an adverbial clause.

1. (Place) He skidded **where** the road curves sharply.
2. (Time) We went home **when** the film had finished.
3. (Reason) He was annoyed **because** he missed the bus.
4. (Condition) **If** it rains, the game will be cancelled.
5. (Condition) You would be sorry **if** that branch broke.
6. (Condition) **If** you had been there, you would have felt sad.
7. (Purpose) I stayed up late **so that** I would welcome my brother when he arrived.
8. (Concession) **Although** the sun was shining in his eyes, John managed to catch the ball.
9. (Manner) He played **as if** his life depended on the result.
10. (Result) She ironed the dress **so** carelessly **that** she burnt it.
11. (Degree) He ran as quickly **as** he could.
12. (Degree) This one is stronger **than** that one is.

3. The position of adverbs

i. We have already seen that when an adverb modifies an adjective or another adverb, it comes immediately before it. *Enough* is an important exception.

Exercise 6

Put the adverb in its right place in the sentence.

Adverbs

1. She was pleased with us. (extremely)
2. He was confident of success. (completely)
3. It was hot in the sun. (very)
4. The music sounded familiar to me. (rather)
5. He took a long time. (unusually)
6. The patient is better now. (nearly)
7. The dress was expensive to buy. (too)
8. He does not speak clearly. (enough)
9. He has powerful shoulder muscles. (tremendously)
10. That path is not wide. (enough)
11. She is better now. (much)
12. He is agile despite his age. (surprisingly)

ii. Adverbs and adverbial expressions showing **place** and **time.** usually come at the end or at the start of a sentence. When they are put at the start, they are often emphasized. Sometimes we put a time expression at the start of a sentence and a place expression at the end, e.g.

> *Last year* he was working *in Accra.*

When both expressions are put at the end of a sentence, the adverbial of place usually comes *before* that of time, e.g.

> He was working in Accra last year.

iii. Adverbs and adverbial expressions of **manner** usually come in these positions:

after the verb: The soldiers crept *cautiously* towards the river.
after an object: He picked up the snake *cautiously.*
earlier in the sentence for special emphasis: Cautiously he moved nearer to the cobra.
in front of the verb when you wish to point out to which word the adverb applies:
He *soon* asked us to come back.
He asked us to come back *soon.*

iv. When two or three adverbials are used together the normal order is Manner, Place and Time, e.g.

I sat	quietly	in the waiting-room	for half an hour.
	manner	**place**	**time**

This order can be changed if you particularly wish to emphasize a point, e.g.

> For half an hour I sat in the waiting-room in fear and trembling.

After verbs of movement (*come, go, run, walk* etc.) we usually put adverbs of place *before* adverbs of manner. This is done because it is more important to know *where* somebody goes than *how* he gets there.

v. Adverbs of **frequency** (answering the question 'How often?') are important because we often use them. Examples include *never, rarely, seldom, hardly ever, occasionally, sometimes, generally, usually, frequently, nearly always, always, often* and *ever*. Other adverbs which are put in a similar position include *quite, just, already, almost* and *nearly*.

These adverbs are usually put in these positions:

a. *Before the verb when it is one word only:*
   She *never* speaks rudely.

b. *After the first part of the verb when it consists of more than one word:*
   He has *never* driven to Kumasi before.
   He has *rarely* been invited.
   He has not *often* driven there before.

c. *After the verb 'to be' when it consists of one word only, and after the first word when it consists of more than one word:*
   It is *usually* hot in the afternoon.
   He has *usually* been top of the class.

d. Notice the positions of adverbs of frequency in questions:
   Will he *ever* recover from the operation?
   Do they *always* work as swiftly as that?
   Why does he *never* come to see us?

Exercise 7

Put *often* in each sentence:

1. He stays there.
2. She is early.
3. He does that.
4. He will be late.
5. We were defeated.
6. It has been broken.
7. They come here.
8. It is flooded.
9. I saw him.
10. It needs repairing.
11. Does he come to see you?
12. Are they as tough as that?
13. Is she as angry as that?
14. He doesn't drink coffee.
15. You won't see him again.
16. Music makes her sleepy.
17. That door sticks.
18. He has not been hurt.
19. It is cool at night.
20. His car breaks down.

Exercise 8

Put the adverb in the sentence correctly. Sometimes there are alternative positions.

1. He has forgotten to bring some. (hardly ever)
2. Do they come this way? (usually)
3. You will see one as good as this. (seldom)
4. He is waiting there when I arrive. (generally)
5. Neither of them is there. (sometimes)
6. I have told them about it. (already)
7. Have they finished painting the house? (nearly)
8. The postman comes before half past seven. (rarely)
9. Importers and merchants are reluctant to lower the price of their goods. (normally)
10. I know he goes fishing. (occasionally)
11. My watch seems to be right. (never)
12. Are they attacked by locusts? (ever)
13. He has told me about the accident. (just)
14. She could have noticed exactly what happened. (never)
15. It has been said that women are more patient than men. (often)
16. If you have finished, I'll explain what really took place. (quite)
17. Have the two men been caught? (already)
18. I am sure he will do that again. (never)
19. Some of them have forgotten to bring their boots. (frequently)
20. He was too slow to catch the centre-forward. (nearly always)

Chapter 18

Agreement

Dogs . . . how to swim

1. Miscellaneous difficulties of agreement

i. Remember that the following words are singular. They take a singular verb and never have an 's' added to them.

furniture, news, apparatus, luggage, information, knowledge, lightning, traffic, equipment, clothing, laughter, thunder, behaviour, shouting, machinery, scenery.

ii. Some problems arise with words which end in *ics*.

   a. Such words as *comics, mechanics, cosmetics* and *tactics* take a plural verb.

   b. Such words as *politics, mathematics, economics, dynamics* and *acoustics* can be used with a singular or a plural verb but only in certain patterns. Consider these examples:

     1. Politics is an uncertain career.

     2. His politics are rather liberal.

     3. Mathematics is my favourite subject.

4. The mathematics of the position are still obscure.
5. Economics is a vital subject.
6. The economics of the project are still being considered.
7. The acoustics of this hall are extremely good.
8. Acoustics is the science of sound and is a factor which must be considered when building a theatre or cinema.

When we refer to each of these sciences as a subject for study, its name is usually regarded as a singular word. When the science is applied to a problem or situation, the name is often used with a plural verb.

iii. There is often confusion over the word *native* so that we have this trouble:

wrong: Both of them are a native of Nigeria.
right: Both of them are natives of Nigeria.

At one time in the past the word 'native(s)' was used to refer to people in a foreign country whose methods of living were different from those of the speaker. It then meant 'savages; uncivilized people' and it is still used in that sense by (i) a few rude or thoughtless people and (ii) ignorant people who have not travelled outside their own country. About two thousand years ago the Romans regarded the Germans and Swiss as savages. The word 'natives' was used (wrongly) by Europeans to apply to people of other lands:

Look at that native brandishing his spear.
The explorer was killed by a lot of natives.
Look! A native is chasing him to kill him.

In each of the above sentences *native(s)* is intended to mean 'a wild and savage man'. In this sense, we can have 'a native' or 'natives'. Fortunately, this use of the word is disappearing.

The second meaning of 'a native' is 'a person who was born in a certain country; a local inhabitant as opposed to a foreigner or an immigrant'. In this sense, nothing is said of a person's character.

George is a native of England.
David and Ifor are natives of Wales.
John and Bill are natives of London.

Notice that in this sense we can use both 'a native' and 'natives'.

iv. *People* can have an 's' on it when it refers to races or nations of people. Compare:

Those people all live in the same house.
The peoples of the world must learn to live together.

v. Notice how *type* and *kind* are used in these sentences:

That is a new type of car.
I saw several new types of cars.
This is a new kind of television set.
There are many different kinds of orchids there.

vi. After *other* we frequently use a plural noun but after *another* we use a singular noun because it means '*one* other'.

There are *other houses* like ours.
There is *another house* like ours.

vii. When *all* = *everything* it is used with a singular verb:

All *is* ready. Let us begin.
I will summarize all that *was* discussed.

If *all* refers to a number of items or people already mentioned, a plural verb is used:

'I've just counted the players. All *are* here.'
'I've checked the tyres. All are O.K.'

2. The Simple Present tense: Make and Makes

He She It Everybody That man	**makes** them	I We They You The men	**make** them

As you already know, the affirmative form of the Simple Present tense ends in 's' when the subject is *he, she, it* or a word which could be replaced by one of them. Otherwise, as in the second box, there is no 's' at the end of the verb.

Exercise 1

Put in the correct Simple Present form of the verb at the top of each list.

(a) **know**

1. We all . . . him.
2. Peter . . . the way.
3. Everybody . . . the tune.
4. Tom . . . your cousins.
5. Who . . . how to do it?
6. The people . . . the truth.
7. She . . . what to say.
8. Dogs . . . how to swim.
9. One of them . . . me.
10. Somebody . . . about it.

(b) **like**

11. Everybody . . . them.
12. Nobody . . . that place.
13. My friend . . . that dress.
14. Which one . . . the film?
15. How many of them . . . tea?
16. Some people . . . to sleep.
17. . . . they . . . your picture?
18. . . . it . . . to eat fish?
19. Mary . . . to play tennis.
20. He . . . to drive.

Exercise 2

Put in the correct form of the Simple Present tense of the verbs in brackets.

1. Mathematics . . . (seem) to be his best subject.
2. Every one of those men . . . (deserve) a reward.
3. A lot of the meat . . . (go) bad if it is left in the sun.
4. Two of the rooms . . . (lead) into the hall but this one . . . (lead) to the kitchen.
5. This . . . (face) south; those . . . (face) north.
6. The weight of his cases . . . (appear) in excess of the allowance unless he . . . (travel) first class.
7. The purposes of the society . . . (conflict) with his interests.
8. Women usually . . . (make) better nurses than men although the latter . . . (claim) to be the superior sex.
9. Wheat . . . (grow) in countries which . . . (possess) a temperate climate but rice . . . (require) a tropical or sub-tropical climate. The latter . . . (exist) in our country.
10. The temperature in that range of mountains . . . (seem) much less than it is here.
11. The acoustics of the hall . . . (affect) the music considerably.
12. The range of his interests . . . (stretch) from sport to modern sculpture.
13. The safety of all the people in these buildings . . . (depend) on a number of factors, most of which . . . (appear) very obvious to me.
14. All that . . . (glitter) is not gold.
15. Courtesy . . . (cost) nothing and often . . . (bring) a reward.
16. He who . . . (laugh) last . . . (laugh) longest.
17. Their house still . . . (lack) something—a supply of piped water. Its absence . . . (make) life difficult at times.
18. Nowadays most young children . . . (know) how to read but sometimes their education . . . (cease) at too early an age.
19. His hair . . . (seem) to be getting thinner each year.

20. One of these houses . . . (belong) to my father but the other two . . . (belong) to my uncle who . . . (live) in another town.

3. Is, are; do, does; has, have

You already know when to use each of the words in the pairs above. The following exercises are revisionary.

Exercise 3

Put *is* or *are* in each blank space:

1. I hope everybody . . . happy today; the holidays . . . about to start and this . . . the end of the term.
2. Some of the branches on that tree over there . . . old and dangerous. . . . there any chance of getting them cut down?
3. Her hands . . . small; the shape of his hands . . . unusual.
4. The traffic . . . at a standstill. Something . . . wrong.
5. All this equipment . . . old-fashioned but some of it . . . still quite useful.
6. . . . the news good today or bad? How . . . the triplets getting on?
7. He wants to buy one of these houses which . . . opposite the school. It . . . in a rather convenient position.
8. Nobody . . . there and nothing . . . ready. Where . . . everybody today? . . . there anything wrong?
9. . . . these the shoes you were looking for?
10. Where . . . the ones you borrowed from me yesterday?

Exercise 4

Put in *do* or *does:*

1. . . . you know his brother? What . . . he do these days?
2. Where . . . she live now? . . . you know her address?
3. It . . . not matter much. What . . . you think about it?
4. Where . . . the organizers live? . . . Mr. Coles know their address? David and John . . . n't know it.
5. . . . all the dust worry you at all? It . . . n't affect me.
6. How . . . they manage to get home so early? . . . somebody give them a lift?
7. When . . . the secretary want to see us? . . . the other members of the committee know about this?

303

Agreement

8. How much . . . do those cost? How many . . . do you want?
9. When . . . do the rest of the team arrive?
10. . . . do your brother's friends want to come as well?

Exercise 5

Put in *has* or *have:*

1. There *have* been a considerable increase in the prices of most kinds of cars but it . . . has not had much effect on sales.
2. Everybody . . . has his own secret ambition.
3. Most of this furniture . . . has an old-fashioned look about it.
4. . . . has anybody been here today? Yes, some people . . . called to see you and there . . . has been a telephone call for you.
5. One of the players who . . . has just got out of that coach . . . has several sticks under his arm.
6. What . . . has come over you? What . . . has happened to you?
7. Where . . . has the rest of the oranges gone? Who . . . has eaten them?
8. Where . . . has the rest of the milk gone? Have Peter's cousins drunk it?
9. An amendment . . . has been passed making it an offence to have an unlicensed gun in your possession.
10. The traffic . . . has increased recently but little . . . has been done to improve parking facilities; indeed, some of the space which was available in the past . . . has now been used for other purposes.

4. This, these; that, those

Exercise 6

a. Put *this* or *these* in front of each word or expression:

1. . . . this equipment
2. . . . this agenda
3. . . . these reasons
4. . . . these two points
5. . . . this audience
6. . . . this crowd
7. . . . kinds of rice
8. . . . this kind of pipe
9. . . . peoples
10. . . . this family
11. . . . this type of problem
12. . . . policemen
13. . . . women
14. . . . this disturbance
15. . . . theorems
16. . . . this climate
17. . . . this grass
18. . . . this weather
19. . . . this money
20. . . . coins

304

b. Put in *that* or *those*:

1. . .*s* regulations
2. all . .*s*. rules
3. all . . . furniture
4. all . . . luggage
5. all . .*s* bags
6. all . .*s* vehicles
7. all . . . traffic
8. in . .*s* ways
9. along . .*s* path
10. . . . scenery
11. some of . . *s*apparatus
12. a lot of . . . crop
13. . . . laughter
14. all . . . information
15. . *s*. excuses
16. all . .*s*. spectators
17. all . . . congregation
18. . . . family
19. . . . suits her
20. . .*s*. suit him

5. Every(body), nobody and none

i. Every(body)

Every is followed by a singular noun and a singular verb, e.g. *Every boy hopes to be successful eventually.* In a similar way, *everybody, everyone* and *everything* are used with a singular verb, e.g. *Everything is satisfactory.*

However, notice the tags at the end of these questions:

a. Everybody is ready, *aren't they?*
b. Everything is ready, *isn't it?*
c. Everyone had a fair chance, *didn't they?*

When we use *everybody* and *everyone* in questions of this type, the tag assumes that the words are plural in meaning although they take a singular verb normally.

ii. Nobody

Nobody and *no one* also take a singular verb but have question tags which assume a plural meaning:

d. Nobody is ready, *are they?*
e. No one had a fair chance, *did they?*

iii. None

Fowler (*A Dictionary of Modern English Usage*) gives this opinion about *none:* 'It is a mistake to suppose that the pronoun is singular only and must at all costs be followed by singular verbs etc.; the Oxford English Dictionary explicitly states that the plural construction is commoner.'

The Concise Oxford Dictionary offers this advice: '*Use none of them is* or *are*, according to the sense required.'

If any were needed, these two authorities will serve to reject the old belief that *none* is always singular. The following are examples of current usage:

a. None of this concerns me.   (singular)

b. None of them are ready yet.   (plural)

c. All the oranges have gone. There are none left.   (plural)

d. None of them really want to go.   (plural)

Some people prefer these alternatives:

b. None of them is ready yet.   (singular)

d. None of them really wants to go.   (singular)

For the time being, therefore, both forms exist and should be expected and accepted.

6. There is and There are

It is necessary for you to be careful when using the expressions *There is/was* and *There are/were*. In these cases the subject follows the verb and is sometimes so far from it that it is easy to use the the wrong form of the verb.

Exercise 7

Put in *is* or *are:*

1. There is, as far as I can see, no particularly pressing problem for us to consider today.

2. There is an endless succession of difficulties in this place. . . Is there any way of improving the position?

3. It seems to me that there are the greatest possible dangers inherent in such a scheme, and that there is a grave risk that the whole project may collapse at any moment.

4. Where there is a will, there is a way.

5. Is there the slightest possibility that the position may improve next year? Yes, there are a number of solutions which may be found, if we have the time.

6. In my village there is a lack of facilities for young people. This may account for the fact that there is more juvenile delinquency there now.

7. Is there as many chairs as there are people?

8. There is quite a crowd of people outside the hotel. I wonder if there is some special reason for such a gathering.

9. There is not much food left, and such vegetables as there are must last for at least two weeks.

10. Here . . .is. a list of the names of the people to be invited. You will find that there are about thirty altogether.

7. The colour of his eyes is . . .

Problems of agreement are often caused by these patterns:

a. **a plural word** *of the* **a singular word** + **a verb**

Example: The **aims** of the cultural society ARE quite interesting.

b. **a singular word** *of (the)* **a plural word** + **a verb**

Example: The **colour** of that boy's eyes IS brown.

In these patterns the subject of the verb is the first noun, or equivalent word, in the group, i.e. *aims* and *colour*, and the verb must agree with them. You must be careful because it is sometimes tempting to make the verb agree (wrongly) with the noun just before it, i.e. *society* or *eyes*. The danger is greatest when the expression is a long one and the writer may forget what his original subject was, e.g.

The **aims** of the society to which most of my friends and brothers belong ARE quite interesting.

Exercise 8

Put in *is* or *are:*

1. One of those rooms .is. my brother's.
2. The leader of the gangsters .is. known to have a criminal record.
3. I was told that the manager of the players . is. not travelling with them.
4. This bunch of bananas is. . too expensive.
5. The greatest problems of this type of mining .are. those connected with equipment.
6. The worst of the problems .is the one which David is trying to deal with.
7. The sharp rise in the price of raw materials .is. partly due to greatly increased demand overseas.
8. The structure of those mountains . is rather unusual.
9. The wild ambitions which constantly flow through his mind are. a source of trouble to him.

inherited from the past.
historical momentum.

10. Many people feel that the congestion in parts of the town ˌⁱs . a legacy of the past.

8. Collective and group nouns

We sometimes want to know whether to say:

i. The team IS playing well today.

　　　　　　or

ii. The team ARE playing well today.

We meet a similar problem in dealing with such words as *audience*, *congregation*, *crowd*, *group* and *family*. With these and similar group nouns we can use a singular or a plural verb according to the sense required. When the team (or other group) is referred to as a single unit, we use a singular verb. When it is considered as a collection of individuals, a plural verb can be used. Compare these sentences:

iii. The audience cheered, clapped and threw their hats up in the air.

iv. The audience is quite a large one for this time of the year.

In (iii) the various actions of members of the audience make us think of the audience as a collection of individuals. In any case, we could *not* say: 'The audience threw *its* hat up in the air.'

Compare these sentences:

v. The Health Committee *are* by no means agreed as to the cause of the outbreak.

vi. The Committee *has* recommended that no action be taken.

Why is a plural verb used in (v) and a singular verb used in (vi)?

9. One (of)

Compare the words in italics:

i. We need one *volunteer*.

ii. One of the *volunteers* is too young.

In (i) we are concerned with one person only. In (ii) we are concerned with one *out of several*. Thus we have these patterns:

　　one + a singular noun
　　one of (*the*) + a plural noun

In each case, the verb will be singular if *one* is the subject:

iii. One player *is* still in the changing-room.

iv. One of the players *is* not here yet.

308

10. One example is . . .

You may sometimes be faced with this awkward construction:
'The rules of hockey are easy to understand on the whole.
However, there are a few rules which can be interpreted in
different ways, thus causing trouble. *One example is the con-
flicting opinions* of referees on the question of obstruction.'
We then have this pattern:

a singular noun IS *a plural noun*
One example   is the opinions . . .

The only solution to this problem is to avoid the construction
by using some other type of expression, e.g. 'One example is the
rule dealing with obstruction. This leads to conflicting opinions
. . .'

Chapter 19

Articles

. . . awkward moment

Please notice that the rules and exercises in this chapter must be supplemented by wide and sustained reading. We learn a language by practising it: by speaking, listening, reading and writing—and NOT by attempting to digest a mass of rules. Subject to this fact, the work below may be of help to you.

1. A or An

We put *an*, instead of *a*, in front of a word if it starts with a vowel sound **when it is spoken** or has a silent 'h' at the front of the word. It is important to remember that the spelling of a word is NOT always a safe guide. For example, *union*, *European* and *uniform* start with a vowel when written but start with a consonant sound (*yew*) *when spoken*.

i. *starting with a 'yew' sound*
   a union
   a European
   a uniform

starting with a vowel sound
   an uncle
   an Englishman
   an umbrella

ii. *the 'h' is pronounced*
   a hotel
   a hill
   a husband

with a silent 'h'
   an honour
   an hour
   an heir

Exercise 1

Put *a* or *an* before each of the following:

1. *an* awkward moment
2. *an* Indian stamp
3. *a* university
4. *a* useful book
5. *a* mirror
6. *an* ex-M.P.
7. *an* African country
8. *a* honeymoon
9. *a* hyphenated word
10. *a* refrigerator
11. *an* honorary appointment
12. *an* exit
13. *a* small egg
14. *a* universal appeal
15. *a* horrible sight
16. *an* Australian book
17. *an* hour's delay
18. *a* helpful person
19. *a* united nation
20. *an* urgent message

Exercise 2

Put *a* or *an* before each of the following:

1. *a* modern hotel
2. *an* encyclopedia
3. *an* umpire
4. *a* hostage
5. *a* hospital
6. *an* onion
7. *a* lettuce
8. *a* chicken
9. *an* ulcer
10. *an* infirmary
11. *an* extremely exciting film
12. *a* very interesting trip
13. *an* honest man
14. *a* unique opportunity
15. *a* unanimous decision
16. *a* healthy person
17. *an* underground railway
18. *a* young lady
19. *a* high hedge
20. *an* independent country

2. No article

We do not use *a*, *an* or *the* in these cases:

a. Before the names of roads, streets, some titles accompanied by a person's name, and plural common nouns used in a general sense.

b. Before the names of towns, cities, provinces and countries (except as noted below) *unless they are used adjectivally.* Compare these examples:

 i. He lives in London. I live in Ibadan.
 ii. He plays for a London football team. She is in the Ibadan hospital.

Note: We put *the* before groups of islands, ranges of mountains and such countries as these:

the United Arab Republic
the People's Republic of China

> the U.S.A   the U.S.S.R.
> the U.K.   the Republic of . . .

We do not put an article before such countries or places as Nigeria, Ghana, Hong Kong, Mauritius, America, England, France, Germany, Italy etc.

c. Before the name of a game after the verb 'play', e.g. 'He plays football. She plays netball. We play hockey.' An article will be required when the name is used adjectivally, e.g. 'This is a hockey ball. That is a badminton net.'

d. Before the name of a meal after the verb 'have', e.g. 'He's gone to have lunch.'

e. In expressions like these:

> at first   next April   get into trouble
> at last   last Monday   in public
> in conclusion   next month   at night

3. The

The definite article is used in these cases:

a. With plural common nouns which are not used in a general sense and refer to particular objects.

b. When we refer to a special person or thing, e.g.

> 'That is *the* camera I wanted to buy.'

c. In front of words which are the only one of their type, e.g.

> the beach   the earth   the ground
> the shore   the left   the north
> the sea   the temperature   the east
> the rain   the climate   the humidity
> the sun   the soil   the dampness
> the moon   the right   the end

d. Before superlatives, e.g. *the finest one there.*

e. Before the names of canals, rivers, seas, oceans, deserts, river basins, mountain ranges, bays and gulfs. We do *not* use an article with capes and lakes if the name of the particular place is given, e.g. 'He went to Lake Emerald, which is near Cape Rushe.'

f. Before *first*, *last* and *next* when the following word is NOT a day or a month. Compare these sentences:

> I'll catch the next bus.
> I'll see you next Monday.

4. A and An

We use *a* or *an* on these occasions:

a. When it means 'any one' and does not refer to a particular object.

b. With occupations, e.g. I am a farmer. He is a mechanic.
Notice that we use *the* when referring to a particular person, e.g. There is the mechanic who repaired my car.

c. When an object is mentioned for the first time. We then use *the* for any further references to it, e.g.

I found *a* wallet. I took *the* wallet to the police station.

We do not use *a* or *an* with uncountable nouns, e.g.
'He drinks milk and eats meat.'

When necessary we can use such expressions as *a bottle of milk*, *a joint of meat* etc.

5. Illnesses etc.

Notice the use (or absence) of articles in the following lists. Imagine that each illness or complaint is used immediately after *He has*

NO ARTICLE	*a* OR *an*	WITH *the*
malaria	a headache	the flu
influenza	a pain in . . .	(the) cramp
smallpox	a bruise on . . .	the stitch
cholera	a scratch on . . .	
typhoid	a sprained . . .	
diphtheria	a broken . . .	
impetigo	a cold	
tuberculosis	a fever	
cancer of the . . .	a bilious attack	
*(the) toothache	an ache in . . .	
*(the) stomach-ache	an ulcer	

Note: toothache and *stomach-ache* can be used with or without *the*.

Exercise 3

Put in *a, an* or *the* OR leave the space empty to show that no article should be used. There are alternatives in some cases.

1. . . . telephone is . . . very important means of communication.

2. There is usually . . . fine weather in . . . British Isles in July.
3. . . . invention of . . . wheel marked . . . step forward in man's efforts to transport things over . . . long distances.
4. . . . tin is mined on . . . large scale in parts of . . . Nigeria.
5. On . . . whole I agree that . . . health of . . . people in this district has shown . . . distinct improvement in . . . last few years.
6. I have friends in various parts of . . . Igboland but they do not all use . . . same dialect.
7. In . . . days of . . . old, . . . transport from one place to another was often . . . problem.
8. We live within . . . easy reach of . . . river so we are fond of . . . fishing and . . . swimming. Whenever I get . . . chance, I go down to . . . river with . . . friend, and we spend . . . pleasant hour there.
9. My uncle is . . . trader but he does . . . little farming with . . . help of his two sons.
10. . . . great many people have tried to discover . . . source of that river but it is not . . . easy task because . . . river seems to come from . . . huge area of . . . swamp at . . . foot of those mountains.
11. . . . uneducated person is at . . . disadvantage if he wants to become . . . trader. He can make some progress but there comes . . . time when he must be able to read and to check . . . figures in . . . account. If he has sufficient money, he can employ . . . educated person to act as . . . accountant or . . . book-keeper for him but he must then rely on . . . honesty and . . . integrity of . . . employee.
12. In his house . . . mere act of . . . disagreement brings . . . retaliation of some kind. Perhaps I should say that . . . 'retaliation' is not exactly . . . right word. It is more accurate to use . . . 'scolding' or . . . 'criticism'. Anyway, . . . atmosphere in that house is not . . . happiest I have seen.
13. I have been told to report anybody offering . . . bribe or . . . inducement of any kind. . . . bribery spreads quickly and is like . . . disease which eats at . . . economic heart of . . . nation.
14. . . . recent increase in . . . tourism in our country has had . . . noticeable effect on . . . few towns but it has not yet made much of . . . impact on . . . mass of people in . . . rural areas.
15. When there is . . . civil war there are usually . . . outsiders who are ready to intervene. In . . . case of . . . Congo, it looks

as if this has been so, but I hesitate to give . . . opinion since I am not aware of . . . facts of . . . situation.

16. My brother returned from school in . . . afternoon and told us that he had to go to . . . Majestic hotel in . . . Lagos in . . . evening. He said he was going to meet . . . representative from . . . foreign firm who hoped to set up . . . factory in this part of . . . country.

17. There was . . . little trouble at . . . new tyre factory on . . . main road to . . . Torquay. During . . . night . . . passer-by saw . . . dull red glow in one of . . . buildings and called . . . Fire Brigade. . . . firemen arrived just in . . . time and discovered that . . . pile of old tyres had caught . . . fire. They soon put . . . fire out.

18. My cousin is studying at . . . university in . . . United Kingdom. He hopes to become . . . engineer when he has passed . . . necessary examinations. He will probably get . . . job with . . . Government or with . . . commercial firm. He is studying . . . electrical engineering at . . . moment.

19. My uncle owns quite . . . area of . . . land not far from . . . tributary of . . . Niger. He is trying to use . . . water from . . . river to irrigate his land.

20. They have gone into . . . woods to collect . . . firewood which they can sell at . . . market. Then they will use . . . money to buy . . . meat, . . . sugar and . . . few other things.

Exercise 4

Put in *a, an* or *the* OR leave the space empty to show that no article should be used. There are alternatives in some cases.

1. In that school they have to speak . . . Yoruba all . . . time.

2. I think Mr. Lee has . . . financial interest in . . . firm which is building . . . new block of classrooms at our school.

3. That shop fell into . . . disrepute when . . . manager started dealing in . . . stolen goods. . . . police soon caught him and he is now serving . . . long sentence in . . . prison.

4. In . . . British Isles there is . . . surprising variety of . . . weather. For . . . example, . . . south-west of . . . England has . . . much milder climate than . . . east coast and . . . midlands. Again, . . . conditions on . . . west coast of . . . Scotland are very different from those on . . . east coast. It would be wrong for . . . tourist to generalize on . . . evidence of one or two places only.

5. It would be . . . fun to give John . . . surprise and not tell him about . . . letter from . . . Ministry of Education until he gets home.

6. My friend has just been awarded . . . scholarship to . . . university in . . . U.S.A. It was awarded by . . . oil company and he was . . . only boy in . . . school to get one. I hope to get . . . scholarship in . . . near future.

7. There was . . . storm last night so I stopped at . . . home and played . . . chess with my brother. He taught me . . . rules and I managed to win . . . third game after he had made . . . careless mistake.

8. When you visit . . . Kowloon, go to . . . shopping arcade under . . . Hotel Miramar. It is in . . . Nathan Street, which is . . . area very popular with . . . tourists.

9. My sister went to . . . Anglican Girls' School but I went to . . . Ibadan Grammar School.

10. George has been transferred from . . . Zamaru to . . . Oil Palm Research Station at . . . Benin. . . . move is . . . promotion for him and will bring . . . increase in . . . salary.

Exercise 5

Write down the letter which appears immediately before the item which must be put in the sentence. If nothing should be added, write 'E'.

1. Each child was given a tooth-brush and a tube of . . . . tooth-paste.
    (A) a   (B) the   (C) some   (D) an   (E) *add nothing*
2. Do you drink . . . tea without sugar?
    (A) the   (B) an   (C) a   (D) some   (E) *add nothing*
3. He is very busy during . . . football season.
    (A) some   (B) the   (C) an   (D) last   (E) *add nothing*
4. What . . . pity! He has missed his bus.
    (A) a   (B) the   (C) an   (D) some   (E) *add nothing*
5. I shall be out during most of . . . morning tomorrow.
    (A) a   (B) the   (C) some   (D) an   (E) *add nothing*
6. I had . . . great difficulty in persuading him to come.
    (A) a   (B) an   (C) the   (D) some   (E) *add nothing*
7. During the holidays we visited . . . Northern Nigeria.
    (A) the   (B) a   (C) some   (D) an   (E) *add nothing*
8. She has . . . advantage of being able to speak several languages.

(A) the   (B) a   (C) some   (D) an   (E) *add nothing*
9. He is learning to be . *a* . mechanic.
   (A) an   (B) the   (C) a   (D) some   (E) *add nothing*
10. If you hurry, you may be able to catch . *the* . last bus.
    (A) an   (B) the   (C) some   (D) a   (E) *add nothing*

Exercise 6

In each blank space put in *a, an* or *the* unless no article is required. If that is the case, leave the space empty.

1. During . . . holidays we cycled from . . . Falmouth to visit
   . . . Jamaica Salt Works along . . . road to . . . Duncans. It is
   . . . distance of about eight miles and took us nearly . . . hour.
   We were not in . . . hurry. We went on . . . A1 road but we
   came back along . . . B11 road although it was . . . longer way
   round.
2. Yesterday evening there was . . . Bible Quiz in . . . hall.
   Teams from several schools in . . . neighbourhood took part.
3. Be careful! . . . current is particularly strong in this part of
   . . . river. There have been . . . number of deaths here
   during . . . past few years through . . . failure of . . . swimmers
   to estimate . . . strength of . . . current.
4. Members of . . . Geographical Society are expected to pay
   . . . certain amount each year. . . . money is used to pay for
   . . . outings to . . . interesting places.
5. . . . Minister of Education is coming here next week to open
   . . . new technical college. It is . . . first of its kind in . . .
   country.
6. . . . traffic situation in . . . centre of . . . town is growing
   steadily worse. I think . . . only solution will be to build . . .
   by-pass round . . . town. This won't solve . . . problem
   entirely but it will bring . . . measure of . . . relief for . . .
   time being.
7. When . . . police inspector reached . . . scene of . . . accident,
   he made . . . note of . . . position of . . . vehicles and asked
   each of . . . drivers to make . . . statement as to . . . cause of
   . . . accident. In their statements they both denied . . .
   responsibility and said that . . . other driver was to blame.
8. Would you like to go to . . . matinée at . . . Lido cinema
   on . . . Saturday? Sonebody has given me . . . complimentary
   ticket to . . . show and I'll pay for you. I think . . . film is
   quite . . . good one. . . . man in . . . street was handing out

317

leaflets advertising it. I've read . . . summary of . . . plot and it seems quite interesting.

9. When my cousin came to stay with us, we took him for . . . tour of . . . district. We went to . . . zoo and to . . . museum. Then we went to visit . . . oil palm estate on . . . outskirts of . . . town. We had quite . . . busy and interesting day.

10. When we go to . . . sea my sister likes to spend most of her time on . . . beach. She is afraid . . . crab may nip her if she goes in . . . water. I used to laugh at her until one day I put my foot on something on . . . sea-bed. I don't know whether it was . . . crab or . . . fish of some kind but it gave me quite . . . bite.

Chapter 20

Comparison

I am taller than you

1. Adjectives

	a **Positive** (one only)	*b* **Comparative** (1 of 2 only)	*c* **Superlative** (1 of 3 or more)
type i	fat easy short	fatter easier shorter	fattest easiest shortest
type ii	careful unusual difficult	more careful more unusual more difficult	most careful most unusual most difficult
type iii	good bad much } many }	better worse more	best worst most

type i: Most monosyllabic adjectives are compared in this way, with *er* and *est*. We compare adjectives of two syllables in a similar way if they have the accent on the second syllable (e.g.

Comparison

sincere) OR end in *er, le, ow* or *y* (e.g. *clever, simple, narrow, wealthy*).

type ii: Most long adjectives are compared in this way with *more* and *most*.

type iii: There are a few adjectives with irregular comparisons. The important ones are given in the table.

Notes

a. better or best?

In most cases the comparative form of an adjective is used when only two things are compared: 'I am taller than you.' It can be used when more than two are concerned:

'I am taller than the other boys in my class.'

In speech we can often hear the superlative used when some people would prefer to use the comparative: 'Both of the rings are nice but I think that one's the best.' This usage is so widespread that it is doubtful whether we can call it an error. However, foreign students are advised to use the comparative on such an occasion.

b. easier than

In many cases the comparative is followed by *than* (and NOT by *then*): 'This is more difficult *than* I thought it was.'

c. the easiest

When an article is used before a superlative adjective, it is usually (but not always) *the:* 'I'll have *the* cheapest ring.'

d. older or elder?

We use *elder* and *eldest* for people in the same family. We do *not* use them for things or animals.

We use *older* and *oldest* for people, animals and things.

In most cases, *elder* and *eldest* are followed by a word such as *brother* or *sister*, or preceded by *the*.

i. John is my elder brother. He is older than me.

ii. You are the eldest in the family. I am the oldest in the class.

e. farther or further?

When in doubt, use *further*. It can have all the meanings of *farther* (which usually refers to distance) and can also mean 'additional' or 'extra'.

f. no comparison

Strictly speaking, we cannot make the comparative and superlative forms of such words as *perfect*, *unique*, *full*, *empty* and *circular*. We cannot have something which is 'more perfect'.

However, when these words are used loosely, or a speaker wishes to stress his point, comparison is used: 'He made a most perfect fool of himself yesterday.' Compare: 'Yes, it's absolutely perfect' in which we could argue that 'absolutely' should be omitted. We can also say (of two tins of petrol): 'This one is fuller than that one.' It would perhaps be more accurate to say: 'This one is more nearly full than that one' but the speed of conversation does not always permit us to think about such niceties.

g. Do not use a double comparative or a double superlative

The most common mistakes in dealing with comparison are shown below:

wrong	**correct**
more taller	taller
most difficultest	most difficult

We cannot put *more/most* before a word AND add *er/est* at the end. That amounts to doing the same job twice and it is quite wrong.

Exercise 1

Look at this table and then answer the revision questions:

	Age	Height	Weight in lbs.	Shoe size	Marks in an English test
Boys					
John	18	6' 0"	175	10	57%
George	16	5' 6"	148	7	53%
David	17	5' 9"	144	9	62%
Girls					
Mary	16	5' 4"	115	4	65%
Susan	15	5' 1"	106	3	56%
Anne	19	5' 6"	121	5	74%

Comparison

a. Answer these questions in complete sentences.

1. Which pupil is best at English? *Anne*
2. Whose shoes are smaller than Mary's? *Susan*
3. Is the average height of the boys more or less than that of the girls?
4. Which girl is better than George at English and the same in height? *Anne*
5. Who has fewer marks for English than Susan?

b. To revise your knowledge of the comparative and superlative, make up similar questions about the table. Ask and answer them in class.

Exercise 2

Put the adjective in brackets into the correct degree of comparison.

1. My mother is far . . . (young) than my father.
2. I am . . . (old) than my brothers and sisters.
3. This was the . . . (cheap) but . . . (reliable) watch I could find.
4. Please take the . . . (great) possible care with this camera.
5. There are several ways of getting there but I think you'll find that this is the . . . (good) road to take.
6. Your handwriting is . *worse* (bad) than mine.
7. Travelling by rail is much *more* (comfortable) than going by car.
8. This is probably the . . . *most* (modern) hotel in the country but is *more* (expensive) than the one I usually stay at.
9. She will be upset. She is . *more* (emotional) than we are.
10. George is the *most* (skilful) of the forwards but he is not the *most* . . . (successful).

2. Adverbs

i. Adverbs of one syllable: *hard—harder—hardest*
ii. Adverbs of more than one syllable: *skilfully—more skilfully—most skilfully*
iii. Irregular adverbs:

badly	*worse*	*worst*
well	*better*	*best*
little	*less*	*least*
much	*more*	*most*

Exercise 3

Write down the letter which appears in front of the item which can be put into the sentence.

1. He plays well but his brother plays even . . . ~A~ B .
   (A) well   (B) better   (C) best
2. I didn't fell very well yesterday but I feel . A . today.
   (A) better   (B) best   (C) worst
3. She never did write very neatly but she is writing even . B .
   neatly nowadays.
   (A) little   (B) less   (C) least
4. During the debate George spoke badly but his brother spoke
   even . . . than he did.
   (A) more badly   (B) most badly   (C) worst   (D) worse
5. Who played . . . of the eleven players?
   (A) better   (B) best   (C) worse
6. My sister cooks much . . . than I do.
   (A) successfully   (B) more successfully   (C) most successfully
7. In the whole class, I think Mary works the . . .
   (A) hard   (B) harder   (C) hardest
8. Of the eight competitors in the javelin event, George threw
   the javelin the . . .
   (A) far   (B) farther   (C) farthest
9. She speaks . . . clearly than her sister.
   (A) less   (B) little   (C) least
10. All three of them can drive but John drives the . . .
    (A) carefully   (B) more carefully   (C) most carefully

3. Some expressions involving comparison

Make sure that you know how to use the following expressions.
If necessary, make up sentences similar in construction to the
models.

i. **as . . . as**
   This case is (*just*) *as* heavy *as* that one.
   David played *as* cleverly and *as* successfully as John.

ii. **not so/as . . . as**
   It's *not so* hot today. (*as it was yesterday*)
   The river is *not as* deep today *as* it was last week.

iii. **with an auxiliary verb**
   He plays better than I *do*.
   He played better than I *did*.

Comparison

> She doesn't speak as well as your sister *does*.
> I can type just as quickly as she *can*.

In conversation the auxiliary verb at the end of the sentence is often omitted. When this is done, the pronoun can be left in the form used when it is the subject of a verb (e.g. *I* and *she*) but it is often changed to the form used when it is the object of a verb (e.g. *me* and *her*). Both of these forms can be heard:

> He plays better than *I*.
> He plays better than *me*.

The second type is more common in conversation.

iv. **the . . ., the . . .**

> *The* sooner he comes, *the* better.
> *The* sooner you start, *the* sooner you'll finish.
> *The* more you do for him, *the* more he grumbles.
> (*The*) least said, (*the*) soonest mended.

Practise in Higher level English
— A. Wong — Greenwood Press.

Chapter 21

Conditional Tenses

If it breaks, Mary will buy another one

1. The Present Conditional tense

Statements

I we	*should	go wait
		(not)
he they	would	play work

Questions

*Should	I we	go? wait?
Would	he they	play? work?

Note: Some people use *would* in place of *should*, particularly in speech and when the use of *should* might suggest an obligation which the speaker does not intend.

The Present Conditional tense is used:

a. In place of the Simple Future tense when the main verb is in a past tense, as in reported speech:

> She said they *would arrive* at eight o'clock.
> I knew I *would* not *find* him in time.

b. To express an unlikely or improbable event, particularly with an 'if' clause which contains a verb in the Simple Past tense. Notice the difference between these two sentences:

possible: If it *breaks*, Mary *will* buy another one.
unlikely: If it *broke*, Mary *would* buy another one.

It is most important that you understand and remember the sequence of tenses in these two sentences.

Exercise 1

The sentences in this exercise are based on the examples in *b* above. Put the verb with *if* in the Simple Present or Simple Past tense. Put the main verb in the Simple Future or Present Conditional tense. The word in italics tells you which type of sentence to construct.

1. (*possible*) If we . . . (develop) the country's resources fully, we . . . (raise) our standard of living considerably.
2. (*unlikely*) If we . . . (fail) to develop the country's resources properly, we . . . (cause) a great deal of hardship.
3. (*unlikely*) If he . . . (drink) too much, he . . . probably . . . (have) an accident.
4. (*possible*) If he . . . (drive) carefully, he . . . (not have) an accident.
5. (*possible*) If that branch . . . (fall) down, it . . . (hit) your bicycle.
6. (*unlikely*) If that tree . . . (fall) down, it . . . (hit) the house.
7. (*unlikely*) If you . . . (score) ten goals, Father . . . (be) astonished.
8. (*possible*) If you . . . (score) a goal, we . . . (be) delighted.
9. (*possible*) If a new university . . . (be) built, there . . . (be) more places available for students.
10. (*unlikely*) If the university . . . (be) closed, there . . . (be) a shortage of professional men eventually.

Exercise 2

Put the verb in brackets into the Present Conditional tense.

1. I knew he . . . (be) early.
2. He told us what . . . (happen).
3. Did he tell you what he . . . (do) if he had a chance?
4. They were certain that they . . . (win).
5. Mary promised that she . . . (phone) this evening.
6. If I had enough money, I . . . (buy) a new house for my parents.

326

7. If you went to the dentist regularly, you . . . (not have) toothache so often.
8. He said that they . . . (not leave) until Thursday.

Exercise 3

The following sentences express possible events. Change them to show unlikely events as in the example below:

> *possible:* If he comes, he will bring you a present.
> *unlikely:* If he came, he would bring you a present.

1. If you fall off, you will hurt yourself.
2. If the flood-water rises any higher, it will come in the house.
3. If she writes more carefully, she will not make so many mistakes.
4. If an election is held now, Mr. Blank will be elected.
5. If income tax is raised, the Government will get more money.
6. You will have a shock if he arrives tonight.
7. That mat will be bleached if you leave it in the sun.
8. She will soon reduce her weight if she goes on a diet.
9. Those plants will die if you don't water them.
10. I'll help him if I can.

2. The Perfect Conditional tense

i. If I had seen Mary, I *would have told* her about the game.
ii. *Would* you *have stopped* to help them if you had seen them?
This tense is formed with *should/would have* + a past participle. It is used to refer to something which might have happened in the past but which did not happen. The other verb in the sentence is often in the Past Perfect tense (e.g. *had seen*). Here are further examples; notice the sequence of tenses involved:

iii. If you had played for us, we *would have won*. (*but we lost*)
iv. If I could have reached the shelf, I *would have got* the box down for you. (*but I didn't*)
v. I'm sure he *would have phoned* you if he could have reached a telephone in time.

Exercise 4

Complete each sentence by adding an expression which contains a verb in the Perfect Conditional tense.

Conditional Tenses

1. If that knife had slipped, *it would have hurt you.*
2. If you had told me that you hadn't enough money, . . .
3. If he had been driving any faster, . . .
4. If that fence hadn't been at the side of the road, *he would have crashed it. run*
5. If the burglar hadn't sneezed, . . .
6. If the party had been on a Thursday instead of on a Friday, . . .
7. If you had asked me to get the things for you, . . .
8. If Susan had been listening carefully, . . . *she would not have made a mistake*
9. If it hadn't been raining, . . .
10. If you hadn't woken me up this morning, . . . *I would have been late.*

328

Chapter 22

The Future

There's something wrong with the radio

1. Going to

We can use *going to* (particularly with verbs of movement) to express future action which has been planned in advance. It also shows that the speaker feels certain that something will happen in the future. When the future action has NOT been planned in advance but is decided upon at the time of speaking, we normally use the Simple Future tense. Consider the following situation and the two possible reactions:

Mrs. Smith: That's a nuisance. There's something wrong with the radio.

Mr. Smith: Yes, I knew that. I'm *going to* take it to the radio shop this afternoon. — (*Planned in advance.*)

OR

Mr. Smith: Oh, drat the thing. It's always going wrong. All right; I'*ll take* it to the radio shop this afternoon. — (*Not planned in advance; he didn't know there was anything wrong with it.*)

a. We can use *am/is/are* + *going to* for future action:

'I'*m going to* buy a new car at the end of the month.'

b. We can use *was/were* + *going to* to show a future intention which happened in the past:

'I *was going to* write to George but now I don't think I will.'

We also use *was/were going to* in indirect speech:

'He said he *was going to* buy a new car at the end of the month.'

Exercise 1

Rewrite these sentences, using *was/were going to* instead of *intended to*:

1. I intended to buy a new watch but I found that I hadn't got enough money with me.
2. I know he intended to write to Mary.
3. I intended to wash the dishes but I forgot all about them.
4. Mary did not intend to buy the shoes at first but she changed her mind.
5. We intended to visit Peter but we were held up by the floods.
6. I intended to switch off the fan but Mary asked me to leave it on.

Exercise 2

Make up a possible answer or response in reply to each of the sentences below. Use *going to* to show future action.

1. What are you going to do on Saturday?
2. I see you've got a puncture in that tyre.
3. You haven't done the ironing yet.
4. What are you going to do this evening?
5. This switch needs repairing.
6. Your shoes need cleaning.
7. Where is your brother going to stay when he goes to London?
8. Isn't it about time you had those brakes repaired?

2. Present Continuous tense

This tense can be used to express future action which has been planned in advance. The future time is nearly always mentioned and it is often in the near future. This usage is particularly common in speech with such verbs as *come*, *go*, *arrive*, *drive*, *fly* etc.

i. I'm going to the market in a minute. Would you like to come?
ii. George is arriving on the four o'clock train this afternoon.
iii. Is he flying to London next week or going by sea?

3. Simple Future tense

Statements		
I We	shall shan't	be in time help them
He You	will won't	be late find him

Questions		
Shall	I we	be in time? help them?
Will	he you	be late? find him?

Note: In statements we can use *will* with any subject but some people prefer to use *shall* after *I* and *we*. In questions we must use *shall* before *I* and *we*.

Broadly speaking, this tense is used to express future action whether or not it is planned in advance. Notice these points:

i. In a time clause, the Simple Present tense is used instead of the Simple Future tense: 'I'll pay him when I *see* him.'
ii. Similarly, the Simple Present tense is used instead of the Simple Future tense in a conditional clause:

'If he *comes* by train, I'll meet him at the station."
iii. The Simple Future tense is often used after *Do you think* when a question is asked about the future:

'Do you think it will rain this evening?'
iv. After *shall* or *will* we use the infinitive without *to* (e.g. *pay*, *meet* and *rain* in the sentences above).

Passive form

The passive form of the Simple Future tense is used when the action is going to be done *to* the subject and not by it, e.g.

The new bridge *will be* formally *opened* on Thursday.
You *will be caught* if you do that.

Exercise 3

Put in the passive form of the Simple Future tense of the verbs in brackets.

331

The Future

1. I'm sure the escaped prisoners . . . soon . . . (catch).
2. We . . . probably . . . (meet) by somebody when we arrive at the station. Then we . . . (drive) to a hotel, I hope.
3. The repairs . . . (finish) by five o'clock.
4. We . . . probably . . . (invite) to Mary's wedding.
5. The soil on the side of that hill . . . soon . . . (wash) away.
6. Many new houses . . . (build) in this town in the next few years.
7. The results of the examination . . . (announce) on Monday.
8. The prisoners . . . probably . . . (release) next year.
9. I'm afraid that tree . . . (blow) down during the night unless the wind dies down.
10. I wonder whether I . . . (pay) at the end of the month.
11. No, I'm sure they . . . (not take) to Kingston tomorrow.
12. I hope the road . . . (repair) in time for the carnival procession.

Questions with tags

These are two of the question forms of the Simple Future tense (active):

i. *expecting the answer 'Yes'*

He will come by train, won't he?	Yes, he will.
You will write to me, won't you?	Yes, I will.

ii. *expecting the answer 'No'*

He won't come by car, will he?	No, he won't.
You won't write to her, will you?	No, I won't.

Exercise 4

Complete the question and give the expected answer.

1. It won't rain, . . .?
2. You won't hurt yourself, . . .?
3. You will pay for me, . . .?
4. It will be open in time, . . .?
5. The men will finish tomorrow, . . .?
6. That medicine won't make me sick, . . .?
7. Those shoes won't quite fit him, . . .?
8. The bus will stop here, . . .?
*9. Nobody will find out, . . .? (Use *they*.)
*10. He will never manage to stop in time, . . .?

Note: *In 9 and 10 use *will* in your question tag because of the negative form of the preceding statement.

332

Exercise 5

Change each statement into a question with a question tag, to fit the answer given in brackets.

1. He will help us.   (Yes, he will.)
2. He will help them.   (No, he won't.)
3. She will telephone tonight.   (No, she won't.)
4. Everybody will be pleased.   (Yes, they will.)
5. That fire will spread to the hedge.   (No, it won't.)
6. You will remember to lock the door.   (Yes, I will.)
7. The oil will leak on to the floor.   (No, it won't.)
8. Your brother will probably win.   (Yes, he will.)
9. The rain will come through the roof.   (Yes, it will.)
10. I shall fall off.   (No, you won't.)

4. Future Continuous tense

We can use the Future Continuous tense on two occasions:

a. To express action which will be in progress at some future time:

'At seven o'clock tonight I *shall be doing* my homework so I shan't be able to come then.'

We *shall be waiting* for you at five o'clock.

b. To express the future without intention, i.e. to replace the Simple Future tense in expressing an action which will happen in the normal course of events and has NOT been specially planned.   Compare these sentences:

with intention: I'*ll make* a point of seeing him about it tomorrow.

without intention: Don't worry. I usually see him every evening so I expect I'*ll be seeing* him tomorrow as well. Then I can tell him about it.

Note: In *a* and *b* we can use *may* in place of *shall* or *will* if we wish to express doubt, e.g. 'I may be waiting for you when you come out of the cinema.'

Exercise 6

Put in the Future Continuous form of the verb in brackets:

1. It . . . probably . . . (rain) when we come out of school.
2. My sister can't come. She . . . (iron) clothes all the afternoon.
3. What do you want to eat? I . . . (get) supper in a minute.
4. George . . . (wait) for us in his car, I expect. I hope our train is not late.

5. I . . . probably . . . (see) Mary this evening. Is there anything you want me to tell her?
6. Peter . . . (arrive) on the one o'clock train.
7. My brother says he . . . (write) to you in the course of the next day or so.
8. In half an hour's time we . . . (go) to bed but in some countries the people . . . just . . . (get) up.
9. We can't use the hall tomorrow evening. The Parents' Association . . . (have) a meeting then.
10. The fishermen . . . (pull) in their net soon. Let's go and see what's in it.

5. Simple Present tense

You may sometimes see or hear the Simple Present tense used to express future action which has been planned in advance, often as a sequence of events:

i. He *goes* to London on Monday, *leaves* for Liverpool on Thursday and *gets* back here on Saturday.
ii. The coach *leaves* the school at seven o'clock tomorrow morning and *returns* at about six o'clock in the evening.

This is not an important usage. The same ideas can be expressed with the Simple Future tense, the Present Continuous tense or with *going to*.

6. Future Perfect tense

i. *non-continuous form: shall/will have* + a past participle

'I *shall have finished* the work by seven o'clock tonight.'

ii. *continuous form: shall/will have been* + a present participle

'By the end of the year I *shall have been working* in the same department for exactly twenty-five years.'

The Future Perfect tense is used to express an action which will be completed or finished by some future time or date. In many cases, the future time or date is mentioned in the sentence and comes after 'by', as in the examples above.

Exercise 7

Put in the non-continuous form of the Future Perfect tense of the verb in brackets:

1. By the end of the year I . . . (save) quite a lot of money.
2. If I go on at this rate, I . . . (put) on twenty pounds by the end of the year. Then I shall weigh more than you.
3. I am sure I . . . (finish) the job by tomorrow evening.
4. The man in the garage says he . . . (complete) the overhaul of your car by half past four.
5. We should be able to put out a good team on Saturday. Both of the injured forwards . . . (recover) by then.
6. Do you think the men . . . (put) in the new water-pipes by the end of the week?
7. By five o'clock this evening the space-ship . . . (travel) eight times round the world.
8. We . . . (use) up all the salt by the end of the week.
9. I think the tide . . . (turn) by seven o'clock.
10. *Do you think she . . . (finish) the ironing by now?

Note: *We can also use this tense with the expression 'by now'.

Chapter 23

The Gerund

It requires considerable skill to build a bridge

In this chapter, check that you are familiar with each of the constructions shown and can use it with confidence. Imitate and practise any with which you are unfamiliar.

A gerund is a word ending in *ing* which is made from a verb but used as a noun, e.g. '*Swimming* keeps you fit.' When necessary a gerund can have some of the qualities of a verb. For example, it can take an object: 'He likes *eating pineapple*.'

We can use gerunds in the following ways:

a. As the object of a verb: 'I like *playing* football.'
b. After a preposition: 'He is good at *drawing* people.'
c. As the subject of a verb: '*Smoking* is bad for you.'
d. After certain verbs: 'This shirt needs *repairing*.'

Exercise 1

Complete these sentences by supplying a gerund and any other words which may be necessary.

1. I like . . .
2. He loathes . . .
3. I enjoy . . .
4. She dislikes . . .
5. He hates . . .
6. He is good at . . .
7. I am tired of . . .
8. She is fond of . . .
9. He's not much good at . . .
10. Is she afraid of . . .?

Exercise 2

Complete these sentences by supplying a gerund and any other words which may be necessary.

336

1. He was accused of . . .
2. He pleaded guilty to the charge of . . .
3. He is clever at . . .
4. She was frightened of . . .
5. They are keen on . . .
6. He is very enthusiastic about . . .
7. She prefers . . . to . . .
8. I don't mind . . .
9. Do you mind . . .?
10. Do you object to . . .?

Exercise 3

Supply a gerund and any other words necessary to complete the sentence.

1. Stop . . .
2. When are you going to finish . . .?
3. That shirt needs . . .
4. I don't think my hair needs . . .
5. I don't remember . . .
6. Don't keep on . . .
7. I can't stand . . .
8. She can't bear . . .
9. It's no use . . .
10. It's no good . . .

Exercise 4

Supply a gerund and any other words necessary to complete the sentence.

1. Would you mind . . .?
2. Would you mind not . . .?
3. Mary told me that she dreads . . .
4. I always try to avoid . . .
5. Unless my tooth aches, I usually postpone . . .
6. That's quite a nice photo. I think it's worth . . .
7. The room was dark so I couldn't help . . .
8. He hadn't done anything wrong so he resented . . .
9. He's got his fishing-rod so he must be going . . .
10. I saw them going to the beach with their towels so they must be going . . .
11. The notice said: 'No . . .'
12. When she heard about the accident, she began . . .

Exercise 5

Compare these two sentences:

The Gerund

i. It is easy *to grow* cucumbers.

ii. *Growing* cucumbers is easy.

Change the following sentences in a similar way. Use a gerund in place of the infinitive in italics. Leave out *It*.

1. It is not very difficult *to learn* to drive a car.
2. It requires considerable skill *to build* a bridge.
3. It is a waste of time *to argue* with them.
4. It is a silly thing *to dispute* the decisions of the referee.
5. It is dangerous *to swim* at the mouth of that river.
6. It requires a great deal of patience *to play* chess.
7. It is asking for trouble *to drive* too near the car in front.
8. It will take us a long time *to paint* the house.
9. It wouldn't be a waste of time *to write* to him.
10. It was a good idea *to hang* the clothes out early.

Exercise 6

Spell the gerunds ending in *ing* which can be made from these verbs:

1. behave	7. quarrel	13. dry	19. transfer
2. rescue	8. label	14. die	20. forbid
3. move	9. signal	15. lie	21. whisper
4. measure	10. cancel	16. tie	22. wonder
5. carry	11. travel	17. refer	23. visit
6. pay	12. shovel	18. commit	24. fasten

Exercise 7

Supply a gerund and any other words necessary to complete the sentence.

1. That scratch on the car is. not worth . . .
2. . . . always takes her a long time.
3. . . . is interesting because it teaches us quite a lot about other countries.
4. He had lost his key but he managed to get into the house by . . .
5. The manager of the hotel was talking to a police sergeant about a guest who had left without . . .
6. I look forward to . . .
7. We're looking forward to . . . because we've never been there before.

338

8. Don't worry. I'm quite used to . . . and I've never had an accident yet.
9. It started to rain so some of the players suggested . . .
10. Ask George if you can borrow his bicycle. I'm sure he won't mind . . .

Chapter 24

The Infinitive

It is difficult to catch a cobra

The forms of the infinitive with which we are here concerned
are:

	active	*passive*
present:	(to) finish	(to) be finished
perfect:	(to) have finished	(to) have been finished

a. Remember *to finish* your homework.
b. Your work must *be finished* before you go out.
c. You ought *to have finished* by now.
d. The new hotel ought *to have been finished* by now.
e. I think I can *finish* in time.

The infinitive can be used with *to* (as in *a*, *c* and *d* above) and it
can be used without *to* (as in *b* and *e* above). Whether or not
you use *to* depends on the particular construction you use.

1. The infinitive after an adjective

i. *It is difficult to catch a cobra.*

Exercise 1

Make up sentences similar to (i), using *It* plus a suitable form
of the verb *to be* plus one of the following: *easy, difficult, wise,
foolish, dangerous, safe, not hard, not simple, not right, wrong,
unwise, impossible, possible, necessary, useless, useful, unnecessary,
helpful, good, bad.*

ii. *She is certain to come by bus.*

Exercise 2

Make up sentences similar to (ii), using one of the following: *certain, likely, unlikely, bound, sure, not bound.*

2. The infinitive after a verb

Remember not *to lock* the door.
Don't forget *to give* him the message.

Exercise 3

Make up sentences in which an infinitive with *to* is used after any suitable form of these verbs: *like, want, wish, hate, start, begin, continue, prefer, prefer not, try, attempt, fail, seem, appear, agree, manage, hope, refuse, learn, happen.*

3. Show me how to do it

An infinitive is used after *how, when, where, what* and *which* in the following sentences:

a. Show me *how to do* it.
b. Please tell me *when to come.*
c. I don't know *where to put it.*
d. I'll find out *what to do.*
e. I'll ask her *which* (one) *to throw away.*

Exercise 4

Complete each sentence by adding *how, when, where, what* or *which* (*one*) + an infinitive with *to* and any other words which may be required.

1. I'm not sure . . .
2. I'll find out . . .
3. Do you know . . .?
4. Did he tell you . . .?
5. Please show us . . .
6. Please can you tell me . . .?
7. I've forgotten . . .
8. I can't decide . . .
9. Go and ask her . . .
10. I want to find out . . .

4. I waited for them to arrive

This pattern is often used:

> *verb + noun/pronoun + infinitive with 'to'*

341

   i. I waited for them to arrive.

  ii. He wanted Peter to lend him some money.

Exercise 5

Complete these sentences by adding an expression which starts with a noun or a pronoun followed by an infinitive with *to*.

1. We are waiting for . . .	7. Tell . . .
2. I have just asked . . .	8. Don't ask . . .
3. Can you arrange for . . .?	9. I'll advise
4. Do you expect . . .?	10. You can count on . . .
5. That salary will tempt . . .	11. I'm depending on . . .
6. She won't allow . . .	12. I'll help . . .

5. The infinitive to show purpose

We can use an infinitive to show purpose, e.g.

a. I locked the door *to stop anybody from getting in.*

b. I want to see Mary *to ask her about the picnic.*

6. Has to = must

We can use an infinitive after *to have* to show an obligation. In this sense 'has to' means 'must'.

a. She has *to go* to the railway station soon.

b. Last night I had *to look after* my baby sister.

c. Next week I shall have *to cut* the grass.

7. Able to and unable to

After *able* and *unable* we use an infinitive with *to*. After *can* we use an infinitive without *to*:

a. I don't think he is able *to lift* that box.

b. I'm sure he can't *lift* that box.

c. Mary says she is unable *to come* tonight.

d. Peter says he can *come* this evening.

8. Only + an infinitive

We can use *only* + an infinitive with *to* when we wish to show a disappointing result:

a. We dashed to the station *only to find* that the train had gone.

b. I went all the way to the Post Office *only to discover* that I had forgotten to take the letters with me.

9. I am instructed to inform you . . .

An infinitive with *to* is used after the following expressions, which are sometimes used in formal letters:

I am instructed . . .   I am obliged . . .
I am requested . . .   I am ordered . . .
I am asked . . .   I am forced . . .

a. I am requested to inform you that your letter is receiving attention.

b. I am forced to remind you that your third instalment is now overdue.

10. The film is about to start

We use the expression *about* + an infinitive with *to* to show that something is going to happen very soon:

a. I was just about to phone you when you phoned me.
b. We must hurry. The film is about to start.

Exercise 6

Complete these sentences by adding an infinitive and any other words which may be necessary. They are based upon the usages mentioned in sections 5 to 10 above.

1. (purpose) He wants a screw-driver . . .
2. (purpose) They are straightening this road . . .
3. (obligation) If you miss the bus you will have . . .
4. (obligation) The referee didn't turn up so I had . . .
5. I don't think he'll be able . . .
6. Mr. Lee phoned to say that he is unable . . .
7. I walked all the way to the market only . . .
8. We went to the sports stadium to see the game only . . .
9. (in a formal letter) Mr. Coles has asked me . . .
10. I am instructed . . .
11. When we reached the field, the referee was just about . . .
12. You'd better bring the clothes in; it's about . . .

11. Too heavy to lift

We can use the pattern *too* + an adjective (or an adverb) + an infinitive.

a. That crate is too heavy (for you) to lift.
b. He drives too carefully to have an accident.

The Infinitive

Exercise 7

Change each sentence so that you convey the same idea by using *too . . . +* an infinitive as in *a* above. In some cases you will have to put some words between the adjective and the infinitive.

1. That log is so heavy that they cannot move it.
2. That bridge is so old that it is not safe.
3. He is so old that he cannot enter the competition.
4. She is so young that she cannot apply for the job.
5. The river was so deep that we could not cross.
6. His shirt is so old and tattered that it cannot be washed any more.
7. He is so cautious that he will not be caught.
8. It is so late that we cannot go now.

12. So + an adjective + as + an infinitive

We can use an infinitive in these expressions:

a. Would you be so kind as *to tell* Mr. Smith that I shall be late tomorrow morning?
b. If you are so rash as *to lend* him money, you must expect to lose it.
c. If you are so stupid as *to do* that, you must expect trouble.

13. She was old enough to apply for the job

We can use an infinitive after an adjective or an adverb followed by *enough*:

a. She was old enough *to apply* for the job.
b. Is the coffee cool enough *to drink* yet?
c. Does he play well enough *to justify* his place in the first team?

14. To be + an infinitive

We can use *to be* + an infinitive to express a plan or an order:

a. It has been agreed that you two are *to go* in this car.
b. Those boxes are *to be taken* to the station in the morning.
c. The aim is *to catch* them red-handed.

15. An infinitive after a noun or pronoun

We can use an infinitive after a noun or pronoun to show what is to be done to the thing concerned or how it will be used:

a. I can't come. I've got some work *to do.*
b. She wants something *to fasten* that parcel with.
c. There are a whole lot of dishes *to be washed.*

16. The infinitive without 'to'

i. The infinitive without *to* is used after *can, could, may, might, must, do, does, did, shall, will, should* and *would*:

a. You can *go* now. The rain may *stop* soon.
b. I didn't *tell* him. He must *have guessed.*

ii. It is also used after *had better* (usually contracted to *'d better*):

a. You'd better *tell* him the truth.
b. I'd better not *let* him see them.

iii. The infinitive without *to* is used after certain verbs in this pattern:

> *verb + noun/pronoun + infinitive*

a. I saw the two men *search* his car.
b. She heard her mother *call* her.
c. Did you see them *open* the door?

Exercise 8

Use each of the following expressions in a sentence of your own. You can use any suitable tense of the first verb in each expression. Put a noun or pronoun in the blank space.

1. let . . . go
2. make . . . stop
3. let . . . start
4 make . . . work
5. watch . . . clean
6. notice . . . take
7. hear . . . call
8. not hear . . . shout
9. not notice . . . put
10. see . . . switch
11. not make . . . pay
12. not let . . . visit

17. The perfect infinitive

active: (to) have finished
passive: (to) have been finished

The perfect infinitive can be used in these ways:

i. *to show that something was not done in the past:*

(a plan) They were *to have brought* it but they forgot.
(a wish) I should have liked *to have seen* him but I missed him.

The Infinitive

(a duty) He ought *to have told* me but he didn't.

She should *have ironed* it but she didn't have time.

ii. *to form the perfect conditional tense with* should, would, could or might (see Chapter 21):

I would *have told* him if I had seen him in time.

iii. *to show that an action was possible in the past:*

Peter could *have played* but he didn't.

He could *have finished* it but he was too lazy.

iv. *with* can't *or* couldn't *to show that an action was not possible in the past, in the opinion of the speaker:*

They can't *have arrived* already.

She couldn't possibly *have done* it.

v. *to speculate about a past action:*

I think he may *have forgotten* what you told him.

vi. *with* appear *or* seem *and verbs such as* is said, is known, is believed *etc.*

He seems *to have lost* something.

They appear *to have been injured.*

He is said *to have been transferred* to London.

Exercise 9

Put in the active form of the perfect infinitive of the verb in brackets:

1. You seem . . . (lose) some weight recently.
2. The men are known . . . (escape) in a grey van.
3. Peter was . . . (bring) the football with him but he had forgotten.
4. They ought . . . (report) that to the police.
5. You ought not . . . (tell) anybody about the scheme.
6. If the river had been deeper, he might . . . (fail) to get across.
7. They can't . . . (arrive) already. The train is not due yet.
8. I'm sure they could . . . (win) if they had wanted to.
9. Mary should . . . (reply) to your letter.
10. He may . . . (leave) it at home.

Exercise 10

Put in the passive form of the perfect infinitive of the verb in brackets:

1. He ought . . . (reward) for his bravery and initiative.
2. The new bridge should . . . (finish) by now.
3. He is said . . . (promote) head of the department.
4. He would . . . (injure) quite seriously if that bush hadn't been in the way.
5. I don't believe it. He can't . . . (give) a scholarship.
6. What's the matter? Oh! That player appears . . . (warn) by the referee.
7. Peter was . . . (invite) but we had to take his name off the list after that letter.
8. I'm afraid the keys may . . . (lose) in the move.
9. Much greater care ought . . . (take) in drawing up the plans.
10. If we had been there, we might . . . (arrest) by mistake.

Chapter 25

Countable and Uncountable Nouns

Fewer and fewer spectators come each week

This is a revision chapter to remind you of the difference between countable nouns and uncountable nouns.

1. Countable nouns

We can count *books*, *letters* and *cars*. These words are countable nouns and we use (*how*) *many*, *a few* and *fewer* in front of them. We can use them in the plural with a plural verb.

$$\left.\begin{array}{l}\textbf{(how) many} \\ \textbf{a few} \\ \textbf{fewer}\end{array}\right\} + \text{a } \textbf{plural} \text{ noun} + \text{a } \textbf{plural} \text{ verb}$$

Examples

How many books are there on the shelf?
A few of the letters are from America.
Fewer and fewer spectators come each week.

If the verb precedes a plural noun, it must agree with it:

There **are**	not **many** some a lot of a **few**	spectators problems flowers

2. Uncountable nouns

We cannot count *envy*, *dirt* and *steel*. These words are uncountable nouns. We do not put *a* or *an* in front of them. We do not add an *s* to the end of them. They are singular words and have a singular verb. We use *much*, *a little* and *less* with them. When we want to express quantity we bring in other words, e.g. *examples* of envy; *piles* of dirt; *bars* of steel.

$$\left.\begin{array}{l}\textbf{(how) much} \\ \textbf{a little} \\ \textbf{less}\end{array}\right\} + \text{a } \textbf{singular} \text{ noun} + \text{a } \textbf{singular} \text{ verb}$$

Examples

How much sugar is there in the tin?
A little of the meat was burnt.
There is less dirt here now.

When the verb precedes an uncountable noun it must agree with it, as in the last example above.

There **is**	not **much** some a lot of a **little**	work water poverty

We can use *a lot of* in front of countable and uncountable nouns so it is a rather useful expression.

Notes:

i. In an affirmative statement we do not usually say: 'There is much sugar in the tin.' This would be changed to: 'There is a lot of sugar in the tin.'

ii. In general, abstract nouns (such as *kindness*, *hatred*, *envy*, *love* and *jealousy*) are uncountable nouns. However, some of them can be used in the plural when they refer to specific acts rather than to the abstract quality, e.g. 'His many *kindnesses* were much appreciated.'

iii. Some words present special difficulties to foreign students:

a. *machinery* has no plural form; it refers to two or more machines or to one machine with various parts. It takes a singular verb.

b. *work* has no plural form when it refers to tasks to be done. Its plural refers to the compositions of authors, musicians etc. and to things created by a man. For example, we could speak of 'The works of Brunel, the well-known engineer.' When we refer to tasks which we must do, we say: 'There IS a lot of work to be done.'

c. *furniture* and *scenery* have no plural form; they both take a singular verb. We can speak of 'suites' or 'items' of furniture. We can refer to 'scenes'. Similarly, *advice* has no plural form except in commercial English where 'advices' is rarely used as a type of technical contraction of 'advice notes'. This usage can be ignored and the singular form, *advice*, used in normal English.

d. *accommodation* and *luggage* have no plural form. They can refer to one or more items and require a singular verb.

e. *people* has two meanings. When it refers to a crowd or to a group of people, it is plural and requires a plural verb, e.g. 'There ARE a lot of people there.' We can also use *people* to refer to a particular race. When there are two or more races in a country we can refer to the 'peoples' (of the world, of Nigeria, of Switzerland etc.)

Exercise 1

Put in *is* or *are*:

1. All the accommodation . . . reserved, I'm glad to say.
2. The scenery around my town . . . particularly attractive.
3. . . . the machinery still in good order?
4. . . . there much work left for me to do?
5. Where . . . all the luggage? Where . . . the cases?
6. Those chairs . . . new but most of the furniture . . . old.
7. Their advice . . . fairly sound, and so . . . his opinions.
8. Their envy . . . not something which worries me.
9. . . . there many lorries on the road today? . . . there much traffic?
10. A few of them . . . old-fashioned. Most . . . modern.
11. A lot of it . . . contaminated in some way but a little . . . all right.
12. There . . . only a few left, I'm afraid.
13. Here . . . a little for you. There . . .n't much left.
14. . . . there many there? There usually . . .
15. There . . . less and less disease in this area each year.

Exercise 2

Put in *much* or *many*:

350

1. There is not *much* . . . advice I can give you.
2. There is not *much* . . . left for me to say, is there?
3. Are there . . . *many* people watching the film?
4. Are there . . . *many* different peoples in your country?
5. Not *much* . . . work remains to be done, thank goodness.
6. How . . . *much* did you pay for that ring?
7. How . . . time is there left? Is there . . . *much* chance that he will come? *many*
8. How . . . *many* times have I told you not to do that?
9. I asked him how . . . *many* employees had been dismissed.
10. There is not . . . *much* consistency in his actions, is there?
11. Do you think there will be . . . *much* trouble in the morning?
12. Luckily for us, there was not . . . *much* traffic on the road.
13. How . . . *many* events are there left to go?
14. . . . *Many* of them are torn or damaged in some way.
15. . . . *Much* of what he says is grossly exaggerated.

Chapter 26

The Present Participle

They were working in the road

Make sure that you are familiar with the constructions shown in this chapter and can use them with confidence. Imitate and practise any with which you are unfamiliar.

1. I watched the [boys] PLAYING football.

In this pattern the present participle refers to the word immediately in front of it.

Exercise 1

Join each pair of sentences by using a present participle as in the example below, and by omitting any words which are not necessary.

Example

> I watched the boys. They were playing football.
> I watched the boys *playing* football.

1. I heard Mrs. Smith. She was arguing with her husband.
2. I noticed two men. They were working in the road.
3. I took a photo of the men. They were cutting down the tree.
4. She spoke to the men. They were painting the house.
5. We noticed George. He was coming out of the cinema.
6. They caught a python. It was stealing a chicken.

Exercise 2

Complete each statement in any sensible way by adding a present participle and such other words as may be necessary.

1. Look at that man . . .	6. Did you notice the men . . .?
2. I saw Mary . . .	7. I saw his dog . . .
3. We heard them . . .	8. They arrested the men . . .
4. I stopped them . . .	9. She noticed a hockey stick . . .
5. I can see Father . . .	10. We saw several rats . . .

2. Anybody (caught/seen) ARRIVING late will get into trouble.

In this pattern the present participle refers to the noun or pronoun which precedes it.

Exercise 3

Put in any suitable present participle:

1. Passengers . . . the services of the steward are requested to press the bell.
2. People . . . in glass houses should not throw stones.
3. Patients . . . to see the doctor should see the receptionist first.
4. Anybody caught . . . to smuggle goods through the Customs may be fined or sent to prison.
5. Motor-cyclists not . . . a helmet stand a greater chance of receiving serious head injuries.
6. Ships . . . through the Suez Canal need to have a pilot on board.
7. Anything found . . . in the corridor should be handed to the duty master.
8. Winds . . . across the Atlantic usually bring rain with them.
9. People . . . in rural areas usually lead a fairly peaceful life.
10. Anybody . . . a free ticket for the show should see Mr. Lee.

3. She is at Mary's house, HELPING her make a dress.

In this pattern the present participle refers to the subject of the sentence although it is not next to the subject.

Exercise 4

Join each pair of sentences by using a present participle and by omitting any words which are not required.

1. She is at Susan's house. She is making a blouse.

353

2. I went to the hall. I hoped to find Peter there.
3. The motorist swerved violently. He hoped to avoid the children in the road.
4. Mary is in the kitchen. She is cooking some fish.
5. They are all sitting in the car. They are waiting for you to come.
6. I stared at the letter. I wondered how I could possibly reply to it.
7. The postman brought the parcel to us. He thought that John lived here.
8. I put my hand on the door. I did not realize that the paint was still wet.
9. I switched on the radio. I did not realize that my brother was trying to do some work.
10. My sister is at home. She is recovering from an attack of fever.

4. (Not) KNOWING that a storm was coming, I got ready to go out

In this pattern the present participle comes before the word to which it refers. Do not use this pattern unless (a) it is quite clear and unambiguous, and (b) the present participle refers to the subject of the following main clause.

In the sentence 'Crossing the road this morning, I saw John' it is not clear whether *crossing* refers to *I* or to *John*. This type of construction should be avoided. In its place we can say: 'When I was crossing the road this morning, I saw John' OR 'I saw John crossing the road this morning'—depending on the sense required.

Exercise 5

Complete these sentences in any sensible way:

1. Not realizing that there was somebody still in the room, I . . .
2. Thinking that the exercise would do me good, I . . .
3. Feeling rather tired, Peter . . .
4. Knowing that she was late, Mary . . .
5. Not looking where I was going, I . . .
6. Hoping that we would be in time to meet the train, we . . .
7. Thinking that there was something wrong with the refrigerator, I . . .

8. Slamming the door behind him, John . . .
9. Pushing our way through the bushes, we . . .
10. Swimming as hard as he could, David . . .

Exercise 6

Make up 10 sentences similar to the pattern dealt with in this section, starting with a present participle or with *not* + a present participle. Check each sentence to make sure that it is not ambiguous.

5. Be + a present participle

We can use *be* + a present participle in such constructions as the following:

question	*possible answers*
What is he doing?	He *may be* cleaning his bicycle.
	He *seems to be* dozing.
	He *must be* sleeping.
	He *could be* visiting his friend.
	He *should be* doing his homework.
	He *ought to be* working hard.
	He *might be* hiding somewhere.

Exercise 7

What do you think each of the following persons is doing now? In your answer use a present participle after one of these: *may be, could be, ought to be, should be, might be.*

1. one of your parents
2. a brother or sister
3. a taxi-driver
4. a shop assistant
5. a policeman
6. a detective
7. an optician
8. a nurse
9. a dentist
10. a farmer
11. a carpenter
12. an electrician

6. Using a present participle as an adjective

We can often use a present participle as an adjective, e.g.

a. I saw a *flickering* light on the side of the hill.
b. He has just signed a very *damaging* statement.

355

Exercise 8

Supply a suitable noun in each case below. Assume that the noun and adjective are used after *I saw* or *I heard*.

1. an insulting . . .
2. a surprising . . .
3. a puzzling . . .
4. an interesting . . .
5. a fascinating . . .
6. a drowning . . .
7. a floating . . .
8. a burning . . .
9. a warning . . .
10. an astonishing . . .
11. a deafening . . .
12. a shining . . .

Chapter 27

The Simple Past Tense

If only I owned all that property!

Regular or weak 'verbs'

Affirmative		Negative			Questions		
I We They	stopped escaped played	I We They	did not (didn't)	stop escape play	Did	I we they	stop? escape? play?

Irregular or 'strong' verbs

Affirmative		Negative			Questions		
I We They	won lost went	I We They	did not (didn't)	win lose go	Did	I we they	win? lose? go?

The Simple Past tense is used on these occasions:

a. to describe a completed past action when the time is mentioned OR when the time of the action is known by the speaker and listener.

b. to describe habitual past action, e.g. *She always walked home.* Even in this case, the time is known because such a sentence as that in the example assumes that the speaker and listener know the period of the habitual action and have referred to it.

The Simple Past Tense

c. in 'unlikely' conditions (see Chapter 21), when the verb in the main clause is in the present conditional tense:

> If that branch *broke*, he would probably hurt himself.

d. in place of the present tense after *It is time . . .*

> It is time you *went* home.

e. after *would sooner* or *would rather* when the speaker refers to another person or thing:

> I would rather you *opened* the box.

f. after *wish* and *if only* when an imaginary or unreal situation is mentioned:

> I wish I *owned* that land.
> If only I *owned* all that property!

(*Note:* The past perfect tense is used when reference is made to past events, e.g. 'If only she *had come* in time!')

Exercise 1

Remember that in the negative and question forms of the Simple Past tense we use *did* (*not*) + the infinitive without *to*. Change the following short sentences into the negative.

1. I saw him.
2. He came home.
3. They went there.
4. We found them.
5. He jumped over it.
6. I lost it.
7. You fastened it.
8. She replied.
9. It rained.
10. They broke it.
11. He hesitated.
12. I stole them.
13. They practised enough.
14. He weighed it.
15. It flew away.
16. She chose the shoes.
17. You corrected it.
18. He paid me promptly.
19. They hurried up.
20. She thought of it.

Exercise 2

If you made any mistakes at all in Exercise 1, change the following sentences into the negative. If you made no mistakes in the previous exercise, you need not do this one.

1. She borrowed it.
2. He taught us.
3. It collapsed.
4. I ate them.
5. She fried them.
6. I knew that.

7. They shot it.
8. He lent me it.
9. They swam all the way.

10. She caught them.
11. I spoke to you.
12. He began in time.

Exercise 3

Change these statements into questions to which the answer can be 'Yes' or 'No'.

1. He made it.
2. They came.
3. You hid it.
4. It worried you.
5. He saved it.
6. You planted them.
7. He got them.

8. She told you.
9. You drove the car.
10. It lit easily.
11. You felt tired.
12. They used it all.
13. You rescued them.
14. You did it by yourself.

The passive form

The passive form of the Simple Past tense is used when the action is done TO the subject. Often we use it because we do not know who has done the action of the verb:

'That window *was broken* during the night.'

Sometimes the person or thing who did the action is mentioned after the preposition *by*:

'I think it was broken *by David*.'

The passive form is made with *was* or *were* + a past participle:

Active Voice	*Passive Voice*
I hit	I was hit
It moved	It was moved
They saw	They were seen

When two passive verbs are used **with the same subject**, we can often leave out *was* or *were* in the second verb as well as the pronoun in front of it:

'He *was congratulated* and *promised* a large reward.'
'The trees *were cut* down and *burnt*.'

Exercise 4

Change these expressions by using the passive form of the verb as in the example:

The Simple Past Tense

Example:
> *Somebody* repaired the radio.
> *The radio was repaired.*

1. *Somebody* closed the bridge last night for repairs.
2. *Some players* broke the badminton rackets during the game.
3. *Somebody* asked me to give you this message.
4. *Somebody* advised us not to go to that shop.
5. *Something* damaged the wind-screen on the way.
6. *Something* blocked up the main drain.
7. *Some men* delivered those crates this morning.
8. *Some men* dredged that canal a few months ago.
9. *Somebody* sold the confiscated goods.
10. *Somebody* told me to come and see you.

Questions with tags

i. *Expecting the answer 'Yes'*

> She sent it, didn't she?
> *She *did* send it, didn't she?* } Yes, she did.

*This is a more emphatic form. We emphasize *did*.

ii. *Expecting the answer 'No'*

> She didn't send it, did she?   No, she didn't.

Exercise 5

Change these sentences into questions to fit the answer given in brackets.

1. You did it.   (Yes, I did.)
2. She did it.   (No, she didn't.)
3. They bought one for you.   (No, they didn't.)
4. The police soon caught them.   (Yes, they did.)
5. I told you.   (No, you didn't.)
6. The weather changed abruptly.   (Yes, it did.)
7. He warned us about the game.   (No, he didn't.)
8. She kept them all herself.   (No, she didn't.)
9. David called to see him.   (Yes, he did.)
10. I repaired it for her.   (Yes, you did.)

Exercise 6

Complete the question and then give the expected answer.

1. He dashed off down the hill, . . .?

360

2. They didn't recover the money, . . .?
3. The new shoes didn't quite fit, . . .?
4. His ambition brought about his downfall, . . .?
5. Their excuses seemed rather weak, . . .?
6. He didn't inspect the guard of honour, . . .?
7. Mary's sister soon got better, . . .?
8. She didn't tell you about it, . . .?
9. He didn't check his work properly, . . .?
10. You found out where they were, . . .?

Chapter 28

The Past Continuous Tense

Everybody was waiting for Mary to say something

<table>
<tr><th colspan="3" style="text-align:center">*Statements*</th><th colspan="2" style="text-align:center">*Questions*</th></tr>
<tr><td>He was
They were</td><td>(not)</td><td>waiting
looking</td><td>Was he
Were they</td><td>waiting?
looking?</td></tr>
</table>

This sense is made with *was* or *were* + a present participle. It is used on the following occasions:

a. To express a past action which was happening when another past action was completed:

> I saw him when I *was walking* to school.
> He lost the key when he *was playing* football.

b. To express two past actions which happened at the same time and which were both continuous:

> They *were playing* football while I *was doing* my work.

c. To show what was happening at some time in the past:

> At six o'clock last night I *was reading* a book.

d. To replace the Present Continuous tense in reported speech:

> *direct:* He said, 'I'm looking for my keys.'
> *indirect:* He said he *was looking* for his keys.

Note: Remember that some verbs are not normally used in continuous forms. (See Chapter 32.)

Questions with tags

i. *Expecting the answer 'Yes'*

She was waiting, wasn't she?   Yes, she was.
They were waiting, weren't they? Yes, they were.

ii. *Expecting the answer 'No'*

She wasn't waiting, was she?   No, she wasn't.
They weren't waiting, were they? No, they weren't.

Exercise 1

Change these statements into questions to fit the answers given in brackets.

1. It was raining quite hard. (Yes, it was.)
2. They were looking for Peter. (No, they weren't.)
3. He was shouting or talking loudly. (No, he wasn't.)
4. They were already playing. (No, they weren't.)
5. The temperature was falling. (Yes, it was.)
6. The passengers were just getting on. (Yes, they were.)
7. Everybody was booing. (Yes, they were.)
8. The river was still rising. (No, it wasn't.)
9. You were making a skirt. (No, I wasn't.)
10. You were repairing the switch. (Yes, I was.)

Exercise 2

Complete the question and then give the expected answer.

1. Most of the spectators were already going home when he scored the equalizer, . . .?
2. The top of the tree was beginning to sway dangerously, . . .?
3. Everybody was waiting for Mary to say something, . . .?
4. Both of the cars were travelling far too quickly, . . .?
5. The water wasn't coming through the door, . . .?
6. My brother and I were sitting quietly over there, . . .?
7. The liner wasn't heading towards the rocks, . . .?
8. The tanks weren't leaking then, . . .?
9. She was watching the television, . . .?
10. A whole lot of rats were eating the rice, . . .?

The passive form

We use the passive form of the past continuous tense to express

The Past Continuous Tense

an action done TO the subject. The action must be in the past and must be unfinished at the time concerned.

a. Mr. Smith must have had an accident. I noticed that his car *was being towed* back to a garage this morning.

b. The prizes *were being awarded* when I arrived at the Sports Meeting to collect Mary.

The passive form of the Past Continuous tense is made with *was/were being* + a past participle.

Exercise 3

Put the verb in brackets into the passive form of the Past Continuous tense.

1. I crossed the road to see what was wrong. Then I saw that two hooligans . . . (arrest) by the police.
2. When I last saw your cat, it . . . (chase) by the dog next door.
3. He told us that he . . . (transfer) to Lagos later in the year but I think there has been a change of plans.
4. Two men burst into the office and tried to grab the money just as it . . . (count).
5. I noticed a lot of Customs' launches round one of the ships, and my uncle told me that it . . . (search) for drugs.
6. Did you notice that those old houses . . . (pull) down yesterday?
7. When the cadets . . . (inspect) yesterday, one of them fainted.
8. I couldn't do the ironing yesterday afternoon because the iron . . . (repair).
9. I suspected that we . . . (follow) so I turned round to have a look from time to time.
10. I'm sorry to say that the injured man died while he . . . (take) to hospital.
11. She told us that the food . . . (provide) by a contractor.
12. The speaker at the road safety talk said that our bicycles . . . (check) by the police at that very moment. This came as a surprise to us.

Chapter 29

The Past Perfect Tense

I was sure that I had locked the door

1. Uses of the Past Perfect tense

Statements
They had (not) finished.

Questions
Had they finished?

The Past Perfect tense is used on these occasions:

i. *To show which of two past actions happened first.* Often the other verb in the sentence is in the Simple Past tense:

a. When they *had finished* their work, they went to the cinema.
b. She put the clothes away after she *had ironed* them.

In many cases the two past actions are mentioned in one sentence but this is not always the case. You may meet a passage like this in a book: 'I went home and sank gratefully into a chair. My feet were sore and my legs felt like lead. I *had walked* nearly thirty miles that day.'

In such a passage, *had walked* is used to show that the action took place before the writer returned to his home. However, if you are not yet confident in the use of the Past Perfect tense, it might be wiser to keep to the pattern shown in *a* and *b* above.

Exercise 1

Inspect each sentence. Then put one verb into the Simple Past tense and the other into the Past Perfect tense. Use the Past Perfect tense for the action which happened first.

1. When I . . . (finish) washing, I . . . (have) my breakfast.

365

2. I . . . (go) to bed after I . . . (lock) the door.
3. When we . . . (dig) the hole, we . . . (throw) all the rubbish in it.
4. When I reached home, I . . . (find) that I . . . (lose) my key.
5. She . . . (tell) me that her sister . . . (go) out already.
6. We . . . (discover) that the wind . . . (blow) down a tree and that it was blocking the road.
7. After we . . . (drag) the tree off the road, we . . . (drive) on.
8. After we . . . (walk) for about an hour, we . . . (stop) for a rest.
9. The fire-engine . . . (arrive) about five minutes after I . . . (telephone).
10. He . . . (deny) that he . . . (steal) the money.

ii. The Past Perfect tense can be used *when it is necessary to refer further back in time*. This often happens in expressions like the following:

> I knew that they *had gone* out.
> I was sure that I *had locked* the door.
> Mary thought the bell *had rung*.
> He discovered that he *had lost* his wallet.

iii. The Past Perfect tense can be used *to express a condition which is impossible* because it refers to a past time when something did or did not happen:

> I would have come if you *had phoned* me (but you didn't).
> She would never have found out if you *hadn't told* her (but you did).

The other verb in the sentence is often in the Perfect Conditional tense. (See Chapter 21.)

iv. The Past Perfect tense is often used *in indirect speech when the introductory verb is in a past tense*. It then replaces a verb in the Present Perfect tense (he *has stopped*) or the Simple Past tense (he *stopped*) in the original speech. (See Chapter 16.)

Direct Speech	*Indirect Speech*
He said, 'I've finished.'	He said he *had finished*.
She said, 'Tom found it.'	She said Tom *had found* it.

v. It is also used after *I wish, I would rather* and *I would sooner* when referring to the past:

> I wish you *had bought* one for me.
> I would rather you *hadn't told* him.

2. Questions with tags

i. *Expecting the answer 'Yes'*

He had already arrived, hadn't he?   Yes, he had.

ii. *Expecting the answer 'No'*

He hadn't already arrived, had he?   No, he hadn't.

Exercise 2

Change those statements into questions which fit the answers given in brackets.

1. The train had already left.   (Yes, it had.)
2. The train had gone already.   (No, it hadn't.)
3. She had shut all the windows.   (Yes, she had.)
4. They had repaired the wall.   (Yes, they had.)
5. The results had already been announced.   (Yes, they had.)
6. You had heard about it before I told you.   (Yes, I had.)
7. He had finished the work already.   (No, he hadn't.)
8. She had gone out already.   (No, she hadn't.)

Exercise 3

Complete the question and give the expected answer.

1. The shop hadn't shut already, . . .?
2. The game had started before you got there, . . .?
3. The milk had gone sour, . . .?
4. You had forgotten something, . . .?
5. The election hadn't been held then, . . .?
6. He hadn't been working there very long, . . .?
7. The rifle had been fired recently, . . .?
8. Peter hadn't told them about it, . . .?

3. The passive form

To make the passive form we put *been* in front of the past participle in the active form:

active	*passive*
he had dismissed	he had *been* dismissed
had he kicked . . .?	had he *been* kicked . . .?

The passive form is used in situations similar to those in which the active form is used BUT it shows that something was done TO the subject and not BY the subject, e.g.

367

i. He *had been dismissed* some months before we met him.

ii. *Had* the guard of honour *been inspected* when you arrived?

Exercise 4

Put the verb in brackets into the passive form of the Past Perfect tense.

1. She said that the new hotel . . . just . . . (open).
2. I read in the newspaper that the men charged with robbery . . . (find) guilty and . . . (sentence) to a long term of imprisonment.
3. I noticed that the wrecked car . . . not yet . . . (take) away.
4. The man on the radio said that the bush fire . . . (bring) under control at last. Many houses . . . (destroy) but no lives . . . (lose).
5. She asked me whether I . . . (invite) to the party.
6. I heard a sudden crash so I rushed out to see whether anybody . . . (injure). I found that part of our fence . . . (knock) down by a car. The vehicle . . . slightly . . . (damage) but nobody . . . (hurt).
7. The policeman warned us that the old bridge . . . (sweep) away by the floods and that a temporary one . . . not yet . . . (build).
8. My cousin told us that he . . . (transfer) to another part of the country.
9. She was very annoyed when she discovered that she . . . (cheat) by the shopkeeper.
10. I asked her whether all the dishes . . . (wash) yet.

4. The continuous form

The continuous form of the Past Perfect tense is made with *had been* + a present participle. It can be used when the first of two past actions was continuous, as in the following examples:

i. We stopped for a rest after we *had been walking* for about an hour and a half.

ii. After he *had been paying for* the car for about four months, he decided to return it to the finance company.

iii. When we *had been living* there for about two months, my mother decided that she did not like the house.

iv. I *had been expecting* him to come by train so I was rather surprised to hear that he was waiting at the airport.

v. That was a really good game. I wish I *had been playing*.

Chapter 30

Prepositions etc.   *see page 17 above*

Notes:

   i. As a matter of convenience, in this chapter prepositions, short adverbs, adverbial particles etc. are considered under one heading.

  ii. Many of the expressions in section 1 have more than one meaning and can be used in different ways. When possible, consider the different uses of each expression, putting it into a suitable context.

1. Some common expressions

Make sure that you understand the meaning of the expressions given in this section, and how to use them in a sentence. If you do not understand an expression, ask somebody to explain it to you or look it up in *A General Service List of English Words* (by Dr. M. West, published by Longmans, Green & Co. Ltd.) or in *The Concise Oxford Dictionary* (published by O.U.P.).

  1. **about**

quarrel about something	to stand about
argue about something	Is Peter anywhere about?
about the biggest	toys lying about the place
about ten o'clock	It came about that . . .
about two feet long	I'm about to start.
to wander about	He's honest about it.

  2. **above**

above all	in the sky above us
He is above cheating.	see page 17 above

above the noise
the flat above him

the above examples
above a thousand

3. across

go across the road
come across something

to get across a river
He lives across the road.

4. after

go after him   look after her   after all
after lunch   after the game   a week after that
He's after something.   She's named after her aunt.

5. against

struggle against
vote against
to be against something
It's against the rules.

to lean against
a law against
protection against
against his conscience

The hills stand out against the sky.

6. ahead

to be ahead of somebody
to get ahead
danger ahead

to look ahead
ahead of them
full speed ahead

7. along

walk along the road
Hurry along, please!
Get along with you!

houses all along the road
He knew it all along.
The launch is along-side.

8. among(st)

to be among(st) friends
among(st) others

Divide it amongst you.
to quarrel among(st)
   themselves

9. around

They are always hanging around (= *about*) the street corners.
all around us   to travel around the country
to wrap something around yourself

10. at

at work
at school
at last
at first
at once
at hand

nothing at all
good at
bad at
to stare at
to laugh at
at London Airport

at sixes and sevens
to be at war with
at three o'clock
at her best/worst
at any rate
at a distance

11. **away**

to run away	to throw away	put it away
to stay away	to be away today	to give away
to drive it away	a mile away	to fade away

12. **back**

to keep it back	to put back	at the back of
to answer back	to hit back	behind his back
to pay back	to come back	to back him up

13. **before**

before the war	Look before you leap.	before long
before 1966	the problem before us	(do it) as before

14. **behind**

behind me	behind the scenes	to be behind with/in
stay behind	behind his back	hide behind the tree
leave it behind	behind the times	to fall behind with

15. **below**

below par	her work is below average	below him
see below	Look below the surface.	below the belt

16. **between**

Stand between them.   It's between one o'clock and five
Between ourselves   past.
the difference between   He lives between London and
a quarrel between   Staines.
Divide it between them.   to choose between

17. **beyond**

beyond the Post Office	beyond all others
beyond my powers	beyond my wildest dreams
beyond any doubt	He went beyond London.

18. **by**

done by Peter	learn by heart	go by bus/rail/air/sea
made by hand	by no means	to tell by looking at
by accident	quite near by	a by-pass; a by-product
Stand by him.	pass by	by the way
by day/night	little by little	paid by the hour
by electricity	by one o'clock	Do it by yourself.

19. **down**

put it down   to let somebody down a cliff
write it down   to let somebody down (= fail to carry out

to calm down	down-stream	your obligations)
to die down	the down train	to run up and down
to fall down	go down the road	to be down to earth
to wear down	pay cash down	down with fever

20. **except**

everybody except Peter   except *for* your friend
This car is the same except *that* the seats are made of leather.
You can't do it except *by* straining yourself.

21. **for**

to pay for	in exchange for	it looks bad for him
to send for	it is difficult for	for all I know
to look for	to wait for a day	as for your friend
to be fit for	for the first time	for fear of
ready for	to go for a swim	for one thing
useful for	to be punished for	enough for us
to work for	a car for sale	good for him

22. **forth**

| to set forth an argument | and so forth |
| to show forth | to set forth (= *start*) |

23. **from**

away from	to escape from	to suffer from
absent from	to come from	from time to time
free from	to start from	from my point of view
different from	to descend from	from that shop
to tell one thing from another		from memory

24. **in**

in the bag	in trouble	in a hurry
in London	in love	in any case
in hospital	in winter	in Spanish
in a new dress	in reply	in front of
to succeed in	to go in	to put your faith in
in pain	in pairs	in case of
in the army	6″ in length	in my opinion
to spend your time in doing something		
in a loud voice	in disorder	in common
in order to	in the face of	to rub it in

25. **into**

rush into the house	to let him into a secret
get into difficulties	to enquire into something
divide into four parts	to marry into a family

26. **near**

    to live near somebody   a near relative
    the day drew near   a near escape
    to come near(er)   a near miss

27. **of**

full of	certain of	kind of him	the last of
made of	south of	the top of	deprive him of
sure of	more of	take care of	within a foot of
kind of	fond of	many of them	cured of
sort of	of course	think of	a man of wealth
good of	less of	King of Sweden	hear of

28. **off**

    the lid is off   set off   a long way off
    leave it off   turn off   to finish off
    take it off   break off   be well off
    switch it off   fall off   it is just off the road

29. **on**

on the table	to congratulate him on	on fire
on Wednesday	to have an effect on	on sale
on the whole	to go on (and on)	to live on
on purpose	to keep on (talking)	to gain on
on the average	to check (up) on	on guard
on the wing	on the occasion of	a loss on
to feed on	on reaching London	a tax on

30. **opposite**

    opposite our school   *Slow* is the *opposite* of *fast.*
    the hotel opposite   at the opposite end
    the opposite sex   on the opposite side
    the opposite house   in the opposite direction

31. **out**

to think out	out of sight	the way out
to throw out	out of town	he is out
to put out	out of training	to divide out
to call out	out of his mind	to pick out
to go out	out of kindness	to hold out
to fall out of	out of stock	to pull out
to fall out with	out of reach	out of joint
to set out	out of practice	to tire out
to find out	to make out	to talk it out

32. over

to fall over	The meeting is over.	to look over a wall
to jump over	over age/weight	covered all over
to turn over	over my head	over two miles
to hand over	waste time over it	roll over and over
to come over	left over	to look over a plan

33. per

ten per cent	£500 per annum	30 miles per hour
ten pounds per month	50p per yard	£1 per person

34. round

to go round	round the corner	to walk round
to turn round	round the bend	round and round
It's somewhere round here.		I'll go round the other way.

35 through

through the window	I got it through Peter.
through the ceiling	through your own fault
all through dinner	It went through London.
wet through (and through)	I couldn't get through (on the telephone).

36. to

too hot to	to refuse to	know what to do
forced to	to allow him to	fix the picture to
need to	to have to	stick it to
ought to	afraid to	fasten it to
the first to	sorry to	pull the door to
hard to	glad to	known to be
easy to	anxious to	I went to see him.
try to	hope to	made to measure
want to	like to	ten to one
to and fro	to the south of	of (no) use to me
go to	kind to	to his surprise

37. together

come together	flock together	together with
hold together	work together	all go together

38. towards

go towards something	towards the end of the month
facing towards something	towards the evening
a contribution towards	How do you feel towards it?

39. under

under the bridge	under the influence of
under the water	under the control of
under the sun	under the impression that
under the threat of	under the age of
put it under	under fifteen
See under *Verbs*.	under a pound
hide under	under a mile
study under	under his arm
under these conditions	under the pretence of

40. up

go up the hill	stand up	up to now
put up with	get up	keep up with
fed up with	climb up	lock up
shut up	add up	catch up (with)
sit up	up-stream	save up	hang up
grow up	an up train	store up	look up
clean up	hurry up	cheer up	pay up
dig up	turn up late	speak up	What's up?
bring up	stay up late	tie up	make it up

41. with

go with him	(dis)agree with	be careful with
take it with you	argue with	be rough with
cut it with this	quarrel with	trade with
mix this with that	the girl with brown eyes	
with regard to	You can do it with an effort.	
with pleasure	with regret	with the exception of
begin with	cover with	made with
filled with	finish with	play with

42. without

without you	without any money	without your help
without end	go without it	without doubt

He went without saying good-bye to anybody.

2. Putting in missing words

Put in any suitable word to complete the sentence. There are alternatives in some cases.

a. 1. I was reading an article . . . the way . . . deal . . . children . . . the home.   . . . my opinion the author was ill-informed.

2. . . . modern times most children learn . . . read . . . an early age. Some are quicker . . . it than others.
3. Mary took care . . . her baby brother while her mother was . . . the market. She was very fond . . . her brother.
4. The taxi-driver seemed . . . drive . . . a terrific speed until we came . . . my uncle's house just . . . of town.
5. I will describe the effect . . . drought . . . the crop . . . which we depend . . . a large extent.
6. He drove northwards . . . London . . . Birmingham and found that the roads were crowded . . . holiday-makers heading . . . the seaside resorts . . . the south coast.
7. I caught . . . . . . Peter who was going . . . the same direction.
8. I look forward . . . a family gathering . . . which I have a chance . . . meet my cousins.
9. Fruit makes a great deal of money . . . the people . . . some rural areas . . . the outskirts of large towns.
10. This hotel has a wonderful view . . . the sea and . . . the evening the sea breeze blows right . . . my room.
11. . . . a large extent, the farming . . . the more barren areas is carried . . . only . . . a small scale.
12. Some of the people live . . . rather difficult conditions and are faced . . . a number of problems . . . which they need advice.
13. That school is well known . . . its sports record . . . a number of years. It seems . . . concentrate . . . games and athletics.
14. Some of the young men . . . our village leave their homes and go . . . seek work . . . a large town.
15. My sister is good . . . making things but she is rather weak . . . mathematics. She is very interested . . . literature.
16. My friend has tried his hand . . . several different jobs . . . the past two or three years. Now he seems to have settled . . . . . . last.
17. The locusts were . . . their way . . . another part of the country but a few fell . . . us. They soon stripped the bushes . . . their leaves. I picked one . . . and held it . . . my finger and thumb.
18. One day, when I was . . . of sight of my elder sister, I fell . . . the river. . . . first I thought I would drown but I pushed . . . my hands and kicked . . . with my feet, and soon learnt . . . swim.

19. . . . ourselves I suspect him . . . trying . . . live . . . his relatives. He never seems . . . do any work.
20. What shall I say . . . reply . . . his letter? Shall I congratulate him . . . his unexpected marriage? I know it was a bit . . . a surprise . . . the family but we can't very well quarrel . . . him.
21. I prefer this one . . . that. It is made . . . silk.

b. 1. What were they arguing . . .?
2. What was she staring . . .? What was she thinking . . .?
3. Which shop did the robbers break . . .?
4. *Who did you give it . . .?
5. *Who did you share it . . .?
6. Where did you get it . . .?
7. What did she object . . .?
8. What did they complain . . .?
9. I wonder what all those people are looking . . .?
10. *Who did you apply . . .?
11. Which player didn't turn . . . for the game?
12. *Who were you referring . . .?
13. What did that man come here . . .?
14. *Who did you borrow it . . .?
15. *Who did she lend her bicycle . . .?
16. Where did this parcel come . . .?
17. *Who is he working . . .?
18. What is this patient suffering . . .?
19. It is still dark. Why did you switch the light . . .?
20. I'm hot. Please switch the fan . . .
Note: *In the questions marked with an asterisk *Whom* can be used in place of *Who*. In normal speech, *Who* is used more often.

c. 1. Don't leave your books lying . . . the place. Put them . . . neatly.
2. My friend lives . . . the flat . . . us. When he is typing, the noise comes right . . . the ceiling but we have got used to it . . . now so we don't complain . . . it.
3. My friend voted . . . the resolution because it conflicted . . . his principles, but I voted . . . it because I am . . . favour of compulsory education . . . to the age . . . sixteen.
4. You can't do that. It's . . . the regulations. You'll get . . . trouble if you are found . . .

5. My father is generally . . . his worst first thing . . . the morning. I am careful not . . . ask him . . . anything then.

6. I shall be away . . . school tomorrow. My brother is coming back . . . the U.K. so we are going . . . the airport . . . welcome him.

7. Divide the money . . . you and don't argue . . . it.

8. He is prejudiced . . . motorists so he will never agree . . . your suggestion . . . speed limits . . . the town.

9. The problem . . . us is impossible . . . solve . . . further information. We don't know enough . . . the situation . . . the moment.

10. I don't think I can be . . . any help . . . you. The matter is . . . my powers. You ought . . . see a lawyer . . . it.

11. You can tell . . . looking . . . that table-cloth that it was made . . . hand. It's a fine piece . . . work.

12. Don't worry . . . the fire. It will soon die . . . If it doesn't, you can put some ashes . . . it. That will put it . . . all right.

13. I must be there . . . time. I don't want to let the other players . . . I know they are relying . . . me.

14. Peter promised . . . pay . . . you if you want . . . go . . . see the cup final . . . the stadium this evening. It won't take us long . . . get ready.

15. The girls have just gone . . . a walk. They won't be long. They've gone . . . Mary's house . . . see how she is getting . . . She is recovering . . . some kind . . . fever.

16. My brother has just gone . . . study . . . the U.S.A. He has promised . . . write . . . us . . . time . . . time. . . . any case, my cousin is there already, and he will look . . . Peter if necessary.

17. I hope he succeeds . . . becoming an engineer. He has always been enthusiastic . . . that type of work. . . . my opinion, he has a natural aptitude . . . engineering.

18. If you get . . . difficulties . . . any kind, let me know. I'll think . . . some way . . . dealing . . . them.

19. As soon as the aeroplane had taken . . . satisfactorily, the stewardess reminded us . . . unfasten our safety belts. Then she brought . . . some magazines . . . us . . . read if we wanted . . .

20. Don't keep . . . grumbling . . . the food. You must just learn . . . be satisfied . . . whatever there is. The hostel steward is only allowed five pence . . . person . . . meal, and it's not easy . . . provide first class food . . . that money.

Chapter 31

The Simple Present Tense

When you drive I always feel nervous

1. Uses of the Simple Present tense

affirmative	*negative*	*questions*
He likes it.	He does not like it.	Does he like it?
They like it.	They do not like it.	Do they like it?

The form ending in 's', e.g. *likes*, is used with *he, she, it* and words which could be replaced by these pronouns.

The Simple Present tense is used on these occasions:

a. To *show habitual action:*

> He always *drives* to work that way.
> *Do* they *like* coffee?

b. In time expressions after **when, until** *etc.*

> Wait until he *arrives.*
> When you *drive* I always feel nervous.

c. In 'possible' conditions after **if** *and* **unless:**

> If he *plays*, we shall probably win.
> I can't come unless my mother *agrees.*

d. To show future, planned action connected with travel:

> She *leaves* for London in March and *returns* in April.
> The expedition *starts* on Monday morning.

e. In place of the Present Continuous tense for verbs which have no continuous form:

> Who *has* the keys now? I *have them.*
> She *knows* how to open the tin.

379

The Simple Present Tense

f. To introduce quotations:

Confucius *says:* 'The truly virtuous man, desiring success for himself, strives to help others succeed.'

g. In dramatic narrative, often used by commentators:

Clay *leads* with his left. Liston *blocks* it and *moves* away. Liston *tries* a right hook. Cassius *counters* with a right to the body.

h. In the following idiomatic expression:

'Why *don't* we *go* to the cinema this evening?'
'Why *don't* we *invite* Mary as well?'

These statements need not be questions. They can be suggestions concerning possible future action.

Warning: When you use the Simple Present tense make sure that your verb agrees with its subject. (See Chapter 18.)

Exercise 1

Put *like it* or *likes it* after each subject:

1. They both *like it*
2. Everybody . . *likes it*
3. Every student . *likes it*
4. Nobody . . *likes it*
5. The goats . . *like it*
6. The women . . *like it*
7. My friend . *likes it*
8. Who . . .? *likes it*
9. I . . *like it*
10. We . . . *like it*

11. Neither of them . . *likes it*
12. None of the boys . . *likes it*
13. The leader of the men . *likes it*
14. The Government . *likes it*
15. My brothers' friend . *likes it*
16. My sister's friends . *like it*
17. The majority . *likes it*
18. Everybody except you . . *likes it*
19. The audience . . *likes it*
20. The spectators . . . *like it*

Exercise 2

Change the following sentences into the negative:

1. She *doesn't* wants them. *want*
2. We know him. *don't*
3. I live there. *do not*
4. Peter knows him. *doesn't*
5. They drink tea. *do not*
6. Your cousin writes very well. *doesn't*
7. He always comes that way. *doesn't*
8. They usually play like that. *don't*
9. It works like that. *doesn't*
10. Eating vegetables makes me fat. *doesn't*

Exercise 3

Change the following statements into questions to which the answer could be 'Yes' or 'No'.

380

1. It costs a lot.
2. She swims well.
3. Frogs like water.
4. They burn easily.
5. It perishes quickly.
6. They know the way.
7. The humidity affects them.
8. Those flowers last a long time.
9. Mary plays the piano.
10. Your cousins often come.

2. Questions with tags

i. *Expecting the answer 'Yes'*

He likes them, doesn't he?
*He does like them, doesn't he? } Yes, he does.

They like them, don't they?
*They do like them, don't they? } Yes, they do.

Note: *The forms marked with an asterisk are slightly more emphatic.

ii. *Expecting the answer 'No'*

He doesn't like them, does he?   No, he doesn't.
They don't like them, do they?   No, they don't.

Exercise 4

Change the following sentences into questions which fit the answers given in brackets.

1. It works properly. (No, it doesn't.)
2. He behaves properly. (Yes, he does.)
3. The train leaves at half past five. (Yes, it does.)
4. They usually come this way. (No, they don't.)
5. The climate affects the situation. (No, it doesn't.)
6. She replies very promptly. (Yes, she does.)
7. You two want some more. (Yes, we do.)
8. Asbestos resists heat. (Yes, it does.)

Exercise 5

Complete the question and then give the expected answer.

1. His car uses a lot of petrol, . . . ?
2. Policemen often work at night, . . . ?
3. Your brother doesn't go to bed very early, . . . ?
4. It doesn't belong to Peter, . . . ?
5. The lift doesn't work, . . . ?

381

The Simple Present Tense

6. The cost of living rises each year, . . .? *doesn't it*
7. She works in an office now, . . .? *doesn't she*
8. Those shops don't close until seven o'clock, . . .? *do they*

3. The passive form

The passive form of this tense is made with *am*, *is* or *are* + a past participle. It is used when the action is done to the subject.

<table>
<tr><td colspan="3" align="center">*Statements*</td><td colspan="2" align="center">*Questions*</td></tr>
<tr><td>I am</td><td rowspan="3">(not)</td><td>invited</td><td>Am I</td><td>invited?</td></tr>
<tr><td>He is</td><td>expected</td><td>Is he</td><td>expected?</td></tr>
<tr><td>We are</td><td>injured</td><td>Are we</td><td>injured?</td></tr>
</table>

i. They *are expected* to arrive this evening.
ii. The gates *are closed* on Sundays.

Exercise 6

Put in the passive form of the Simple Present tense of the verbs in brackets.

1. I . . . (instruct) to inform you that you . . . (require) to submit your claim by the end of this month.
2. Our house . . . (paint) once every four years.
3. This room . . . (clean) out every day. The chairs . . . (put) on top of the desks, and the floor . . . (sweep) thoroughly.
4. The Star Ferry gates . . . (close) when the ferry is full. Then passengers . . . (force) to wait a few moments for the next ferry.
5. These machines . . . (make) in Germany but they . . . (assemble) here. They . . . (use) quite a lot nowadays.
6. A lot of concrete . . . (need) for the new housing schemes. Some of it . . . (import) but some . . . (manufacture) locally.
7. When new land . . . (clear) for settlement, the trees . . . often . . . (burn) down. The ashes . . . (dig) into the ground to act as a fertilizer.
8. The files . . . (keep) in these cabinets over here. Copies of letters . . . (put) in the files. Circulars . . . (duplicate) on this machine. The accounts . . . (check) in that department over there. Invoices . . . (issue) by the same department.

382

9. My car *is serviced* (service) nearly every month. The battery *is checked* (check) more frequently. The wheels *are changed* (change) round from time to time. If necessary, weights *are attached* (attach) to the wheels so that they *are balanced* (balance) properly.

10. Stamps *are sold* (sell) at this counter but enquiries *are dealt* (deal) with over there. Licences *are issued* (issue) at the next counter. When a new post office *is opened* (open), you will not have to wait so long.

Chapter 32

The Present Continuous Tense

There's something wrong with that dog

1. Uses of the Present Continuous tense

affirmative	*negative*	*questions*
I am going.	I am not going.	Am I going?
It is raining.	It is not raining.	Is it raining?
We are winning.	We are not winning.	Are we winning?

The Present Continuous tense is used on these occasions:

a. *To express a present temporary action*, i.e. one which is happening now but which may be temporary and may stop eventually:

> She *is cooking* the dinner at the moment.

b. *To express future action which has already been planned*. We often say the time when this action will take place:

> He'*s leaving* for Accra tomorrow morning.
> I'*m buying* a new car next week.

c. *For an action which happens many times so that it is virtually a habit*. The verb is often accompanied by a word such as *always* or *continuallly*:

> He *is* always *complaining* about the noise.
> The prisoners *are* continually *trying* to escape.

Note: Remember that some verbs are not normally used in the continuous form. These include *have* (when it means to *own*, *possess* or *suffer from* an illness), verbs of thinking, (e.g. *think, know, believe, realize, remember, forget, understand, mean* etc.), verbs of the senses (e.g. *see, notice, recognize, hear, smell*), verbs of emotion (e.g. *like, dislike, wish, want, desire, love, hate,*

384

refuse, forgive etc.) and *own, possess, belong, owe, keep, seem, appear* (= *seem*), *contain, matter, keep* (= *continue*), *concern* and *consist of.*

It is a common mistake to try to use *have* in a continuous form when it means to *own, possess,* or *suffer from.* On such occasions the Simple Present or Past must be used:

i. 'Who *has* your bicycle now?' — 'Peter *has* it.'

ii. 'Who *had* the book last week?' — 'Mary *had* it all the time.'

iii. My brother was absent for four days because he *had* influenza.

We can use the Present Continuous form of *to have* when **future** action is concerned. Compare the following:

iv. 'Which one are you having?' (This means: 'Which one will you have?' or 'Which one would you like?')

v. 'Which one have you got?' (This means: 'Which one is in your possession now?')

Referring to the future, we can also say:

vi. He is having a party next Saturday.

vii. We are having a holiday next Monday, I believe.

Exercise 1

Put in the correct form of *to have.*

1. She . . . her breakfast at the moment but I don't think she will be going to school because she . . . the toothache and ought to see a dentist.
2. The telephone rang while I . . . a bath so I just let it go on ringing.
3. Last week Peter . . . an attack of fever.
4. Who . . . the keys now? . . . you . . . them? (Use *got.*)
5. Mary . . . my watch. Who . . . yours?
6. The staff . . . a dinner tomorrow evening.
7. There's something wrong with that dog. Do you think it . . . rabies?
8. What . . . we . . . for dinner tomorrow?

2. Questions with tags

i. *Expecting the answer 'Yes'*

They are waiting, aren't they? Yes, they are.

ii. *Expecting the answer 'No'*

They aren't looking for me, are they? No, they aren't.

Exercise 2

Change these statements into questions to fit the answers given in brackets.

1. The game is just starting. (Yes, it is.)
2. The water is still rising. (No, it isn't.)
3. The passengers are coming now. (Yes, they are.)
4. It is starting to rain. (Yes, it is.)
5. Your brothers are playing today. (No, they aren't.)
6. You are writing to David. (No, I'm not.)
7. The chief clerk is looking for them. (Yes, he is.)
8. She is still working for you. (No, she isn't.)
9. I'm taking too much. (No, you aren't.)
10. You are waiting for your brother. (Yes, I am.)

Notice the alternative answers to some questions:

i. I'm going too fast, aren't I? $\begin{cases} \text{No, you aren't.} \\ \text{No, you're not.} \end{cases}$

ii. He's looking for me, isn't he? $\begin{cases} \text{No, he isn't.} \\ \text{No, he's not.} \end{cases}$

There is no difference in the occasions on which these answers can be used. You must recognize both forms but you are advised to use one type only in your own answers.

Exercise 3

Complete the question and give the expected answer.

1. He isn't looking at all well, . . . ?
2. The outbreak of cholera is spreading, . . .?
3. These trees are suffering from some kind of disease, . . .?
4. She isn't catching them up, . . .?
5. The air-conditioning system is functioning well, . . .?
6. The results are coming out on Monday, . . .?
7. The irrigation channels are improving the crops, . . .?
8. The smoke isn't getting in your eyes, . . .?
9. You two boys aren't playing with that machine, . . .?
10. I am getting thinner and thinner, . . .?

3. The passive form

The passive form of this tense is made with *am/is/are* + *being* + a past participle. It is used when the action is being done to the subject now OR is going to be done to it in the future.

active	*passive*
he is paying	he is being paid
we are inviting	we are being invited

Exercise 4

Put in the passive form of the Present Continuous tense of the verbs in brackets.

1. Can you wait a moment, please? Your radio . . . (repair) now. It is nearly ready.
2. A new fence . . . (put) up round our school.
3. Don't worry about the smoke. A lot of rubbish . . . (burn) over in that corner of the compound.
4. Fewer and fewer snakes . . . (catch) in this district each year.
5. More and more cars . . . (import) each year.
6. He . . . (transfer) to another town next month.
7. My brother . . . (discharge) from hospital at the end of the week.
8. I think his case . . . (hear) at the magistrate's court on Monday.
9. The man told me that those trees . . . (cut) down soon.
10. We . . . (take) round the new factory tomorrow morning.
11. . . . Peter . . . (invite) to the wedding?
12. . . . anybody . . . (appoint) to fill the vacancy caused when Mr. Lee retired?
13. . . . your brothers . . . (present) with their certificates next week?
14. The new block . . . formally . . . (open) on Saturday.
15. The damaged ship . . . (tow) to the nearest port.

Chapter 33

The Present Perfect Tense

I've been playing football for some years

1. Uses of the Present Perfect tense

Statements		
He has	(not)	arrived
We have		finished

Questions	
Has he	arrived?
Have we	finished?

The Present Perfect tense is used on these occasions:

a. To express a past action when the time is not mentioned.
In most cases, if the time is mentioned the Simple Past tense must be used. This is a most important rule. It is a very common mistake to use the Present Perfect tense with a time expression. The following examples are correct:

    i. I *have* never *seen* him before.   (Present Perfect)
    ii. I *saw* him when he was in Lagos.   (Simple Past)
    iii. He *has been promoted.*   (Present Perfect, passive)
    iv. He *was promoted* yesterday.   (Simple Past, passive)

b. With **just, already, recently, never, yet** *and (in questions) with* **ever:**

    Have you ever *heard* from your cousin?
    They *have* recently *been repaired.*

c. To answer questions which contain a verb in the Present Perfect tense:

'Where *have* you *been?*' 'I'*ve been* to see Peter.'
'What'*s happened?*' 'She'*s lost* her watch.'
d. *To express an action which began in the past and is still taking place:*

'I'*ve played* football for some years (and still play).

He'*s worked* here ever since I can remember (and still works here).

The same idea is sometimes expressed by means of the continuous form of the tense:

I'*ve been playing* football for some years.

He'*s been working* here ever since I can remember.

Exercise 1

Make up sentences containing the adverb shown below and the Present Perfect tense of the verb in brackets.

Example: just (close)

I have just closed the door.

1. recently   (apply)
2. just   (go)
3. almost   (finish)
4. completely   (waste)
5. already   (reply)
6. finally   (agree)

7. just   (explain)
8. already   (mend)
9. recently   (give)
10. almost   (recover)
11. finally   (repay)
12. completely   (exhaust)

Exercise 2

Put in *never* and the Present Perfect form of the verb.

1. He . . . (forget) his wallet before.
2. They . . . (play) that tune before.
3. She says she . . . (have) an accident yet.
4. I . . . (see) a bird like that before.
5. She . . . (pay) back that money I lent her.
6. They . . . (grasp) the significance of the situation.
7 The price of tin . . . (rise) so high, as far as I can remember.
8. We . . . (have) any snow in our country.

2. The continuous form

The continuous form of this tense is made with *has/have* + *been* + a present participle. It is used for an action which has been happening for some time and is still continuing or has just stopped. It is often used with *since* (+ a definite date or point of time) or *for* (+ a length or period of time):

> I *have been waiting* for you for twenty minutes.
> *Has* she *been working* there very long?
> They'*ve* only *been playing* for a few minutes.

Exercise 3

Put in the continuous form of the Present Perfect tense of the verb in brackets.

1. He . . . (promise) to bring it for a long time but he hasn't brought it yet.
2. David . . . (clean) the car for the last quarter of an hour. He still hasn't finished.
3. What . . . you . . . (do)?
   I . . . (tidy) up the kitchen.
4. What . . . they . . . (discuss) for so long?
   Oh, they . . . (try) to find a way of preventing the river from flooding.
5. I . . . just . . . (help) Susan to wash the dishes.
6. The cost of living in that country . . . (rise) steadily for some time now.
7. Peter . . . (attend) the out-patients department of the hospital for several weeks now.
8. I . . . just . . . (plant) some flower seeds.
9. Those two men . . . (sit) in that car for the last half-hour.
10. How long . . . you . . . (wait) for us?

3. Questions with tags

i. *Expecting the answer 'Yes'*

> He has seen them, hasn't he?   Yes, he has.
> He has been fighting, hasn't he?   Yes, he has (been).

ii. *Expecting the answer 'No'*

> You haven't seen them, have you?   No, I haven't.
> You haven't been fighting, have you?   No, I haven't (been.)

Note: In the reply to the continuous form, *been* is often omitted.

Exercise 4

Change these statements into questions to fit the answers given in brackets.

1. It has stopped.   (Yes, it has.)
2. They have started.   (No, they haven't.)
3. The cause of the accident has been puzzling him for some time.   (Yes, it has.)
4. He has changed his tactics a lot.   (No, he hasn't.)
5. They have been waiting for us.   (No, they haven't.)
6. She has improved considerably of late.   (Yes, she has.)
7. You have filled in that form.   (No, I haven't.)
8. That food has upset you.   (Yes, it has.)

Exercise 5

Complete the question and then give the expected answer.
1. His train hasn't arrived yet, . . .?
2. You haven't been fooling around with those wires, . . .?
3. She hasn't been wearing those shoes, . . .?
4. David has just opened an account at the bank, . . .?
5. That shirt has shrunk, . . .?
6. The foundations have moved slightly, . . .?
7. The baby hasn't swallowed the button, . . .?
8. They have already finished the work, . . .?

4. The passive form

Statements	Questions
He has (not) been informed.	Has he been informed?
We have (not) been chosen.	Have we been chosen?

The passive form is made with *has/have* + *been* + a **past** participle. It is used when the action is done to the subject. Often we have to use it because we do not know who has done the action:

Two windows *have been broken.*
A watch *has been stolen* from the classroom.

Exercise 6

Put the verb into the passive form of the Present Perfect tense.
1. Peter . . . not . . . (drop) from the team yet.
2. A goal . . . just . . . (score).
3. The floor . . . not . . . (wash) yet.
4. Somebody . . . (injure), I think.
5. . . . an ambulance . . . (summon)?

6. . . . the men . . . (pay) yet?
7. . . . you ever . . . (vaccinate)?
8. A new record for the 100 metres . . . just . . . (set) up.
9. The lift . . . not . . . (repair) yet.
10. Most of the rubbish . . . (take) away and burnt.
11. His brother . . . (award) a scholarship at the university.
12. I don't think the applications . . . (deal) with yet.

Chapter 34

Personal Pronouns

the tragedy

Subject	*Object or after a preposition*
I found the keys	They caught **me.**
He knows the way.	Do you know **him?**
She wants the book.	I congratulated **her.**
It eats fish.	We brought **it.**
We are hungry.	He spoke to **us.**
You look fine.	I saw **you.**
They are late.	I found **them.**

Exercise 1

Say the pronoun which we can use in place of each word or expression below when it is the *subject* of a verb. Then put *has, have, is* or *are* after the pronoun and make a sentence.

Example: the results.

> *They.*   *They* are better than we had expected.

1. the mistakes
2. his father's friends
3. my niece
4. the range of hills
5. David's sister
6. Mary's brother
7. the proprietor
8. the baby
9. the results of the experiment
10. swimming
11. swimming and wrestling
12. my friend and I
13. Peter and Mary
14. the dog
15. the cat's ears
16. the cost of the articles

Exercise 2

Say which pronoun we can use in place of each word or

393

expression below when it is the object of a verb or follows a preposition. Put *He heard about* in front of the pronoun to make a sentence.

1. the tragedy
2. your successes
3. the song
4. Peter and I
5. David and Mary
6. the disaster
7. the children
8. his ambition
9. the result of the tournament
10. the rise in exports
11. his jealousy
12. John and his friend
13. the cockroaches
14. the disastrous fire
15. the floods
16. their claims

Exercise 3

Put a suitable personal pronoun in each blank space:

1. I looked at the rifle but . . . seemed rather rusty to . . .
2. We tried to put out the flames but had to retreat when . . . threatened to surround . . .
3. Mary went to her father and asked . . . if . . . would lend . . . some money because . . . wanted to buy a dress.
4. My cousin had a pain in her shoulder so . . . went to see a doctor about . . .
5. I gave him the pineapples and . . . put . . . in his car.
6. The referee's decision puzzled the spectators. . . . shouted out their comments and showed that . . . disagreed with . . . and his decision.
7. The dangers involved in travel in outer space may not be obvious to us yet but . . . should not under-estimate . . .
8. I knew the effect which air currents would have on the aeroplane when we passed over the mountains, so . . . was not surprised when . . . made . . . fall sharply and then rise again.
9. When Mary had finished with the magazines . . . took . . . round to her friend and gave . . . to . . .
10. Peter and I asked Susan whether . . . would like to come with . . . when . . . went to the exhibition.

Exercise 4

Choose the right pronoun from the brackets.

a	*b*
(we, us)	**(they, them)**
1. *It's . . .	1. Give me . . .
2. . . . saw him.	2. Are . . . yours?

394

3. Were . . . in time?
4. He went with . . .
5. Shall . . . help him?
6. Can you tell . . . now?
7. Help . . . do it.
8. Are . . . all ready?
9. Tell . . . the truth.
10. He works near . . .

3. Put . . . here.
4. Where are . . . now?
5. Who are . . .?
6. He is very fond of . . .
7. *It's . . .
8. Send . . . to me.
9. Did . . . lose . . .?
10. Here . . . are.

Note: In *a*1 *It's us* is far more common than *It's we.* Similarly, most Englishmen would use *It's them* in *b*7.

Chapter 35

Possessive Pronouns

My bicycle is older than your bicycle

Possessive adjectives	*Possessive pronouns*
It is *my* car.	It is **mine.**
It is *his* house.	It is **his.**
It is *her* ring.	It is **hers.**
This is *its* collar.	(not used)
It is *your* book.	It is **yours.**
It is *our* house.	It is **ours.**
It is *their* cat.	It is **theirs.**

Notes:

a. We do not use a noun after a possessive pronoun.

b. We do not put an apostrophe on any of the possessive adjectives or *pronouns*. An apostrophe is used with *its* **only** when it means *it is* or *it has*, e.g. 'It's been a tiring day.'

Exercise 1

Write these sentences in another way, using a possessive pronoun as in the example.

Example: Those books belong to her.
　　　　　Those books are **hers.**

1. That watch belongs to Mary.
2. They belong to my cousin's father.
3. That bicycle over there belongs to the daughter of my neighbour.
4. Which of them belongs to me?

5. I think this one belongs to Peter and me.
6. Those shovels belong to the men.
7. That ladder belongs to you.
8. How many of them belong to that girl?

Exercise 2

Put a possessive pronoun in place of the words in italics.

1. *My bicycle* is older than *your bicycle.*
2. *Their car* is not as reliable as *Peter's car.*
3. Whose is this—*his book* or *your book?*
4. I'm sure this is *my key.* It can't be *Mary's key.*
5. That's not *our cat.* It must be *their cat.*
6. Your car is longer than *your brother's.*
7. Shall we go in your car or in *our car?*
8. This is our coach and that is *the visitors' coach.*
9. I don't think that is *my sister's.*
10. I know it's *your key* or *your brother's key.*

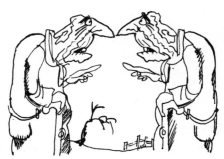

The old man was talking to himself

Chapter 36

Reflexive and Emphasizing Pronouns

I	I enjoyed **myself** at the party.
he	He nearly cut **himself** with the knife.
she	She felt cross with **herself**.
it	The cat licked **itself**.
one	One must learn to protect **oneself**.
you (singular)	You look as if you have strained **yourself**.
we	We nearly lost **ourselves** in town.
they	They soon dressed **themselves**.
you (plural)	Make sure you behave **yourselves**, boys.

In the sentences above, the words in bold type are called reflexive pronouns. They are used when the action of the verb refers back to the subject. In particular, they are used with such verbs as *behave, enjoy, exert, hurt, strain* and *injure* if there is no other direct object, e.g.

   i. We enjoyed the party.
 ii. We enjoyed ourselves at the party.

It is quite wrong to say: 'We enjoyed at the party.'

    The most common ways in which reflexive pronouns are used are:

a. as the direct object of a verb:

    She cut *herself* with that knife.

b. as the indirect object:

    Susan made *herself* a skirt. (= 'made it *for herself*')

c. after a preposition:

The old man was talking to *himself.*

Warning: Notice that only the plural forms—*ourselves, yourselves* and *themselves*—end in *ves.* There is no form ending in *selfs.*

Emphatic or Emphasizing Pronouns

When reflexive pronouns are used to emphasize a noun or pronoun, as in the following examples, they are called *emphatic* or *emphasizing* pronouns but it is not important to remember this name.

i. I want to speak to the culprit *himself*—and to nobody else.
ii. The President *himself* is coming to visit the school.
iii. I *myself* gave him permission to go.
iv. I gave him that book *myself.*
v. He is not very interested in stamps *himself* but his brother collects them.

Exercise 1

Put in a suitable reflexive pronoun:

1. We hurt . . .
2. They lost . . .
3. It scratched . . .
4. She did it by . . .
5. I broke it . . .
6. You will hurt . . ., David.
7. My brother made . . . sick.
8. You should enjoy . . ., girls.
9. Did they behave . . .?
10. He made . . . a book-case.

Exercise 2

Put in a suitable reflexive pronoun:

1. They have organized . . . very efficiently.
2. It's no good trying to persuade . . . that you are right, John.
3. She proved . . . be an excellent cashier and worthy of trust.
4. Never mind. You can comfort . . . with the thought that you are not the only ones to have suffered in that way.
5. Under such circumstances, I suppose one can congratulate . . . on having escaped alive.
6. The silly goats lost . . . on the hillside.
7. He blamed . . . for having been so careless.
8. Mary and I excused . . . and hurried away to get our things packed for the journey.

9. Those men consider . . . to be superior to anybody in the village.
10. I shall never convince . . . that what I did was right.
11. Listen, Peter. Just ask . . . this: 'What else could I have done?'
12. Two of the passengers managed to drag . . . clear of the wreckage.
13. He is always holding . . . up to us as an example to follow.
14. The majority of the candidates allowed . . . sufficient time to finish all the questions properly.
15. It is time for Peter and me to start thinking about . . . for a change.
16. The contractors agreed amongst . . . that they would not tender for the job.
17. Calm . . ., Peter! There's no need to get so excited.
18. No, please don't disturb . . ., gentlemen. I just want to get that book.
19. I suppose one should guard . . . against that sort of trick.
20. She can think . . . lucky to have got any money at all.

Exercise 3

Put in a suitable reflexive or emphasizing pronoun:

1. Suit . . ., John. You can take it or leave it.
2. The engine . . . is all right but the body of the car is very rusty. I can see . . . getting rid of this soon.
3. She . . . is very pleasant but her husband is a miserable fellow.
4. Leave them alone. They can do the job by . . .
5. The injury . . . is not too serious but if he gets pneumonia as well, he will be in serious trouble.
6. We can't help you financially. I'm afraid we're not very well off . . . at the moment.
7. I'm not much of a player . . . but I'll give you a game.
8. The hotel . . . is quite nice but it's in rather an isolated place.
9. I think I'll make . . . a new dress. My sister made one for . . . so I ought to be able to do the same.
10. If we find the ring, we may get . . . quite a nice reward.

Chapter 37

Relative Pronouns

Those men went up into space

1. Defining and non-defining clauses

The clause introduced by a relative pronoun may be defining or non-defining. It is important to recognize the difference between these because the intonation and punctuation used for a non-defining clause are different from those used with a defining clause.

i. *a defining clause*

This describes a preceding noun or pronoun and tells the listener which particular object we are concerned with:

> The boy *who found the wallet* received a reward.
> I gave some money to the boy *who had found the wallet*.

In each case the defining clause is necessary to make it clear which boy we are speaking about. No commas are used with the defining clause and the voice is not noticeably lowered.

ii. *a non-defining clause*

This adds to our knowledge of a noun or pronoun but is not essential because, without it, we already know which particular object we are concerned with:

> My brother, *who found the wallet*, received a reward.
> I gave some money to Peter, *who found the wallet*.

If we leave out the non-defining clause, the listener will still know which boy was concerned. The clause is thus not essential to an understanding of the sentence. In speech it is marked by a lowering of the voice; in written work it is separated from the rest of the sentence by a comma (if it occurs at the end) or by two commas (if it comes in the middle of the sentence).

2. Who

When it is a relative pronoun, *who* is used to say something about *a person*—and not about an animal or lifeless thing.

  i. The man *who lives next door* is a police officer.
 ii. I want to speak to the player *who is putting on his boots*.
iii. I lent my pump to the girl *who works in the office below* and she lost it.

Exercise 1

In the blank space put any suitable relative clause starting with *who* + a verb as in the examples (i) to (iii) above.

1. The boy . . . is my cousin.
2. The teacher . . . is absent today.
3. The policeman . . . is a brave man.
4. The driver . . . has been taken to hospital.
5. I want to speak to the girl . . .
6. He told us about some soldiers . . .
7. That is the taxi-driver . . .
8. Peter knows the man . . .

Exercise 2

Join each pair of sentences to make one longer sentence. Use *who* and leave out the words in italics.

1. The men have been arrested. *They* tried to break into the shop.
2. The man is a friend of ours. *He* owns that garage.
3. I was reading about the two men. *Those men* went up into space.
4. The man didn't give his name. *The man* telephoned this morning.
5. I took a photograph of the lady. *She* awarded the prizes.
6. Did you thank the man? *He* gave you a lift.
7. I really must write to the people. *They* want to buy our house.
8. The doctor is Peter's uncle. *He* came to see you in hospital.
9. They have dropped the player. *That player* let in two goals last time.
10. The reporter sent in that news item. *He* invented most of it.

3. That and Which

That is often used in place of *who*, particularly in speech:

i. I know the boy *that* found it.

That and *which* are both used to start a relative clause which tells us something about an animal or a lifeless thing:

ii. The book *that is lying on the table* belongs to John.

iii. The tree *which is blocking the road* was blown down during the storm last night.

iv. She has a cat *which drinks coffee*—when it gets the chance.

In sentences like (ii), (iii) and (iv), *which* is slightly more formal than *that*. In speech, *that* is more common. In writing, *which* is more common. However, notice the following:

a. Which is used in non-defining clauses rather than *that:*

Her new shoes, *which* are rather like yours incidentally, seem extremely comfortable and look very smart.

b. Which, and not *that*, is used after a preposition:

The train in *which* we travelled was a fast one.

c. There are three ways of constructing sentences like that in *b* above, in which a preposition is involved:

i. The train *in which* we travelled was a fast one.

ii. The train *that* we travelled in was a fast one.

iii. The train we travelled in was a fast one.

All three methods can be used in speech but (iii) is most common. Methods (i) and (ii) are found more in writing.

d. Which, and not *that*, can be used as a connective relative:

He spent more than he earnt—*which* inevitably led to disaster.

In trying to put out the fire, she picked up a tin of liquid and tipped it on the fire—*which* was the worst thing she could possibly have done because the tin was full of paraffin.

Exercise 3

Combine each pair of sentences in TWO different ways, as in the example. First make the type of sentence (without a relative pronoun) used in speech. Then make the more formal type (with *which*) used in written work. Leave out any words in italics.

Example: That is the knife. I cut myself with *that knife.*

    i. That is the knife I cut myself with.

    ii. That is the knife with which I cut myself.

1. This is the camera. I took the photographs with *this camera*.
2. That is the shop. She works in *that shop*.
3. I'll show you the place. You must start from *that place*.
4. Peter told me the method. He catches most fish by *that method*.
5. This is the range of hills. We must go through *them*.
6. Have you got the box? The camera came in *a box*.
7. I'm trying to remember the name of the hotel. We usually stop at *that particular hotel*.
8. I'm afraid that's a problem. We can't do anything about *it* at the moment.
9. There is a price. I can't go beyond *that price*.
10. That is the alley. They disappeared down *there*.
11. I think this is the key. They are looking for *this key*.
12. This is the central point. Everything depends on *this*.
13. That is the corner. He was looking round *that corner*.
14. I'll tell you about the amendment. I objected to *it* very strongly.
15. We came to the foot of the mountain. We intended to climb up *it*.

4. Whose

Whose is used to show possession, ownership or the relation between two people. Although it can be used after things it is normally used only in connection with people:

I know the girl *whose* brother won the championship.
There is the man *whose* house was burnt down.

Exercise 4

Complete each sentence by adding a sensible statement made up of *whose* + a noun + some more words.

1. The motorist . . . got into trouble.
2. I want to speak to the student . . .
3. Do you know the boy . . .?
4. The girl . . . was taken to hospital.
5. The man . . . reported the theft to the police.
6. He can visit my uncle . . .
7. I'll write to my cousin . . .
8. You know there was a fire last night? Well, that's the man . . .
9. You remember that accident by the station? Well, that's the boy . . .
10. The competitor . . . will be the winner.

Exercise 5

Join each pair of sentences to make one longer sentence. Use *whose* and leave out the words in italics.

1. That is the man. *His* dog bit me.
2. I want to see the girl. *That girl's* watch was lost yesterday.
3. I'm looking for the person. *His* car is parked outside.
4. Tell us about the passenger. *His* luggage was searched.
5. That's the boy. *His* pen was broken.
6. Those are the people. *Their* house is opposite Peter's.
7. I'll introduce you to the man. *His* support for the scheme is essential.
8. That's the player. I kicked *his* leg accidentally.
9. I've forgotten the name of the girl. I borrowed *her* hockey stick.
10. Here comes the man. You chased *his* dog away.
11. We've had a letter from the referee. We rejected *his* report.
12. I must speak to the manager about the assistant. He put forward *the assistant's* name for promotion.

5. Whom

We use *whom* in the following ways:

a. As the object of a defining relative clause:

> The girl **whom** *we chose* is Mary's cousin.
> The boy **whom** *you saw* happens to be my brother.

However, in speech and in writing we can leave out *whom:*

> The girl *we chose* is Mary's cousin.
> The boy *you saw* happens to be my brother.

Notice that we cannot use *who* in place of *whom* in this construction when it is used in formal English. *Who* is sometimes used in speech but some authorities claim that this is wrong. The best method in this case is to omit the relative pronoun.

b. As the object of a non-defining relative clause:

> Mary, **whom** *you probably met yesterday evening*, is my friend's cousin.
> I'll introduce you to Peter, **whom** *some people regard as our best forward*.

In non-defining clauses, *whom* cannot be omitted.

Relative Pronouns

c. After a preposition:

> The boy *from* **whom** I borrowed it lives here.
> The girl *to* **whom** you spoke is Peter's sister.

This type of expression is used in speech and in writing but there are alternative forms which are used in speech:

> The boy that I borrowed it from lives here. ⎫ *fairly common*
> The girl that you spoke to is Peter's sister. ⎭

> The boy I borrowed it from lives here. ⎫ *very common*
> The girl you spoke to is Peter's sister. ⎭

Exercise 6

Join each pair of sentences in TWO different ways. First make the type of sentence which is very common in speech. Then make the more formal type in which *whom* follows a preposition. Leave out any words in italics.

1. That's the boy. I spoke to *him*.
2. This is the patient. The doctor is very worried about *her*.
3. We must write to the contractor. They depend on *that contractor*.
4. I'm going to a dinner with the people. I work with *them*.
5. What was the name of that boy? You borrowed the books from *him*.
6. Tell us about the officer. You served under *him* in the army.
7. That is the police sergeant. The thieves were arrested by *him*.
8. Don't worry about the boys. You were arguing with *them*.
9. I'll point out the shop-assistant. I heard the news from *her*.
10. Where is the centre-half? The whole team has been built up around *that fellow*.

Appendix A

A Suggested Reading List

Notes:

1. Most of the following books are available in editions which should not cost more than fifty pence or so.

2. From time to time notice the author's skill at narration, description, plot construction and characterization, and consider how he achieves his effect.

3. If you find that you do not like a book in this list, cross it out. Add any others which you have found interesting and consider worthy of inclusion.

4. *In addition to these books, you should try to read some good novels published by your own countrymen or written by them and published elsewhere.*

1. Chinua Achele: *Things Fall Apart* and *No Longer at Ease*
2. Margery Allingham: *Tiger in the Smoke*
3. Jane Austen: *Pride and Prejudice* and *Northanger Abbey*
4. H. E. Bates: *Fair Stood the Wind for France*
5. Adrian Bell: *Corduroy*
6. Karen Blixen: *Out of Africa*
7. Ray Bradbury: *Golden Apples of the Sun*
8. Paul Brickhill: *Reach for the Sky*
9. Charlotte Brontë: *Jane Eyre*
10. Emily Brontë: *Wuthering Heights*
11. John Buchan: *The Thirty-Nine Steps* and *Prester John*
12. F. S. Chapman: *The Jungle is Neutral*
13. Sir Winston Churchill: *My Early Life*
14. Sir Arthur Conan Doyle: *The Adventures of Sherlock Holmes*

15. Joseph Conrad: *Lord Jim, The Secret Agent, Mirror of the Sea*
16. Stephen Crane: *The Red Badge of Courage*
17. A. J. Cronin: *The Citadel*
18. Charles Dickens: *Great Expectations* and *Oliver Twist*
19. Julian Duguid: *Green Hell*
20. Alexandre Dumas: *The Count of Monte Cristo*
21. Gerald Durrell: *The Bafut Beagles*
22. C. O. D. Ekwensi: *Burning Grass* and *The People of the City*
23. Rowena Farr: *Seal Morning*
24. C. S. Forester: *The African Queen*
25. E. M. Forster: *A Passage to India* and *Where Angels Fear to Tread*
26. William Golding: *Lord of the Flies*
27. Robert Graves: *Goodbye to All That*
28. Graham Greene: *Brighton Rock*
29. Sir Arthur Grimble: *A Pattern of Islands* and *Return to the Islands*
30. Sir H. Rider Haggard: *She* and *King Solomon's Mines*
31. Thomas Hardy: *The Mayor of Casterbridge*
32. L. P. Hartley: *The Go-Between*
33. Ernest Hemingway: *The Old Man and the Sea*
34. Thor Heyerdahl: *The Kon-Tiki Expedition*
35. Geoffrey Household: *Rogue Male*
36. David Howarth: *The Sledge Patrol*
37. Richard Hughes: *High Wind in Jamaica*
38. Sir John Hunt: *The Ascent of Everest*
39. Hammond Innes: *The White South*
40. Helen Keller: *The Story of my Life*
41. Rudyard Kipling: *Kim*
42. F. Kitchen: *Brother to the Ox*
43. D. H. Lawrence: *Sons and Lovers*
44. Camara Laye: *The Dark Child*
45. Laurie Lee: *Cider with Rosie*
46. Doris Lessing: *African Stories*
47. Betty Macdonald: *The Egg and I*
48. Wolf Mankowitz: *A Kid for Two Farthings*
49. Richard Mason: *The Wind Cannot Read*
50. W. Somerset Maugham: *The Summing Up* (on the craft of the writer)
51. Gavin Maxwell: *Ring of Bright Water*
52. Nicholas Monsarrat: *The Cruel Sea*
53. E. Mphaelele: *Down Second Avenue*

54. R. K. Narayan: *The Guide* and *The Man-Eater of Malgudi*
55. George Orwell: *Animal Farm* and *1984*
56. Alan Paton: *Cry, the Beloved Country*
57. Dorothy Sayers: *Murder Must Advertise*
58. John Schaefer: *Shane*
59. Nevil Shute: *A Town Like Alice* and *Pied Piper*
60. Wole Soyinka: *The Lion and the Jewel*
61. Howard Spring: *Fame is the Spur*
62. John Steinbeck: *The Grapes of Wrath* and *The Pearl*
63. Rosemary Sutcliff: *Eagle of the Ninth*
64. Jonathan Swift: *Gulliver's Travels*
65. R. H. Thouless: *Straight and Crooked Thinking*
66. J. Tickell: *Appointment with Venus*
67. Mark Twain: *The Adventures of Tom Sawyer* and *Huckleberry Finn*
68. Jules Verne: *Twenty Thousand Leagues Under the Sea*
69. H. G. Wells: *The Time Machine, The Invisible Man, War of the Worlds, Mr. Polly*
70. Eric Williams: *The Wooden Horse*
71. Henry Williamson: *Tarka the Otter*
72. John Wyndham: *The Day of the Triffids, The Kraken Wakes, The Midwich Cuckoos, *The Crysalids*

*Particularly recommended

Appendix B

Topics for Composition

A. Those already set by examining authorities.

B. Further topics for consideration.

A. *Those already set by examining authorities: the University of London* (L) *or the University of Cambridge* (C).

1. Myself—in twenty years' time. (L)
2. The future of my country. (L)
3. Hopes and plans for your future education. (L)
4. What do you think will be your greatest problem when you leave school? (C)
5. What I am looking forward to most in life. (C)
6. The next few years. (L)
7. My country and its achievements. (L)
8. The most important problem facing your country today. (L)
9. Explain, for the benefit of a foreign visitor, the appearance and value of the paper money and coins of your country. (C)
10. The treasures of my country. (C)
11. Strange customs. (L)
12. Traditional stories of my country. (L)
13. A memorable harvest. (C)
14. Describe what you have seen while watching some craftsman of your country at work. (C)
15. Old customs of your country that are disappearing. (C)
16. The women of my country. (L)
17. Educational opportunities in my country. (L)
18. Describe your first day at a new school. (L)
19. Give an account of some recent technical achievement in

410

your country, for example, the building of a dam, bridge, airport, university or other building. (C)
20. Games and recreations peculiar to your country. (C)
21. What changes could, in your opinion, be introduced in your country to improve ONE of the following?
    i. the marketing and sale of goods;
    ii. the maintenance of law and order;
    iii. housing;
    iv. diet.
22. Proposals for improving my town or village. (L)
23. Why I am proud of my town or village. (L)
24. Describe the means of communication and travel in your country. (L)
25. Describe a journey you have made by boat, pointing out what made it particularly interesting. (L)
26. My journey to this examination centre. (L)
27. Describe an interesting journey you have made recently, and show why you found it interesting. (L)
28. Recent developments in travel. (L)
29. Describe your first visit to a strange city. (L)
30. Describe your first visit to a town. (C)
31. A hurried journey *or* an exciting chase. (C)
32. A holiday, festival *or* celebration in honour of a great event in the history of my nation. (L)
33. Describe a special school occasion, for example, Prize Giving, Speech Day, or other annual event, at which you were present. (C)
34. A strange journey. (L)
35. The form of travel I like best. (L)
36. Man's treatment of animals. (L)
37. Animals in the service of man. (L)
38. The place of animals in the life of man. (C)
39. Preparing for a holiday. (C)
40. The best way to spend a week's holiday. (L)
41. If you were given enough money to take a month's holiday at any place in your country or in a neighbouring country, where would you go? Give reasons for your choice. (C)
42. Describe EITHER (a) a famous place you have visited, OR (b) a place which gives you great pleasure. (C)
43. My likes and dislikes. (L)
44. The kind of entertainment I most enjoy. (L)
45. The kind of music I like best. (L)

46. How I earn my living. (L)
47. My best friend. (L)
48. A character sketch of a person you will never forget. (L)
49. Describe in detail some hobby or interest of your own which you find both enjoyable and useful. Give your reasons for thinking that it is useful. (C)
50. Fire (C)
51. Patience (C)
52. The value of learning a foreign language. (L)
53. The benefits and pleasure I hope to derive from my study of English OR French OR German. (L)
54. The value of learning ONE of the following:
    i. how to play a musical instrument;
    ii. how to give first-aid treatment;
    iii. how to read a map and use a compass. (C)
55. Describe clearly the proper way to use ONE of the following: (a) a dictionary; (b) a hand-weaving loom; (c) a potter's wheel; (d) a microscope; (e) a paper pattern for making a garment. You are NOT required to describe the appearance of the item you choose. (C)
56. A new pupil at your school has asked you how he (or she) can do ONE of the following: (a) borrow books from the school library; (b) join a school club or other school organization. Explain clearly what he (or she) must do, and what rules have to be observed. (C)
57. Describe an accident in which you were involved, or which you witnessed, and say what effect it had on you. (L)
58. The scene I like best, in town OR country. (L)
59. The countryside near where you live. (L)
60. Write a clear description of the surroundings and outward appearance of your school. (C)

B. *Further topics for consideration.*

61. Write about any cartoon, illustration or photograph which you have seen in a newspaper or magazine.
62. Briefly describe any programme which you have recently seen on television or heard on the radio and which you enjoyed. Explain what you liked about it.
63. Describe some of the problems, hardships and pleasures to be found in any occupation which interests you.
64. Describe some of the things you like to do in your leisure time.

65. Give an account of some of the ways in which your country OR your part of it has changed in the last few years.
66. 'When I saw the grim look on her face, I knew there was going to be trouble. . . .' Develop and complete the story of which this is the start.
67. Write a story which starts: 'The funniest moment I can remember occurred . . .'
68. Write one of these dialogues:
    a. between two neighbours, one of whom has complained about the noise from the other's radio;
    b. between two boys or two girls who are planning a trip during the holidays;
    c. between a mother and daughter OR between a father and son when the older person is explaining how something should be done.
69. Write about somebody you admire and explain which qualities you particularly admire.
70. Describe a storm you have experienced yourself.
71. You have seen an article in a newspaper attacking the latest fashions in women's clothes. Write an article defending or attacking these fashions. Give reasons for your opinions.
72. Write an eye-witness account of any historical event as if it were happening now with you watching it.
73. Write a speech for delivery in a debate either for or against the motion 'That school holidays should be shortened and homework abolished.'
74. Gold.
75. Clothes.
76. Games.
77. Snakes.
78. Curiosity.
79. Types of toys.
80. Laziness.
81. Write an account of yourself as seen through the eyes of another person.
82. Write a report for a school magazine of any important event at school. It can describe a Sports Meeting, the visit to your school of an important person, Speech Day or any other event you choose.
83. Write a short story in which you are one of the characters concerned.

84. Give an account of the life of any wild animal in which you are interested.
85. Describe a place or district which you dislike and say why you dislike it.
86. Write about what you hope to get out of life OR what you hope to contribute to your fellows.
87. Describe a quarrel which you have witnessed or in which you were involved. You can use dialogue when necessary.
88. Describe the sort of person you hope to marry one day.
89. Make up a set of rules for use with ONE of the following:
    a. a league competition for any sport;
    b. an Art competition;
    c. a competition in which different kinds of food are to be judged.
90. Write a criticism of a book which you have enjoyed. Do not tell the story.
91. Use the following notes as the basis for an article in your school magazine on 'Road Safety'. You can use as much or as little of the following information as you like, and you can introduce new material if you wish.
    a. The annual total of casualties on the roads is high and increasing.
    b. Increases in industrialization and population will mean a rise in accidents on the road unless plans are made now to make the roads safer.
    c. Accidents can be caused by people using vehicles, by the machines themselves, by faulty roads, by the absence of road signs or by bad ones, by pedestrians, by weather conditions and by other causes such as animals.
    d. Each cause should be tackled systematically at national level.
    e. In addition, propaganda and education are required in and out of school.
    f. The biggest single factor will remain—errors of judgment by drivers. Legislation may be necessary to enforce greater care and consideration for others.
92. Assume that you have been asked to help to compile a brochure for tourists. Write an account, to be put in the brochure, of the tourist attractions of EITHER your own district OR your country as a whole. In writing your account, you can deal with any or all of the following points as well as any others which may be relevant.

a. What are the major attractions of the district or country as a whole: shopping, facilities for sport or relaxation, pleasant climate, scenery, hunting, old buildings or what?

b. Are there any special attractions in the town(s)? What are shopping facilities like? Are there any special ceremonies, processions or other town events?

c. Are there any interesting buildings in the town(s) which attract tourists?

d. Are there any special attractions in the rural areas? If so, what are they? What about the scenic beauty, if any? What about farming, rural crafts and customs, wild-life, and other things which might attract tourists?

e. Are there any special attractions connected with the sea, rivers or lakes? Are there opportunities for bathing, swimming, fishing etc.?

f. What is the general attitude of your people to tourists? Are they very friendly and helpful?

g. Are transport facilities good in your country so that tourists can enter easily and travel about easily?

h. Sum up the tourist attractions briefly, reminding your readers of the major ones.

93. A foreign magazine has invited you to write an article describing the progress and developments in your country in the last ten years. Write the article, dealing with the points below when they are relevant. You may add further material if you wish to do so. It is emphasized that you are not obliged to deal with all of the points below but you should try to present an accurate general picture of progress and developments in the last ten years.

a. Trade, industries and employment.

b. Agriculture.

c. Fishing.

d. The development of natural resources, e.g..mining etc.

e. The social services: education, health, housing, social welfare.

f. Public utilities: transport, water, electricity etc.

g. The police and armed forces

h. The general standard of living

i. Sport

j. Political stability—or any changes—if this is relevant to the subject

94. Write an account, to be sent in to a local newspaper, of any

game or match which you have seen recently. Be sure that you deal with the following points:

a. When and where was the game played? Was it a league or cup match?

b. Which teams were playing and what was the final result?

c. Give a general account of play in each half, i.e. before and after half-time. Give the half-time score.

d. If possible, describe how the goals or points were scored and say who obtained them.

e. Describe any specially exciting incidents.

f. At the end, give the final score again.

Acknowledgements

We are grateful to the following for permission to reproduce copyright material:

The Proprietors of *Australia and New Zealand Weekly* for the review of 'Australia, Her Story' by Kylie Tennant, published in issue dated 31 October 1964; British Overseas Airways Corporation for an extract from *BOAC Travellers Digest*; Cassell & Co. Ltd and Little, Brown & Company. Publishers for extracts from *Atlantic Conquest* by Warren Tute, copyright © Warren Tute 1962; the author for 'Meta Village Chiefdoms' by E. M Chilver, published in *The Nigerian Field*, Vol. XXX, No. 1, January 1965; The Clarendon Press for extracts from *Concise Oxford Dictionary* and *Dictionary of Modern English Usage* by F. G. and H. W. Fowler; Miss D. E. Collins and Cassell & Co. Ltd for an extract from *The Secret Garden* by G. K. Chesterton; Rupert Hart-Davis Ltd for an extract from *The Bafut Beagles* by Gerald Durrell; William Heinemann Ltd and The Viking Press Inc. for an extract from *The Grapes of Wrath* by John Steinbeck, copyright © 1939 by John Steinbeck; the Executors of the Ernest Hemingway Estate, Jonathan Cape Ltd and Charles Scribner's Sons for an extract from *A Moveable Feast* by Ernest Hemingway; the Controller of Her Majesty's Stationery Office for an extract from *The Examining of English Language* (8th Report of the Secondary Schools Examinations Council 1964); the author for an extract from *Rogue Male* by Geoffrey Household, published by Chatto and Windus Ltd; the author and the Hogarth Press Ltd for an extract from *Cider with Rosie* by Laurie Lee; the author, Sidgwick & Jackson Ltd and Random House, Inc. for an extract from *Flight Into Space* by Jonathan Norton Leonard; the author and William Heinemann Ltd for an extract from *The Summing Up* by W. Somerset Maugham; The Nigerian Field Society for extracts from *The Nigerian Field*, Vol. XXX, No. 1; the Nevil Shute Norway Trustees, William Heinemann Ltd and William Morrow and Company, Inc. for an extract from *A Town Like Alice* by Nevil Shute (published in the U.S.A. under the title *The Legacy*); Penguin Books Ltd for an extract from *Your Money's Worth* by Elizabeth Gundrey; P & O-Orient Lines for an extract from *ORIANA News* No. 975 and from their pamphlet entitled *The Cocos-Keeling Islands*; Warner Publicity Ltd for an extract from *Malaya Peninsula* by Malaysian Airways, and the author and Michael Joseph Ltd for an extract from *The Chrysalids* by John Wyndham.

We are also grateful to the following examination boards for permission to reproduce questions from past examination papers: University of Cambridge Local Examinations Syndicate, the Senate of the University of London, Metropolitan Regional Examinations Board, and the Welsh Joint Education Committee.